The Authors

Michael Buckley was raised in Australia and now lives in Canada, where he teaches and does freelance writing. He spends part of each year on the road. Michael kicked off his travelling days back in the '70s with a year's overland trip through Asia, India and the Middle East to Europe. His main asset is his big feet, which he puts in everywhere. He co-authored *China – a travel survival kit*.

Robert Strauss was born in England. During the '70s he travelled for several years in Europe and Asia, including a visit to the Tibetan communities in Dharamsala (India) and Nepal. After completing a degree in oriental languages in 1981, Robert made several visits to China and spent his time teaching, travelling and writing between England, Germany, Portugal and China. He will be working on the up-date of *China – a travel survival kit* and was last seen in Hong Kong, en route to Siberia.

Acknowledgements

Michael Buckley and Robert Strauss travelled overland by truck from Chengdu to Lhasa in mid-'85. Michael then took the road to Kathmandu, with an excursion to Everest base camp en route, and Robert hitched south-east to Samye, north to Golmud, then east to Xining. Assembly of this project required the dexterity of one of those multi-armed tantric deities, ready to grab bits and pieces from the complex sources available. Information of the practical kind relied largely on the authors' saddlebags, and on interviews with other travellers to the region. With two writers on the case, a second opinion was refined from the material – where personal comments are included you'll just have to guess whose they are.

The authors were helped along by a host of travellers and others. They would particularly like to thank the Library of Tibetan Works & Archives, Dharamsala, for assistance with illustration material.

Special thanks to J M Yates who engineered transfer of material to disc in his Kaypro cubbyhole in Vancouver; to Laurie (USA) for listening and support; to Rocky, Manna and the Phoenix crew (Hong Kong); Bing (UK); the convoy crew – Ed, Dave, Christine and Meghan (USA); Annette (USA); Jim (USA); Alexis, Thomas and Samuel (UK). Among those who had input, and many thanks to them: Captain Snappo (Canada), Geoff Bonsall (Hong Kong), Geoff Flack (Canada), Ken Fraser (Canada), Peter Sevcik (Czechoslovakia), Elizabeth Kim (USA), Bhuchung K Tsering (Dharamsala), Marcia Keegan (USA), Bradley Rowe (UK), Sarah and Johnny Capes (Australia), Scott Harrison (USA), Howard Gabel (USA), David Nemtean (Canada), Sylvia Schriever (Canada), John Hammer (USA), Earl Cooper (USA), Martin Weis (USA), Karen Hipkins (USA), Gillian Currie (UK), Elizabeth-Anne Malischewski, Tord Andersson and Kristin

Olsson (Sweden), and Knut Andersen (Norway).

From the Publisher
Back in the Autonomous City of Richmond (The Land of Bitumen), dreaming of 'The Land of Snows', was a hardworking Lonely Planet team. The line-up follows: Richard Everist, editing; Tina Shearman, mapping; Richard Holt and Fiona Boyes, paste-up; Sue Tan, indexing and proof reading; Ann Logan, typesetting; and George Bouchahine, supplies.

A Request
All travel guides rely on new information to stay up-to-date. Things change – prices go up, good places go bad, new places open up – nothing stays the same. Tibet is likely to change rapidly so if you find things better, worse, cheaper, more expensive, recently opened or closed, or simply different, please write and tell us about them and help make the next edition even better. We love getting letters from travellers out 'on the road' and, as usual, the most useful letters will be rewarded with a free copy of the next edition, or another LP guide if you prefer.

Lonely Planet Newsletter
To make the most of all the letters and information that come into Lonely Planet, we publish a quarterly newsletter with extracts from many of the letters we get, plus other facts on air fares, visas, etc. It's packed with down-to-earth information from writers with the best possible qualifications – they've been there. Whether you want the latest facts, travel stories, or simply to reminisce, the LP Newsletter will keep you in touch with what is going on. It comes out in February, May, August and November (approximately). To subscribe, write to Lonely Planet in either Australia or the USA; a year's subscription costs $10 A$ in Australia, US$ in the USA, write to:

Lonely Planet Publications
PO Box 88, South Yarra
Victoria 3141, Australia
or
Lonely Planet Publications
PO Box 2001A, Berkeley
CA 94702, USA

Contents

INTRODUCTION 7

FACTS ABOUT THE REGION History – Tibet Today – Early Travel & Exploration – 9
Population & People – Economy – Administration – Geography – Fauna & Flora
– Climate – Religion – Customs – Culture – Festivals & Holidays – Tibetan
Language – Chinese Language – Place-names & Geographical Terms

FACTS FOR THE VISITOR Visas – Consulates & Embassies – Documents & 81
Paperwork – ATPs, PSBs & Open Cities – Open Cities & Sites – Customs –
Money & Costs – Health – Film & Photography – General Information – Reading
– Tourism & Information – Tours & Trekking – Itineraries & Timing – Places to
Stay – Food & Drink – Things to Buy & Trade – What to Take & How to Take It

GETTING THERE & AWAY International Exit/Entry Points for China – Round-the- 112
world Tickets – Overland Through Asia

GETTING AROUND Helicopter – Rented Vehicles – Bus – Trucks & Trucking – 119
Offbeat Options

LHASA Around Lhasa 125

YARLUNG VALLEY MONASTERIES & SITES Ganden Monastery – Mindolin Monastery – 150
Samye Monastery – Zêtang & Nêdong – Destinations With Tough Access

GYANTSE & CHUMBI VALLEY Gyantse – Yadong Route & Chumbi Valley – Yadong 157

SHIGATSE 164

SAKYA 170

TREKKING IN THE EVEREST REGION Xêgar Route & Pang La – The North Face – 175
Everest Base Camp – Nangpa La – Kharta – Makalu & Everest East Face –
Xixabangma Base Camp

NEPAL ROUTE Lhasa to Kathmandu – The High Road – Shigatse to Lhazê & Sakya 188
– The Tingris – Xêgar – Xêgar to Tingri West – Tingri West – Tingri West to
Nyalam – Nyalam to Zhangmu – Zhangmu – Friendship Bridge – Kodari –
Tatopani – Tatopani to Kathmandu – Staging-point Kathmandu – Onward from
Kathmandu – Kathmandu to Lhasa

SICHUAN ROUTES Staging-point Chengdu – Chengdu to Lhasa Overland –Chengdu 203
to China – Lhasa to Chengdu Overland – Hong Kong to Chengdu –Burma Side-
door – North Route via Chamdo – Kangding to Dêgê – Dêgê –Border Bridge –
Chamdo – Chamdo to Nyingchi – Nyingchi to Lhasa – South Route via Markam

YUNNAN ROUTE Kunming to Dali – Staging-point Dali – Dali to Markam 220

QINGHAI ROUTES Qinghai Province – Qinghai-Tibet Highway – Lhasa to Golmud – 225
Staging-point Golmud – Staging-point Xining – Around Xining – Xining to
Maniganggo – Yushu

XINJIANG ROUTES Lhazê to Shiquanhe – Tsaparang – Mt Kailas & Lake Manasarovar 244
– Shiquanhe to Kashgar – Staging-point Kashgar – The Karakoram Highway

GLOSSARY 251

INDEX 254

STOP PRESS – VISAS

Immediately before this book went to press in early 1986 there was a significant liberalisation of regulations concerning access to places in China. There are now 244 places in China open with a passport visa only. This means Alien Travel Permits (ATPs) are almost obsolete since only 40 places require them. Lhasa, Golmud, Dali and Kashgar do not require ATPs. This may have implications for travel from Nepal to Tibet, and for other possible entry-points to China. The China-Pakistan border may be open to individuals by the time this book is published; a Pakistan visa will be necessary. Further changes in Chinese regulations are likely.

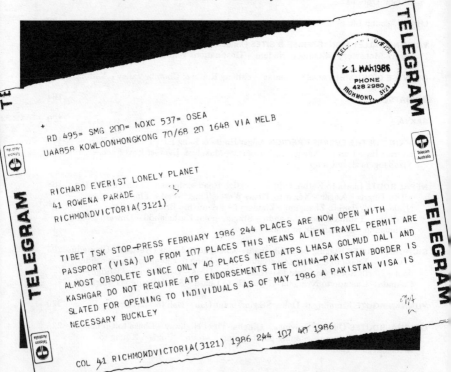

TELEGRAM

2 1. MAR 1986
PHONE
428 2980
RICHMOND, 3121

RD 495= SMG 200= NOXC 537= OSEA
UAA858 KOWLOONHONGKONG 70/68 20 1648 VIA MELB

RICHARD EVERIST LONELY PLANET
41 ROWENA PARADE
RICHMONDVICTORIA(3121)

TIBET TSK STOP-PRESS FEBRUARY 1986 244 PLACES ARE NOW OPEN WITH
PASSPORT (VISA) UP FROM 107 PLACES THIS MEANS ALIEN TRAVEL PERMIT ARE
ALMOST OBSOLETE SINCE ONLY 40 PLACES NEED ATPS LHASA GOLMUD DALI AND
KASHGAR DO NOT REQUIRE ATP ENDORSEMENTS THE CHINA-PAKISTAN BORDER IS
SLATED FOR OPENING TO INDIVIDUALS AS OF MAY 1986 A PAKISTAN VISA IS
NECESSARY BUCKLEY

COL 41 RICHMONDVICTORIA(3121) 1986 244 107 40 1986

Introduction

A land of superlatives, Tibet once held claim to being the most expensive destination in the world to visit. In the Victorian era the price was probable death – meted out either by the elements or by bandits; by the 1980s the price was reduced to a group tour arm and a leg. It sounds almost irreverent to say it, but Tibet on $10 a Day has finally become possible. The opportunity for high adventure, however, has not changed a whit.

For the present, Lhasa is officially open to independent travellers and there is a 'soft opening' of the Lhasa-Kathmandu Highway, with the sites of Shigatse, Xêgar and Zhangmu along the way. Other sites are due to open, and trek-tours are diving into little-known nooks and crannies. Official permission for the rest of the 'rooftop' is as impossible as it always was. In the spirit of the early explorers, however, travellers have taken up that challenge. With Lhasa readily accessible, crazy new dreams have taken shape – riding a horse to the holy mountain Kailas, trekking to Everest base camp at the north face, mountain-biking the high passes and camping out with nomads . . . In the short time (since September 1984) that Tibet has been open to individual travellers, safaris like these have rapidly materialised.

The Chinese call the place 'Xizang', which translates literally as 'Western Storehouse' (perhaps a passing reference to the dumping of radioactive wastes in the Tibetan Himalayas?). Western Storehouse is pretty bland – 'Wild West' might be more appropriate. Roaming the wastelands are shaven-headed lamas, hardy yak-herders, leathery horsemen, demolition-derby truck drivers, aloof Chinese on military manoeuvres, snot-nosed urchins, nomad women with long tresses smeared in yak-butter, proud Khampas (tribespeople) with chunks of turquoise dangling, and assorted unwashed pilgrims begging for Dalai Lama pictures. Living on this harsh plateau Tibetans have learnt to endure incredible hardships with a great sense of humour and easy-going hospitality.

Tibet is a very special place. There's only one drawback to visiting – it makes other places seem dull by comparison. The Land of Snows is, to be sure, changing fast – hotels are on the rise, a blackmarket exists, roads are being paved, monks hold tourists to ransom for temple-photos . . . and the Chinese seek to recoup their heavy subsidies to Tibet by fleecing every traveller. But behind all that is the medieval magic of the land, the temples and the people – none of which appear to be of this planet. It makes you sad to leave, and as you do, you're already plotting your return.

The three great religious kings (clockwise from top):
Songtsen Gampo, Tri Ralpachen and Tri Songdetsen

Facts about the Region

When the iron bird flies and horses run on wheels, the Tibetan people will be scattered like ants across the world and the Dharma will come to the land of the Red Man.

Padmasambhava, 8th century

The Empire

Written records of Tibetan history have survived from the 7th century AD but it is known that nomad tribes populated Tibet as early as the 2nd century BC. Known as the Chiang and the Sumpa, these tribes roved as far as Chinese Turkestan. An excavation near Chamdo in 1977, however, set the clock much further back with the discovery of neolithic remains some 50,000 years old. Chronology, names, facts and figures of Tibetan history are obscure and often dubious. Part of the confusion is that the Tibetans employed an element and animal cycle to compute dates.

The cornerstone of the emerging Tibetan civilisation was the Yarlung Valley area, about 80 km south-east of Lhasa. There, according to tradition, the union of a monkey and a she-devil created the Tibetan race. Around 600 AD the warrior-king of Yarlung, Namri Songtsen, began the work of unifying the clans of Tibet. It was his son, Songtsen Gampo, who consolidated an empire and established Tibet as a military power to be reckoned with and feared. Songtsen Gampo ruled from roughly 627-650 AD, and moved his base to the Lhasa region. He is credited with adapting Sanskrit for a Tibetan alphabet, and with drafting Tibet's first code of law. At this time, Nepal was briefly reduced to a vassal state, and in addition to his three Tibetan brides, Songtsen Gampo acquired a Nepalese princess (Bhrikuti Devi) and a Chinese princess (Wen Cheng). As the story runs, under the united persuasion of these two princesses (both devout Buddhists), Songtsen tried to incorporate the existing Tibetan Shamanist religion (known as Bon) into the Buddhist scheme of things. He constructed two temples in Lhasa to honour the princesses – one temple being the Jokhang.

The 7th and 8th centuries saw the continued meteoric rise of a Tibetan empire. It extended into Kashmir, China proper, Turkestan, Sikkim, Bhutan, Nepal, and Upper Burma. Tibet maintained constant pressure on China, with skirmishes along China's western border regions. By the late 7th century Tibet had gained a strong influence over central Asian trade-routes – including brief control of the Silk Road oases of Kashgar, Khotan and Kucha. The Chinese strongly contested these incursions, and in 763 the Tibetans, by way of reply, sacked the Tang Dynasty capital of Changan (Sian, or Xian). How Tibet could support these diverse and complex military operations remains something of an enigma.

The Tibetan ruler at this time was Trisong Detsen, who held power from 755-797 and is regarded as the greatest of the kings. Indian tantric master Padmasambhava was brought to Tibet during his reign and is said to have founded Samye Monastery (circa 775 AD), the first Buddhist university. Large numbers of Sanskrit tantras and texts were translated into Tibetan, and the primacy of Indian Buddhism over Chinese Buddhism was firmly established.

The Dark Ages

Around 815 Tritsug Detsan (known as Ralpachen) took the throne. In 821-22 he concluded a peace-treaty with the Chinese, but his domestic affairs were far from peaceful. In contrast with previous kings, Ralpachen tried to enforce strict Buddhist orthodoxy. The simmering mix of the old,

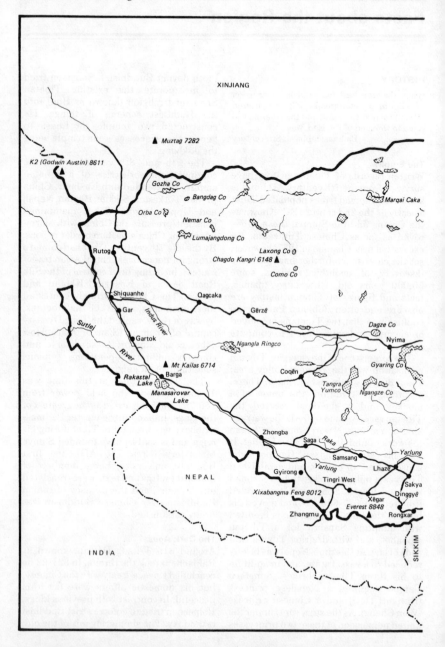

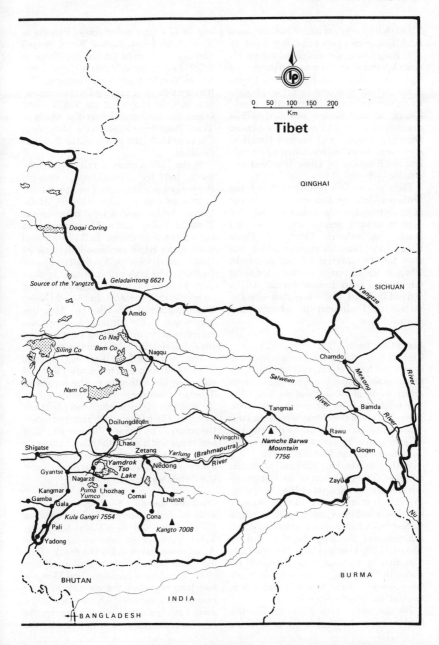

Tibetan Bon religion and of Indian-based Buddhism now came to boiling-point. In 836 Ralpachen was assassinated by his elder brother, Langdarma, who succeeded him and changed tack completely. Under pressure from Bon priests, he suppressed Buddhism in central Tibet and in a mad frenzy of destruction razed Buddhist monasteries, relentlessly persecuted Buddhist monks, and burned Buddhist scriptures. In 842 he was killed by a monk, and the Kingdom of Tibet dissolved into chaotic factions.

For close on four centuries, Tibet was broken up into lay and monastic pockets of influence. Established in the mid-9th century around present-day Zanda and Burang in western Tibet, the Guge Kingdom became an enclave which was vital for the survival of Buddhism. In 1042, at the invitation of the Guge royal family, the great Indian scholar Atisha arrived in Tibet. He is credited with the revival of Buddhism in western and central Tibet.

Rise of the Sects

From the 9th to the 20th centuries, time seems to have stood still in Tibet. A recovery was made, but there was to be no return to the glorious era of the kings. On the religious front great changes took place, but since the changes were derived from India, it could hardly be regarded as a Renaissance. Tibetan translators rapidly assimilated Indian Buddhist texts.

With the Muslim invasion of India, however, Tibet was cut off and began to develop its own brands of Buddhism. By the 12th century three Buddhist lineages or schools had emerged – the Nyingmapa (oldest order, founded by Padmasambhava, 8th century), the Kagyupa (founded by Marpa, 11th century) and the Sakyapa (founded by Drokmi, 11th Century). Of these, the Sakyapa, whose rising fortunes were linked with Mongol diplomacy, became the most influential.

By the early 13th century, Tibetan leaders had submitted to Genghis Khan, who in 1249 appointed Sakya Pandita as Viceroy of Tibet. Kublai Khan himself became a convert to Tibetan Buddhism in 1270. From roughly 1200 to 1350 Tibet was welded back into a political unit, with the core area being Yarlung-Lhasa-Shigatse, although the control of the Sakya grand lamas did not extend over the whole of Tibet. With the collapse of the Mongols in China in 1368, the power of the Sakyapa declined.

In the 14th century, a reformist movement led by Tsongkhapa, strongly challenged the Sakyapa. The new school, known as the Gelukpa (Yellow Hats) gained the support of local rulers in the Tsangpo Valley, and of Mongol chiefs at the northern frontiers. In 1578 Mongol ruler Altan Khan conferred the title of Dalai Lama (Ocean of Wisdom) on Sonam Gyatso, third high priest of the Gelukpa Sect. The title was posthumously conferred on his two predecessors. In 1641-2 Gushri Khan, leader of the Khoshot Mongols, intervened in the struggle between the religious sects in Tibet and established the 5th Gelukpa Dalai Lama as ruler.

The 'Great Fifth' (Lobsang Gyatso, 1617-1682) managed to reunify Tibet and extended his authority to the fringes of Tibetan territory. He instituted a 'harmonious blend of religion and politics', a system which is generally referred to as a theocracy. The Great Fifth visited China and reopened trade with India. During his reign many monasteries were erected – symbols of a new centralised power – and the Potala was rebuilt.

The Great Game

With its strategic buffer position between the populous nations of China and India, Tibet increasingly became a pawn in Asian power plays. After the death of the 5th Dalai Lama, Tibet was plunged into chaos by Mongol factions. The Mongols had long regarded the country as their domain and occupied Lhasa twice in the early 18th century (1705-1708 under the Khoshot Mongols and in 1717 under the

Dzungar Mongols). The Manchu Emperors (Qing Dynasty) saw Tibet as the key to controlling the fierce Mongols, and in 1720 the Emperor Kangxi sent a Chinese army to deal with them. Both the Mongols and the Chinese attempted to interfere with the selection and fate of the Dalai and Panchen Lamas. In 1707 Latsang Khan (Khoshot Mongols) sent the licentious 6th Dalai Lama on a journey to Litang, where he disappeared. Latsang then selected a 25-year-old monk (rumoured to be his natural son) as a puppet Dalai Lama – a choice that caused an uprising among the Tibetans in 1717. Meanwhile, the Tibetans had discovered the 7th Dalai Lama, a child-reincarnation from Litang, who was subsequently captured by Chinese troops in 1720.

The Chinese tore down the walls of Lhasa in 1720, quartered a large garrison within Tibet, and annexed part of Kham Province to Sichuan. They left two Qing Viceroys to direct foreign relations. During Manchu overlordship, there was loose supervision through imperial represent-atives (ambans) in Lhasa. Tibet turned to China for support in 1788 when faced with an invading Gurkha army which wanted to settle trading, territorial and religious issues. After chasing each other back and forth, the Gurkhas and the Tibetans made a peace agreement in 1792. In the process, the power of the Chinese ambans in Tibet increased considerably. The door to Tibet was closed by the Manchus.

Meanwhile, the states of Sikkim, Bhutan and Ladakh had splintered to become distinct political units. By the mid-19th century, Manchu power in Tibet was waning and in 1856 when another Gurkha army invaded Tibet the Chinese did not help. The Nepalese exacted an annual tribute from the Tibetans. From 1806 to 1875, the Dalai Lamas were short-lived and the 9th, 10th, 11th and 12th Dalai Lamas did not live to assume full power. Some died in suspicious circumstances and power was held by the regents.

The stage was set for the Russo-British

rivalry which was known in Asia as 'The Great Game'. The British Raj feared that the Russians had designs on Tibet as a gateway to India. In 1888 there was a border dispute between British Sikkim and Tibet but the Tibetans retreated. In 1900 a lama called Dorjieff was reported to have delivered a letter from the Dalai Lama to the Czar of Russia. This episode confirmed British paranoia – Dorjieff was a Buryat Mongol by birth, and thus a Russian citizen. There were also rumours of a secret Russo-Chinese treaty con-cerning Tibet.

In 1903-4 a British expeditionary force under Francis Younghusband invaded Tibet and reached Lhasa. The reality of this game was that the Tibetans could not hope to resist superior British technology – in one engagement some 600 Tibetans were mowed down by Maxim guns. The 13th Dalai Lama fled to Mongolia, where he remained for four years, and the British coerced the Tibetans into signing an agreement on trade and border rights. Oddly enough, after the slaughter inflicted by the British on the Tibetans, the two nations became best of friends – after all, which two peoples spend more time drinking tea? In 1910 when the Chinese invaded Lhasa, the 13th Dalai Lama fled to India under British protection.

Captain O'Connor, British trade agent at Gyantse early in this century, described the ordinary Tibetans as 'simply agri-cultural people, superstitious indeed to the last degree, but devoid of any deep-rooted religious convictions or heart-searchings, oppressed by the most monstrous growth of monasticism and priest-craft which the world has ever seen'. Those who bowed to the yoke of the nobles and officials were generally well-treated but those who did not were submitted to hideous punishments which included the putting out of eyes and flaying alive.

Interlude

The 13th Dalai Lama, Thupten Gyatso

(1876-1933), returned to Tibet in 1912. The Manchu (Qing) Dynasty had fallen in China and Tibet expelled Chinese troops and officials from its territory, with a rough borderline being established at the Mekong-Salween divide. The president of the new Chinese Republic, Yuan Shikai, sent the Dalai Lama a telegram announcing that he would restore the Dalai Lama's rank. The Dalai Lama replied that he already had that rank, and that he had resumed the normal government of his country. This was regarded in Tibet as a declaration of independence. Earlier in 1912 Yuan Shikai had stated that the Chinese would not relinquish their hold on previous Manchu territory, including Mongolia, Xinjiang and Tibet. Chinese claims over Tibet dated from 1720 but a weak Chinese Government could do little to enforce them.

Tibet's claim to independence was not formally recognised by other nations. Independence in Tibet carried a de facto status derived from British policy on Tibet. To sort out territories the British arranged the Simla Conference (1913-14) where Tibet tried to gain recognition for its independent status, and where China asserted its claim over Tibet. The upshot was that the British formulated a compromise solution where Tibet had autonomy within Chinese suzerainty (not sovereignty) – a solution that would not now be recognised as legal. This was done to allow the Chinese to save face and to give the Tibetans assurance that the Chinese would stay out. Tibet signed the Convention, but the Chinese did not, thus releasing the Tibetans from any obligation to China. The conference established the Tibeto-Indian borders (the McMahon Line), but left the Chinese-Tibetan borders in limbo. Since China refused to sign the Convention, it paved the way for independent trading between Britain and Tibet.

There followed 20 years of peace in Tibet – Tibet remained neutral through both world wars. During this time, the 13th Dalai Lama experimented with modernisation; officers of the Tibetan army were given training by the British, Tibetan students were sent to England, a hydro-electric plant was constructed in Lhasa, and the first motor-car rumbled across the High Plateau. Reforms and modernisations did not, however, affect the majority of the people, who were impoverished serfs. Thupten Gyatso died in 1933. He was succeeded by the 14th Dalai Lama, Tenzin Gyatso, who was born in 1935. Tenzin Gyatso was enthroned in 1940, with effective power held by the Regent, the Abbot of Reting Monastery. In 1941 Reting Rinpoche decided to go on a religious retreat, and handed over the Regency to the Dalai Lama's senior tutor, Taktra Rinpoche. Taktra Rinpoche's period in power was marked by corruption and in 1947 there was a minor civil war in Lhasa when monks at Sera Monastery violently protested the detainment of Reting Rinpoche (who died in prison shortly after).

Chinese Invasion

In 1947 India won its independence, thus removing any British deterrent to a Chinese invasion of Tibet. The new Communist government, assuming power in 1949, wasted little time in asserting its claims. In October 1950 the Chinese advanced from Sichuan toward Chamdo, which they captured. Another Chinese contingent moved from Xinjiang into western Tibet. The Dalai Lama had mobilised a force of 12,000 men to meet the Chinese but the Tibetans were poorly equipped and would have been easily defeated. The 14th Dalai Lama, then 15 years old, had the choice of negotiating with the Chinese, resisting them, or fleeing to India. The first course was chosen, although the Dalai Lama had no part in the initial negotiations. The captured governor of Chamdo, Ngapo Ngawang Jigme, signed a 17-Point Agreement for the 'peaceful liberation of Tibet' in May 1951.

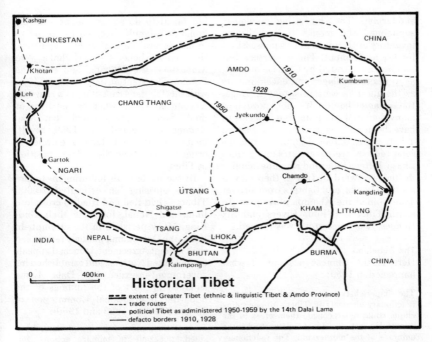

Historical Tibet

▬▬▬ extent of Greater Tibet (ethnic & linguistic Tibet & Amdo Province)
- - - trade routes
▬▬▬ political Tibet as administered 1950-1959 by the 14th Dalai Lama
▬▬▬ defacto borders 1910, 1928

Under the 17-Point Agreement, Tibet would continue to be self-governed under the Dalai Lama, but China would provide the military backbone and conduct foreign relations. Ostensibly, the status quo would remain intact – religious freedom and the Tibetan language were guaranteed – but any Tibetan claim to independence was relinquished. The Chinese proposed that roads, schools, hospitals and light industry be introduced – which met with the Dalai Lama's approval. In 1954 the Dalai Lama made a visit to China, at which time Mao Zedong confided ominously 'Religion is poison.'

At first the Tibetans welcomed the reforms as a break from the feudal past, but the honeymoon was short-lived. China had been quietly carving off pieces of Tibet and donating them to neighboring provinces. Amdo, to the north, had been incorporated into Qinghai and treated as part of China. Likewise, large sections of

Kham, to the east, were donated to Sichuan, Gansu and Yunnan Provinces. Monastic lands were confiscated, tribal lands were collectivised, and it soon became apparent that the Chinese idea of schooling was very different from the Tibetan idea. Road building did not benefit the Tibetans – it enabled the Chinese military to get around. Food shortages developed with the influx of Chinese settlers and road-builders. Tibetans had little empathy for the zeal of Maoism, and alongside the construction of hydro-electric stations, experimental farms and roads, armed resistance took place at various places from 1954-59.

The main uprisings took place in Kham, where the Chinese made the fatal mistake of trying to disarm the tribesmen – the Khampas. In February 1956, the Chinese People's Liberation Army (PLA) laid siege to the Monastery of Litang which was defended by several thousand monks and farmers. The Chinese had previously summoned the monks to compile an inventory of the monastery's possessions for tax assessment. The monastery was bombed and strafed by Chinese aircraft, as were other villages and encampments as the guerrilla warfare spread to Dêgê, Batang and Chamdo. It is not known how many died in the fighting, but it seems to have been full-scale warfare in eastern Tibet, with a number of Chinese atrocities reported by refugees streaming into Lhasa. Fifteen thousand Khampa families drifted westward to Lhasa, then moved south to Lhoka, and fighters from all over Tibet joined the Khampa movement. In south Tibet the 'Four Rivers and Six Ranges' resistance group was formed.

The Rebellion

Here is the Chinese account of what happened in 1959:

The imperialists and a small number of reactionary elements in Tibet's upper ruling clique could not reconcile themselves to the peaceful liberation of Tibet and its return to the embrace of the motherland. The reactionary elements were intent upon launching an armed rebellion, negating the agreement and detaching Tibet from China. Abetted by the imperialists, they continued to sabotage and create disturbances. Despite the central government's consistent persuasion and education, they finally launched an armed rebellion in March, 1959.

But, contrary to their desires, this rebellion accelerated the destruction of Tibet's reactionary forces and brought Tibet onto the bright, democratic, socialist road sooner than expected.
Beijing Review, 27 June , 1983

According to the Tibetans, in early March 1959 the Dalai Lama (then 23 years old) was invited to a cultural performance without his usual bodyguards. Thousands of refugees from Kham, who had flooded into Lhasa, mounted spontaneous mass demonstrations against the Chinese, concentrating their numbers at the Norbulinka and outside the Potala. The Dalai Lama attempted to placate them, but failed to do so, and along with his immediate family, decided to escape to India. Several days after his departure, the Chinese shelled the Norbulinka, Sera Monastery, the Jokhang, and even the Potala. The fighting lasted three days, with the Tibetans caught up in a religious fervour, not caring whether they lived or died. Some sources claim that Mao Zedong engineered the 1959 revolt, including the Dalai Lama's escape, in order to strengthen the Chinese position in Tibet.

By the end of 1959, following the failure of the uprising, an estimated 20,000 Tibetans had fled and tried to cross into India and Nepal, following their God-King. Many perished in the attempt. In India, the Dalai Lama publicly renounced the 17-Point Agreement, launched appeals to the United Nations, and established his government-in-exile. The Dalai Lama summed up part of the findings of the impartial International Commission of Jurists (Geneva, 1959 and 1960):

Tens of thousands of our people have been killed, not only in military actions, but individually and deliberately. They have been killed without trial, on suspicion of opposing communism, or of hoarding money, or simply because of their position, or for no reason at all. But mainly and fundamentally they have been killed because they would not renounce their religion. They have not only been shot, but beaten to death, crucified, burned alive, drowned, vivisected, starved, strangled, hanged, scalded, buried alive, disemboweled and beheaded. These killings have been done in public. Men and women have been slowly killed while their own families were forced to watch, and small children have even been forced to shoot their parents.
The Dalai Lama, *My Land & My People*, 1962

The Cultural Revolution

The period from 1959 until the easing of Chinese policy in Tibet around 1979 is not history but a horror-story – the obliteration of history. Recovering from the vicious reprisals of 1959, Tibet was hurled

Top & Left: Ganden Monastery near Lhasa – completely destroyed (RS)
Right: Defaced fresco at Norbulinka, Lhasa (MB)

Top: Younger initiates debating at Sera Monastery (MB)
Left: Butter lamps at Jokhang Temple, Lhasa (MB)
Right: Monk at Palkhor Choide Lamasery, Gyantse (MB)

headlong into the madness of the Cultural Revolution (1966-76) which hit Tibet harder than any other part of China.

With the flight of the Dalai Lama, the Chinese dissolved the remnants of the Tibetan Government, and although the Tibetan Autonomous Region (TAR) was set up in 1965, it was autonomous in name only. Ngapo Ngawang Jigme, a leading collaborator with the Chinese, was named as its head. China now had complete administrative, political and economic control of Tibet and the role of the monasteries had been completely eliminated. While China claimed that there were bumper harvests under the newly organised system of communes, thousands of Tibetans starved to death while the harvests were shipped off to feed Chinese. The socialist transformation of Tibet was accelerated and the communes were ordered to grow winter wheat (a Chinese food) instead of the traditional barley.

A number of misconceptions have arisen about what happened during the Cultural Revolution – not that a particularly clear picture is possible anyway. First, it would appear that monasteries, castles, and historic buildings were dismantled before the onset of the Cultural Revolution, which gives a different slant to the destruction. And second, although there was a large influx of Red Guards in Lhasa in 1966, it would appear that most of the destruction was carried out by young Tibetans who had joined rival Red Guard factions. The Chinese stood in the background orchestrating the orgy. There seems to have been some method in the Red Guards' madness as items of value within the temples were designated for shipment to China before the destruction. Scriptures were burned in bonfires, the buildings were dynamited, and local communes were invited to cart off the timber and stones that were left.

All forms of Tibetan customs and worship, public and private, were banned – including barter. Tibetans were com-

pelled to memorise passages from Mao's Little Red Book, and participate in Mao Thought Study classes. Those who erred were subjected to *thamzing* (struggle session), a refined form of public torture and humiliation which could easily result in death. Large numbers of Tibetans died in labour-camps and prisons. There are no figures, but one source claims that 10,000 persons died between 1960 and 1965 in Drapchi prison in Lhasa.

It is most likely that the young Tibetans who joined Red Guard factions had not the slightest idea what the differences between the two main factions were. Faction-fighting, which continued until 1969, combined with famine, provoked Tibetan uprisings in various parts of Tibet which were directed against the PLA. Khampa rebels, from their base in Mustang, Nepal, continued to mount attacks from across the border. In 1970, with the Red Guards gone, but the Cultural Revolution far from over, another wave of arrests and executions took place in a 'class-cleansing' campaign.

'About Face'
When the dust settled on the '60s and '70s, thousands of monasteries had been destroyed – and because of the sand-papering winds of Tibet they look like they've been that way for thousands of years. For the people, the wounds will take much longer to heal, if that is ever possible.

The turn-around in Chinese policy started in 1979, three years after the death of Mao Zedong and the fall of the Gang of Four. In 1979 General Ren Rong, Chinese Communist Party (CCP) chief in Tibet for the previous 10 years, was dismissed in disgrace by Beijing. At the same time, Beijing started to open a dialogue with the Dalai Lama's government-in-exile, allowing delegations from Dharamsala to visit Tibet. Far from being the conciliatory gesture the Chinese expected, these delegations roused the feelings of the Tibetans to a fervour. One delegation was expelled for giving the 'wrong speech'. The reports of the delegations were hardly flattering, and neither were those of foreign pressmen who were allowed to visit in 1979.

In 1980 top-ranking CCP chiefs Hu Yaobang and Wan Li toured Tibet, and Beijing admitted that it had made a number of mistakes in its attitude toward the Tibetans. Yin Fatang, a relatively liberal-minded military man, was given the reins; unlike many of his subordinates, he could speak Tibetan. In the years that followed, taxes were waived, state subsidies were increased, communes were dismantled, farmers were permitted to grow the crop of their choice, and herders were allowed to graze livestock as they wished. A few monasteries were reopened following restoration, and freedom of worship was somewhat restored. These were gestures towards a new Chinese 'hands off' policy on Tibet. Yin Fatang publicly appealed to the Dalai Lama and Tibetans in exile to return to Tibet for a visit or re-settlement. In 1984 he threw the region open to investment by Tibetans in exile, and promised to foot the bill for schooling their children in Tibet.

These concessions were taken with a grain of salt by the Dalai Lama's government-in-exile. 'Once bitten by a snake you feel suspicious even when you see a piece of rope,' was the way the Dalai Lama put it. In 1982 negotiations, members of the Dalai Lama's cabinet visited Beijing to demand the withdrawal of Chinese troops, enlargement of the territory's present borders, and terms for autonomy similar to those being offered to Taiwan. The Chinese, upset by the reaction of the Tibetan people to the Dalai Lama's delegations in Tibet in 1979 and 1980, made it clear that if the Dalai Lama were to return he would be based in Beijing and only allowed occasional visits to his homeland. In Beijing he would hold a desk job as one of the Vice-Chairmen of the National People's Congress, China's rubber-stamp parliament.

Government-in-exile

The Dalai Lama's government-in-exile is a continuing source of embarrassment and irritation to the Chinese. The Dalai Lama has travelled frequently throughout both the east and the west, and has gained considerable sympathy for his cause, which is not only greater freedom for Tibet but world peace in general. Countries that previously refused him entry (such as the USA and France) now welcome him, although they do not officially recognise his government. The Dalai Lama has even been favourably received in Communist bloc countries.

There are a number of offices representing the Dalai Lama's government: in New Delhi, New York, London, Switzerland, Tokyo and Kathmandu. The function of these offices is to keep the world informed of the situation in Tibet, to promote a deeper understanding of that situation, to foster awareness of all aspects of Tibetan culture, and to seek aid and assistance for the needs of Tibetans in exile. Through a network of Tibetan foundations, institutes and monasteries abroad, the government-in-exile has been quite successful in publicising its case.

The main exile centre in Dharamsala (India) has kept Tibetan customs and culture alive. A Council of Ministers (the Kashag) and the Assembly of the Tibetan People's Deputies supervise a number of departments and councils, and maintain links with the 40-odd Tibetan refugee settlements in India, Nepal, Sikkim and Bhutan. Tibet's famous monasteries – such as those of Sera, Drepung, and Ganden – have been built anew in south India, where the majority of Tibetan refugees have settled.

TIBET TODAY

The question of Tibet is far from resolved. Hefty state subsidies have certainly improved the lot of the Tibetans recently, but on the whole they're not happy with Chinese rule. Members of a determined pro-independence underground thrust appeals to the UN into the hands of journalists who visit Lhasa. Tibetans who talk to foreign journalists have been detained, as have some Tibetan exiles when they have visited their homeland. Beijing will not tolerate any mention of independence and is prepared to deal harshly with offenders – Tibetans are executed for anti-Chinese agitation. How this can be reconciled with the policy of allowing greater autonomy is a problem which has not yet been resolved. Although some concessions have been made by the Chinese in the '80s, it is a little too early to tell how sincere and far-reaching the gestures are. For instance, the Tibetan language has yet to be restored in secondary schools, and to general use. The restoration of religious freedoms has unavoidable political overtones even though it may only be a showcase for attracting tourism. Whether Beijing will tolerate a full return to religious 'superstition' remains to be seen. Transient pilgrims often take three months to get to Lhasa or Shigatse, and this does not sit well with the Chinese who have been trying to settle the nomads. Proselytising of Tibetan Buddhism is restricted by Han cadres.

In September 1985 a 'celebration' of Tibet's 20 years as an autonomous region took place in Lhasa. Since 1983 the Chinese had been building new schools, hotels, sports facilities, roads and other projects around Lhasa in preparation. At the last minute the Chinese government informed foreign reporters and governments that the show would be closed to them. It also announced that foreign pressmen would be screened for future trips to Tibet due to the unsatisfactory reporting that had occurred (some of which was based on the Chinese media). In Delhi, hundreds of Tibetan refugees gathered outside the Chinese Embassy to demand a cancellation of the ceremonies. A letter presented by a member of the government-in-exile demanded an internationally-supervised referendum on self-

Tibet Celebrations Amid Tight Security

LHASA, September 2 (AFP).

Political activists were put behind bars and foreigners kept out of bounds at the official celebrations to mark the 20th anniversary of Tibet becoming an autonomous region of China began here 'peacefully' amid tight security.

The celebrations began yesterday with a parade in a large park in front of the Potala Palace here. and an Agence France Presse reporter who entered the city said extraordinarily tough security measures were taken and the police presence was so strong that there were almost as many policemen as civilians in the crowd.

According to Tibetan sources, political activists have been arrested and are being kept out of the way until the celebrations end on Thursday and there were also rumours among Tibetans that a bomb was found in Lhasa's telex centre.

Everybody entering Lhasa was frisked, and foreigners were kept out of the city during the celebrations. Access to the high-ranking officials' area of the park was carefully controlled, only those with special passes being allowed to enter.

Agence France Presse, 2 September, 1985

determination in Tibet and called the event a grave provocation: 'What is there to celebrate? Tibet today is a graveyard of a rich and unique civilisation.'

Meanwhile, back in Lhasa, a CCP official was quoted in a local newspaper: 'For the upcoming celebration it is necessary to strictly control guns, ammunition, explosives and other toxic agents and to strengthen education for personnel carrying guns or pistols so they can avoid losing them or having them stolen.' A dress-rehearsal for the event featured PLA men lying prone on the rooftops with machine-guns. Security for the four-day event was extraordinarily tight, with thousands of Chinese police and army personnel in evidence. There were reports of Lhasa residents and visiting Tibetans from India being arrested.

For security reasons no programme was given out – radio and television stations announced the scheduled activities at the last minute. The Tibetans themselves were neither invited, nor expected, to attend the festivities. In the midst of this, the Panchen Lama showed up from Beijing, causing hysterical scenes as Tibetans sought his blessing. It was the second appearance of the Panchen Lama on Tibetan soil since 1965.

When they weren't busy monitoring ammunition, the Chinese announced plans to distribute 80,000 alarm-clocks, 10,000 metres of silk and 400,000 boxes of tea to the needy. *China Daily* and the Chinese media spewed forth an avalanche of reports and statistics about the new Tibet and all telephone links into Lhasa were suspended to effectively bar foreign reporters from any coverage. Top-ranking CCP delegate Hu Qili delivered a speech on the building of a new socialist Tibet. He said that Tibet was entering a phase of social stability and unity, but underlined the fact that 'Tibet is part of our motherland's sacred territory that cannot be put asunder'. This message was backed up by Wu Jinghua, who replaced Yin Fatang as Beijing's CCP chief in Lhasa in mid-1985. Presumably the message was given in Chinese although the Panchen Lama had earlier stated that reports or speeches given in Chinese should be translated into Tibetan.

This non-event – the 20th anniversary of the Tibetan Autonomous Republic – encapsulates the present situation. The Tibetans are outraged, but the Chinese choose to ignore them, steadfastly believing that the socialist transformation of Tibet has been a complete success.

EARLY TRAVEL & EXPLORATION
Filling in the Blanks

In 1979, when the first foreign tourists were permitted a peek at Lhasa by the Chinese, only 1200 westerners had ever seen the Holy City (including some 600 invading members of the Younghusband expedition of 1903-4). Just getting there was a major accomplishment but if you stayed you were guaranteed a bestseller: *Three Years in Tibet* by Ekai Kawaguchi, 1909; *Twenty Years in Tibet* by David Macdonald, 1932; *Seven Years in Tibet* by Heinrich Harrer, 1953 ... The west lusted after the blank spaces on the map.

The first westerners to enter Tibet were Jesuits. In 1642 a Portuguese missionary, Antonio de Andrade, made a difficult journey from Delhi to Tsaparang, the capital of Western Tibet (Guge Kingdom, close to the present-day Zanda), for a reconnaissance of the heathen. His retinue endured blinding snowstorms and was baffled by the unknown phenomenon of altitude sickness. The following year Andrade returned to set up a mission, which was sacked by the King of Ladakh in 1630. Another mission, which was set up in Shigatse, was caught up in the rivalry between the Yellow and Red Hats (opposing religious orders) and was also abandoned.

In 1661 the first Jesuits reached Lhasa. They were the priests John Grueber and Albert D'Orville who had set out from Peking to reach Rome overland. D'Orville died in India, but Grueber eventually reached Rome. He was the first European to see the Potala (an earlier version of the present one), and he filed a report on Tibetan living conditions. He noted, with some distaste, that sought-after 'curative' pills in Lhasa were in fact made from the Dalai Lama's excrement.

In 1716 two more Jesuit priests,

Ippolito Desideri and Emmanuel Freyre also reached Lhasa. They had set off with the intention of re-establishing the Tsaparang mission. Freyre left shortly after arriving and Desideri found himself the sole European in Lhasa – until three Capuchin monks suddenly popped up and demanded that he withdraw. The Capuchins, who had previously tried to establish a Lhasa mission in 1708, were back again. In 1718 Rome awarded the Tibetan parish to the Capuchins, but the news did not reach Lhasa till much later. Desideri hung on, remaining in Tibet for five years, dodging Capuchin priests, Yellow Hats and Mongol princes, and working on a book which 'exposed Lamaism'. In 1721, after the downfall of the Dzungar Mongols in Lhasa at the hands of the Chinese, Desideri could no longer ignore orders from Rome and he departed for India. The Capuchins, under Orazio della

Penna, struggled on until 1745, when they were tossed out. The number of converts by the year 1733 was given as seven.

The only others to attempt a Christian conversion of Tibet were two French Lazarists, a century later. In 1844-46 Abbe Huc and Joseph Gabet journeyed from Peking via Koko Nor to Lhasa, stayed several months, and were thrown out by the Chinese Amban. If the Jesuits and the Capuchins had accomplished little else, however, they had aroused the west's curiosity about this mysterious kingdom. Atlas-publishers eagerly snapped up any surveying morsels that the missionaries had.

A remarkable journey was made by the independent Dutch adventurer Samuel Van de Putte, who from 1725-35 crossed Tibet twice in caravans – from Ladakh via Lhasa to Peking and back again, in disguise. Despite their value he ordered

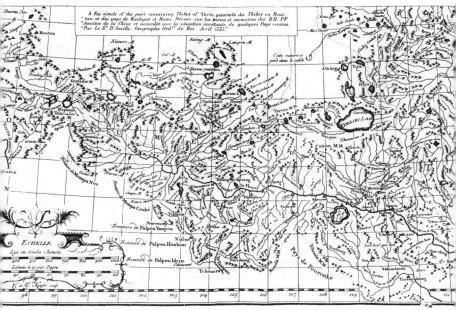

D'Anville map of 1733

his notes destroyed, and all that remains from the journeys is a sketch-map (now in a Dutch museum) and some indecipherable scraps of paper.

A map of Tibet was published in Paris in 1733 by Jean D'Anville, as part of a collection on China, based on the Great Lama Survey ordered by the Chinese Emperor Kangxi. The lamas had been trained by early 18th century Jesuit missionaries. It was the D'Anville map that George Bogle, a British East India Company envoy, used on his mission to Shigatse in 1775. The British East India Company saw Tibet as a back-door for trade with China, which was cut off by the xenophobic Manchus. They were also interested in Tibetan borax and other minerals (gold!) and the feasibility of selling English cloth. George Bogle was dispatched with a multi-purpose mission that included plans to bring back a live pair of mountain-goats (famous for their soft wool), and any rare plant or seed samples.

Bogle and his retinue set off through Bhutan, where word was received from the Tashi Lama (Panchen Lama) that no *fringy* (Tibetan – foreigner) would be allowed into Tibet. Bogle managed to beat the odds, and he reached Gyantse where he had an audience with the Tashi Lama. He then travelled on to Shigatse and managed to gain the Tashi Lama's confidence to the degree that he married one of the Lama's sisters. Shigatse was as far as Bogle got; he was refused permission to enter Lhasa, and was told that any trading would have to be arranged through the Chinese court. A follow-up mission under Samuel Turner, in 1783, did little to advance the case of the East India Company.

With the outbreak of war between Nepal and Tibet in 1788, the position of the Chinese in Tibet was greatly strengthened. Tibet's doors became as tightly closed as China's, and Chinese troops were stationed in Lhasa, Shigatse, Xêgar and Phari (Pali) by 1793. No Englishman would reach Lhasa for over a century – with one exception.

Thomas Manning

In the winter of 1811, Thomas Manning, a most eccentric individual traveller, arrived in Tibet. Frustrated in his attempts to get to Peking from Canton, the Englishman decided to try his luck from India. The prize of visiting Lhasa fell to a man who never wanted it – Lhasa simply got in his way. He bumbled through to the Holy City intent on getting to Xining and thence to Peking, where he hoped to advance his study of Chinese. He hated travelling, had no financial backing, and made no preparations (he did take along a pair of ice-skates, in anticipation of winter sports in the Himalaya). For company he had a Chinese servant, a sullen character with whom he argued much of the way and finally fired in Lhasa.

Manning refused to tell a soul of his exploits; the only records are letters, and a short journal that was rescued after his death and published in 1876. Although he was considered the foremost Chinese scholar in Europe, Manning published only a slim volume of Chinese jokes in translation. Among the unpublished material, there was a paper on the consumption of tea in Bhutan, Tibet and Tartary, and his Tibetan journal. The journal was not intended for the public and mostly contains trivia of a personal nature.

He started his trip in Calcutta and made his way up through Phari (Pali) where he fell in with a Chinese general. The general's escort force badly needed medical attention. Manning set up an impromptu clinic, though his qualifications as a physician were dubious. As luck would have it, the general and his entourage were headed for Gyantse. Two bottles of cherry brandy, donated to the cause, got Manning a ticket that far. The general even persuaded Manning to have some warmer Chinese clothes made up. Between Phari (Pali) and Gyantse, Manning mentions a lake which he sized up for skating:

The lake was frozen; at least that part we were next, and would certainly have borne me. My skates were not many miles off . . . We stopped but a few minutes and proceeded on to where the lake becomes a river . . . There were many fine, fat ducks on it, which were very tame, and let us come close to them. The people of Tibet never disturb them: they eat no birds, but, on the contrary, let the birds eat them. The sun here was burning hot. There were a few miserable-looking houses scattered about, looking like ruins of villages, as the Tibet houses often do, and a few patches of arable land.

Manning now assumed a role as a Chinese physician, although nobody took his disguise seriously even though he wore Chinese spectacles. His copious beard was out of character with the disguise but he could not bring himself to part with it:

He (the Chinese general) was greatly taken with my beard, and seemed as if he could never sufficiently admire it. He adverted to it both then and afterwards on other occasions. He named such and such a mandarin, such a one he thought had better moustaches; in fact, I had kept mine cut short in India, for convenience of eating soup and drink, and they were not yet full grown.

Setting up shop in Gyantse, Manning dispensed herbal remedies, opium, and solution of arsenic, to the needy. Then astonishingly, he was, with the assistance of his friend the general, allowed to proceed to Lhasa:

The road here, as it winds past the palace is royally broad; it is level and free from stones, and combined with the view of the lofty towering palace, which forms a majestic mountain of building, has a magnificent effect. The roads about the palace swarmed with monks; its nooks and angles with beggars lounging and basking in the sun. This again reminded me of what I have heard of Rome. My eye was almost perpetually fixed on the palace, and roving over its parts, the disposition of which being irregular, eluded my attempts at analysis. As a whole it seemed perfect enough;

but I could not comprehend its plan in detail. Fifteen or twenty minutes now brought us to the entrance of the town of Lhasa.

If the palace exceeded my expectations, the town as far fell short of them. There is nothing striking, nothing pleasing in its appearance. The habitations are begrimed with smut and dirt. The avenues are full of dogs, some growling and gnawing bits of hide which lie about in profusion, and emit a charnel-house smell; other limping and looking livid; others ulcerated; others starving and dying, and pecked at by the ravens; some dead and preyed upon. In short, everything seems mean and gloomy, and excites the idea of something unreal. Even the mirth and laughter of the inhabitants I thought dreamy and ghostly. The dreaminess no doubt was in my mind, but I could never get rid of the idea; it strengthened upon me afterwards.

Shortly after his arrival in Lhasa, Manning obtained an unprecedented audience with the seven-year-old Dalai Lama (IX), which he records as a moving experience. Manning was allowed to remain in Lhasa for four months – but having contracted rheumatism, he never put on his skates, indeed, he seems to have forgotten about them. He was now running very low on funds, though his medical practice in Lhasa provided some income. Not all his patients benefited. He mentions in his journal that the Grand Lama's personal physician complained of a 'general debility' – Manning prescribed an oily mixture, a glass of wine, and a Spanish-fly blister, and then dryly notes: 'He died.'

Suddenly, around February 1812, the journal stops after some ominous reflections on the prospect of torture. It seems that he was rumoured to be a spy, and that the Chinese emperor had sent for his head. Manning quickly repaired to India.

In 1817 he joined a British Embassy delegation to Peking as an interpreter, on the condition that he was allowed to keep his flowing beard, although he did agree to dispense with his long Chinese gowns. He finally reached the city of his dreams – Peking – but only stayed briefly, as the mission was aborted following an argument over protocol. Sorely disappointed, Manning returned to England where he lived in a cottage devoid of furniture but containing the best Chinese library in England. Quixotic to the end, he spent his time in study and meditation. His beard, now waist-length, had turned white. He died in 1840.

The Age of Explorers

Manning added zero to geographers' knowledge of Tibet, which was embarrassingly slim. By the 1860s the British, who had taken the lead as topographers in Tibet, still had no precise location for even Shigatse or Lhasa. Motives for venturing into these uncharted snowlands, however, were now much more complex. The missionaries had (almost) given up, the British and the Russians were intent on reconnaissance, and a motley crew of unauthorised explorers, mystics, mountaineers, geographers and plain sensationalists came to the fore (some never came back from the fore). Tibet continued to exert a peculiar fascination for travellers of the Victorian era. With the mysteries of the Nile solved and Africa trampled over, Tibet's rivers and mountains remained untouched. With the discovery in 1852 that Mt Everest was the highest mountain yet sighted, fascination increased.

Most of the footwork for the British reconnaissance of Tibet was undertaken by Indian agents, known as pundits. Posing as holy men, these remarkable agents mapped out much of the unknown terrain and for the first time accurately gauged the position and elevation of Lhasa. The reconnaissance was carried out between 1865 and 1885, with some of the strangest equipment ever used by surveyors including adapted prayer-wheels and rosaries, and marked logs which were dumped in rivers and traced when they were discovered in India. The results of the surveys revealed that the old D'Anville map, based on Jesuit survey methods, was inaccurate. Nain Singh (code-named

'Number One') was awarded the Royal Geographical Society's gold medal for his charting of Central Tibet and the goldfields of Western Tibet. A protégé, Kishen Singh (code-named A K) prepared a highly detailed map of Lhasa, and mapped large tracts of Tibet, including Amdo Province.

Toward the turn of the century, the efforts of explorers to bluff their way through to Lhasa intensified. Lhasa had become as difficult a goal as Mecca. In 1889-90, explorer Henri D'Orleans joined another Frenchman, Bonvalot, for an expedition into central Asia. Their goal, starting from Moscow, was Haiphong, via China and Tibet. They were stopped and turned back just short of Lhasa, but D'Orleans managed to take many photographs of northern and eastern Tibet, which were among the first published (1892). Even the greatest explorers of the age – Russian Nicholai Przhevalsky (entered Tibet 1879) and Swede Sven Hedin (entered Tibet 1896) – failed to make it to Lhasa, despite repeated attempts. The only outsider who did succeed before 1903 was the Japanese Buddhist, Ekai Kawaguchi, who travelled to Lhasa in disguise (1899-1901) by way of Mt Kailas.

In 1903-4 the British invaded Tibet, with a force of 100 Englishmen, 1100 Gurkhas and Sikhs, 10,000 porters, and some 20,000 beasts of burden. The force forged through to Lhasa on the excuse of dealing with trade problems. The expedition forcefully opened the door to Tibet and took some of the lustre off Lhasa as a destination. Although the British withdrew by 1908 they left behind trade-agents and other links. In 1905 an obscure academic journal, known as *National Geographic*, published its first photo-essay – pictures of Tibet taken by two Russian explorers. Sven Hedin, the famous Swedish explorer, gave up on the idea of getting to Lhasa and instead shifted his attention to the riddle of Mt Kailas' rivers. Mt Kailas was believed to be the source of the Indus, the

Brahmaputra, the Sutlej and the Ganges rivers. From 1907-8 he mapped and travelled the mountainous regions of western Tibet.

Limited numbers of adventurers – some now famous, others not – managed to gain access to Tibet after 1904, including hefty groups with the British Everest expeditions in the 1920s. The exploits of some of the 20th century adventurers appear in other sections of this book.

The problem of mapping out Tibet is certainly not solved, even in the mid-'80s – unless you have access to Chinese military mapping. Heinrich Harrer and Peter Aufschnaiter provided the basis for modern knowledge of Lhasa and parts of Tibet with maps which were completed in the 1940s. Since then the Chinese have radically changed the face of Tibet, and changed place-names to Pinyin. With Tibet's closure from 1950-79, geographers were reduced to air force defence maps and Landsat photos for their data and there have still been very few major scientific expeditions to Tibet, bar the Chinese ones.

Tibetan Postal System

Between 1913 and 1950, Tibet asserted its independent status by controlling its own affairs, bearing its own flag, and by issuing its own currency, passports and stamps. Its claim was not formally recognised by world powers, although Tibetan passports were accepted as legal documents by the USA, the UK and India. Just how fragile Tibet's status became is demonstrated by its bizarre postal system.

The Tibetan mail which has survived from the late 19th century consists of traders' mail, religious mail and Chinese official mail. It was carried by runners; the monasteries, for instance, had their own runners. With the British invasion of 1903-4, one of the concessions extracted from the Tibetans was the right to set up telegraph and post offices. There were four British post-offices: Pharijong (Pali), Yatung (Yadong), Gyantse and Gartok, with the earliest starting around 1906. The British were not permitted to establish a post-office in Lhasa. Surviving mail from Gartok is extremely rare – only four pieces have been found (in

Delhi, 1980, by the present writer!), plus a few cancels.

The postal system for external mail was primarily used by Nepalese and Indian traders, and was written in Hindi, Nepalese and English. Delivery was accomplished by runners – there were also ponies used, and in the 1930s a Dodge truck operated on part of the route to India. The runners, like most Tibetans, were illiterate and they could only identify traders' mail by handmarked symbols on the envelopes. The mail could be delivered in a very short time: from Lhasa to Phari took four days. From Phari, the mail would go over the Indian border to Siliguri. Officials in Lhasa used to subscribe to newspapers in Calcutta, which might arrive a week or so later. Considering the altitude of the passes along the route, the runners did a remarkable job. Phari's post-office, mounted on top of a hill at 4600 metres, was for a while manned by a diabolical postmaster who delighted in asking Indian troops garrisoned there for their names and addresses as they puffed through the door.

In 1910 the 13th Dalai Lama, who had fled to India, asked the British company of Waterlow to design a Tibetan stamp. Waterlow produced some proofs with the Lion of Tibet on them; the symbol of the Dalai Lama. These were rejected by the Tibetans, but they kept the proofs, and when the Dalai Lama returned to Tibet, the Waterlow design was copied for the first Tibetan stamp issue of 1912. The Dalai Lama could not be placed on a stamp as it might get trodden underfoot, which would bring dishonour on him. Besides, who was going to strike his head with a great metal franking hammer?!

Tibetan stamps were a very haphazard affair. The 1912 issue, done in five values, was printed off woodblocks of 12 stamps. Tibetan cancels never bore dates, so only if they were used in combination with Indian or Nepalese postage could the date be determined. The random print-runs were never announced. The 1914 issue of stamps was not discovered by the west until 1942. In the 1933 issue, which was used till the mid-1950s, the printers seemingly had no control over the inks. One setting of the four trangka green stamp of 1933 has 17 different shades. The printer would produce a run of several hundred sheets – the next time a printing was needed, the correct shade might not be available in the market-place, so it would be doctored with another colour of ink. When postage-values changed, and there was no new stamp issued to cover the rates, a larger value stamp would be cut up or torn up into, say, a ½ trangka or a ¼ trangka – and added to other stamps to make up the correct postage. Due to paper shortages, envelopes were reused by turning them inside out. Sometimes stamps were entirely ignored for internal postage, a gift to the postmaster would do the trick.

If you were living in Lhasa in the 1930s and you wanted to get a letter to England, life got complicated. There was no British post-office in Lhasa and Tibet was not a member of the International Postal Union (it's not clear if they ever applied). What you had to do first was get the letter to the British post-office in Gyantse and you therefore needed two sets of stamps – Tibetan, and Indian. Alternatively, you could address the letter care of a trader in Gyantse, who would affix the Indian postage, forward the letter, and bill you. In Lhasa, by the first method mentioned, they'd cancel the Tibetan postage and forward the item to the Tibetan post-office in Gyantse. Somehow the letter would then get across town to the British post office in Gyantse, and then go on to Yatung and India, and the letter would enter the inter-national postal system. Incoming mail was virtually impossible to orchestrate unless you could address it to a trader in Gyantse or Pharijong, who would affix the Tibetan postage and forward the letter. In the process, the actual stamps would be dwarfed by a selection of wax seals, handstamps, chops, registration-marks and cancellations. Red wax seals could only be used by Incarnate Lamas. Few of the Dalai Lama's letters went beyond Sikkim, they were carried by private runners, and enclosed ceremonial silk scarves and perhaps a small bag of gold-dust. They could only leave the Potala on auspicious dates.

After 1947 the Indian Government, now independent, continued to operate the old British post-offices within Tibet until the mid-50s, although the Chinese established their own post-offices as early as 1951. The Chinese issued, in 1952, a series commemorating the 'peaceful liberation of Tibet' to be followed in 1956 by a series on the opening of the Xinjiang-Tibet and Qinghai-Tibet highways, and in 1961 on the Rebirth of the Tibetan People – but these stamps were not circulated in Tibet itself very much. In Dharamsala, the Dalai Lama authorised a private set of stamps, designed by an Australian. By the early 1950s, stamp collectors were rushing to buy any Tibetan postage, and the Tibetans reprinted sheets from 1912 and 1914-18 to deal with the export market. The majority of fake Tibetan stamps and covers started to appear in the 1950s, although this hobby goes back to 1920 (and is still going strong). Buyers who are offered **earlier Tibetan stamps in Kathmandu, and no doubt soon within Tibet, will probably be offered forgeries nine times out of 10.** Covers are now forged to the point where only a handful of world experts can tell the difference.

– Geoffrey Flack

POPULATION & PEOPLE

Accurate population figures for Tibet are nearly impossible to discover. Even simple figures for the populations of Lhasa or Shigatse vary considerably. In the July 1982 Chinese census, the pop-ulation of Tibet was given at 1.89 million. This figure presumably includes the Han settlers and technicians living in Tibet (estimated at 150,000), but does not include the number of Chinese troops stationed there (estimated from 100,000 to 300,000 and up), nor the mobile population of Han construction workers and businessmen who travel to Tibet in the summer. The same census gave the number of Tibetans within China at 3.87 million, which means that a minimum of two million Tibetans live outside Tibet. They are scattered in a number of autonomous prefectures in Qinghai, Gansu, Sichuan and Yunnan.

The problem with statistics is determ-ining which Tibet is being talked about. There are two identifiable Tibets: political Tibet (post-1950) and ethnographic Tibet.

1912 1/2 Trangka stamp, 1933 2/3 Trangka stamp

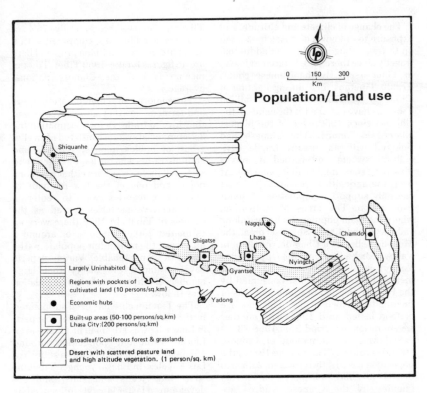

Population/Land use

0   150   300
Km

Shiquanhe

Nagqu

Shigatse   Lhasa   Chamdo

Gyantse   Nyingchi

Yadong

Largely Uninhabited

Regions with pockets of
cultivated land (10 persons/sq.km)

● Economic hubs

▣ Built-up areas (50-100 persons/sq.km)
● Lhasa City:(200 persons/sq.km)

Broadleaf/Coniferous forest & grasslands

Desert with scattered pasture land
and high altitude vegetation. (1 person/sq. km)

Present-day political Tibet covers an area of 1.2 million square km so that according to the Chinese census there would be roughly one person per square km in Tibet. Ethnic and linguistic Tibet encompasses a much wider area, including slabs of Qinghai, Sichuan, Gansu and Yunnan Provinces, which fell within the Tibetan realm as recently as 1949. Historically speaking, the net is much wider than that: the Sherpas are Tibetan in origin, although they've been in Nepal for five centuries; the peoples of Sikkim and Bhutan are Tibetan in origin; and the peoples of Zanskar and Ladakh are also closely linked.

Added to this complex picture are the Tibetan communities in exile, with an estimated 100,000 Tibetans scattered in settlements around India and Nepal. A fraction of the incoming refugees were also transplanted to countries like Switzerland and Canada (because of the mountains!). The Indian Government has adopted a policy of settling refugee Tibetans in widely scattered areas to prevent any political agitation, thus posing a real problem for the Dharamsala government-in-exile as it can establish no large base. There are Tibetan settlements in Himachal Pradesh, Assam, West Bengal (Darjeeling), Dharamsala, Ladakh, Mysore and Madhya Pradesh. In Nepal there are settlements at Mustang, Pokhara, Jumla, Namche Bazaar, and a few in the Kathmandu Valley. In addition, there are several thousand Tibetan refugees living in Bhutan and Sikkim.

The change of climate and altitude, and exposure to unknown diseases took a toll on those settling in India – an additional tragedy since there were far greater losses in Tibet itself. By the Chinese count, 87,000 Tibetans died during fighting in 1959. By the Tibetan count 1.2 million Tibetans have perished at the hands of the Chinese since 1950. One of the biggest killers was famine. The Chinese had tinkered with an already fragile agricultural system and turned it into a disaster – some might call it genocide. At best, the agricultural resources of Tibet can only support a population of about two million. The areas of cultivation, where the main populations lie, are along valleys in the Lhasa-Shigatse area, the Mekong Valley near Chamdo, the Chumbi Valley near Yadong, and the Upper Indus Valley toward Shiquanhe. In 1959 Tibet's meagre harvest was either consumed by the PLA or shipped to China and tens of thousands of Tibetans died. This shortage of food lasted until 1963, with another severe rationing period from 1968-73.

Following the turnabout of Chinese attitudes towards Tibet in the 1980s, the population has slightly recovered. Although there is no child-limit placed on Tibetan families by the Chinese (cadres are restricted to two children), the infant mortality rate in Tibet is high (estimated well in excess of 150 per 1000 births). From 1953-1959, by Chinese figures, the population declined 7%. The final word on the statistics game is a report in *China Daily* that says that between 1964 and 1982, the population of the Tibetan minority increased 54.7%.

Life expectancy is around 40 for Tibetans (as compared with 65 in China proper and as compared with 30 under the Dalai Lamas). Polygamy and polyandry are tolerated by Peking; a man can marry two sisters, or several brothers may share a wife, although this is now rare. Originally these arrangements were considered a way of keeping family property intact. The Chinese are trying to re-educate the

Tibetans on this score. Fully 75% of Tibetans are illiterate, compared with a 32% illiteracy rate in China proper. There are no figures for pre-1950 Tibet. Tibetan income is half the Chinese national average.

The majority of Tibetans are herders and farmers – as they always were – and they love to trade. Before occupation the Tibetan social system consisted of an elite group of nobles, monks, generals and administrators who ran large estates – and serfs. A Tibetan was born either a serf or a noble, and one of the few methods of jumping categories was to enter a monastery. Monasteries served as the schools of Tibet. In 1950 there were an estimated 200,000 monks, or around a quarter of the male adult population (the statistics are not reliable). Various experts have advanced the theory that large numbers of celibate monks kept population growth low.

The Tibetan elite has been supplanted by the Chinese who live, for the most part, in Lhasa. Towns are small in Tibet – even Lhasa (estimated population around 150,000) would barely rate as a suburb of Los Angeles. In Lhasa, younger Tibetans sport blue jeans and suits, and are developing a faster lifestyle influenced by video movies. Chinese civilians stick to the main towns of Tibet: Lhasa, Shigatse, Chamdo, Nagqu, Yadong, and Shiquanhe. Army bases are dotted at intervals along major roads, sometimes as close as every 100 km.

The Dalai Lama, in an article in *Tibetan Review* (August 1985) raised the question of whether the Chinese are attempting, by assimilation, to outnumber the Tibetans. This is the case in present-day Mongolia and Manchuria, where Chinese settlers now vastly outnumber the original native populations, or minority groups. He points a finger at Qinghai Province (once the Tibetan region of Amdo): 'The area where I was born, the Kokonor region of northeastern Tibet, now already has a population of 2.5 million Chinese and only

700,000 Tibetans, according to a recent Chinese newspaper report.'

The exact origins of the Tibetans as a race are sketchy. Ethnologists generally place them in the Tibeto-Burman group, identifying several types. The Chinese have encouraged marriage between the Han and the Tibetans to water things down (forcibly during the Cultural Revolution) but the Tibetans have resisted the idea. There are several Tibetan sub-groups distinguished by linguistic variation: the Qiang (numbering around 100,000, living in upper Sichuan), the Monba (around 7000) and the Lhoba (around 2000). The Monba and the Lhoba inhabit scattered areas around the Bhutan-Tibetan border, with the main grouping of the Monbas around the town of Cona in southern Tibet.

Formerly, in the outlying areas of the Tibetan realm, there were tribal groupings, clans and nomads, who were beyond the power of Lhasa. Walking through Barkhor Bazaar in Lhasa, you can see some of these people on pilgrimage to the Holy City. From the fringes of Tibet, and from Qinghai Province, come nomad women, with their braided hair done in 108 strands (a holy number). The waist-length tresses must be redone at least once a week and smeared with yak-butter. From deep in Qinghai Province come the Golok nomads, who are ethnically Tibetan, but have little respect for politics – Chinese, Tibetan, or otherwise. They wear greasy sheepskins, yak-hide boots, and often sport felt bowler hats (the bowler hat is a legacy of the British invasion of Tibet; this surprising fashion is shared by the peoples of the Bolivian altiplano). From eastern Tibet come the quick-tempered Khampas – the men have tassels of red yarn braided through their hair, and a dagger, which is not entirely decorative, hanging off their belts. Mixed into this kaleidoscope are Nepali and Kashmiri traders, and the odd Muslim from Xinjiang.

The general situation in Tibet has led to the misconception that the Tibetans are a primitive people – an attitude that the Chinese certainly hold. Tibetan levels of hygiene may not appear to have changed since the 15th century but Tibetans may choose not to wash for a number of religious and practical reasons: washing removes sacred body oils, there may be no plumbing, and it may simply be too cold. One has to consider that the Tibetans developed a type of culture well suited to their ecological zone, and to their dispositions. For centuries, theirs was an isolated civilisation, and it is unfair and irrelevant to judge them by jet-setter standards. Centuries ago, Tibetans developed a code of protecting their wildlife and flora far in advance of the west (a code broken by the Chinese). The Tibetans are struggling to adapt to the ways of the modern world and they're remarkably cheery and friendly people considering what they've weathered. Though they may appear ragged and unkempt, they definitely have their pride.

The Tibetans are direct, open and honest in their dealings. They have a great sense of humour, they're self-reliant, amazingly hardy, and have none of the shyness or coolness that the Chinese bring to bear on foreigners. Tibetan women have fairly high status, although they still do heavier work than men. Unlike the Chinese, if curious Tibetans gather to look at a foreigner, they will break the ice immediately – sometimes faster than you thought possible. Very few Tibetans speak English and those that do are likely to be older folk, educated in India, who have lived through the holocaust. There are other ways to communicate; the Tibetans are great traders for a start, and they love to play with your toys! Sometimes you can find Nepalese visitors or traders who will act as intermediaries.

ECONOMY

The events of the 1960s and '70s – the formation of communes, the redistribution of land and animals, the ban on barter, and the attempt to grow winter wheat (a

Chinese food) instead of the traditional barley – brought about economic collapse in Tibet. The Chinese reluctantly started to admit this in 1980 after a visit by top-ranking Hu Yaobang, who was clearly shocked. As a result, new policies were formed: the household has been restored as the basic unit of production; 90% of agricultural families have been given land leases for between 30 and 50 years; communal animal stocks have been broken up and 95% of families have received animals to raise; the winter wheat policy has been abandoned and barley, the crop Tibetans have grown for hundreds of years, reinstated; and free markets, tourism and cross-border trade with Nepal and India have been encouraged. It was recently announced that the Chinese government would not levy taxes on Tibetan farmers nor require state purchases of agricultural goods before 1990.

At present, a massive capital works programme is in progress, requiring over US$215 million to be spent on 43 special building projects including generating stations, hotels, libraries, schools, art museums, trade centres and children's centres. None-the-less, economic policy in Tibet was blasted in a critique which appeared in a Shanghai economic journal in 1985. It stated that Tibet had received more than US$3 billion in subsidies since 1952 and now had nothing to show for it. Like an anaemic patient requiring constant blood transfusions, Tibet has become totally dependent; every yuan created in Tibet swallows 1.2 yuan in subsidies. Together with the soaring costs of bureaucracy (dominated by Han administration), estimated at US$57 million for 1984, this is hardly a recipe for recovery. The national target in China for the year 2000 is to quadruple output; in the case of Tibet, this would require, at the present rate, more transfusions of state funds to the tune of US$1.53 billion.

Agriculture & Forestry

Tibet has about 228,000 hectares of farmland (limited by climate and elevation). The main crops are highland barley, wheat, rapeseed, broad beans, buckwheat, corn and rice. Although wooden ploughs and yaks are still used, mechanised equipment is being introduced. Estimates put the number of tractors in the region at 10,000. Irrigation systems and reservoirs are being built and proved their value during an unprecedented drought in 1983. Strong sunlight produces extraordinary yields: cabbages weighing 28 kg; potatoes weighing two kg each; 6000 kg of barley per half hectare compared with a normal yield of 2000 kg.

The forestry industry is now concentrating on the extraction of lumber from the forests along the middle and lower parts of the Yarlung Zangbo (Brahmaputra), which cover 6.32 million hectares and represent 1.43 billion cubic metres of timber. The various vegetation belts contain a wealth of species including many varieties of pine, spruce and fir. The main load carried by truck convoys leaving Tibet is timber – in phenomenal quantities.

Animal Husbandry

Tibet is one of the largest pastureland areas in China with over 13.3 million hectares providing for 21 million head of livestock including yak, cattle, Tibetan sheep, goats, horses, mules and donkeys. Yaks, the 'ships of the plateau', are the mainstay of the traditional Tibetan economy. In China, the main areas where these comical creatures are found are on the Qinghai-Tibet plateau and in parts of Gansu, Xinjiang, Sichuan and Yunnan provinces. There are three types of yak: the wild yak, the *dzo* (a cross between cattle and female yaks) and the domesticated yak.

The dzo is docile, strong and hardy so it is valuable for farm work, riding and as a pack animal. Yaks supply milk; a mature female yak (*dri*) produces milk for four to seven months, with a higher fat content than cow's milk. Yak meat is tender and lean and is the principal meat eaten by Tibetans in cooked, wind-dried, semi wind-dried and almost raw forms. Yak dung is collected and dried for use as fuel. The hair and the hide are used for making thread, blankets, clothing, boots, tents and yak-hide boats. A wild, adult male yak weighs one ton, double the weight of a domestic one. China has approximately 12 million yaks, 85% of the world's total. In the Tibetan Autonomous Region alone, there are four million.

Tibetans rely on the yak – its hair, hide, dung, bone, meat, milk, yoghurt, cheese and butter – for their livelihood (including transportation and ploughing) and yet they are hypocritical about the slaughter of yaks. With the harsh climate and lack of fresh vegetables, eating yak meat is a necessity – but butchers, along with boatmen (whose boats are made of yak-skin), and disposers of the dead, are relegated to the lowest levels of society. Muslim butchers are used in places like Lhasa, as Muslims have no qualms about the taking of life. Another solution was for herdsmen to stuff the yak's breathing apparatus with mud, and come back a few hours later to find . . . a dead yak.

Mining & Mineral Resources

Tibet has an extraordinary wealth of minerals which have hardly been exploited. The Tibetans were extremely superstitious about mining, believing that if the earth were disturbed, ill-fortune would befall the Dalai Lama and the crops would fail. Gold was extracted for centuries at the Thok Jalung goldfields in western Tibet, which led to a story of a race of gigantic black ants which mined for gold. This reference appears to be to Tibetan gold-miners who covered themselves in black yak-hair blankets for protection against the desert winds, and either attacked strangers venturing too close, or let loose huge black mastiffs on them.

Tibet's untapped mineral resources include oil-shale, asphalt, coal, iron, manganese, magnesium, tin, copper, lead, zinc, salt, arsenic, borax, sulphur, mica, graphite, talc, gypsum, jade, radium, and titanium. The world's largest lithium mine is in northern Tibet with a lithium deposit amounting to half the world's known total. There are also deposits of uranium and plutonium which are, naturally, of crucial importance.

Industry

Before the 1950s, industry was only really present in the form of a mint and an ammunition factory in Lhasa, and various regional handicraft centres which produced religious products. Tibet now has 215 small and medium-sized industries employing 69,000 workers, producing over 80 kinds of products and accounting for 20% of total production in Tibet. The Chinese justify the high percentage of Han Chinese workers (between 30% and 50%) with the excuse that most Tibetans are illiterate and have no more than four years schooling, thus making it necessary for them to be trained by Han workers.

The Chinese government has recently announced plans for a massive drive to develop western China. One popular proposal is that western China (covering over 60% of the country's total land mass but supporting only 28.5% of the total population), should first provide the eastern part of China with raw materials to support eastern industry and then set up their own manufacturing industry later.

Linzhi, 440 km to the east of Lhasa, is a much vaunted industrial centre and its showpiece is the Linzhi Wool Textile Plant. This factory moved to Linzhi from Shanghai with 642 workers and technicians in 1966, and produces copious amounts of woollen blankets, woollen fabric and knitting wool. The present workforce numbers about 1300; about 50% are Tibetan. The industry around Lhasa includes power plants, machinery plants, printing shops, chemical factories, woollen textile plants, leather processing factories, grain processing factories and carpet factories.

The present emphasis is on light industry, individual businesses, free markets and more autonomy for management in order to produce goods for consumption by the region's own population. The handicraft industry, producing articles such as aprons, rugs, butter-tea urns and yak saddles, is provided with state subsidies for gold and silver, exemption from taxes and low-interest loans. In 1984 the output of the handicraft industry was 30 million yuan.

Energy

Hydro-electric power stations are presently under construction in many parts of Tibet to tap part of the enormous power generating capacity of rivers originating in Tibet. There are plans to build the world's largest hydro-electric power station, at the turning point of the Yarlung Zangbo (Brahmaputra), with a generating capacity of 40 million kilowatts.

The exceptionally high altitude in Tibet creates intense solar radiation. The solar radiation observatory set up on the East Rongbuk glacial basin at 6000 metres has measured a direct solar radiation co-efficient seldom found in the world – 1.8 calories per square cm per minute. If the solar energy striking a square metre was concentrated, it would boil 10 kg of water from 0°C to 100°C in less than an hour! Lhasa averages 3000 hours of sunshine annually and solar energy is already in use. Portable solar hot-water heaters and solar ovens are made and used locally.

High-temperature hot springs are found all over Tibet. At Yangbajain, three geothermal generators can now supply Lhasa with over 8000 kilowatt hours of energy. Wind energy is also being explored. Two wind belts have been identified and experimental wind power stations near Nagqu have proved successful.

The Military

A factor often missed by reports (particularly Chinese ones) on Tibet is the cost of the continued military presence. Estimates put the number of PLA troops in Tibet at between 100,000 and half a million. Roads used almost solely by gigantic military convoys and garrisons in border areas are a reminder of Tibet's strategic importance. There are at least nine military airfields (Gonggar, near Lhasa, functions as the sole civilian one), 11 radar stations and three nuclear bases. It is reported that Tibet has become one of China's largest Inter-continental Ballistic Missile (ICBM) bases, capable of targeting India and other areas near the Indian Ocean. Nuclear testing was carried out in various areas in 1982, and Chinese officials referred to 'severe atmospheric pollution' when Tibetans were evacuated after a test at Lop Nor in March 1982.

ADMINISTRATION

Before the Chinese occupation, the Dalai Lama was the supreme religious and temporal head of the government of Tibet. During the Dalai Lama's absence or minority, a regent (*gyaltsab*) appointed by the Tibetan National Assembly, ruled on his behalf. Next in line were two prime ministers (*silons*), one a monk and one a layman. Beneath them was the secular administration, the Council of Ministers (*Kashag*), composed of four ministers (*kalons*), one of whom was a monk, the rest being secular officials.

Parallel to the Kashag was the ecclesiastical administration, the Department of Religious Affairs (*Tse Yigtsang*), headed by the Lord Chamberlain (*Chikyab Khenpo*) and four secretary-generals (*drungyik chemo*) – the entire departmental staff was composed of monks. The secretary-generals dealt with the affairs of all monastic officials from their selection, training, appointment and transfer, to dismissal. They also served, together with four heads (*tsipon*) of the Finance and Revenue Departments, as joint chairmen of the Tibetan National Assembly (*Tsokdhu Gyezon*), the highest deliberative body of the Tibetan State, composed of 350 members. The other assembly was the Working Committee (*Tsokdhu Rakdhu*) composed of approximately 60 members of the National Assembly. The decisions of the assemblies were forwarded to the Dalai Lama for acceptance or rejection. At regional level there were seven major administrative units with individual governors. Below them there were more than 240 districts (*dzongs*) each with a district-commissioner (*dzongpon*).

Since 1965, Tibet has been administered as an autonomous region (*zizhiqü*) of China. The region is divided into five prefectures (Ngari, Shigatse, Shannan, Nagqu, Chamdo) and 71 counties with Lhasa considered a municipality. The old provinces of Amdo and Kham have been divided up into Qinghai province and autonomous prefectures in Gansu, Sichuan and Yunnan provinces. The most important bodies, effectively in charge of Tibet, are the Communist Party Committee and the People's Government. The Political Consultative Committee is little more than a rubber stamp outfit. In 1985, the First Secretary of the Chinese Communist Party in Tibet, Yin Fatang, was discharged and replaced by Wu Jinghua. Wu is not a Tibetan but a member of the Lolo minority and he does not speak Tibetan. However conciliatory Wu's approach may seem, it does not answer the question of why Tibetans cannot be found to fill posts such as this.

GEOGRAPHY

Almost as large as western Europe in area, Tibet has borders with India, Nepal, Sikkim, Bhutan and Burma. The northern plateau of Tibet is called Chang Tang, a rocky, arid desert stretching 1300 km from west to east at an average altitude of 4000 metres and comprising nearly half of the country. It is bounded to the north by the Kunlun and Tanggula mountains beyond which lies the Qaidam basin; to the west a barrier is formed by the Karakoram and Great Himalaya mountain ranges. The Chang Tang has no river systems; merely brackish lakes which are the remnants of the Tethys Sea which covered Asia Minor some 100 million years ago.

Highest of the world's mountain ranges, the Himalaya are also the youngest. They

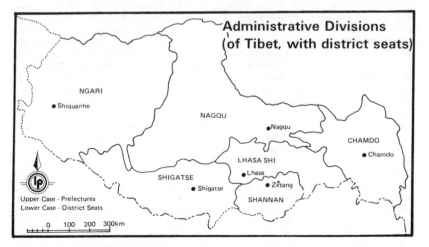

Administrative Divisions of Tibet, with district seats)

NGARI
● Shiquanhe

NAGQU
●Nagqu

CHAMDO
● Chamdo

LHASA SHI
● Lhasa

SHIGATSE
● Shigatse
● Zetang

SHANNAN

Upper Case - Prefectures
Lower Case - District Seats

0   100   200   300km

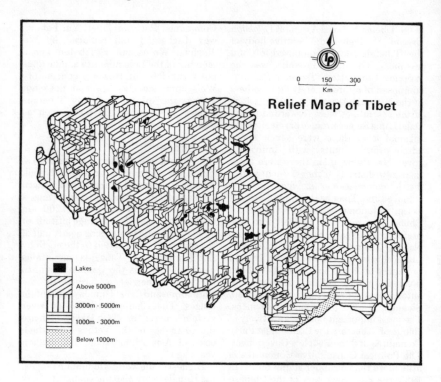

Relief Map of Tibet

0   150   300
Km

Lakes

Above 5000m

3000m - 5000m

1000m - 3000m

Below 1000m

were formed by a collision of the Indian and Asian continental plates some 50 million years ago. The Himalaya, Tibet's natural mountain border for centuries, have the world's highest snowline, and more than 17,000 glaciers. The south-eastern part of Tibet is closed off by mountain ranges running north to south and divided by three of the major rivers of Asia: the Yangtze, (at 6300 km the longest river in China), which continues across China to Shanghai; the Mekong which enters Laos and Thailand; and the Salween which runs south into Burma.

Separated from the Himalaya by the Yarlung Zangbo (Brahmaputra) River, which flows east through the lowland valleys of southern Tibet, is the Kailas mountain range. It runs east from above Lake Manasarovar. In the south-west,

near Mt Kailas, are the sources of four major rivers: the Indus, which flows westward across Kashmir to Pakistan; the Brahmaputra, which flows east, joins the Lhasa river and drops down into north-eastern India; the Sutlej, which flows south to western India; and the Ganges, which flows south and across northern India. The Yellow River rises in the Bayan Har mountains in north-eastern Tibet (or rather Qinghai province) and continues 5460 km across the north of China to empty just south of Tianjin.

The largest lakes in Tibet are Manasarovar, in the west; Tengri Nor (Nam Co) in the north-west; Yamdrok Tso in central Tibet; and Koko Nor (Qinghai Lake) in the north-east (Qinghai province).

FAUNA & FLORA
Alpine Zone

This zone, from 5000 metres up to the permanent snowline, has plenty of hardy plant and animal life. Among the plants are saussurea, gentian, rock-jasmine and sandwort which are rare flowers with special forms and structures. Rock-jasmine and sandwort are cushion plants. A cushion plant has crowded stems and leaves, is wind-resistant, can keep and accumulate heat quicker under direct sunshine, and loses heat slower at night.

Lower forms of plants such as snow algae, glacial-lake algae, moss and lichen are well adapted to the alpine environment. Lichens can survive extremes of climate fatal to other plants and excrete acids to break down rock substances for a foothold. Lichens, however, cannot survive in large cities – the air pollution kills them! It takes lichens about 25 years to grow to a diameter of two cm; lichens have been known to live up to 4500 years. Known as the 'pioneer plant', the lichen forms large colonies and prepares rock surfaces and soils for colonisation by other plants, especially the mosses. The acid excreted by the usnea, a low-altitude lichen, is an excellent antibacterial substance. Lichen acid is also used as a fixer to control the evaporation of industrial perfumes.

Animal life in this zone includes the alpine wild goat or ibex and the Himalayan marmot (its local name is 'snow pig') which scurries around satisfying an enormous appetite for food (which is stored as fat in preparation for hibernation). The snow-grouse stays up around the snowline even during the most bitter winters. Brown bears roam this zone in search of marmots which they catch by digging into their burrows with their strong forelegs.

Among the insects is the sandwort noctuid, a tiny moth, clothed with fluff, which is a bad flier. During high winds it folds its wings and lies on its side in the shelter of cushion plants. There is also an alpine grasshopper with defunct wings.

Highly prized in Tibetan and Chinese medicine, the Aweto (Chinese Caterpillar Fungus) is a brownish caterpillar three to four cm long that looks like a silkworm. A precious tonic made from it is supposed to be good for debility, coughing, lumbago, and other complaints.

Although it was believed for a long time that no birds flew over the high peaks of the Himalayas, griffon vultures have been seen flying at 9000 metres near the summit of Everest. Yellow-billed choughs are often seen at Everest base camps at about 7000 metres. Snow pigeons and bar-headed geese have also been sighted flying over peaks at 8300 metres.

Grassland Zone

The grassland zone extends up to 5000 metres and the vegetation varies according to the soil moisture. In the grassland, 4500 metres and upwards, apart from spear grass, glacier sedge and big-ear sedge, there are other plants such as dune blue-grass and pennisetum which are found on the sand and gravel deposits of dried lake basins. Rushes are often found in the marshlands near rivers or lakes. On the dry slopes, the drought-resistant pea-shrub develops into large clusters of cushions. On scree slopes there are cold and wind-resistant plants such as dwarf stone pines, rock-jasmine and sandwort.

Saltwater lakes of the grasslands contain a scaleless carp (known locally as 'naked carp') and several species of stone loach, also scaleless. During the summer many of the islands in rivers and lakes are visited by birds like the bar-headed goose, ruddy shelduck and brown-head gull which breed in large numbers. Wild asses (*kiang*) and gazelles graze the pastures together with marmots, pikas and other rodents. The commonest birds in this zone are the snowfinch and the Tibetan rosefinch.

Forest Zones

The dwarf-twisted forest is a zone which occurs at approximately 4000 metres and

Sunbird

has different types of vegetation depending on exposure to sun and moisture. On the shady and wet slopes evergreen rhododendrons bloom in vermilion, pink and yellow in May and June. Pipits, robins and wheatears are birds typical of this zone. An essence made from Himalayan rhododendrons (of which there are at least 300 species) is an excellent cure for bronchitis. On the sunnier slopes there are species of juniper. The higher this zone extends, the stronger the wind – which leads to the predominance of dwarf-like rhododendrons which hug the ground with twisted branches. The snow grouse inhabits these dwarf-twisted groves as does the pika, a rodent a little smaller than a hare.

From about 4000 metres downwards there is a zone with needle-leaved and deciduous trees. Different types of trees favour different altitudes. From 3700 metres to 4000 metres birches, rhododendrons and other deciduous trees prosper. In the lower part of the needle forest, the Tibetan fir is found in abundance until the zone grades off into mountain ashes, campbell maples and other broad-leaved trees. In the needle-leaved areas the forest is inhabited by musk deer and in the broad-leaved areas by the Asiatic black bear.

A mixed needle and broad-leaved forest zone occurs between approximately 3100 metres and 2500 metres. The predominant tree species are the Chinese hemlock (a needle-leaved tree) and the broad-leaved oak; other species include the mountain ash, campbell maple, birch, hornbeam maple, holly, and wild peach. Shrubs and herbs growing here include daphne (a shrub which provides pulp for high quality paper), Chinese magnolia vine, Jack-in-the-pulpit and ginseng. In the warmer climate, exotic monkeys (such as rhesus macaques and langurs) swing around the trees, and brilliantly coloured sunbirds extract nectar from blooms.

An evergreen broad-leaved forest zone occurs from approximately 2500 metres to 1600 metres – the upper part of the forest is dominated by the tropical oak, and the lower part has an abundance of lianas and specialised plant-forms. In the clearings, bamboos and Euphrates poplars thrive whilst red-abdomened squirrels, monkeys, rhesus macaques and langurs leap around. Red pandas and barking deer are also found here. Species of medicinal herbs which thrive in this environment include seven-leaved grass, figwort or mock ginseng, and solomon seal. The roots, stems, leaves and flowers of the epiphytic fern (which grows on the daimyo oak) are all used for medicinal purposes. There is a tree which yields industrial oil, and a tree which produces varnish. The Machilus (laurel family), tropical oaks and camphor trees are prized for their fine timber.

A recent survey by Chinese zoologists in Tibet pointed out the urgent need for nature reserves to protect the 12 top-protected species which include the wild yak, Asiatic wild ass, snow leopard and black-necked crane. Apparently the black-necked cranes have been decimated by the practice of collecting their eggs for use as a delicacy; only 1000 remain.

Langur

CLIMATE

In southern and eastern Tibet, the Himalaya act as a barrier against the rain-bearing monsoons, and rainfall decreases as you travel north. The central region of Tibet sees only 25 to 50 cm of rain a year (Sikkim, by contrast, sees some 500 cm). Snowfall is far less common in Tibet than the name 'Land of Snows' implies. The sun is quick to melt off snowfalls. Temperatures can vary from below zero during the early morning and evening to a sizzling 38°C at midday. In the north and west of Tibet rainfall becomes even scarcer, but fewer than 100 days in the year are frost-free and temperatures plummet as low as −40°C. Northern monsoons can sweep across the plains for days on end, often whipping up duststorms, sandstorms, snowstorms, or (rare) rainstorms. In the summer, the snowline in the north and east lies between 5000 and 6000 metres; in the south, even higher at 6000 metres.

Weather conditions can get exceedingly rough, and although there's plenty of sunshine, you can get roasted and frozen in the course of a day. In the summer, dust is a big problem, and it can get *very* hot during the day. In the winter, temperatures are much lower, and overland routes are often impassable for weeks on end. In the late autumn, there can be lengthy transport delays due to washouts, mudslides and flooding.

It is really not possible to recommend a best time to visit – you'll cop the weather, and lots of it, no matter what time of year. Spring (May to June) tends, however, to have the best weather conditions. From May to mid-September the climate is at its best in the Lhasa area. Travellers have been through Lhasa in February, in the winter, and found it's not too bad, once they get over the initial shock of the piercing cold (invigorating!).

If you want to go on to catch the Nepalese trekking season, you'll find that the timing is likely to be at loggerheads with the better seasons in Tibet. The best trekking season in Tibet is March to June, when it doesn't get too hot. In Nepal, however, the best trekking season is October through April (this is the cold season but there's little rain). Nepal has a monsoon season from late June to September.

The Wild & the Woolly

For many years there have been reports in the Himalayas of strange humans, under such aliases as the Yeti, Wild Man, Yeren (in Chinese), Migyu (in Tibetan), Abominable Snowman, Hairy Man, and Big Foot.

China now has its very own Wild Man Research Society which staged a successful exhibition in September 1985 of a Hairy Man which was, in fact, a rare macaque or short-tailed monkey (the first captured in 100 years), 1.06 metres high and weighing 92.5 kg. This Hairy Man was caught in Xinning county (Hunan Province) after harassing two girls and was then taken on a tour of neighbouring counties as a curiosity. The Wild Man Research Society recently published a report which considered the natural habitat of the Wild Man to be the virgin forests of the Himalayas at about 4500 metres. The Abominable Snowman may be a Wild Man who occasionally forages above the snowline. The report cites several eye-witness accounts.

Nai Qiong, a 40-year-old Tibetan from Chengtang village near Dinggyê in Southern Tibet, went on a hunt in the forests in 1968. One evening he decided to stay overnight in a cave large enough to accommodate four people. After his meal he lay down next to a fire. At about midnight he was awakened by shouts and somebody/thing throwing stones at him. At the entrance to the cave stood an extremely tall animal with a body covered in white fur and its two eyes gleaming brightly in the light of the fire. The animal continued throwing rocks and emitting strange, menacing sounds. Somebody/thing was also throwing rocks from above and there was more grunting coming from the surrounding area. Nai Qiong, not surprisingly, was scared witless and threw all the wood he could find onto the fire. The animal was obviously scared of the fire and stayed away, finally departing at the first light of dawn.

Another story concerns an official at the village of Boqü which is close to Zhangmu at an altitude of 2300 metres and has a subtropical climate. In the autumn of 1976, this official was asleep in his wooden house when he was wakened at midnight. What he saw by the light of the moon, standing in front of his bed, was a tall Wild Woman covered in chestnut-coloured fur with two massive breasts. She was, according to the official, eyeing him with what was clearly a strong desire to mate. The frightened official leapt out of bed and ran to his colleague's room. They both returned and although the Wild Woman was exceptionally strong, she meekly submitted to capture and was tied to a post. In the morning she had slipped the ropes and fled.

In 1972, a group of PLA soldiers were out on patrol in dense forest when one member of the patrol became separated from the others, who suddenly heard his screams. When they raced back to look for him, he had disappeared. Various attempts to find him proved fruitless until, several months later, another group out on patrol suddenly heard shouts coming from a cave above them. About 50 metres above them, at the entrance to the cave, they saw a person shouting. In desperation, this person jumped and was killed instantly when his head hit a rock. The patrol examined the body and discovered it was their missing colleague. His uniform was in tatters and his hands and feet were covered with strips of animal skin. While they were examining the body, a Wild Woman appeared on the scene but swung off on a liana when she saw what had happened.

The report summed up its findings: the Wild Man is stronger than modern man and averages 1.80 to 1.90 metres in height. The body is covered with thick fur which can be 12 cm long and either chestnut-brown or golden-brown in colour. The face is not covered with hair. The feet measure 35 cm and the eyes are extremely bright. The body exudes a strong smell of garlic. The faeces occur in much larger quantities than that of modern man and contain animal bones, seeds and fruit peel. Wild Men climb trees, swing easily from branch to branch and can walk erect. They live in natural caves in the forests but do not know how to use fire and are scared by it. Their main sources of food are small mammals and forest fruits and vegetables. They possess feelings and express fear, satisfaction or anger with special noises. They appear to have an interest in including modern man in their sex life.

RELIGION

For centuries, Tibetans have followed their own forms of Buddhism – ancient forms from India that interacted with the existing folk religions. In spite of intense repression and persecution during the Cultural Revolution, religion is surfacing again as the focal point of Tibetan life.

Prior to the introduction of Buddhism, the native religion in Tibet was a form of shamanism called **Bon**, which relied on priests or shamans to placate spirits, gods and demons. Magic was a strong element used to control the spirits of mountain passes, soil, water and springs or sacred mountains. Animals and even humans were used in sacrificial rites; demonic forces were invoked or expelled through black magic. According to Bon, the world was divided into three spheres: heaven, earth, and the underworld. Heaven was occupied by gods or Lha, Nagas were the masters of the earth, and the underworld was inhabited by a group of demons called Tsen. There were numerous spirits – the tent god, the house god and the hearth god among them – and many legends connected with the mountain gods. The centre of Bon religion appears to have been the Shang Shung kingdom in western Tibet, and there were possibly both Hindu and Iranian influences.

With the arrival of Buddhism there began a long struggle for religious supremacy. Bon adopted many Buddhist ideas, and gradually came to resemble Buddhism, however, Bon also gave its own twist to Buddhism in the process. One of the elements of ancient Tibetan religion was the use of oracles, and the State Oracle, used by the government of the Dalai Lama, survived the test of time. The dominant religion of Tibet became a form of Buddhism which exhibited differences from forms of the religion practiced elsewhere.

The founder of **Buddhism** was Siddhartha Gautama, the son of King Suddhodana and Queen Mahamaya of the Sakya clan. He was born around 563 BC at Lumbini

Toenpa Shenrab, a Bon version of Sakyamuni

on the border of present-day Nepal and India.

In his 20s, Prince Siddhartha left his wife and new-born son to follow the path of an ascetic. He studied under several masters, but he remained dissatisfied and spent another six years undergoing the severest austerities. He gave a graphic account of himself: 'Because of so little nourishment, all my bones became like some withered creepers with knotted joints; my buttocks like a buffalo's hoof; my backbone protruding like a string of balls . . . ' Realising that this was not the right path for him, he gave up fasting and decided to follow his own path to Enlightenment. He placed himself cross-legged under a Bodhi tree at Bodhgaya and went into deep meditation for 49 days. During the night of the full moon in May, at the age of 35, he became 'the enlightened or awakened one' – the Buddha.

Shortly afterwards, Buddha delivered his first sermon, *Setting in Motion the Wheel of Truth*, at the Deer Park near Sarnath. Then, as the number of his followers grew, he founded a monastic community and codified the principles according to which the monks should live. The Buddha continued to preach and travel for 45 years until his death at the age of 80 in 483 BC. To his followers, Buddha was also known as Sakyamuni (the sage of the Sakya clan). Buddhists believe that he is one of the many Buddhas who appeared in the past – and that more will appear in the future.

Approximately 140 years after Buddha's death, the Buddhist community diverged into two schools: **Hinayana** (the Lesser Vehicle), and **Mahayana** (the Greater Vehicle). The essential difference between the two was that Hinayana supported those who strove for the salvation of the individual, whereas Mahayana supported those who strove for the salvation of all beings. Hinayana prospered in South India and later spread to Ceylon, Burma, Thailand, Cambodia, Indonesia and Malaya. Mahayana spread to Inner Asia, Mongolia, Siberia, Japan, China and Tibet.

Vajrayana Buddhism is a tradition associated with Mahayana, and is the form of Buddhism most often associated with Tibet. Vajrayana (the Diamond Vehicle, or Mantrayana, or Tantric Buddhism) recognizes Nirvana (the release from the cycle of mortal existence and rebirths) and samsara (the consequential succession of lives and rebirths) as propounded in the Mahayana tradition. Vajrayana Buddhism emphasizes life in the fast lane, with the object of reaching Nirvana within one lifetime instead of enduring countless rebirths. In mountaineering terms, it can be compared to the perilous direct ascent of a sheer face, as opposed to a safer indirect route.

Among the early Tantric practices were meditation on corpses, use of wine, and esoteric sexual rituals. The sexual intertwining of male deities and their consorts symbolized liberation – wisdom and compassion joined to eliminate opposites. Only the strongest followers, having gained great powers, would use these practices, which were considered a most dangerous path. Sexual imagery is now used in Kalachakra Tantra meditation procedures (practitioners include the Gelukpa, Sakya, and Kagyupa Schools). It is only a small part of the training, and it is often misconstrued by westerners. Tibetans simply view this meditation technique as a key to dealing with the more subtle levels of the mind.

The Introduction of Buddhism

Buddhism gained a firm foothold in Tibet during the reign of King Songtsen Gampo (circa 605-650 AD). Songtsen Gampo's two queens, Bhrikuti Devi from Nepal and Wen Cheng Konjo from China, were devout Buddhists. Their united persuasion led to the spread of Buddhist doctrine and the construction of the Ramoche and Jokhang temples. The king sent his minister, Thonmi Sambhota, to India to devise a Tibetan script and alphabet, thus opening the way to a systematic translation of Buddhist scriptures.

The Bon priests were not well disposed toward Buddhism although it had many similarities to their own practices. They feared that their religion would be absorbed for this very reason. Skilful interpretation of a smallpox epidemic in the 7th century, to which a royal queen had fallen victim, resulted in the expulsion of Indian teachers and many of their Tibetan followers. During the reign of King Trisong Detsen (755 – 797 AD), the power struggle reached a critical intensity between, on one hand, Buddhism and the imperial family, and on the other, the powerful alliance of the Tibetan aristocracy and the Bon religion. Although the Buddhist monks were superior to the Bon priests in doctrinal debate, they were no match for them when it came to magic. Seeing their power threatened by an Indian scholar imported by Trisong Detsen, Bon priests seized on the occasion of the destruction of the palace on red hill (the early Potala) by lightning as a signal for violent opposition, and demanded that the new teacher return to India.

A second attempt at transplanting Tantric Buddhism was made by the Indian wizard Padmasambhava, who established Samye Monastery, with the first Tibetan Buddhist monks being ordained around 767 AD. Padmasambhava (also known as Lopon Rinpoche) was said to have been born in a lotus bud, and then adopted by an Indian king. He renounced any claim to a throne, and was banished from his country. For many years he wandered, seeking religious knowledge from many centres and teachers, until he became a master of the tantric way, famed for his miracles. A complex figure, Padmasambhava was said to be a man of the world with a private life devoted to wine and women. He incorporated some of the black magic of Bon into Tantric Buddhism, including the use of oracles. Padmasambhava conquered the demons set up by Bon magicians and proved the might of his tantric learning. Having established Samye Monastery, he spent many years travelling all over Tibet preaching his brand of Buddhism. Not long after his death, a bitter political dispute developed between the Chinese and Indian Buddhists in Tibet. Trisong Detsen decided to settle this issue and a debate was held at Samye in 792. The Indian Buddhist team prevailed and the Indian school (Mahayana) became the accepted one in Tibet.

King Tri Ralpachen (817-838) was the last of the three religious (Buddhist) kings. During his reign, translation work was continued on a huge scale under a commission composed of Indian and Tibetan scholars. In his efforts to promote Buddhism by force he alienated himself from his court, consisting largely of Bon followers, and was eventually assassinated by his brother Lang Darma. Lang Darma, who reigned 838-842, was known as the 'Evil King' as he attempted to completely snuff out Buddhism in an orgy of persecution.

The rebirth of Buddhism, over 100 years later, was initiated in western Tibet, where Tsaparang and Toling became centres of Buddhist learning under the patronage of the kings of Guge, particularly Yeshe O. Rinchen Sangpo (958-1055) also did much to revive Buddhism. He visited India several times and studied under many teachers, mastering Buddhist philosophy, various tantras, and the Kalachakra. He brought Indian scholars to Tibet, and with their co-operation, translated an immense number of scriptures into Tibetan. One of the most important of these was the *Kalachakra*, a doctrinal text which was introduced around 1026. It had links with astrology and chronology (the Tibetan calendar is based upon it), and was adopted by later sects, including the powerful Gelukpa school. Rinchen Sangpo encouraged the construction and rebuilding of temples and monasteries in western Tibet (notably Toling), Ladakh, Lahaul and Spiti. Under his direction, Buddhism was strengthened in central Tibet, and both the central and western regions were visited by the Indian scholar Atisha, between 1042 and 1054.

Atisha (also known as Jowo Je) was born in Bengal, the son of a prince, and married early, becoming the father of nine children. He is said to have been almost 30 when he abandoned his princely rights and took his vows as a monk. He travelled as far as Burma and Afghanistan and studied in many different schools. After reluctantly taking his leave from the university of Vikramashila in India, Atisha reached Toling in 1042, and set about translating texts with Rinchen Sangpo.

Atisha emerged as a major force in the revival of Buddhism. He greatly strengthened the monastic tradition and its disciplines, but he accepted Indian Tantric practices which the Tibetans had found to their taste. It was during this second period of the diffusion of Buddhist doctrine that the various schools of Tibetan Buddhism were instituted. A tradition derived from Atisha, the Kadampa sect, formed the basis for the reforms of Tsongkhapa, who founded the Yellow Hat

sect. From the 14th century onwards, increasing isolation from India, which had started during the Muslim invasions of the 12th century, led to the development of the separate sects attached to individual masters or monasteries.

Sects

There are numerous sects in Tibetan Buddhism, the most important of which are the Nyingmapa, Kagyupa, Sakyapa, and Gelukpa. Some western scholars divide Tibetan Buddhism into Red Hat and Yellow Hat sects, according to the colour of the hats worn by the lamas. The Nyingmapa, Kagyupa and Sakyapa are referred to as Red Hat sects, while the Gelukpa are called the Yellow Hat sect. Some Tibetan scholars prefer the term 'old translation school' for the Red Hat sects, and 'new translation school' for the Yellow Hat sects, thus illustrating the origin of the differences which are not as radical as the coloured hats might suggest. In fact, the yellow hats have a red lining, and the red hats have a yellow lining!

The business of religion in Tibet is a slippery subject. In real religious terms there is little sectarian conflict, but when religion is combined with politics, there is. In Tibet it is extremely difficult to separate the course of religion, politics and history, so that the different forms of Buddhism or the schools are often conveniently viewed as being rivals, which in fact they are not. Fierce rivalry did come about, but it had to do with political jockeying, not religious differences. In the 17th century, the Gelukpa sect, backed by the Mongols, assumed a dominant role in politics and effectively ruled Tibet through their leader, the Dalai Lama, from 1642 until the Communist occupation of the 1950s.

Nyingmapa Sect (ancient, old) This is the oldest sect, dating back to the time of Padmasambhava who hid secret doctrines in different places during his wanderings in Tibet. These secrets (*terma*) were discovered by men such as Orgyen Lingpa (died 1379) who reportedly found the biography of Padmasambhava. According to this biography, Padmasambhava concealed 108 scriptures, 125 tantric images and five rare essences between the region of Mt Kailas and China. Once discovered, these terma were compiled into books. The teachings of the Nyingmapa are compiled in 61 volumes and are divided into nine sections or vehicles. The first three are dedicated to the 'Body of Emanation' and were proclaimed by the Buddha. The following three elucidate the doctrine of the lower tantras and are ascribed to the 'Body of Enjoyment in Heavenly Paradises'. The last three deal with the highest tantras. Mindolin monastery (south of Lhasa, close to Zêtang), one of the three most important monasteries of this sect, is now under renovation.

Kagyupa Sect (oral transmission) This sect was founded by Marpa (1012-1098) who was born in southern Tibet. After learning Sanskrit, he sold all his worldly possessions and went to India where he met Naropa, a disciple of Tilopa and a famous Vajrayana teacher, who initiated him into tantric doctrines. Marpa returned to India twice for spiritual guidance and to study sacred books of the Vajrayana tradition, which he translated into Tibetan.

Marpa's most famous disciple was Milarepa (1040-1123), Tibet's most revered poet. At an early age Milarepa became embroiled in a family feud. When his mother refused to marry her late husband's brother, the man became enraged and seized all their property, leaving her destitute. Milarepa's mother encouraged him to seek revenge by learning black magic from a sorcerer, which he then used to kill his enemies and destroy their wealth. Although this pleased his mother, Milarepa was plagued by remorse and finally sought out Marpa to help him atone for his crimes. Marpa subjected Milarepa to gruelling tests before initiating him and giving him responsibility for transmission of the doctrine. Milarepa then spent six years in solitude, meditating in a cave. His only clothing was a light, cotton robe, hence his name Mila-repa, cotton-clad Mila. After returning home to find his mother dead, his home in ruins, and his sister dressed in rags, he decided to lead the life of a hermit and search for final liberation. The rest of his life was spent in the mountains where he achieved his goal of final liberation. The songs and poetry he left behind, known as *The Hundred Thousand Songs of Milarepa*, are revered by Tibetans.

Gampopa, a disciple of Marpa and Milarepa, founded a subsect of the Kagyupa; the Karmapa sect. Gampopa's disciple, Dusum Khenpo, was the first incarnation and founder of the main Karmapa monastery at Tsurphu (near Lhasa) in 1189. Another subsect, the Drukpa, is now found in Bhutan and Ladakh. The 16th Gyalwa Karmapa (head of the Kagyupa sect) was born in Tibet in 1924. After fleeing Tibet in 1959, he founded Rumtek monastery in Sikkim as

Marpa

his principal seat in exile. He died in Sikkim in 1981.

Sakyapa Sect (grey earth) For a description of this sect, and Sakya monastery, refer to the Sakya section.

Gelukpa Sect (the Virtuous) The origins of this sect can be traced to the Kadampa sect which was founded by Atisha. Tsong Khapa (1357-1419), also known as Je Rinpoche, was responsible for reforms which led to the founding of the Gelukpa.

Tsong Khapa was born of nomad parents in Amdo, at what is now the centre of Kumbum (Taersi) monastery. At seven he took the vows of a novice and by the age of 16 he had learnt all his teachers could offer, so they sent him to central Tibet for higher studies. He showed special interest in logic and composed a famous work called *Lam-rim* (the Graded Path to Enlightenment). As his group of followers began to increase rapidly, he built the monastery at Ganden in 1409 to provide a base for his new sect, which required adherence to monastic discipline.

Studies at Ganden, where he was the first abbot, encompassed various Buddhist schools, non-Buddhist philosophical systems and tantras. The actual practice of these tantras was only open to those monks who had already mastered theoretical learning. Monks had to observe absolute celibacy (in contrast to the Sakyapa sect which required its abbots to marry) and abstain from liquor and narcotics. A system of 253 vows was introduced for the monks, leading gradually to higher levels of renunciation. Drepung Monastery (built in 1416) and Sera Monastery (built 1419), together with Ganden Monastery, formed the three main centres for the Gelukpa, and their influence on state affairs was emphasized by the term 'the three pillars of the state'.

Shortly after the death of Gedun Drub (the 1st Dalai Lama), the Gelukpa introduced the system of reincarnation,

Tsongkhapa

which was largely a method of staying on top politically. Gedun Drub, who was the nephew of Tsong Khapa, became abbot of Ganden in 1438, and thus the supreme head of the Gelukpa. It was Gedun Drub who, to honour his teacher and predecessor, Khedrup Je, founded Tashilhunpo Monastery in Shigatse, which later became the seat of the Panchen Lama (see the Shigatse chapter for details on the Panchen Lama). Tsong Khapa had foretold that Gedun Drub would be the first of a succession of reincarnations of Avalokitesvara. At the same time, he predicted that the abbots of Tashilhunpo would be the successive reincarnations of Amitabha.

Dalai Lamas

I	Gedun Drub	1391-1474
II	Gedun Gyatso	1475-1543
III	Sonam Gyatso	1543-1588
IV	Yonten Gyatso	1589-1617
V	Ngawang Lobsang Gyatso	1617-1682
VI	Tsangyang Gyatso	1683-1706
VII	Kesang Gyatso	1708-1757
VIII	Jampel Gyatso	1758-1805
IX	Luntok Gyatso	1806-1815

X	Tshultrim Gyatso	1816-1837
XI	Khedrup Gyatso	1838-1856
XII	Trinle Gyatso	1856-1875
XIII	Thupten Gyatso	1876-1933
XIV	Tenzin Gyatso	1935-

The dates of birth and death for the Dalai Lamas differ from source to source. The title originated in the 16th century, when the chief priest of the Gelukpa, Sonam Gyatso (the 3rd Dalai Lama) visited Mongolia and converted the Mongolians, for the second time, to Buddhism. The Mongolian ruler, Altan Khan, embraced Buddhism as the national religion and conferred the title of Dalai Lama on Sonam Gyatso. This title was applied retrospectively to the two previous heads of the Gelukpa who, like Sonam Gyatso, had been recognized as successive reincarnations of Chenrezig (Avalokitesvara). *Dalai* is a Mongolian translation of the Tibetan *Gyatso* meaning ocean, thus the full title means Ocean of Wisdom. In China and the west, this is the title used for the leader of the Gelukpa, but most Tibetans generally use terms such as *Gyalwa Rinpoche* (Victorious One).

The present Dalai Lama is the 14th and although the Dalai Lama represents the highest bodhisattva, there are many other incarnations, called *tulku*, usually descended from the founder of a monastery. A tulku is discovered and verified through local oracles, omens and common opinion and, if necessary, a final decision is made by the Dalai Lama. There are four grades of tulku, the highest of which, a regent, is chosen to act during the minority of the Dalai Lama.

Discovery and verification of a Dalai Lama is a complicated process. Often the dying Dalai Lama will give an indication of his rebirth; sometimes children may come forward of their own accord or are recognised because of special powers or behaviour. Searches are conducted in secret to investigate predictions from oracles, strange signs and phenomena. Lhamo Latso, the oracle lake near Lhasa, famed for the visions seen in its waters,

has often been consulted. Children chosen as likely candidates are subjected to a range of tests. In one test, for example, they are asked to select, from a variety of objects, those which once belonged to the deceased Dalai Lama. The child may well identify persons from his previous life or show knowledge of a different dialect. Another system, instituted by the Chinese, involved the use of a lottery, with a name drawn during a special ceremony.

Once selected, the Dalai Lama was brought to Lhasa around the age of six and trained at the Gelukpa colleges. He might, in time, develop an interest in the teachings of the other sects, which all accept him as temporal and spiritual head of Tibet. The Dalai Lama was expected to complete his Gelukpa training and take his final examinations at the age of 18. Thereafter he was ceremoniously put in charge of the affairs of government.

Historically, the Regents, who were in charge of the Dalai Lamas, could and often did, exercise more than their fair share of authority. From the 6th to the 12th Dalai Lama, the respective Regents became so powerful that none of the Dalai Lamas even reached the age when they could assume control of state affairs.

The 4th Dalai Lama, Yonten Gyatso, was born (as predicted by the 3rd Dalai Lama) as a son of the Mongol King, Altan Khan. This forged a strong link between the Mongolians and the Tibetans which was opposed by the Chinese during the Ming dynasty.

The 5th Dalai Lama (Ngawang Lobsang Gyatso), also known as 'the Great Fifth' is renowned for his military exploits and political astuteness, both of which preserved Tibet's independence against Chinese and Mongolian pressure. Under his rule, the Gelukpa sect assumed a dominant role which maintained religious unity in Tibet until occupation by the Chinese in the 1950s. The 5th Dalai Lama started construction of the Potala, which was completed many years after his death. It was kept secret to ensure its completion.

During his reign, out of gratitude to his teacher, Losang Chogyan, he created the office of Panchen Lama. The 5th Dalai Lama bestowed land and farms on the Panchen Lama, near Shigatse, where Tashilhunpo monastery was founded.

The 6th Dalai Lama, Tsangyang Gyatso, was a strange combination of spiritual and earthly attributes. As a young man he developed a taste for the ladies and is said to have slipped out of the Potala at night to visit the houses of ill-repute in the village below. The Lukhang (House of the Serpent), on an island in the lake behind the Potala, was one of his favourite trysting places. Clearly though, his love, as portrayed in his poetry, was not merely physical, but also contained a higher element derived, perhaps, from tantric practices. His death remains a mystery. Some accounts say he had a son by a special love and the high monks, fearing the office of Dalai Lama would become hereditary, drove him into exile in Inner Mongolia and imprisoned his lover and their son. Other accounts maintain that the Chinese used his unorthodox lifestyle as an excuse to intervene and invited him to Peking. On the way he disappeared at Litang (some say at Gunga Nor near Qinghai Lake). This explains the absence of a tomb for the 6th Dalai Lama in the Potala.

The 7th Dalai Lama, Kesang Gyatso, was born in Litang, as prophesied by the 6th Dalai Lama. He was quite different in nature to his predecessor and retreated further and further into a saintly life of solitary contemplation. He left most affairs of state to the Regent, the Panchen Lama and the Chinese who used this chance to obtain a tighter grip on political affairs – a precedent which can be followed to present times.

As a result of intrigue and dissension between the Tibetans and Chinese, from the 7th to the 13th Dalai Lama, only one reached his majority. Many of them were poisoned, but the strangest death was that of the 12th Dalai Lama, whose regent organised the collapse of his bedroom ceiling on his head.

The 13th Dalai Lama, Thupten Gyatso, was a shrewd reformer and proved himself a skilful politician when Tibet became a pawn in the Great Game between Russia, China, and Britain. He was also responsible for restoring discipline in monastic life and increasing the number of lay officials to avoid excessive power being placed in the hands of the monks. Legislation was introduced to counter corruption among officials, a national taxation system was established, and a police force was created. As a result of his contacts with foreign powers and their representatives

Poem by the 6th Dalai Lama

In the short walk of this life
We have had our shares of joy
Let us hope to meet again
In the youth of next life

he showed an interest in world affairs and introduced electricity, the telephone and the first motor car to Tibet. Nonetheless, at the end of his life in 1933, he saw that Tibet was about to enter a dark age:

Very soon even in this land of the harmonious blend of religion and politics . . . acts may occur forced from without or within. At that time if we do not dare to protect our territory, our spiritual personalities including the victorious Father and Son [Dalai Lama and Panchen Rinpoche] may be exterminated without trace, the property and authority of our Ladangs [residences of reincarnated lamas] and monks may be taken away. Moreover, our political system , developed by the three Great Kings will vanish without anything remaining. The property of all people, high and low, will be seized and the people forced to become slaves. All living beings will have to endure endless days of suffering and will be stricken with fear. Such a time will come.

The present Dalai Lama, the 14th, was born on the fifth day of the fifth month of the Wood Hog Year of the Tibetan calendar (6 June 1935) in Amdo near the monastery of Kumbum (Taersi, in Qinghai province). Many portents led to his discovery. The head of the deceased 13th Dalai Lama, lying in state, had turned toward the east. Three letters, a monastery with a jade-green roof, and a house with turquoise tiles were seen in the waters of the oracle lake (Lhamo Latso) by the Regent in 1935. Search parties scoured Tibet and one which had travelled north-east found a house with turquoise-green tiles near the monastery of Kumbum, which had a jade-green roof. The leader of the group disguised himself as a servant, but the moment he entered the house, the youngest child of the family jumped into his lap and requested his rosary – one which had belonged to the 13th Dalai Lama. On being shown a whole variety of religious objects (drums, rosaries, walking sticks) the young child selected only the ones which had belonged to the deceased Dalai Lama. The three letters *ah*, *ka* and

The 14th Dalai Lama, Tenzin Gyatso

ma seen in the oracle lake were interpreted as meaning Amdo (for the province) and *ka-ma* for the monastery of Karma Rolpai Dorje, close to Taersi.

The Chinese governor of the area demanded a huge ransom to let the boy go to Lhasa; 300,000 Chinese dollars. After several years of bargaining, the money was paid and the child set off with his parents in a large caravan which took over three months to reach Lhasa. En route, the Tibetan National Assembly declared the child the 14th Dalai Lama and on 22 February 1940, the formal ceremony of instalment on the Lion Throne was held in Lhasa.

From the age of six, the Dalai Lama received strict religious training and

The 14th Dalai Lama, Tenzin Gyatso   (Photo: Marcia Keegan)

learnt to read and write. At the age of 13 he was formally admitted to Drepung and Sera monasteries to attend debates and practice dialectical discussion at large meetings. He then continued with studies of Buddhist thought and took the preliminary examinations at each of the three monastic universities (Sera, Drepung and Ganden) at the age of 24. A year later he took his final examinations and received his degree as Master of Metaphysics. His time was divided between the Potala (winter residence) and the Norbulinka (summer residence) where he had time to tinker with a motor generator and cars which had belonged to his predecessor.

Although the accepted age for a Dalai Lama to assume control of the state from his regent was 18, the Tibetan cabinet, dismayed by the Chinese occupation of eastern Tibet, made a special request for him to assume control at the age of 16. As the Chinese threat to Lhasa became clear, the National Assembly requested the Dalai Lama to avoid personal danger by staying near the Indian border at Yadong. After the signing of the Sino-Tibetan Agreement in 1951, the Dalai Lama returned to Lhasa. Within a few years the Chinese had firmly established themselves in Tibet. In 1954, the Dalai Lama and the Panchen Lama visited Peking. Smouldering resentment amongst Tibetans led to a series of revolts which culminated, in 1959, in a full-scale uprising against the Chinese in Lhasa. On 17 March 1959, the Dalai Lama, disguised as a soldier, escaped from the Norbulinka with members of his family and an armed escort, to start a long trek into exile in India.

Since then, the Dalai Lama has formed a government-in-exile at Dharamsala in India and has become an eloquent spokesman for Tibet as well as a rallying point for Tibetan exiles and their culture. For the Chinese, he is a distinct embarrassment. The Chinese have made several offers for his return but are unwilling to grant him residence in Lhasa. They would prefer that he stayed in Peking, at a safe remove from the fervently dedicated Tibetans. The last word belongs to the Dalai Lama himself:

Message for Beijing

"I AM encouraged to note that the Chinese leaders are more open-minded and moderate compared to those in the past.

"I hope that they will try to understand better the real situation in Tibet and, based on that understanding, adopt a policy that is pragmatic and morally principled.

"It is my belief that in human society it is not sufficient just to satisfy the basic needs such as food and shelter and clothing . . . freedom is essential and basic. For the Tibetan people, freedom is an inalienable right.

"It is good that the Chinese have recently been taking some interest in the history of Tibet. The history of a nation is naturally based on historical records and nowhere is there a single record that states that Tibet has at any time been a part of China.

"There have been periods when the Mongols and Manchus had some influence over Tibet but then, where is there a nation which has not experienced such influences be it military, religious, cultural or through the marital relationship of its rulers?

"Such influences and acts of aggression have been used in the past, as well as in the present, by stronger powers to claim sovereignty over weaker nations. But the Tibetan people have never voluntarily agreed to become part of China.

"I call on unbiased and impartial scholars of international law to give their opinion on this aspect of the Sino-Tibetan relationship. China has the right to its own happiness and prosperity but not at the expense of another nation or people."

—Times Service.

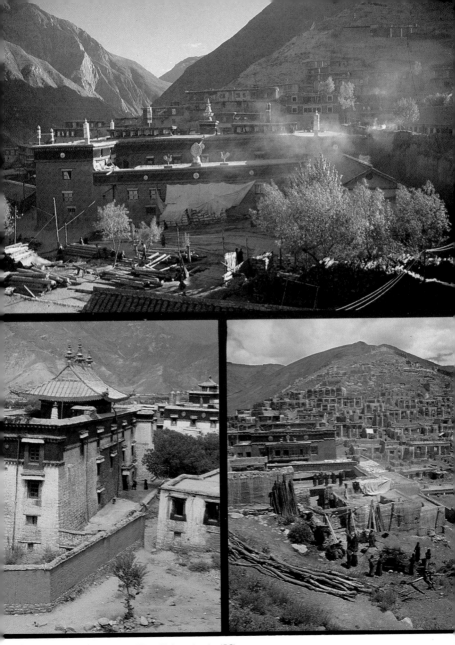

Top: Dege Printing Lamasery, Tibet-Sichuan border (RS)
Left: Sera Monastery, Lhasa (MB)
Right: Jiegu Monastery, Yushu, Qinghai (RS)

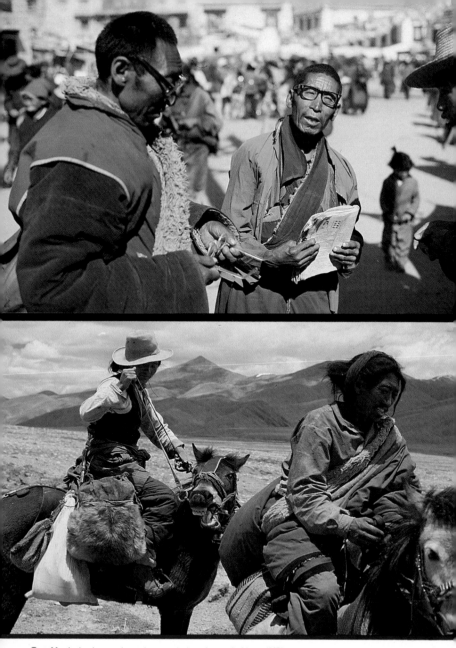

Top: Monks buying ready made prescription glasses in Lhasa (MB)
Bottom: Khampa horsemen from eastern Tibet

Living Buddhas

While the Dalai and Panchen Lamas are the most important incarnations, there are hundreds of other 'living buddhas' or 'tulkus' in Tibetan Buddhism. Heads of monasteries were – and still are, to some extent – appointed as recognised incarnations of their (celibate) predecessors, a system that goes back to the Karmapa sect in the 12th century. The first head of the Karmapa sect prophesied that his successor would be incarnated. It has been prophesied that the 14th Dalai Lama will be the last of the lineage, and the Dalai Lama himself has indicated that he does not think it is possible for another reincarnation to appear in India, and therefore, he will be the last Dalai Lama. On the other hand, it is said that as long as there are believing Tibetans, there will always be reincarnations. Five reincarnations have been born in Switzerland and recognized as Rinpoches – they now live in Sikkim and India. Other tulkus have been found in India and France.

In the past, exceptional children have been sought out and discovered according to various oracles, signs and portents. There was probably some pulling of strings and legs to gain these considerable positions of power. The temptation to falsify incarnations resulted from the great benefits, material and otherwise, available to the incarnation's family. With the last of the Rinpoches fading away, the question is: Who will know enough to look for the signs, portents and oracles? And with a new generation of Tibetans who live in exile and are increasingly westernised, another more serious question arises: Will the incarnation-select want to take up the position?

One solution to this is altering the method of selection. Traditionally the Dalai Lama's senior tutor, the Ganden Tri Rinpoche, and head of the Gelukpa school, is appointed as head-abbot of Ganden Monastery. Yongzin Ling Rinpoche (1902-1983), the old head-abbot of Ganden, was recognized by the 13th Dalai Lama and the State Oracles of Nechung and Gadong as the reincarnation of his predecessor, and was enthroned at the age of seven as the 97th throne-holder to Ganden since Tsongkhapa. In 1959 he fled to Dharamsala, and toured Europe and North America during the 1970s and 1980s to teach. In late 1983 he died at Dharamsala. In a new selection method, his successor was appointed by the 14th Dalai Lama and enthroned in Dharamsala in March 1984. The new scheme of things is that the Ganden throne-holder is appointed, usually for a period of seven years, from the senior retired abbots of Dharamsala colleges. The 98th Ganden Tri Rinpoche is Jamphal Shenphen, born in Kham in 1921. He became a Geshe at Ganden Monastery, and escaped from Tibet in 1959.

Since the death of the 16th Gyalwa Karmapa in Sikkim in 1981, there has been a crisis among the Kagyupas. The 16th Gyalwa Karmapa, head of the Kagyupa School, was born in 1924, and enthroned as a child in the monastery of Tsurphu to the north-west of Lhasa. In 1959 he escaped to India and in 1962, at the invitation of the royal family of Sikkim, founded Rumtek monastery in Gangtok, which became his principal seat. On his death in 1981, the Tibetan government-in-exile sent letters to the heads of the different sub-sects of the Kagyupa, and the four high-ranking lamas who jointly hold the seat at Rumtek Monastery in Gangtok, requesting them to elect a new leader. There was no reply from Rumtek, and with all the sub-sects of the Kagyupa, the matter is still disputed.

Gods & Saints

The Tibetan Buddhist directory of gods and saints, consisting of myriad deities imported from India and innumerable local creations, is so vast that it cannot be described in full detail here. The following is intended as a broad outline of who's who at the cosmic party, and just how many arms, legs, and heads they have.

NEW TRIJANG RINPOCHE ENTHRONED

A two-and-a-half year old boy has been enthroned in Dharamsala on 10 June 1985 as the reincarnation of Kyabje Trijang Rinpoche, the Dalai Lama's junior tutor who passed away on 9 November 1981 at the age of 80.

The boy, Tsering Gyurme, was born on 15 October 1982 in Dalhousie, north India. His father's name is Sonam Topgyal and mother's Lobsang Dolma. The father used to teach carpetweaving at the Tibetan Handicraft Centre in Dalhousie. At present he is the store-keeper of a restaurant run by the centre. He hails from Phenpo, central Tibet and has four other children.

The search for Trijang Rinpoche's incarnation started in March 1983 under the guidance of the Dalai Lama who used divination to determine that the incarnation is most likely to be found in north-western India. By the end of last year eight likely candidates were discovered. In April this year there was a short list of three. On 23 April the Dalai Lama confirmed the candidate from Dalhousie as the true incarnation. The other two candidates were from Ladakh and New Delhi.

On 17 May the steward and other officials of the House of Trijang formally approached the parents of Tsering Gyurme to request them to hand over the charge of the boy to them. On 10 June, the new Trijang Rinpoche was brought to Dharamsala and enthroned him in the presence of the entire Tibetan population of Dharamsala who streamed in endless queues to receive his blessings.

Trijang Rinpoche will be taken down to Ganden Monastic University in south India next year to begin his monastic education.

— Tibetan Review, June 1985

Buddhas Buddha Sakyamuni, the historical Buddha of this age, is generally ranked highest, but there are thousands of other Buddhas:

Buddha Sakyamuni is usually shown seated on a lotus throne, legs crossed, with the fingertips of his right hand touching the earth. His head reveals fixed marks of identity: a bump of wisdom on top of the head, often crowned with a precious jewel; three auspicious lines on the neck; ear lobes elongated and split; and a dot in the centre of the forehead, symbolising the third eye of spiritual wisdom.

Adibuddha is the Supreme Buddha, the source of all other Buddhas, but at least three separate forms are recognized depending on individual sects. The form recognised in the Gelukpa sect is *Vajradhara*.

Buddha Maitreya is the future Buddha (Tibetan: *Champa*), often depicted standing, or sitting on a throne, flanked by or holding the Wheel of Dharma on the right, and a libation jug with a plant, on the left.

Dhyani Buddhas The Vajrayana deities from India are usually divided into five basic families, each with a Buddha at its head. There are five Celestial Buddhas, each with a Shakti (female consort) and an attendant Bodhisattva. *Amitabha* (Tibetan: *Opame*) is the Buddha of Boundless Light, the Great Buddha of the West, often seated in a contemplative pose, holding a bowl of ambrosia, with peacocks in attendance below. The Panchen Lama is a reincarnation of Amitabha. The other Celestial Buddhas are: *Akshobya*, the Buddha of the East; *Ratnasambhava*, Buddha of the South; *Amoghasiddhi*, Buddha of the North; and *Vairocana*, Buddha of the Centre.

Bodhisattvas These are beings who compassionately refrain from entering Nirvana in order to save others. Some of the ones most commonly worshipped in Tibet are:

Avalokitesvara (Tibetan: *Chenrezig*) is the patron saint of Tibet. A form of Avalokitesvara is *Shadakshari*, of whom the Dalai Lama is an incarnation. Shadakshari is said to live in a paradise called Potalaka which is symbolised by the residence of the Dalai Lama in Lhasa which bears the same name. Avalokitesvara is represented with up to 11 heads and from two to 1000 arms. The many heads are said to have burst from an original head as a result of contemplating the suffering of living beings. In his cosmic form, he is given 11 heads (eight represent the cardinal directions and intermediate points; the other three signify the zenith, centre and nadir). The head at the top is that of *Amitabha* (the parental Buddha of Avalokitesvara). The 1000 arms which form a mandala around his body, represent omnipresence. The palm of each hand is marked with an eye to symbolize the vision of the cosmic god.

Manjusri (Tibetan: *Champai Chang*) is representative of divine wisdom and is depicted with from one to four heads and from two to eight arms. He holds a sword and a book.

Vajrapani (Tibetan: *Chana Dorje*) is one of the oldest Bodhisattvas in the Buddhist pantheon. He bears a thunderbolt and a bell. He is often depicted clothed in a tiger skin, with serpents writhing around his arms and feet.

Tara (Tibetan: *Dolma*) is the spiritual consort of Avalokitesvara and possesses 21 forms. One form, Green Tara, is identified with Princes Bhrikuti, the Nepalese wife of Songtsen Gampo; another form, White Tara, is identified with Princess Wen Cheng, the Chinese wife of the same king (himself identified as a reincarnation of Avalokitesvara).

Mahasiddhas, Saints & Lamas The cult of the Mahasiddhas (perfected beings) in Tibet recognises 85 Mahasiddhas, all of whom were Indians. They are virtually always male historical figures; unorthordox

Avalokitesvara

teachers, yogis, or wandering mystics. Mahasiddhas are usually depicted wearing a loin-cloth, sitting on an animal skin, their eyes bulging with mystic power and their hair drawn up in a top-knot. The following are especially revered:

Nagarjuna, the 1st century AD founder of the Madhyamika school of Buddhism, is portrayed like a Buddha, with seven serpents forming a hood above his head. *Padmasambhava* was an 8th century tantric master. The patron saint of Nyingmapa, he is portrayed in the lotus posture, dressed in brocade, with a crown on his head. In his right hand is a *dorje* (thunderbolt), in his left is a skullcap, and in the bend of his left elbow he supports a flaming trident.

Rinchen Sangpo (958-1055) was a prodigious translator and religious master. He is depicted in the meditation posture seated on a lotus, dressed in a long yellow robe.

Atisha (982 – 1054) was an Indian teacher, credited with the founding of the Kadampa sect. He is portrayed in red clothing with a monk's hat.

Marpa (1012-1098), a Tibetan guru, is shown with a book and a skull.

Milarepa (1040-1123), a great Tibetan mystic and poet, is shown with his right hand at his right ear. He wears a red sash over his shoulder.

Tsong Khapa (1357-1419) was the founder of the Gelukpa sect. He is shown dressed in red, with a yellow hat. The lotus flower on his left shoulder contains a book, the one on the right contains a sword.

Dharmapalas These gods are Protectors of the Faith (Tibetan: *Chokyong*). Some were imported from India and others, originally Bon deities, were conquered and transformed by Padmasambhava into Buddhist protectors:

Mahakala (Tibetan: *Gonpo*) is the most important Dharmapala, with a shrine in virtually every Tibetan monastery. He is a form of the Hindu god Shiva, and is highly revered by nomads in Tibet as the 'Protector of the Tent'. Mahakala is usually depicted in a black or white form with six arms either cradling a staff with a severed head or holding the symbols of his power to defeat hostile demons: a snare, a trident, a rosary of skulls, a chopper to cut off the demons' life roots and a skullcap to hold their blood. His head is framed with a ring of fire (representing cremation) and his face is crowned with a shock of hair. He is the Sakyapa sect's patron deity.

Yama was originally an ancient Hindu god of death. Yama plays a more important role in the Tibetan pantheon, as Lord of the Dead and King of Religion. He is always shown in a terrifying pose, with the head of a buffalo, riding naked on a blue bull. His head is adorned with rings of severed heads and a diadem of skulls.

Yamantaka is the slayer of Yama, an angry form of Manjusri (divine wisdom). He is shown ringed with fire, with nine demonic heads (the principal one is that of a buffalo, the ninth, at the top, that of a benign Bodhisattva). His 34 arms swirl out in all directions holding emblems such as skullcups, daggers, swords, choppers, and drums. His 16 legs trample on assorted creatures of the world as he indulges in the cosmic dance of destruction. Yamantaka is evoked and appeased during the New Year festivals in special ceremonies performed by both Sakyapa and Nyingmapa sects.

Lhamo is the protective goddess of both the Gelukpa sect and of Lhasa, usually depicted in blue or black, riding on a mule with a human skin thrown over its back. A Gelukpa text describes her as follows:

She is of dark-blue colour, has one face and two hands. Her right hand wields a club adorned with a thunderbolt, which she lifts above the heads of oath-breakers, the left hand holds in front of her breast the skull of a child born out of an incestuous union, full of substance possessing magic virtues, and blood. Her mouth gapes widely open and she bares her four sharp teeth; she chews a corpse and laughs thunderously.

Yidams Whereas Dharmapalas are protectors of religion, Yidams protect the individual in the role of guardian deities – a type of guardian angel. Each monastery, family or individual has a Yidam. The Gelukpa sect adopted, as their Yidam, *Vajrabhairava* (a cosmic and angry form of Manjusri), and the Sakyapa adopted *Hevajra*. Hevajra has the usual assortment of arms, legs and heads (16, four, and eight respectively), and though he has a fearful black countenance with a skull necklace, his inner nature is tranquil – when embracing *Nairatmya*, his consort. At the time of initiation, the lama will decide on an individual's Yidam which the individual will then carry with him, often as an image on a *thangka* (scroll) or in a *gau* (portable shrine). Yidams are not restricted to a terrifying form, there are also angry and even benign forms.

Dakinis These are a class of demi-goddesses, the female counterparts of male Dakas. The Tibetan expression for Dakini (*Khandoma*) means 'sky-walking woman', which explains the belief that they can fly. Since Dakinis are also regarded as embodying wisdom, in both celestial and mortal forms, they play an important role as spiritual guides for Mahasiddhas. In tantric initiation, the expression dakini is used to describe the female partner who thus takes on a human or superhuman aspect. Dakinis are usually depicted as naked virgins, often with a necklace of skulls around their necks.

Local Deities & Lokpalas Many of the local Tibetan gods which were already resident in the mountains, forests, lakes, rivers, sky and underworld were co-opted into the Buddhist religion. Other common subjects of worship are the four demon kings, guardians of the four directions, known as the *Lokpalas*. They come from the slopes of Meru, the cosmic mountain at the centre of the universe (associated with Mt Kailas in western Tibet): *Vaishravana*, the Regent of the North; *Dhritarashtra*, the Regent of the East; *Virudhaka*, the Regent of the South; and *Virupaksha*, the Regent of the West.

Monasteries

Several centuries after Buddha Sakyamuni's death, wandering assemblies of monks in India started to settle in permanent monastic institutions which gradually served two important functions, as centres of learning and as places of retreat. In time, this form of co-habitation required organisation, rules and administration.

The establishment of Buddhism in Tibet would have been impossible without the establishment of monasteries which became a dominant element in political, religious and cultural life. Even today, monasteries (although most are ruined or under reconstruction) form focal points in the sweeping Tibetan landscape and appear to be gradually regaining a sad fraction of their former importance.

The Tibetan word *gompa* means 'place of meditation'. It is probable that small hermitages (some still exist) were the origins of some of the large monasteries. Other monasteries, such as Samye, were constructed on new sites, usually in solitary and lofty positions in the mountains, in accordance with the advice of astrologers. They varied in size from communities numbering a dozen monks to huge monastic cities such as Drepung, Sera and Ganden, inhabited by many thousands of monks.

Monasteries were usually endowed with estates which were farmed by tenants who, in return for use of the land, provided taxes and provisions. As a result, trading and commerce became vital sources of income. Devout pilgrims and visitors often provided offerings of money, and the monks could leave the monastery to perform rituals for which they received payment. Monasteries on trade routes also charged caravans for the provision of pack animals and guides.

The smallest monastery consisted of a single room which functioned as an assembly room, library and shrine. The larger monasteries consisted of several temples, meditation rooms, living quarters for the abbot, living quarters for the monks, storage rooms and outhouses. The design generally followed a standard pattern with a *Lhakang* (a hall housing the principal deity), a *Dukhang* (a hall of assembly for the monks) which adjoined the *Gonkhang* (an inner chapel, often underground) reserved for the Yidam and other guardian deities. The Gonkhang is usually in total darkness, and has an atmosphere of awe and mystery: monks chant constantly to ward off hostile forces and images, painted on a black background, make everything seem even spookier. Gonkhangs usually contain images of Dharmapalas, especially Yamantaka and Mahakala, and chortens containing the relics of abbots or lamas. Monasteries also have a library (*Kanjur-Lhakang*), a large kitchen, a courtyard (surrounded by a gallery) for religious dances, and other rooms to store ritual objects, dance masks, food and materials.

Monasteries are often surrounded by walls. On the roof are cylindrical victory banners (*Gyaltsan*), often in the form of gilded metal cylinders filled with prayer slips. A common symbol seen on the upper walls or roof is the Wheel of Dharma flanked by two deer (signifying Buddha's first sermon at Sarnath in India). Often seen on the exterior wall is the *Namchuwangdan*, an intricate monogram containing seven syllables surmounted by the crescent moon, the sun and the flame of wisdom. This is considered a mantra of great power as it represents the human body in micro-cosmic form.

The Lhakang and Dukhang usually have an entrance hall with the guardians of the four directions (Lokpalas) on the wall facing the main shrine and other instructional wall paintings such as the Wheel of Life on the other walls. A set of steep steps usually lead into the main temple. Inside, a hall of pillars houses a large statue of the main deity (often Sakyamuni or Maitreya) opposite the entrance. These statues, often made from gilded bronze or copper, are consecrated by sealing mantras (prayers), jewels or coins inside. Right and left of the main statue are statues of bodhisattvas, saints, previous abbots or patrons. On the altar in front of the statues stands at least one butter lamp and seven offering bowls: the first, second and sixth are filled with water; the third contains flowers; the fourth holds incense; the fifth is a butter lamp; and the seventh holds aromatic substances. Other items include a large copper bowl filled with a mound of rice or barley (symbol of Meru, the cosmic mountain) and various dough effigies (*torma*) made from barley-flour, butter, honey or sugar. Pilgrims and visitors leave gifts such as coins, banknotes, greeting scarves (*khata*), bracelets or, as a sign of the times, digital watches!

Monastic Life

At any age a male can join a monastery. A sponsor, who is usually a friend or relative, arranges for a teacher and residence. The entrant is then expected to take the pre-novice vows of a *rapjung* (the first of three grades of monk). He receives training, works, studies and takes part in ceremonies that start at dawn and may continue into the night. Between the age of 15 and 25 monks take 36 further vows to become a *getsul*. Full ordination as a *gelong* requires a minimum age of 20 and observance of 250 rules. The rapjung monk wears brownish-red robes; the getsul and gelong monks wear red.

Within a monastery only a small proportion of the monks are gelongs and even fewer are *lamas*. In Tibetan, the term lama corresponds to the Sanskrit 'guru'; strictly speaking, this term is reserved for 'perfect' teachers. Non-student monks can train as craftsmen, look after the monastery's land, do the accounts and handle the business and financial matters. Other monks work in the kitchens or perform general cleaning and maintenance duties.

The daily timetable, rituals, festivals and ceremonies of the major sects all follow the rules of the *Vinaya* (Sanskrit: that which leads) text. Every two weeks the assembled monks recite the rules, with a pause after each one, to allow any monk who has transgressed to confess and receive punishment. The most important rules, punishable with expulsion if broken, concern sexual intercourse, theft, murder and exaggeration of one's miraculous powers; other rules, in seven groups, deal with lesser transgressions such as lying and drinking.

The structure of administration varies from sect to sect but in general the *khenpo* (abbot) directs the teaching, presides over the assembly and liturgical acts, and monitors the education of the monks. The *kyorpon* checks whether students have memorised their allotted scriptural passages, and the *chotrimpa* is responsible for monastic discipline.

In the Geluk tradition, studies are divided into five groups, each requiring several years for completion. The first, *Namdrel*, is the study of logic; the second, *Parchin*, is a comparative study of Buddhist scriptures; the third, *Oumah*, is the study of the path between extremes; the fourth, *Sunyata*, is the study of non-existence or voidness; the fifth, *Dzo*, is the study of metaphysics. Various classes of degrees are awarded by monasteries, the best known being the *Geshe* degree system of the three great monastic universities (Drepung, Sera and Ganden). The Geshe degree is conferred on supreme masters of the five major topics of Buddhist philosophy after passing through at least 17 classes in a minimum of 20 years.

Statistics for the number of monasteries and monks before the occupation of Tibet by the Chinese in the 1950s vary according to political viewpoints. Before the 1950s there were at least 2500 monasteries. No reliable statistics are available for the present status but reports indicate that at best only 10% of the monasteries (and monks) are still active. The Chinese Religious Bureau, a state-run agency that oversees all spiritual activity in Tibet, has 35 members – seven are Chinese, the rest are Chinese-appointed Tibetans. This bureau allocates funds for the reconstruction or renovation of monasteries and screens aspirant monks who also undergo literacy tests and background checks before permission is given. Since the quotas of monks fixed by the bureau for the monasteries are low, many aspirant monks are rejected. Today, it is too early to assess the veracity of a reported religious revival. Full restitution of the monastic system is one thing, show-case Buddhism is definitely another.

On Pilgrimage

Tibetan Buddhism has permeated every facet of life in Tibet, and its iconography is still apparent to a considerable degree – despite Chinese attempts to change Tibetan culture. There are altars in nomads' tents, private homes, temples and monks' cells – some complex, some simple – draped with scarves and other offerings. Every altar has at least one butter-lamp, which is supposed never to go out. On special occasions, or in large monasteries, there may be hundreds. The lamps are usually made of copper or brass, but sometimes they are silver, or gilded. They have a wide bowl to hold yak butter, and a twist of cotton for a floating wick. The bulbous stem rests on an inverted lotus. Butter-lamps used to be a favourite gift to be offered to a monastery, and many of them are inscribed with details of the donor and the weight of silver used. The finest lamps were made in Dêgê.

Many pilgrims who come to Lhasa still travel incredible distances, performing *kjangchag* – prostrating themselves all the way. This is hard to imagine, but the body is thrown forward on the ground, spread-eagled with the hands outstretched, and the pilgrim arises out of the dust and continues the next prostration from the place where the hands last touched the ground. This is meant to be healthy and holy, and is popular during the fourth month of the year, the month of Buddha's birth (May). Senior prostrators might attempt a gruelling prostration-circuit of holy Mt Kailas. *The Canterbury Tales* were never like this! In order to gain merit, without discomfort, some wealthy (and lazy) devotees used to hire prostrators to do the full Kailas dirt-circuit for them. *Korlam*, or circumambulation of sacred places in a clockwise direction, reflects the religious belief that man revolves around Buddha in the same manner as the planets move around the sun.

A tradition derived from the custom of offering garments to deities is the offering of a white ceremonial scarf, the *khata*, during visits to monasteries and shrines and as a greeting (it is also offered during marriage and death ceremonies). *Tsa tsa* are votive plaques, which used to be mass-produced in clay from bronze moulds. The earliest forms were used to consecrate chortens and were stamped with magic formulas. They are still common and can be found painted or unpainted on altars, chortens, or carried in a portable shrine. They are popular souvenirs for pilgrims visiting a monastery.

The *manichorkor* or prayer-wheel, is a specialty of Tibetan Buddhism, and can be turned by hand, hot air, wind or water. Prayer-wheels vary in size from the hand-held version to the huge wooden cylinders, sometimes numbering hundreds, in monasteries or temples. As they spin, the scrolls contained in the cylinders release several million prayers and invocations to the heavens, and gain the wielder merit. *Rosaries* usually consist of 108 beads, the holy number, and are used to recite the name of Buddha 100 times (the extra beads are in case you become forgetful or lose some). The largest bead indicates the completion of the cycle. Rosaries are made from many materials: turquoise, amber, coral, wood, seeds and bone.

If any pilgrim needed further reminders, *prayer-flags* are seen gracefully fluttering from bridges, tents, rooftops, rock-cairns

at the top of high mountain-passes, or virtually any high point. Prayers are written on the cloth, and these are fluttered to the heavens. The colours used on prayer-flags have an astrological significance. Each year is named after the six elements, with each element having its own colour; red being fire, and yellow being earth.

Spirit-traps are used to protect buildings against evil spirits or demons. They are usually made from the skull of a dog, sheep or goat supported by a willow-rod framework interwoven with straw and woollen threads in special patterns. Once the demons are caught in the threads of the trap, they are destroyed by burning the entire trap. More than one traveller has freaked upon discovering a skull hanging in his dormitory room above the bed.

Water has a fundamental place in Indian mythology and Buddhism. In Tibet, all lakes are considered sacred, the habitat of *Lu* (water spirits) and are venerated by circumambulation. For washing, ritual initiation and offerings to deities, different types of water vessels are used. Visitors and pilgrims to places of worship who make offerings or present a khata, receive water in their cupped hands which they drink and rub on their foreheads.

A land like Tibet presents the curious eye with a thousand questions. There are many ritual objects – dorjes, drilbus, phurpas – which are used in tantric rituals, or seen held by ferocious Buddhist deities in temple frescoes. Putting fire in the eyes of monks and pilgrims are a host of landmarks and icons. These include:

Mandalas

The meanings and functions of a mandala are many. It is considered, primarily, to contain the essence of religion; it is a symbol of both the mind and the body of Buddha. The main use of a mandala is in meditation. Following the strict rules of a written description, a mandala usually depicts deities or symbols arranged around a central figure. The entire assembly is enclosed by a rectangular building with a door in each wall pointing to one of the four main points of the compass. The circular perimeters of the mandala include flames, thunderbolts, cemeteries and lotus petals. The person meditating contemplates the mandala according to his training, and perhaps follows the instructions in the written description until he temporarily occupies the place of the central figure, thus acquiring some of its attributes and powers.

Mani-walls

These walls are generally a metre high and can vary in length from a metre to several km. Slates, stones and boulders are carved or painted with inscriptions (often the *Om Mani Padme Hum* mantra) and images of deities (often that of Avalokitesvara), and piled on top of each other. The walls are considered holy objects – pilgrims circumambulate or prostrate around them in a clockwise direction.

Thangkas

Thangkas are religious paintings, rectangular shaped, usually on cotton or linen that can be rolled up. Red or yellow silk is used for the border, and plain blue silk or Chinese brocade serves as a mount. Sometimes the bottom of the mount has a small, rectangular patch known as the *thang-so*, which serves as an 'entrance' to pass into the subject of the painting. Two sticks are attached to top and bottom so that the thangka can be rolled up and transported. Ease of transport was important for nomads and it's probable that Buddhist monks used thangkas as mobile illustrations of their religion. Special pattern-books give exact iconographic instructions for painting (thangkas by numbers?). The colours were made from minerals and plants in complicated processes which were kept secret between master and disciple. Before use, thangkas

were consecrated. Since they were not waterproof, a mirror image was sprinkled with water instead. A mantra, often written on the reverse of the thangka, was also part of the consecration ritual and on the reverse of some thangkas there is even the handprint of the officiating monk.

Chortens

The chorten (Sanskrit: *stupa*) is a particularly striking symbol of Buddhism. The origin of this structure is traced to the death and cremation of Buddha. Buddha's ashes were divided among eight lords who took them home and built eight stupas to house the relics. In Tibetan Buddhism, a chorten generally symbolizes the mind of Buddha, one of the 'three supports'; the other two supports are the book (symbolizing the word) and the image (symbolizing the physical plane). Chortens vary in design and size from those a metre high to the many-storeyed structures such as the one in Gyantse. In its standard form the rectangular base of the chorten represents the earth element; the spire represents the fire element; the crescent symbolizes the air element; and the ball of flame on the top represents the ethereal element. The rings (either seven or 13) around the spire signify the seven or 13 stages of heaven. The chorten resembles a cosmic mandala: the central shaft represents Meru, the cosmic mountain, and each of the sides of the rectangular base respectively represent the four cardinal directions.

Shambhala & Shangri-La

Most Tibetans have not heard of Shangri-La, but James Hilton (the author of *Lost Horizon*, 1933) probably based his story about Shangri-La on the Tibetan legend of Shambhala. The Shambhala legend was first heard by Jesuit and Capuchin missionaries who stumbled into Tibet, and who probably served as models for Hilton's characters. In *Lost Horizon* a Capuchin monk called Perrault had made his way into the valley of Shangri-La and attempted to convert the residents. Instead, he had been converted to Buddhism, and some 200 years later, as High Lama, this wizened gentleman was still alive to tell a new recruit the rules. The main luxury at Shangri-La was Time – that slippery gift that often eludes westerners. Shangri-La was a repository of the best of eastern and western knowledge, preserved for:

a time when men, exultant in the technique of homicide, would rage so hotly over the world that every precious thing would be in danger, every book and picture and harmony, every treasure garnered through two millenniums, the small, the delicate, the defenseless – all would be lost . . .

There are several Tibetan versions of the legend of Shambhala, but they run in the same pattern. Somewhere to the north of Tibet is a kingdom ringed by impenetrable snowcapped mountains and cloaked in mist. In this sanctuary, poverty, hunger, crime and sickness are unknown, and people live 100 years. In the city of Kalapa there is a glittering palace where the sacred Kalachakra teachings are kept. According to the legend, about 300 years from now, when Lhasa lies under water, the world will erupt in chaotic warfare. When the last barbarian thinks he has conquered the world, the mists will lift from Shambhala and the King of Shambhala will ride forth to destroy the forces of evil. The King will establish a new Golden Age of a 1000 years.

Tsong Khapa and other great Tibetan wizards and sages are thought to have visited Shambhala in the past. When the Golden Age dawns it is said that the tomb of Tsong Khapa at Ganden will open up, and he will live again to teach true wisdom. A number of ancient, surrealistic Tibetan guidebooks have been written on how to get to Shambhala. Some Tibetans believe Shambhala is a mystical Nirvana of the Gods; others think it is real, but that the journey is not external but internal, and that the war with ignorance is in your own heart.

CUSTOMS
Marriage

Traditionally, the compatibility of a couple was assessed by an astrologer and a lama. After the marriage contract was signed, there was an official ceremony at the bridegroom's home. The bride's family would then raise prayer-flags on the roof of the bridegroom's home.

Amongst nomads it is customary for the parents of a son to start looking for a bride when he is about 18. Once a likely bride is found, a long series of visits are arranged and gifts like scarves, butter, cheese and meat are exchanged. If all goes well an astrologer is asked to fix an auspicious date for the marriage. On the day, the groom's family sends a group to the bride's home where her family pretends the visitors are unwelcome and uninvited. The bride's parents stay behind, while the bride leaves with the visitors to return to the groom's home on a specially decorated horse or even a white yak. On arrival at the groom's home, the bride pretends to be unhappy but finally accepts the gift of a pail of milk offered by her mother-in-law and flicks a drop of milk into the air for good luck. The marriage is concluded with a great feast. Snowfall during the marriage procession is considered an evil omen for the bridal pair.

Polyandry is rare now. It was practiced previously on a limited scale, to ensure that a family's possessions and land remained undivided. The eldest brother's wife sometimes married the younger brothers as well.

Burial

Burial is performed, if possible, according to the advice of an astrologer who will assess which of the elements the body will return to – earth, air, fire, water or wood. Sky burial is the commonest form. The body is blessed, tied up in a cloth in a sitting position, taken to a site out in the open on a mountainside and systematically cut up as food for the birds. The bones are pounded together with tsampa and this mixture is also left for the birds. Whatever the vultures leave uneaten is buried or burned. Burial in the earth is rare and is used only if the birds will not eat a body – a very inauspicious sign. Cremation is also a rare form of burial since wood is a scarce and expensive commodity in many parts of Tibet. Lamas may be cremated and their ashes placed in a chorten in their monastery. Water burial is reserved for small children and paupers. A wood burial requires the corpse to be placed in a hollow tree trunk. Embalming is reserved for high lamas.

Bardo

Preferably before the moment of death, the dying person starts to receive last instructions for his passage towards rebirth, from a monk. According to the famous Tibetan scripture, *The Tibetan Book of the Dead*, between death and rebirth lies the world of Bardo which is divided into seven stages, each further subdivided into seven. During the 49 days of Bardo, the soul of the deceased, guided by monks, seeks to follow the right path towards liberation.

Jewellery & Dress

Many Tibetans in Lhasa are adopting western or Chinese clothing, but elsewhere traditional dress is still the norm and varies considerably from one part of Tibet to another. Men and women often wear the *chuba*, a heavy cloak made from sheepskin or woollen cloth which is tied at the waist with a broad cloth belt. Colourful boots of leather or felt with leather soles are also worn.

In former times, and it still holds true to some extent, wealth was portable – it was worn in the form of jewellery. A high-ranking official's wife might have worn $20,000 worth of gems. Elaborate head-dresses and silk costumes weighed down wealthy wives; the massive peaks of false hair and bamboo supported an array of pearls, amber, turquoise and coral. Slung around the lady's neck were further rows of pearls, charm-boxes, talismans and other protection against mishaps. It's a wonder these women could move. Elaborate hairdos with long braided tresses and beautiful silver hair-bands studded with turquoise, coral and amber are still to be seen among the nomad women of Tibet.

Coral is admired by the Tibetans because it comes from the sea, and few Tibetans have seen the ocean. Likewise, they value shells, which were once a form of currency in Tibet. Tibetan men, especially the Khampas, also wear ornaments. Ancient superstition says that a man without an earring will be reincarnated as a donkey. Khampas normally wear their hair in two strands, plaited with red cord, wound around their heads. Tradition used to frown on bareheaded women, which might explain the profusion of different types of head-gear. Head-gear varies regionally; felt stetsons (made in Tianjin) are popular, as are fox-fur hats. Among the men, the monks and abbots of old Tibet invented a variety of hats to denote different ranks and schools.

Charms & Amulets

Talismans, in the form of charm-boxes or amulets, have long been used by the Tibetans to ward off evil spirits, and to clear obstacles in the wearer's life. The *Gau* or portable shrine is a container that houses the image of a deity, or mantras, or other small items. These miniature shrines can be found in nomad tents, monasteries, homes, and are often worn around the neck or fastened to a crossbelt, especially by travellers or pilgrims. The top is leaf-shaped, and through a window in the centre an image, wrapped in silk, of the owner's deity can be seen.

In former times, the most valued additions to a charm-box were nail-parings from the Panchen Lama or the Dalai Lama, or a hair from a high lama's head (or a scrap of his food, or a piece of his robe). When the English under Young-husband invaded in 1903-4, Tibetan soldiers performed mad acts of bravery in the belief that their talismans would protect them against bullets. The talisman-issuing lamas insisted that the talismans had failed because they were for deflecting copper bullets, and obviously the British machine-guns had used some other kind of metal.

Popular talismans are based on the eight lucky Buddhist symbols: the Wheel of Dharma (the Law), the Umbrella of Power and the Twin Golden Fishes (symbols of happiness), the Conch-Shell Trumpet (symbolising the spread of the doctrine), the Sacred Vase (containing the elixir of immortality), the Palbu (a mystic knot symbolising meditation), the Holy Lotus (symbolising Buddha and purity), and the Victory Banner (or canopy, symbolizing the victory of Buddhism). Other good luck symbols include the inverted swastika (Tibetan: *yung-trung*) and various animals, real and mythical. Amulets are often tied in with astrological calculations. The right amulet can come to the rescue of a married couple whose charts do not match.

CULTURE
Music
There are three approximate categories of Tibetan musical instruments. The wind instruments include the long ceremonial trumpets (the *Dong* or *Chodong*, which are up to five metres in length), the conch-shell trumpet, and the human thigh-bone trumpet. The sounds made by these instruments were used to drive away evil spirits, and also to summon monks to assemble for religious services. The human thigh-bone trumpet was used in exorcism and was capable of subduing gods or demons. Traditionally, the best bones came from Brahmins, particularly 16 year old Brahmin girls, but any source was acceptable, including victims of accident or disease. Tiger's thigh-bone trumpets also appear to have been used in old Tibet. There are several types of drums such as the double-sided type

struck with a curved stick, or the hand-drum. The *damaru*, which came from India was made of wood – or occasionally from two human skulls – and attached to the waist of the drum were two leather balls which struck the surface of the drum as it was twirled. The stringed instruments include several types with curved necks and waisted bodies.

The religious function of music in Tibet is to symbolise primordial sounds, eternity, the cycle of birth and death; to call the monks to ceremonies; to introduce or end magic formulas; and to accompany liturgical texts. For this religious music a type of notation is used which relates the music to the accompanying words and indicates how long it is to be played. There is also a long tradition of folk music with songs sung in chorus or individually, for example, to accompany specific types of work such as house-building (stamping the earth on the roof or the floors) or loading pack animals.

Literature
Most ancient Tibetan literature is devoted to translations of Buddhist texts from India. These books are regarded as sacred since the book is a symbol of Buddha's word. Most of the books are written on local, handmade paper with illuminations in the centre or at the ends of the page. The wooden covers are carved on the outside and painted on the inside. Some of the most valuable books are written on black paper with gold or silver script and are illustrated with miniature paintings.

The two most important collections of Buddhist scriptures are the *Kanjur* and *Tenjur*. The *Kanjur*, or *Translation of the Buddha Word*, contains works supposedly representing Buddha's words and is divided into six sections containing 1055 titles in 108 volumes. The sections are: Tantra, Prajnaparamita, Ratnakuta, Avatamsaka, Sutra, and Vinaya. The *Tenjur*, or *Translation of Teachings*, is a collection of 225 volumes with 3626 texts divided into three groups: Stotras (hymns of praise), commentaries on Tantras, and commentaries on Sutras.

Other religious works include the *Collection of Sayings of the Kadampa Saints, The Jewel Ornament of Liberation* by Gampopa (a disciple of Milarepa) and *The Great Account of the Stages on the Path* by Tsong Khapa.

Popular literature includes heroic epics such as *Gesar* (reportedly the world's longest historical poem), legends of the saints, fairy tales and the *Hundred Thousand Songs of Milarepa*. Storytellers used to be a common sight. Lama-manis, a type of mendicant traveller, would move from place to place showing thangkas illustrating Buddha's life and reciting stories (sometimes also on popular themes) in a sing-song voice all day. Gesar-tellers were often illiterate but gifted with incredible powers of memory, and capable of reciting stories in minute detail for days or even weeks.

Dance & Drama

Cham dances, a form of religious, masked dance or pantomime, are the most important form of Tibetan dance. These dances are performed at set times in the monastery courtyard by monks wearing luxurious brocade dress and masks of wood, metal or leather. Saints and Dharmapalas from tantric Buddhism are honoured in these dances which take place, for example, at New Year, on Padmasambhava's birthday or at solstices. Apart from seeing ritual exorcisms, purification and prayers, onlookers are also acquainted with the appearance of terrifying deities and thus prepared, if only partly, for Bardo. Some Cham dances are a combination of dance and dialogue – a well-known Cham dance of this kind is *The Conversion of the Hunter by Milarepa*.

Architecture

The nomads (Tibetan: *drokpa*) live in yak-hair tents which are high and spacious with room for six or more people. Near the entrance is a stone kitchen range which serves as a campfire. The smoke is let out through an aperture in the roof. Some camps are protected by a low wall of stone.

A standard Tibetan house is one or two storeys high with a flat roof and floors of earth, beaten hard on a bedding of brushwood. Heavy logs and wooden pillars support the floors. The outside walls are made of earth or stone (round stones are not used) laid on mortar made from mud. Windows may use glass or waxed paper and are protected by wooden shutters. Living quarters are usually above the ground floor. A more opulent house could be three or more storeys high with panelled walls, and ceilings and pillars painted with ornate pictorial designs. In areas in eastern and southern Tibet, such as the Chumbi valley, where sloping roofs are constructed with pine shingles kept in place by stones, the houses bear a resemblance to Swiss chalets.

Painting & Sculpture

Tibetan painting and sculpture is religious in inspiration and is renowned for its thangkas, mandalas and statues. Patrons, usually monasteries or wealthy laymen, employed painters and sculptors, often monks, to create artworks for ritual use or private devotion. The monks would often write commentaries on deities in the wide-ranging Tibetan pantheon and corresponding images were fashioned. The aim of the artist was not to be individually creative but to develop the traditional style he had learned. Many Tibetan works are anonymous; the painter worked according to iconographic pattern-books or consulted a lama who could locate the appropriate text. The earliest influences on painting and sculpture in Tibet came with Buddhism during the reign of the Pala dynasty in India creating the Pala-Tibetan style. Other influences, between the 14th and 16th centuries, came from Nepal and China and resulted in Tibeto-Nepalese and Sino-Tibetan styles.

Medicine

Tibetan medicine is based on the Indian Theory of Humours. The humours – bile, wind, and phlegm – correspond to greed, wrath and torpor, meaning that a physical imbalance is also a spiritual imbalance. In Tantric Buddhism the mind and body are one. The main diagnosis in traditional Tibetan medicine is done by reading the pulse to determine which humour flow has been blocked or is excessive. Tibetan medical practitioners have shown that a diagnosis using this method can be just as accurate as one revealed by elaborate western equipment.

Surgery was not used by Tibetan lama-doctors. It was banned after a 7th century king's mother died after an operation. Methods that were used included hot and cold compresses, blood-letting and cauterization, as well as a variety of exorcisms, prayers and herbal remedies. The Tibetan system is at once medieval and modern. From sky-burials, the Tibetans gained detailed knowledge of the nervous and circulatory systems far earlier than the west. These findings can be seen in medical thangkas and are expounded in voluminous Tibetan medical treatises. Again, far in advance of the west, the Tibetans understood conception, and the growth of the embryo. Then they went one step further to come up with a theory of evolution (fish metamorphosed to reptiles and mammals), predating Darwin by several centuries. This theory is backed up by an ancient Tibetan legend which says that the Tibetan race descended from the union of a monkey and a she-devil.

In the 16th century, a medical college (Tibet's second) was founded across from the Potala, and called Chagpori. Over 1000 herbal remedies were prescribed. Some were revolting concoctions, and others still puzzle western doctors because they appear to work. As a cure-all, pills made from the excreta of the Dalai Lama or the Panchen Lama (or both) were used, but they could only be afforded by the very rich. Tibetan lama-doctors had no answer for the scourges of later centuries – influenza epidemics and smallpox epidemics. The prescription for syphilis (prevalent in Tibet in the 19th century) was mercury, peacock's feathers, gold-dust and pounded land-crabs boiled together. Western medicine, introduced by the British-run hospital in Gyantse (early in the 20th century) amazed Tibetan lama-doctors with the cures wrought for eye-diseases.

As may be gathered from the preceding, Tibetan medicine is a highly complex and esoteric subject, with an approach that has completely mystified westerners. For the sceptical, Buddha predicted that in our time 18 diseases (one of them cancer) would become prevalent due to two causes – low moral conduct, and pollution. In Lhasa there is a Tibetan hospital where the traditional approach is practised, along with some modern equipment as back-up. In Dharamsala, the secrets of the Tibetan healing-sciences are better preserved and propagated.

FESTIVALS & HOLIDAYS

Virtually every month, at every full or new moon, there are local or national festivals in Tibet:

New Year Festival

The first day of the first month of the Tibetan calendar (usually February or early March) is celebrated all over Tibet. Monasteries, chortens and shrines are visited at dawn and offerings are made. Three days after the New Year Festival, the *Great Prayer* (Tibetan: *Monlam*) festival begins. This festival celebrates the victory of Buddha over his six opponents and used to last about three weeks in Lhasa. During the following month the *Lesser Prayer* festival is held.

Buddha's Anniversary Festival

Known as *Saka dawa*, the 15th day of the fourth month (approximately May) of the Tibetan calendar is celebrated as the anniversary of Buddha's birth, enlightenment and death. In Lhasa, the Jokhang is packed with worshippers praying to Sakyamuni.

The Incense Festival

This festival takes place on the 15th day of the fifth month (approximately late June). Apparently, on this day evil ghosts prowl around looking for a human spirit. However, if the spirit is really happy, the ghosts are unable to take possession. Tibetans dress up, wander around and party hard enough to repel the spirits.

The Xuedun Festival

Literally the *Yoghurt Banquet*, this festival takes place between the end of the sixth and the beginning of the seventh month (approximately mid-August).

The Washing Festival

This festival takes place during the beginning of the seventh month (approximately early September) and lasts about a week. Everybody in Lhasa goes to the river to wash themselves and their clothes. According to a legend, bathing like this can cure sickness of any description.

The Ongkor Festival

Literally *Looking Around the Fields*, this festival takes place at the end of the seventh month (approximately late September) to ensure a good harvest. Tibetan opera, horse-racing and archery are common events. Reportedly, the town of Zêtang puts on a spectacular show.

Tsong Khapa's Festival

This festival takes place on the 25th day of the 10th month (approximately late November) to celebrate the anniversary of the death of Tsong Khapa. Butter-lamps are lit and left on windowsills and rooftops.

Banishing the Evil Spirits Festival

This festival occurs on the 29th day of the 12th month (approximately late January).

Evil spirits are exorcised into ritual soup and left outside with burning straws.

TIBETAN LANGUAGE

Tibetan is classified as part of the Tibeto-Burmese language group within the Sino-Tibetan language family. Although there are many regional dialects and sub-dialects, they are mutually intelligible. The Lhasa dialect is considered the lingua franca and has two distinct, social levels of speech – ordinary and honorific – but the honorific form is now falling into disuse.

Although there may have been a Tibetan script in earlier times, it was the introduction of Buddhism in Tibet during the 7th century which created the need for a written language so that Sanskrit canonical texts could be translated into Tibetan. King Songtsen Gampo sent his minister Thonmi Sambhota with a delegation to India where he produced a script for Tibetan based on the Sanskrit alphabet.

The Tibetan alphabet is written with 30 consonants and four vowels plus six symbols used for Sanskrit words. There are four types of script: two for general use, one for Buddhist textbooks, and one for ornamental use.

English is not commonly spoken in Lhasa, although there are a few Tibetans, often those who have been to India, who speak excellent English. Many Tibetans also speak Mandarin – less by choice than by the force of circumstances, which includes the education system. Certainly, outside of Lhasa, you will find a knowledge of the Tibetan language invaluable. However skimpy your efforts may seem, it's still worth downing a couple of cups of beer (Tibetan: *chang*) and letting rip – the Tibetans love it.

The pronunciation provided for the following phrases is approximate and based on Lhasa dialect.

General Phrases

Yes (there is/are)
doo

No (there isn't/aren't)
mindoo

Yes
rei

No
marei

Hello
toshi dili

Goodbye
kelichoo

Where are you from?
keirang kenei rei?

I'm from (America)
nga (america) nei yin

Britain
injilang

Thank you
to duo chay

How are you?
keirang gusu dipu yin bei?

I'm fine, thanks
nga dipu yin, to duo chay

I want this
nga di gaw

I don't want this
di ma gaw

What is this?
di karei rei?

Is this . . .?
di . . . reibei?

Do you have . . . ?
. . . doogay?

Where is the . . . ?
. . . kaba to?

How much is this?
dila gong kazei rei?

Demonstrative Pronouns

this	*di*
that	*paki*
these	*ding zu*
those	*pang zu*

Adverbs

slowly	*kali, kali*
quickly	*diyok po, diyok po*
here	*diroo*

there	*paroo*
up	*yala*
down	*mala*

Personal Pronouns

I	*nga*
you	*keirang*
he, she	*kong*
we	*nga zu*
you	*keirang zu*
they	*kong zu*

Numbers

1	*jay*	༡	གཅིག
2	*nie*	༢	གཉིས·
3	*song*	༣	གསུམ·
4	*shee*	༤	བཞི·
5	*nga*	༥	ཕ·
6	*zhu*	༦	དྲུག
7	*doo*	༧	བདུན·
8	*jiay*	༨	བརྒྱད·
9	*gu*	༩	དགུ·
10	*choo*	༡༠	བཅུ·
11	*chuk jay*	༡༡	བཅུ·གཅིག
12	*chong nie*	༡༢	བཅུ·གཉིས·
13	*chuk song*	༡༣	བཅུ·གསུམ·
14	*choob shee*	༡༤	བཅུ·བཞི·
15	*chur nga*	༡༥	བཅོ·ཕ།
16	*choo zhu*	༡༦	བཅུ·དྲུག
17	*chub doo*	༡༧	བཅུ·བདུན·
18	*chob jiay*	༡༨	བཅོ·བརྒྱད·

19
   choo gu ༡༩ བཅུ་དགུ་
20
   nie shoo ༢༠ ཉི་ཤུ་

30
   song shoo ༣༠ སུམ་ཅུ་
40
   sheep shoo ༤༠ བཞི་བཅུ་
50
   ngap shoo ༥༠ ལྔ་བཅུ་
100
   gya ༡༠༠ བརྒྱ་

Adjectives

big	*chembow*
small	*choongchu*
beautiful	*dzaybo*
delicious	*sheembo*
good	*yagudoo*
bad	*yagumindoo*
cold	*trangmo*
hot	*tsabo*

Food

I'm hungry	*nga troko toki doo*
I'm thirsty	*nga kakam gee*
food	*kalak*
barley	*nay*
roasted barley	*tsampa*
milk	*oma*
meat	*sha*
fish	*nya*
egg	*gonga*
onion	*tsong*
rice	*dray*
vegetables	*tsay*
tea	*cha*
fruit	*shing tong*

Question Words

where	*kaba*
when	*kedu*
how many/much	*kazei*
who	*su*
why	*karei yin na*

People

mother	*ama*
father	*papa*
parents	*pama*
child	*pu goo*
boy	*pu*
girl	*pumo*

Time

today	*deening*
tomorrow	*sengyi*
yesterday	*kasa*
now	*tanda*
morning	*shao pei*
evening	*guan da*

Hiring Transport

We want to hire a (bus)
   nga zu (gong gong chee che) dala lege yin
minibus
   mian bao che
jeep
   jipu
landcruiser
   fengtian
taxi
   choo zu che
truck
   mo che
horse
   da
donkey
   poon goo
yak
   ya

on (Monday)
   (sandawa) shiu pei
Tuesday
   sanmingma
Wednesday
   sanlagba
Thursday
   sapubu
Friday
   sapasang
Saturday
   sapemba
Sunday
   sanyima

We want to stay at
(Gyantse)
  nga zu (Gyantse) dei gi yin
One person wants to return
  mi chee zu lo yongki yin
We don't want to return
  nga zu lo yongki min
What is the price per (day)?
  (nima) reirei kong kazei rei?
kilometre
  gong li
What is the total price?
  donbei guomu kazei rei?

Trucking
Where are you going?
  keirang kaba tega?
I'm going to Lhasa
  nga Lhasa zhukini
When are you going?
  keirang kedu tega?
What time are you going?
  keirang chuzui kazei la tega?
Have you got a spare seat?
  kupkia dongba du ke?
Have a cigarette
  shie da chu
I don't smoke
  nga taman tinge mai
I don't feel well
  nga subu dipu mindoo

Please, I want to take a photo
  gong bu masson nga barji gyage yin
What time are you going?
  keirang kedu tega?
I'm a tourist
  nga nian jie la yombei
What is your name?
  keirang ming karei rei?
My name is . . .
  nga ming . . . yin
I don't understand
  ha ko ma song

Vocabulary

amber	*boshay*
backpack	*depei*
beer	*chang*
belt	*ge ra*
black	*nagu*
book	*teb*
boots	*somba*
bone	*roogo*
bracelet	*dro tun*
bridge	*sam ba*
candle	*yang la*
cave	*trak poo*
cheese (dried)	*choora gambo*
chicken (meat)	*cha sha*
coral	*chee ru*
cup	*mok*
doctor	*amje*
dog	*kee*
east	*shar*

Tibetan Alphabet — 30 consonants, plus four vowels (at right), written from left to right in four

far	*gyang bo*	restaurant	*sa kang*
felt	*ching ba*	road/trail	*lamga*
fire	*may*	rock	*do*
firewood	*may shing*	rock cave	*dra pu*
fur	*o sha*	room	*kang mee*
gold	*say*	rug (Tibetan)	*per rum*
green	*jang gu*	sheep	*lug*
guide	*lamga chay ngen*	silver	*ngoo*
hat	*sha mo*	south	*lho*
hawk	*cha*	spoon	*turma*
hospital	*men kang*	snake	*drool*
hotel	*dren kang*	snow	*kang*
hot spring	*choo tsha*	snow leopard	*sik*
hour	*choo dze*	star	*kar ma*
iron	*ja*	statue	*gu*
knife	*tee*	store	*tshong kang*
leather	*gaw*	sun	*nyee ma*
lake	*tso*	temple	*lha kang*
matches	*moo see*	Tibet	*per la*
meat (dried)	*sha gambu*	Tibetan (people)	*per pa*
medicine	*men*	Tibetan (language)	*per kay*
moon	*dawa*	turquoise	*yu*
monastery	*gompa*	vulture	*ge*
mountain	*ree*	water (boiled)	*choo kema*
mountain pass	*la*	weather	*nam shi*
much/many	*mang bo*	Westerner	*inji*
mule	*dray*	west	*nub*
near	*nie bo*	white	*gaa bo*
nomad	*drogpa*	wind	*loongbo chembo*
north	*chang*	wool	*pay*
photo	*bar*	Yak/cow cross	*dzo*
rain	*char pa*	yellow	*say bo*
red	*maa mo*	yoghurt	*sho*

different kinds of script.

CHINESE LANGUAGE

Nothing reveals the role of the Chinese in Tibet more clearly than the sad necessity to include this section. Hotel staff, truck drivers, restaurant owners, shopkeepers, CITS officials, PSB officers and, of course, party cadres owe their positions either to the fact that they are Chinese or to their ability to speak Chinese. In Tibet, where proficiency in Chinese is a key to power and preferential treatment, linguistic chauvinism is alive and kicking.

Spoken Language

Although there are eight major dialects in China, the official dialect promoted as a lingua franca is the Beijing dialect which the Chinese refer to as *Putonghua* and Westerners as Mandarin. Since many of the Chinese in Tibet come from provinces such as Gansu, Sichuan, Shaanxi and Guangdong, you will also hear dialects from these areas. However, Mandarin is understood by almost all the Chinese and, to a lesser extent, by many Tibetans, especially in towns. In the remote areas of Tibet, away from the roads, nomads and villagers are refreshingly ignorant of Mandarin and you will have to try your Tibetan.

Spoken Mandarin makes do with about 400 syllables which are provided with tones. These tones are crucial for meaning. Without mastery of tones, your efforts at Chinese will be unintelligible, so it is worth practising the tones in the phrases given here with someone who speaks Chinese.

Written language

Written Chinese draws on a fund of approximately 50,000 characters which were originally pictographs. Literate Chinese have a command of at least 5000 characters and a knowledge of at least 1500 is required to read a newspaper.

Most of the characters used today have two components. The phonetic component provides a rough indication of pronunciation and the root component, also called the radical, provides the meaning. Modern Chinese uses around 214 radicals and dictionaries usually list characters under these. For example, many characters connected with trees, forests and wooden products or structures contain the radical for 'tree'.

Characters are all written with a basic stroke system which makes use of up to 13 basic strokes. Some characters are written with just a few strokes, others require as many as 20. One further complication is the use within China (but not Taiwan or Hong Kong) of simplified characters intended to speed up literacy, particularly in rural areas.

Pinyin

A phonetic system known as pinyin was introduced in China during the 1950's to romanise the Chinese language. The Place-names and Geographical Terms section of this chapter provides further details of this system. Mandarin uses four basic tones which are represented in pinyin as follows:

— first tone (high level)
⁄ second tone (rising)
∨ third tone (falling-rising)
∖ fourth tone (falling).

So, for example, mā 妈 means mother, má 麻 means hemp, mǎ 马 means horse and mà 骂 means to scold. An unmarked syllable receives no stress and is skated over with no particular tone.

Although pinyin helps foreigners get their bearings in the language, it is of little use unless tones and intonation are correct as well. The phrases given below are provided with pronunciation and tones using pinyin. For a more detailed language guide to Chinese, try Lonely Planet's *China Phrasebook* which is part of a series of *Language Survival Kits*.

There are some peculiarities in pinyin that take some getting used to:

X is pronounced 'sh' so that Xêgar is pronounced 'Shergar'

Q is pronounced 'ch' so that Qinghai is pronounced 'Chinghai'

Zh is pronounced 'j' so that Zhangmu is pronounced 'Jangmu'

C is pronounced 'ts' so that Moincêr is pronounced 'Mointser'

Z is pronounced 'ds' so that Lhazê is pronounced 'Lhadse' or 'Lhatse'.

There is also considerable variation in vowel-sounds between pinyin and regular English sounds. On the other hand, places like Chengdu, Shanghai and Lhasa sound roughly the same as the spelled form.

General phrases

Yes (there is/are)
yǒu
有

No (there isn't/aren't)
méi yǒu
没有

Yes
shì
是

No
bù
不

Hello
nǐ hǎo
你好

Goodbye
zài jiàn
再见

Where are you from?
nǐ cóng nǎli lái?
你从哪里来？

I'm from America
wǒ cóng měiguo lái
我从美国来

Britain
yīng guo
英国

Thank you
xièxiè
谢谢

How are you?
nǐ hǎo ma?
你好吗？

I'm fine, thanks
wǒ hǎo, xièxiè
我好，谢谢

I want . . .
wǒ yào . . .
我要....

I don't want . . .
wǒ bù yào . . .
我不要....

What is this?
zhè shì shénmo?
这是什么？

Is this . . . ?
zhè shì . . . ma?
这是....吗？

Do you have . . . ?
nǐ yǒu . . . ma?
你有....吗？

Where is the . . . ?
. . . zài nǎr?
......在哪儿？

How much?
yào duōshǎo qián?

要 多 少 錢 ？

Sorry
duì bu qǐ

对 不 起

Trucking

Where are you going?
nǐ dào nǎli?

你 到 哪 里 ？

I'm going to Lhasa
wǒ dào Lāsā

我 到 拉 萨

When are you going?
nǐ shénmo shihòu qù?

你 什 么 时 候 去 ？

What time are you going?
nǐ jǐdiǎn zhōng qù

你 几 点 钟 去 ？

Have you got a spare seat?
nǐ yǒu kōng zùo ma

你 有 空 坐 吗 ？

Have a cigarette!
chōu yān ba

抽 烟 吧

I don't smoke
wǒ bù hùi chōu yān

我 不 会 抽 烟

Go ahead! (help yourself, don't stand on ceremony)
bù kèqi

不 客 气

How much do you want from here to Golmud?
cóng zhèli dào Gě-ěr-mù nǐ yào duōshao qián?

从 这 里 到 格 尔 木
要 多 少 錢 ？

Let's go! (Let's roll!)
zǒu ba

走 吧

Get out (of the cab)
xià chē

下 车

Get in (the cab)
shàng chē

上 车

What are we doing now?
xiànzài wǒmen zùo shénmo?

现 在 我 们 做 什 么 ？

Can I help?
wǒ nèng bu nèng bāng nǐde máng?

我 能 不 能 帮 你 的 忙

The truck's broken down
chēzi huàile

车 子 坏 了

We need to fill up with petrol
wǒmen yào jiā yóu

我 们 要 加 油

Don't smoke
bú yào chōu yān

不 要 抽 烟

We need to fill up with water
wǒmen yào jiā shuǐ

我 们 要 加 水

Let's eat!
chī fàn ba

吃 饭 吧

Have a rest!
xiūxi ba

休 息 吧

Wait a moment!
  děng yīxià
等 一 下

Where's the toilet?
  cèsuǒ zài nǎr?
厕 所 在 哪 儿 ?

I want to take a photo
  wǒ yào zhào ge xiàng
我 要 照 个 相

Would it bother you to stop here for a photo
  máfan nǐ zài zhèli tíngchē zhào ge xiàng
麻 烦 你 在 这 里 停 車 照 个 相

Is this alright?
  zhèli hǎo bu hǎo?
这 里 好 不 好

Here is just fine
  zhèli hǎo
这 里 好

Take it easy! (said to the person leaving)
  mànmàn zǒu
慢 慢 走

I don't feel well
  wǒ juéde bù shūfu
我 觉 得 不 舒 服

I've got a headache
  wǒ tóu téng
我 头 疼

altitude sickness
  gāo shān fǎn yìng
高 山 反 应

What's the name of this place?
  zhèige dìfang jiào shénmo mìngzi?
这 个 地 方 叫 什 么 名 字

How far is it from here to . . . ?
  cóng zhèli dào . . . yǒu duōshao gōnglǐ?
从 这 里 到 ..... 有 多 少 公 里

Hiring transport

We want to hire a (bus)
wǒmen yào zū jià (gōnggong qìchē)
我 们 要 租 架 公 共 汽 车

minibus
  xiǎo xíng gōnggòng qìchē
小 型 公 共 汽 车

jeep
  jǐpǔ
吉 普

landcruiser
  fēngtiān
豊 田 ·

taxi
  chūzū chē
出 租 车

truck
  kǎchē
卡 车

Yak-hide boat
  niú pí chuán
牛 皮 船

horse
  mǎ
马

donkey
  lú
驴

yak
  máo niú
毛 牛

Monday
  xīngqī yī 星 期 一

Tuesday
  xīngqī èr 星 期 二

Wednesday
  xīngqī sān 星 期 三

Thursday
  xīngqī sì 星 期 四

Friday
  xīngqī wǔ 星 期 五

Saturday
  xīngqī liù 星 期 六

Sunday
  xīngqī rì 星 期 日

We want to hire a taxi on Monday
  xīngqī yī wǒmen yào zū jià chū zū chē 星 期一我们要租架出租车

We want to stay at Gyantse overnight
  wǒmen yào zài Gyantse zhùsù 我 们 要 在 江 孜 住 宿

One person wants to return
  yīge rén yào húi lai 一 个 人 要 回 来

We don't want to return
  wǒmen bù yào húi lai 我 们 不 要 回 来

What is the price per day?
  měi yī tiān zūfèi yào dūoshao? 每 天 租 费 要 多 少

kilometre
  gōnglǐ 公 里

What is the total price?
  yígòng yào dūoshao qián? 一 共 要 多 少 钱

Food

I'm hungry
  wǒ è 我 饿

I'm thirsty
  wǒ kǒu kě 我 口 渴

food
  fàn 饭

pork
  zhū ròu 猪 肉

beef
  níu ròu 牛 肉

Yak meat
  maó níu ròu 毛 牛 肉

mutton
  yáng ròu 羊 肉

duck
  yā 鸭

dumpling (plain)
  mántou 馒 头

dumpling (filled with meat)
  bāozi 包 子

dumpling (filled with meat and vegetables)
  jiǎozi 饺 子

rice
  dà mǐfàn 大 米 饭

fish
  yú 鱼

tea
  chá 茶

water (boiled)
  kāi shuǐ 开 水

soup
  tāng 汤

vegetables
  shū cài 蔬 菜

peanuts
  huā shēng 花 生

beancurd
  dòufu 豆 腐

beer
  píjiǔ 啤 酒

milk
  niú nǎi 牛 奶

egg
  jī dàn 鸡 蛋

onion
  cōng 葱

I'm a vegetarian
  wǒ chī sù 我 吃 素

Demonstrative Pronouns

this (one)
  zhèi (ge) 这 个

that (one)
  nà (ge) 那 个

these (ones)
  zhèi (xie) 这 些

those (ones)
  nà (xie) 那 些

Adverbs

slowly
  mànmàn de 慢 慢 地

quickly
  kuài kuàide 快 快 地

here
  zhèlǐ 这 里

there
  nàlǐ 那 里

Personal pronouns

I
  wǒ
我

You
  nǐ
你

He
  tā
他

She
  tā
她

It
  tā
它

We
  wǒmen
我们

You (pl.)
  nǐmen
你们

They
  tāmen
他们

Question words

where
  zài nǎr
在 哪 儿 ?

when
  shénmo shihou
什 么 时 候 ?

how much (money)
  dūoshao qián
多 少 钱 ?

who
  shúi
谁 ?

why
  wèi shénmo
为 什 么 ?

People

mother
  mǔqin
母 亲

father
  fùqin
父 亲

parents
  fùmǔ
父 母

child
  háizi
孩 子

boy
  nán hái
男 孩

girl
  nǔ hái
女 孩

Time

today
  jīntiān
今 天

tomorrow
  míngtiān
明 天

yesterday
  zuótiān 昨天

now
  xiànzài 现在

morning
  shàngwǔ 上午

afternoon
  xiàwǔ 下午

evening
  wǎnshàng 晚上

the day after tomorrow
  hòu tiān 后天

Countries

Canada
  jiānádà 加拿大

Australia
  aòdà lìyà 澳大利亚

Germany
  xīdé 西德

France
  fǎgúo 法国

Tibet
  xīzāng 西藏

India
  yìndù 印度

Nepal
  nípō ěr 尼泊尔

China
  zhōng gúo 中国

Numbers

one
  yī 一

two
  èr 二

three
  sān 三

four
  sì 四

five
  wǔ 五

six
  liù 六

seven
  qī 七

eight
  bā 八

nine
  jiǔ 九

ten
shí 十

eleven
shíyī 十一

twelve
shíèr 十二

thirteen
shísān 十三

fourteen
shísì 十四

fifteen
shíwǔ 十五

sixteen
shíliù 十六

seventeen
shíqī 十七

eighteen
shíbā 十八

nineteen
shíjiǔ 十九

twenty
èrshí 二十

thirty
sānshí 三十

forty
sìshí 四十

fifty
wǔshí 五十

one hundred
yī bǎi 一百

Hotel

hotel (hostel)
lǚshè 旅社

guest house
zhāodài suǒ 招待所

hotel
fandian/lǚguǎn 饭店/旅馆

hotel (higher grade)
bīnguǎn 宾馆

I want a single room
wǒ yào yì jiān dāng rén fáng 我要一间单人房

I want a double room
wǒ yào yì jiān shuāng rén fáng 我要一间双人房

I want to stay in a dormitory
wǒ yào zài sùshè zhùsù 我要在宿舍住宿

How much per day?
měi tiān yào duōshǎo qián? 每天多少钱?

I want something cheaper
wǒ yào piányi de yì diǎn 我要便宜一点的

Too expensive
  tài guì
太贵

Where is the toilet?
  cèsuǒ zài nǎr?
厕所在哪儿

Ladies
  nǚ
女

Gents
  nán
男

Is there any hot water?
  yǒu rè shuǐ ma?
有热水吗？

Is there a bathroom?
  yǒu xǐzǎo jiān ma?
有洗澡间吗？

water (boiled)
  kāi shuǐ
开水

washbasin
  liǎn pén
脸盆

Trains

hard seat ticket
  yìngxí piào
硬席票

hard sleeper ticket
  yìng wò piào
硬卧票

soft sleeper ticket
  ruǎn wò piào
软卧票

I'm going to Xining tomorrow and want to buy a (hard sleeper ticket)
  wǒ míngtiān dào Xīníng, xiǎng mǎi yī zhāng (yìng wò piào)
我明天到西宁，想买一张硬卧票

How much is it?
  yào duōshao qián?
要多少钱？

When does the train leave?
  huǒchē shénmo shíhòu kāi?
火车什么时候开

Buses

I want to take the bus to Zetang
  wǒ yào zuò gōnggòngqìchē dào Zétāng
我要坐公共汽车到泽当

When does the bus leave?
  qìchē shénmo shíhòu kāi?
汽车什么时候开？

How much is the ticket?
  chēpiào yào duōshao qián?
车票要多少钱？

Places

Public Security Bureau (PSB)
  gōng ān jú
公安局

China International Travel Service (CITS)
  Zhōngguó guójì lǚxíngshè
中国国际旅行社

Civil Aviation Administration of China (CAAC)
  Zhōngguó mín yòng háng kǒng zǒng jú
中国民用航空总局

bus station (long distance)
  (cháng tú) qì chē zhàn
train station
  huǒchē zhàn
airport
  fēijī chǎng
post office
  yóu jú

长途汽车站
火车站
飞机场
邮局

PLACE-NAMES & GEOGRAPHICAL TERMS

Tibet is a Tower of Babel when it comes to place-names. There could be variants in Tibetan itself, as well as Nepali, Sanskrit, Hindi, or Chinese (pinyin) translations, to which can be added the mayhem of more conventional English spellings used by early foreign travellers and explorers. Given the complexities of scholarly transliteration of Tibetan, and the fact that most modern cartographers employ pinyin when covering the Tibetan region, the pinyin system for romanising Mandarin has been used in this book for place-names. The Tibetans, of course, do not adhere to pinyin any more than they would wish to adhere to Chinese. Some of the more familiar English spellings for place-names have been retained. The place-names in *italics* are the *pinyin* versions:

Chamdo – *Qamdo*
Gartok – *Garyarsa*
Gyantse – *Gyangzê*
Lake Manasarovar – *Mapam Yumco*
Mt Everest – *Qomolangma Feng*
Mt Kailas – *Kangrinboqe Feng*
Mt Namche Barwa – *Namjagbarwa Feng*
Pali – *Pagri* , (and *Phari* in historical terms)
Rakastal – *La'nga Co*
Sakya – *Sag'ya*
Shigatse – *Xigazê*
Tibet – *Xizang*
Tingri West – *Xêgar*, (there are two Tingris – the other one to the east retains the pinyin spelling)
Tsaparang – *Zanda County*
Yamdrok Tso – *Yamzho Yumco*, (lake)

In addition, some geographical features such as rivers and mountain ranges have been referred to in both pinyin and the more familiar conventional spellings. These include the Yangtze River *Jinsha Jiang*, the Salween River *Nu Jiang*, the Sutlej River *Xiangquan He*, the Mekong River *Lancang Jiang*, the Tsangpo-Bramaputra River *Yarlung Zangbo Jiang*, the Yellow River *Huang He*, and the odd item like Takla Makan Desert (instead of *Taklimakan Shamo*), or Khunjerab Pass (instead of *Khunjirap Daban*).

The great snag with the pinyin system is that you may be looking at Tibetan sounds that have been modified into the Chinese system of pinyin where that particular sound doesn't exactly match. The pinyin system of romanisation, in addition, continues to fox English speakers. *Xêgar* is pronounced Shergar, *Nagqu* is pronounced Nagchu, *Zhangmu* is pronounced Jangmu, *Qinghai* is pronounced Chinghai, to mention a few oddities. The letter 'v' in pinyin is only used to render a foreign sound. In addition to these quirks, pinyin makes use of several diacritical marks. There is a glottal stop (') which marks a slight break – as in *Xi'an* (these stops are often ignored in this book, so it would be rendered Xian). There are two diacritical marks – the umlaut and the circumflex – which are used for rendering sounds from local dialects, or from national minority languages. The umlaut is equivalent of the good old German umlaut, as in München. There is no equivalent in English, but the sound similar to the 'u' in the French 'tu' (and not so far from the 'ew' in the English 'few'). Hence *Qüxü*, by the time it comes out in near-English format would sound roughly like Chushui. The circumflex is roughly equivalent to the 'e' in the French 'je', so that *Dêgê* would be pronounced Derge.

With the large number of variant spellings for place-names and monasteries in Tibet, it is often quite difficult to track down what an older book on Tibet is referring to (this is not made much easier by the fact that there are often *two* places with the same name in pinyin – like two Gyirongs). There are several places that approximate to Gar, the old capital of western Tibet. The winter seat was GarDzong (now corresponding to the pinyin *Gar*), and the summer seat was Gartok (now corresponding to *Garyarsa*), with the two capitals being about 65 km apart. Their role, in any case, has been supplanted by *Shiquanhe*, the new Chinese creation which functions as the capital of the Ngari region.

To help clarify pinyin usage (or Tibetan terms changed into pinyin), here are a few geographical terms:

Tibetan Geographical Terms

caka – lake (also *co, tso, ringco, yumco, nor*)
chema – sand
chumi – spring
dzong – fort (also *zong*)
gompa – lamasery or monastery (also *gonpa*)
kang – ice, snow (also *gang*)
la – pass, hill
ri – peak
tang – plain, plateau
zangbo – river (also *chu*)

Tibetan Compass Points

Chinese Geographical Terms

dao – island (also *yu, zhou, sha*)
feng – mountain(s), peak(s)
gaoyuan – (high) plateau
hai – lake, sea, wetland (also *hu, yanhu*)
he – stream, section of stream, river (also *gou, qu, shui, yuan, jiang*)
pendi – basin, depression
pingyuan – plain
quan – spring
shamo – desert
shan – mountain(s), peak(s)
shankou – pass
sheng – province
shi – municipality
yiji – ruins
zizhiqu – autonomous region
zizhixian – autonomous county
zizhizhou – autonomous prefecture

Chinese Compass Points

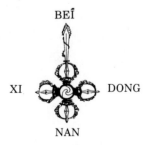

Monastery Names
A simple phonetic spelling has been

adopted for Tibetan terms and monastery names in this book – without any diacritical markings. The correct scholarly transliteration of Tibetan (Pelliot Transcription) has little meaning for the average mortal, and employs a highly complex system of markings with prefixes which are not pronounced. Drepung Monastery comes out as *hBras-spüngs*, and Tashilhunpo Monastery is given as *bKra'-shis-lhun-po*.

Tibetans tend to think in terms of monasteries just as much as towns – the towns for them *are* the monasteries. Thus the Jokhang Temple is synonymous with Lhasa, and Tashilhunpo Monastery is synonymous with Shigatse. To assist with this unique form of direction-finding, here are some of the major temples (remaining) with Tibetan script:

Monastery or Temple	**Location**	**Tibetan Script**
The Potala	Lhasa	རྩེ་པོ་ཏ་ལའི་ཕོ་བྲང་།
Jokhang	Lhasa	ཇོ་ཁང་།
Ramoche	Lhasa	ར་མོ་ཆེ།
Sera	Lhasa outskirts	སེ་ར་ཐེག་ཆེན་གླིང་།
Drepung	Lhasa outskirts	འབྲས་སྤུངས།
Ganden	40 km East of Lhasa	དགའ་ལྡན་རྣམ་པར་རྒྱལ་བའི་གླིང་
Samye	Samye	བསམ་ཡས་གཙུག་ལྷ་གང་།
Changzhusi	5 km South of Zêtang	ཁྲ་འབྲུག་ལྷ་ཁང་།
Tashilhunpo	Shigatse	བཀྲ་ཤིས་ལྷུན་པོ།
Sakya	Sakya	ས་སྐྱ་དགོན།
Chamdo	Chamdo, East Tibet	ཆབ་མདོ་བྱམས་པ་གླིང་།
Toling	Zanda, West Tibet	མཐོ་གླིང་།
Taersi	26 km from Xining	སྐུ་འབུམ།
Youning	50 km from Xining	དགོན་ལུང་བྱམས་པ་གླིང་།

Top: Detail from fresco at Drepung Monastery, near Lhasa (MB)
Left: Rock carving at rear of Drepung Monastery (MB)
Right: Repainted fresco detail from Potala Palace, Lhasa (MB)

Facts for the Visitor

VISAS

There are several methods of getting a Chinese visa. A long-winded one is to get it from home-base, where Chinese consulates and embassies still continue to deny that China is open for individuals. You can cable the Foreign Independent Travel Division (FIT) at the China International Travel Service (CITS) in Beijing (FIT Division, CITS, Head Office, 6 Changan Avenue, Beijing, Telex 22004 CIFITCN); state your name, sex, age, itinerary, duration of visit, proposed entry point, nationality, and request a visa. At the same time you have to remit a sum of money to the Bank of China – inquire from your nearest consulate, it's usually around US$20. If CITS sends back a letter of confirmation to the consulate on your home-turf, then you run back down to the consulate to request that the visa be issued. Visas are not normally issued to those holding Israeli, South Korean or South African passports, but having a Taiwanese visa in your passport is not a problem. If you're going to Taiwan, the People's Republic of China (PRC) visa *is* a problem, so some travellers have requested the visa to be issued on a piece of paper attached to the passport. Visas require a blank page in your passport, two photos, and an application.

The less you seem to know about China, the better the visa issued. Journalists, those with a religious background, and other similarly suspect mortals may be screened. Several subtle differences exist in the types of visas which are issued, even when the visa comes from the same source. Group-tour visas can be issued that specify Zhangmu (on the Nepal-Tibet border) on the visa, hence allowing entry there. Other group-tour visas actually include Lhasa on the visa, so those in the group do not need an Alien Travel Permit (ATP). An ATP is an additional travel document which can only be issued in China, and allows travel to sites which are not normally open with passport visas only (see Documents & Paperwork section, this chapter).

Hong Kong Visas

A far easier method of getting your visa is to front up in Hong Kong, where visas are readily dispensed within 24 hours by a number of travel agents. The Chinese Embassy in Kathmandu and other places in Asia will not issue visas to individuals but they will issue to groups. Some travellers have had their passports forwarded to Hong Kong, even from home-base, so that they can get the visa before travelling, thus avoiding the need to pass through Hong Kong (and perhaps, for example, making it possible to get in through Kathmandu – although this may backfire). The main drawback to this procedure is that when a visa is issued in Hong Kong, it applies almost immediately, and you are expected to enter through Hong Kong. The Chinese won't object if you fly from Hong Kong to other points like Beijing or if you enter by boat from other points (like Xiamen, Wuzhou, Zhanjiang, or Haikou), but they are not bound to respect an entry from Kathmandu since you do not have an Alien Travel Permit (ATP) with Lhasa on it when you get to the border at Zhangmu. In theory you must enter at a city which is open with a passport only (ie that does not require an ATP). *See also Stop Press page 6.*

Visas are apparently dispensed in Hong Kong by the Visa Office of the Ministry of Foreign Affairs of the People's Republic of China, 287 Queen's Rd East, Central Hong Kong (tel 5-744163). You cannot approach them directly, although it appears that some nationalities favoured by China (Norway, Sweden and Denmark) have been able to do this.

There are a number of travel agents in Hong Kong licensed to operate visa applications. Some agents pass through bigger agents and it's all terribly incestuous, so don't bother investigating further. They'll get your visa and that's all you have to worry about. Visas are normally issued for one month. A few of the travel agents that travellers have dealt with include:

Phoenix Services Agency, Room 603, Hanford House, 221D Nathan Rd, Tsimshatsui, Kowloon (tel 3-7227378, or 3-7233006). Near London Theatre and the Jordan MTR, this place comes highly recommended. It's HK$70 for a visa in two working days, HK$100 for an express visa (in by 11 am, back next day), and HK$150 for a same-day visa (in by 11 am, back by 5 pm). This agency is a good source of current information on China and Tibet, and will arrange transport for you into mainland China, as well as handling worldwide flights. Open 10 am to 6 pm Monday to Friday, and 10 am to 3 pm Saturday, closed Sunday.

Traveller's Hostel, 16th Floor, Block A, Chungking Mansions, Nathan Rd, Tsimshatsui, Kowloon (tel 3-687710). This place has similar rates and services to Phoenix. It has run-down accommodation, and is one of the main meeting and information exchange points for budget travellers passing through Hong Kong. Check their noticeboards for travelling companions or if you want to exchange reading materials.

Traveller Services, Room 704, Metropole Building, 57 Peking Rd, Tsimshatsui, Kowloon (tel 3-674127), offers visas, airfares and other services, including a few dubious ones involving Taiwan connections. It's an offshoot of the Traveller's Hostel, although it's a separate business.

Wah Nam Travel, Room 1003, Eastern Commercial Centre, 397 Hennessey Rd, Wanchai (tel 5-8911161) with a branch-office at Room 602, Sino Centre, 582-592 Nathan Rd, Kowloon (tel 3-320367) will get a visa for HK$80 in four working days,

for HK$115-HK$130 in two working days, and for HK$200 same-day (in by 10.30 am, back by 5.30 pm).

China Travel Service, with a convenient branch at 1st Floor, 27-33 Nathan Rd, Kowloon (tel 3-7219826, Foreign Passenger Department) is across from Chungking Mansions. They are part of the official Chinese tourist set-up, and their visas are pricey: a visa for HK$120 in three working days, for HK$170 in two working days), and for HK$220 express (in by 3 pm, back next day by noon). Their main branch is at 2nd Floor, 77 Queen's Rd, Hong Kong Central (tel 5-236222).

Hong Kong Student Travel Bureau (HKSTB), Room 1024, 10th Floor, Star House, Salisbury Rd, Kowloon (near Star Ferry) (tel 3-694847). HKSTB won't get you a visa by itself, but they will do a combination: HK$380 for a visa plus an express train or overnight ferry (or hovercraft) to Canton; HK$300 for a visa plus a train ticket to Canton via Shenzhen and an escort service to Shenzhen; HK$510 for a visa, a train ticket to Canton, lunch in Canton and one night in a hotel there. Similar packages can be arranged through Traveller's Hostel, Phoenix Services Agency and Trinity Express. HKSTB also has an office at 8th Floor, Tai Sang Bank Building, 130-132 Des Voeux Rd, Central (tel 5-414841). Check out their booklets and international flights.

Trinity Express, Basement Shop No 15, New World Centre, Salisbury Rd, Tsimshatsui, Kowloon (tel 3-7239761 or 3-683207) offer a next-day visa for HK$150; and a same-day visa for HK$350 (in by 1 pm, back by 6 pm). Trinity Express has, like Wah Nam, a direct line through to Chinese officials, and Trinity claims to issue a multiple-entry super-deluxe visa, valid for six months, for HK$700, in four working days.

On The Spot Visas

As of 1985, a brand new ball-game popped up: the Chinese announced that should you arrive at Beijing, Tianjin, Shanghai, Hangzhou, Fuzhou, Xiamen, Guilin, Kunming or Xian by air, or at Manzhouli, Erenhot (Erlan) or Shenzhen by train, you would be issued a visa on the spot. The visa costs quoted were Y10 for one month, Y30 for six months, and Y50 for one year! One passport photo is required. Apparently this state of affairs is mainly aimed at foreign businessmen whose time and patience are short. However, several regular travellers have put the system to good use. A female traveller, arriving in Beijing from London (told she was mad by British Airways officials), demanded a one-month visa – and she got it. She carried a one-page outline of the new visa situation, as promulgated by the Chinese Embassy in London, in case there were any complications upon arrival.

A few travellers have stepped off the Trans-Mongolian in Erenhot without visas and been given one month (a visa, that is!) which is then extendable for at least one more month. All of the places previously listed for air or train entry are wide open, meaning that you don't need an Alien Travel Permit to get to them. When you arrive, you get the Chinese visa, and can also pick up your ATP.

Extensions & Exit Permits

Chinese visas are generally issued for one month in Hong Kong, with validity commencing almost immediately. Visas are extendable within China for another month, at any Public Security Bureau (PSB), at a cost of Y5. Some travellers have managed to get more than one month on the initial visa. It is difficult, but not impossible, to get a second extension on the initial visa – it depends on which PSB you deal with. In certain parts of China, such as Xinjiang, extensions are easier to come by than in others.

To go out of China by an unusual land border, you need an exit permit, which is a stamp in your passport, costs Y5 and is obtainable from a PSB. You need one of these if you're going through to Kathmandu from Lhasa, and you can get it at the Lhasa PSB on the spot. In theory your original visa cannot be extended after you have got an exit permit stamp in your passport. Exit orders are issued to naughty travellers – this is a pack up your bags and piss off stamp, as opposed to a regular exit permit.

CONSULATES & EMBASSIES

Tibet is smack in the middle of some of the world's most fascinating travel areas and trekking destinations. Whether you can slip across the borders is a different story (group-tours are starting to do this). The only border open officially is the Nepalese one, and the only consulate in Tibet is the Nepalese one in Lhasa. Nepal itself presents little problem for visas. You can pick a Nepalese visa up in Lhasa within one day, issued for varying periods (seven days to one month, renewable in Kathmandu) for Y35, and the visa gives you three months leeway for getting to Nepal. The full-page visa issued by the Royal Nepal Consulate-General in Lhasa is a rather exotic addition to your passport. Right at the border, at Kodari, you can get a Nepalese visa on the spot for 180 Rps, valid for seven days, and renewable for 23 days in Kathmandu.

The main consulate and embassy junctions for possible connections within Asia are at Hong Kong, Beijing, New Delhi and Kathmandu. You can get a Burmese visa at these places (also the Nepalese and Thai visas). The Nepalese and Burmese visas each require four passport photos, so you should take a supply along. Burmese visas can be slow to get, but are issued the same day in Hong Kong, Kathmandu or Bangkok. You can stay up to two weeks in Thailand without a visa (transit). All Trans-Siberian visa-wrangling should be done in Beijing if you're heading back to Europe from there. There are US and Japanese consulates in Shanghai, and there is a new US consular office in Chengdu.

Since the assassination of Indira Gandhi, Indian officials have tightened up regulations for visas – all nationalities which previously did not require visas now have to apply for them. If you have a visa for India, no special permission is needed to enter Kashmir, Ladakh or Zanskar. As for entering Sikkim and Bhutan from Tibet – forget it! It's a refugee route only. Bhutan is a closed shop; it is possible to get permission to enter Sikkim from within India.

DOCUMENTS & PAPERWORK

Apart from your passport, the most valuable document you will carry in China is the Alien Travel Permit (ATP), a cardboard folder that you get from any Public Security Bureau (PSB) at one of the 107 cities and sites in China open with a passport only. The ATP gives you access to additional sites (some 180 at the last count). You need an ATP with Lhasa on it to get to Lhasa. This is a formality; additions for up to 20 sites are available from any PSB for Y1.

The ATP is useful evidence of your identity since it's written in Chinese, and you had to show your passport to get it. You might try and have 'student' added to your ATP – that addition would go a long way. ATPs can be used in hotels or for bicycle rental as a kind of security deposit, and it's no great loss if it goes missing.

It's useful to carry an International Health Certificate. If you're coming from an infected area, you will have to show it upon entry into China (for the relevant inoculations). Anything else that looks vaguely official is useful in China and Tibet – including business cards, an international driver's licence, even credit cards (although they have limited practical use!). The more plastic, chops and seals on it, the better. Travellers can often get around tourist-pricing by showing a student identity card. In theory these are only of use if you're a student in China, although International Student Identity Cards (ISIC) with the Taiwan imprint on them have been persuasive (fake ones have incurred fines of up to Y200 in places like Guilin). Youth Hostel cards sometimes have the desired effect but there's no guarantee they will work; it depends on who you're dealing with.

Also useful, for your own security, is a photocopy of pages at the front of your passport, a spare copy of addresses, and copies of travellers' cheque numbers, liberally sprinkled around your person and your baggage. You're on your own in Tibet – it's a long way to embassy-land. Within China, keep a few bank transaction receipts in order to reconvert currency upon exit. You must show your customs declaration form upon exit, but there's no control over how and where you spend your money.

STOP PRESS

In early 1986, after this chapter had been written, there were numerous changes in the regulations concerning visas and ATPs. See Stop Press on page 6.

ATPs, PSBs & OPEN CITIES

Travel within China is restricted to a list of some 285 cities and sites, but the list will probably expand in the future. Of the 285 sites (in late 1985), 107 are open without a permit (ie passport only), and the remainder are open with an Alien Travel Permit (ATP). You need an ATP with a Lhasa entry on it to enter Tibet and you can get one from any Public Security Bureau (PSB) within China – some travellers have picked up their ATP from the Jinjiang Hotel in Chengdu. The branch of the PSB you deal with is the Foreign Affairs Section, and they probably speak some English. If in doubt go armed with a map showing Chinese characters of the places you want on your permit, or get someone to write the characters down for you. ATP additions cost Y1.

ATPs are valid for the length of the visa in your passport, so if your visa is renewed, so is your ATP. As the ATP is written in Chinese, add your own English version to keep track. The ATP is not sacred – if you don't like what's on it, or haven't got the right stuff, just arrange to lose it in the nearest of the 107 cities where you can ask for another one. On leaving China you may be asked to surrender your ATP. There is one important rider on your ATP – it shows modes of travel: Plane, Train, Ship, and Car. You will normally be expected to travel by plane or rail within China, but it is important that you try and get a permit that is valid for 'Car', which means all road transport, since transport within Tibet is by road. If you mention overlanding to Tibet in say Chengdu, then the PSB will immediately strike 'Car' off your permit. If you accumulate entries on your ATP and there's no further space, pieces of paper will be attached to it with a staple or paperclip.

Out of Bounds

Within Tibet, only Lhasa is officially open with an ATP. The road to Kathmandu is open in theory, if you have an exit permit stamped in your passport next to the Chinese visa, with the sites of Shigatse, Xêgar and Zhangmu being OK to stop at. There seems to be a hands-off policy in Tibet (in contrast to the rest of China), and you can generally do as you please and ignore restrictions, as long as what you do is not too outrageous. The only time I had to show an ATP in Tibet was at Zhangmu on the border. Travellers coming in from Kathmandu have managed to score ATPs in Zhangmu and Shigatse, although in theory those places aren't even open with an ATP.

Rita's rule of the road: When in doubt – split! If you do get caught out of bounds (which is more likely to happen in Qinghai), several things may happen. Your passport may be confiscated and returned to you at an 'open' city or site; you may be given an exit-order and told to leave China; or you may be fined; or you

may be told to write a self-criticism. Within Tibet, there are PSBs at Lhasa, Shigatse and Zhangmu. You may not run into Foreign Affairs Bureaus elsewhere, except in Qinghai. If you are turned back along a route, it will be back to where you came from, and travellers have sometimes used this to their advantage by proferring the wrong originating point (this is the 'backward travel theory', as first devised in *Alice in Wonderland*).

One method of getting around restrictions is to assemble your own private group, rent a vehicle in Lhasa (preferably a government vehicle) and head off – it's dubious if anyone will stop you. Whether you do get stopped depends largely on where you sleep the night. If you pass *through* a closed place, but don't stay the night, chances are you won't get nailed. For the same reason, any day-trips from Lhasa in any direction should be OK as long as you don't stay out the night. If you do stay out the night, create a state of maximum confusion. One duo, upon entering closed towns in Qinghai where they intended to stay the night, immediately went to visit the local government offices (not the PSB) to introduce themselves (one of the travellers spoke Chinese). Then, when the PSB came to bang on the hotel door, they replied gleefully that they'd already been given a tour of the town thank you, and did not need the PSB to show them around. If you get close to sensitive military areas, which is quite likely to happen in parts of Tibet, you might get hauled over the coals.

Confessions

If you have been particularly naughty, you will be asked to write a self-criticism (both authors have qualified for this task). This does not prevent you continuing on your merry way – it's just a face-saving device for Chinese officials. Favourite phrases that satisfy are of the grovelling variety: 'My ancestors would be ashamed of me' – that kind of thing. It appeals to the ancestor-fixated Chinese ego (there was an apocryphal advertising billboard in Canton that bore a slogan, 'Bring back your ancestors with Coke!').

One traveller was stopped dead in his tracks in Xiahe (Gansu) before the full official opening, and was busy writing his self-criticism when the PSB noticed he'd extended his own visa. This is the highest level of naughtiness conceivable to the Chinese. The traveller, undaunted, immediately added to his confession: 'In addition to the above, I must confess I have altered the contents of my passport, for which I humbly . . . ' The PSB fined him Y800 for forgery, gave him an exit-order, then gave him an extension! He had pleaded that several weeks were necessary for him to get from Xiahe to Canton. Sickness is one of the best excuses, or perhaps high-altitude hallucinations.

Some have refused to write self-criticisms. There was the exceptional case of an American with a dog-skin round his neck who, with a similarly-attired accomplice, was picked up at a site outside Lhasa. They were both told to write self-criticisms, refused, and were threatened with a fine of Y5, which would double every day until it was paid. After three weeks of stalemate, the PSB changed it to a straight Y30 fine. The next day the fine was delivered in dirty 10-fen bills – the American said he had begged them in the marketplace. PSB gave the pair exit-orders, but they managed to get those cancelled elsewhere, and got their visas extended somewhere else.

Open Listings

The lists of open cities are haphazard affairs – many PSBs in China don't have the full list, or they may not have an updated list. One traveller managed to get Shigatse on his ATP – but Shigatse is not officially open. Some PSBs will refuse to give you certain places that are known to be open, and other PSBs will actually give you closed places, not knowing any better. Sometimes only the capital of a particular province is authorised to give certain additions within that province.

In 1985 a large number of new places (some 130 of them) opened up for permit-holders – a lot of them being in boring old Guangzhou Province. For a place to be open, it must first be proven to Beijing that there is adequate tourist infra-structure; transport, hotels, facilities, sights. A listing is just that – it doesn't tell you how interesting a place is. It could consist of a bunch of tombs, or a dam blessed by the venerable Mao. Another Lonely Planet guidebook, *China – a travel survival kit*, will give you ideas on inter-esting places. These tend to be villages or minority peoples' areas, of which very few are open. By using those places that are open as stepping stones, you can get to closed places.

OPEN CITIES & SITES

In the following 1985 list, those places in UPPER CASE are wide open (ie passport only – there are 107 of these places) and those places in lower case require ATP endorsements. (Co = County – which often encompasses a huge undefined area).

MUNICIPALITIES
BEIJING, SHANGHAI, TIANJIN

SOUTH-WEST CHINA
GUANGXI PROVINCE BEIHAI, GUILIN (incl YANGSHUO), LIUZHOU, NANNING (Capital) WUZHOU, Beilu County, Binyang Co, Guiping Co, Guixian Co, Luchuan Co, Rongxian Co, Wuming Co, Xing'an Co.

GUIZHOU PROVINCE ANSHUN, GUIYANG (Capital), Kaili, Liupanshui, Qingzhen Co, Shibing Co, Zhenning Bouyei-Miao Auto-nomous Co (Huangguoshu Falls), Zhenyuan Co, Zunyi.

YUNNAN PROVINCE KUNMING (Capital), SHILIN (STONE FOREST, LUNAN YI AUTONOMOUS CO), Chuxiong, Dali, Jing-hong Co, Menghai Co, Naxi Autonomous Co (Lijiang), Qujing, Simao Co, Tonghai Co, Yuxi.

Provinces of China

1 Xinjiang
2 Tibet
3 Qinghai
4 Sichuan
5 Yunnan
6 Gansu
7 Ningxia
8 Inner Mongolia
9 Shaanxi
10 Guizhou
11 Guangxi
12 Shanxi
13 Henan
14 Hubei
15 Hunan
16 Guangdong
17 Jiangxi
18 Anhui
19 **Beijing Mun**
20 **Tianjin Mun**
21 Shandong
22 Jiangsu
23 Zhejiang
24 Fujian
25 Shanghai Mun
26 Liaoning
27 Jilin
28 Heilongjiang
29 Hebei

Hainan

SICHUAN PROVINCE CHENGDU (Capital), CHONGQING, EMEI CO, LESHAN, Dazu Co, Fengjie Co, Guanxian Co, Meishan Co, Wanxian Co, Wushan Co, Xindu Co, Yunyang Co, Zhongxian Co.

SOUTH CHINA
GUANGDONG PROVINCE (incl HAINAN) CHAOZHOU, FOSHAN, GUANGDONG (Capital), GAOYAO CO, HAIKOU, HUIZHOU, JIANGMEN, SHANTOU, SHAOGUAN, SHENZHEN, ZHANJIANG, ZHAOQING, ZHONGSHAN, ZHUHAI, Anding Co, Baisha Co, Baoting Co, Boluo Co, Changjiang Co, Chengmai Co, Danxian Co, Dapu Co, Deqing Co, Ding'an Co, Dongguan Co, Dongfang Co, Fengkai Co, Fengshun Co, Haifeng Co, Heyuan Co, Huaiji Co, Huidong Co, Huiyang Co, Ledong Co, Lingao Co, Lingshui Co, Lufeng Co, Luoding Co, Maoming, Meixian, Nanhai Co, Qionghai Co, Qiongshan Co, Qiongzhong Co, Sanya, Shunde Co, Sihui Co, Tunchang Co, Wanning Co, Wenchang Co, Xingning Co, Xinxing Co, Yunfu Co.

WEST & NORTH-WEST CHINA
TIBET AUTONOMOUS REGION Lhasa (Capital), Lhasa-Kathmandu road-route.

QINGHAI PROVINCE HUANGZHONG CO (incl TA'ER LAMASERY), XINING (Capital), Golmud, Gonghe Co, Ledu, Lenghu, Mangya. Qinghai Lake is open, however in practice, the lake and bird-island Niaodao seem only to be open for arranged CITS tours since the whole place is a nature reserve (tours run from Xining).

GANSU PROVINCE LANZHOU (Capital), Dunhuang Co, Jiayuguan, Jiuquan Co, Linxia (Labulong Monastery), Tianshui Co, Yongjing Co, Xiahe (Labrum).

NINGXIA HUI AUTONOMOUS REGION YIN-CHUAN (Capital), Zhongwei Co.

XINJIANG AUTONOMOUS REGION URUMQI (Capital), Kashgar, Shihezi, Turpan Co.

CENTRAL CHINA

SHAANXI PROVINCE XI'AN (Capital, incl LINTONG CO), XIANYANG (incl QIANXIAN CO, LIQUAN CO, XINGPING CO & YANG-LING – all tomb sites), YA'AN, Baoji, Hancheng.

SHANXI PROVINCE TAIYUAN (Capital), Datong, Fanzhi Co, Linfen, Wutai Co, Yuncheng.

HENAN PROVINCE ANYANG, KAIFENG, LUOYANG (incl LONGMEN), ZHENGZHOU (Capital), Gongxian, Huixian, Linxian, Nanyang, Puyang, Pingdingshan, Sanmenxia, Wenxian Co, Xinxiang, Xinyang (Jigong Shan), Yuxian.

HUBEI PROVINCE JIANGLING CO, SHASHI, WUHAN (Capital), XIANGFAN, YICHANG, Ezhou, Danjiangkou, Huangshi, Jingmen, Shiyan, Suizhou, Xianning.

HUNAN PROVINCE CHANGSHA (Capital), HENGYANG, XIANGTAN, YUEYANG, Hengshan Co, Xiangtan Co (incl Shaoshan), Zhuzhou.

ANHUI PROVINCE BENGBU, HEFEI (Capital), HUANGSHAN CO, JIUHUASHAN (QING-YANG), TUNXI, WUHU, Anqing, Chaohu, Chuzhou, Chuxian, Fengyang Co, Huaibei, Huainan, Jingxian Co, Ma'anshan, Shexian Co, Tongling Co, Xiuning Co.

JIANGXI PROVINCE JINGDEZHEN, JIU-JIANG (incl LUSHAN), NANCHANG (Capital), YINGTAN, Ganzhou, Jinggangshan Co, Pengze Co (Dragon Palace Cave).

COASTAL CHINA

HEBEI PROVINCE CHENGDE, QINHUANG-DAO (incl SHANHAIGUAN & BEIDAIHE), SHIJIAZHUANG (Capital), ZHOUXIAN CO, Baoding, Handan, Tangshan, Zunhua Co (Dongling Tombs).

SHANDONG PROVINCE JINAN (Capital), JINING (incl QUFU & YANZHOU COUNTIES), QINGDAO, TAI'AN (incl TAISHAN), WEIF-ANG, YANTAI, ZIBO, Kenli (Shengli Oilfield).

JIANGSU PROVINCE CHANGZHOU, LIAN-YUNGANG, NANJING (Capital), NANTONG, SUZHOU, WUXI, YANGZHOU, ZHENJIANG, Changshu, Huai'an Co, Huaiyin, Xuzhou, Yancheng, Yixing Co.

ZHEJIANG PROVINCE HANGZHOU (Capital), NINGBO, SHAOXING, WENZHOU, Deqing Co (Mogan Shan), Huzhou, Jiaojiang, Jiaxing, Jinhua, Putuo Co (incl Shenjiamen & Mt Putuo District).

FUJIAN CHONG'AN, FUZHOU (Capital), QUANZHOU, ZHANGZHOU, XIAMEN.

NORTH & NORTH-EAST CHINA

INNER MONGOLIA AUTONOMOUS REGION BAOTOU, ERENHOT, HOHHOT (Capital), MANZHOULI, Dalad Banner (Xiangshawan), Dongsheng, Hailar, Tongliao, Xilinhot (Abagnar Qi), Zalantun (Butna Qi). Some grassland areas north of capital Hohhot are open through arranged tours with Hohhot CITS.

LIAONING PROVINCE ANSHAN, DALIAN, DANDONG, FUSHUN, JINZHOU, SHEN-YANG (Capital), YINGKOU, Benxi, Chaoyang, Fuxin, Liaoyang, Tieling.

JILIN PROVINCE CHANGCHUN (Capital), JILIN, YANJI, Antu Co (Changbai Shan region), Baicheng, Liaoyuan, Siping, Tonghua.

HEILONGJIANG PROVINCE DAQING, HAR-BIN (Capital), QIQIHAR, Hegang, Heihe, Ichun (incl Taoshan hunting grounds), Jiamusi, Jixi, Mudanjiang, Qitaihe, Suifenhe, Tongjiang, Wudalianchi.

OTHER In addition to the places mentioned, certain routes are 'open'. These include the Kathmandu-Lhasa road, sections of the coast between Shanghai and Dalian, sections along the Yangtze River from Shanghai to Chongqing, and the road from Beijing to Tianjin is open to foreigners in their own cars from June to September. Some mountain areas open to foreign climbers are listed in the trekking section of this book. Other demarcation zones are transit points to an open destination – if a town pops up along a particular route, it may be OK to stay there the night and move out next morning. Previously, this included railway stations in closed towns where travellers had to wait to change trains for an open destination. City-limits of places are often not clearly defined. Given that Beijing Municipality is roughly the size of Belgium, there is plenty of scope for the devious mind. If you speak Chinese, new vistas open up with fast talking. Er, sorry, change that to *speak fast Chinese*.

CUSTOMS

Chinese customs are generally more interested in what you take out rather than what you bring in. On the bringing-in score, anything that is detrimental to China's politics, economy, culture, and ethics is prohibited – whether it be in printed form, film or tapes. This is a pretty wide net, but you need not concern yourself about it too much as they're more interested in nailing Hong Kong smugglers (who traffic in 'Yellow Music' and other 'pornographic materials') than you. Chinese customs may be quite interested in your reading material; this could be mere curiosity, but several travellers have had Dalai Lama pictures confiscated. It's legal for Tibetans to have these and flaunt them, but when travellers bring them in, that's a different story. As a travelling pilgrim you're permitted to have *one* Dalai Lama picture for personal use. As for a Tibetan flag – well, you're on shaky ground there! There have been a few instances of book-confiscation – Fox Butterfield's *China, Alive in the Bitter Sea* was confiscated at Beijing Airport – but there's no real pattern here.

On entry into China you are allowed four bottles of spirits, two cartons of cigarettes, 72 rolls of still film, and 3000 feet of eight mm cine-film. Cigarettes and liquor are quite cheap in Chinese Friendship Stores, they sell around the tax-free rate – but film is more expensive than in Hong Kong. Permission for video recorders seems to vary.

Customs will ask you to itemise your valuables to prevent resale – these include camera, lenses, watch, Walkman, radio and so on – and you will have to show these same items plus the accompanying form upon exit. Such items are expensive within China. Customs will also ask you to declare all your currency, but there's no check on how you spent your money or where. You need at least one bank-exchange receipt to reconvert Chinese currency into hard currencies when you leave.

When leaving the country you may get a more thorough glance through your baggage. Coming from Tibet, customs will be looking for items bought on the free market. Anything that looks antique (in theory over 100 years old) has to bear an official seal from a Friendship Store or official outlet, or they will confiscate it. Apparently there was a little scam going on at Lhasa's Gonggar Airport; locals would sell travellers trinkets, airport officials would confiscate the trinkets, and sell them back to the locals who would then . . . oh, never mind. Airports are not supposed to be customs checkpoints, since you're still in the same country, but with the Chinese paranoia about skyjacking, your stuff can pass through a thorough security check (airport X-ray machines and guard-devices can sometimes find embarrassing items in travellers' pockets!).

MONEY & COSTS

Tibet need not be an expensive proposition. Getting there by air can be pricey, as on Chinese airlines (CAAC) you have to pay a tourist surcharge, with tourist money. If you arrive overland somehow, it's considerably cheaper. Discounting the airfare business, you can survive in Tibet on US$10 a day, with the costs being higher in Lhasa. Hotels and truckstops are cheap, and there is rarely haggling over

1940's Tibetan currency, 10 Sang banknote

dormitories as there is in the rest of China. Food, when available, is not too expensive. The biggest expense is *organised* transport – hiring a vehicle for the run to the border from Lhasa, or paying for internal airfares. Depending on your lifestyle, you should be able to get by on US$5 to US$15 a day. If you want to splurge, and are buying souvenirs, there is no upper limit.

The unit of currency used in China is *Renminbi* (RMB, People's Money), which comes in denominations of 1 yuan, 2 yuan, 5 yuan, and 10 yuan (paper bills). The yuan is divided into 100 fen (1 fen, 2 fen, 5 fen bills), or 10 jiao (also called 'mao' and issued in 1, 2 and 5 jiao bills, which is equivalent to 10, 20 and 50 fen). There are coins valued at 1, 2 and 5 fen.

There is a different money-system for foreigners and travellers in China. They are expected to use a lucre called *Foreign Exchange Certificates* (FECs or *Waihuizhan* – lovingly referred to by local Chinese as *Waihui*). These are issued in denominations (all crisp paper bills) of 10 fen, 50 fen, 1 yuan, 2 yuan, 5 yuan, 10 yuan, 50 yuan and 100 yuan, and bear English on them. The last of the big spenders, foreigners are hit with a double-pricing system where they are forced to pay for items like hotels and transport in FECs rather than in RMB. Within China you are largely forced to pay for big bills in FECs, and you can use RMB on the streets. Within Tibet, it's still largely a RMB economy. It's not illegal to be in possession of RMB, and if you get off the track in China or Tibet you should have a quantity of RMB as the locals won't know what your FECs monopoly money is. Besides which, FECs will instantly indicate that you are a foreigner, which may not be something you wish to draw attention to.

You might like to request the Bank of China for one payment (a small amount) in RMB (not FECs). You then have a receipt showing that you changed money into RMB, and if you have that, you can justify having large amounts of RMB (which came from other sources) in your pocket. Foreigners teaching in China are often paid in RMB, or half in RMB and half in FECs – and they can then argue that they can only pay their bills in RMB. The Bank of China at Zhangmu was mostly issuing RMB to incoming travellers from Kathmandu – so they also had an RMB argument. Although most bills in Lhasa (apart from rented transport) can be paid in RMB (including the Friendship Store there), the situation is slowly changing – No 1 Guesthouse now wants FECs whereas before it would take RMB.

FECs and RMB are not exactly interchangeable in value. FECs are more highly rated than RMB since FECs are the 'hard currency' used to buy TV sets or for saving money. Therefore, there is a black market between FECs and RMB.

You can reconvert your left-over FECs into foreign currencies upon departure from China (you have to present one money-exchange voucher). You can also reconvert RMB into foreign currencies if you argue for a few hours. It is illegal to take RMB out of the country, but you are allowed to take out as many FECs as you want, if you plan to return.

In late 1985, the yuan was devalued, and exchange rates for FECs against foreign currencies were:

USA	US$1	= Y3.19 FECs
UK	£1	= Y4.60 FECs
Australia	A$1	= Y2.23 FECs
Canada	C$1	= Y2.33 FECs
Germany	DM1	= Y1.22 FECs
Hong Kong	HK$1	= Y0.40 FECs
Japan	Y1000	= Y15.14 FECs

Within China, Friendship Stores, CAAC, taxi-drivers, state-run hotels, and anything to do with China's official tourist set-up will demand payment in FECs. Increasingly, so will the railway system. However, anything on the free market is fair game for RMB, and generally in Tibet you can use RMB. In shops, say in Chengdu, items can be sold in both RMB and FECs, with differing prices – an item like cigarettes might go for Y3 RMB, or Y2 FECs.

Travellers' Cheques & Credit Cards

Travellers' cheques are accepted within China (and in Lhasa and Shigatse) – but stick to major companies when getting cheques issued. American Express has an office at the Beijing Hotel in Beijing, otherwise the nearest American Express offices are in Kathmandu and Hong Kong. There are 36 cities within China that have emergency cheque cashing for American Express at the Bank of China, and there are eight cities where you can get travellers' cheque refunds at Bank of China main branches: Beijing, Shanghai, Tianjin, Guangzhou, Shijiazhuang, Xian, Qingdao and Hangzhou.

Getting travellers' cheques cashed within China is never a problem; your hotel will help you out day or night. In Tibet, however, you have to load up when you spot a bank – there aren't many outlets around. Credit cards are not widely accepted in China – it's strictly a cash economy. The major cities (the eight previously listed) will probably accept Visa, Mastercard and American Express – and it may be possible in Nanjing and Kunming. Don't count on it.

Black Market

There is a booming black market in the major capitals of Chinese provinces between RMB and FECs. In Canton there is also a black market in Hong Kong dollars (up to double the official exchange rate), and in US dollars (70% and up). The Muslims in Xinjiang are eager for US dollars or FECs as funds for the traditional journey to Mecca. The main RMB/FECs black market is on the streets near major hotels or tourist attractions in Canton (major), Shanghai (limited), Beijing (limited), Xian (major), Guilin (major-major), Chengdu (major) and Lhasa (OK). Rates fluctuate from place to place, but in 1985 they were within the 150-175 RMB for 100 FECs range, with higher rates being offered in Canton and Guilin. The huge rise in black-marketing is perhaps explained by the new accessibility of goods. Some of the FECs will be used in Friendship Stores, but there are now a lot more places where FECs can be used than previously. In Chengdu there was a photography store where Ektachrome 100 film was sold for Y10.50 FECs, or Y31.50 RMB!

The blackmarket dealers are getting very slick – watch yourself. A favourite trick is for a group of money-dealers to home in on a traveller, all thrusting wads of bills. Do not make a deal under these conditions – you will lose out. As the group clusters, someone blows a whistle as if it's a police raid, and they all scatter, trying to force you to make a fast deal. You will find that the big wad of bills you thought was 10s is actually mostly 5s (wrapped on the inside of the wad). If you do a deal, make sure you count the money first. In Guilin, apparently, a couple of farmers were arrested in a Friendship Store for using counterfeit FECs they had been sold.

It should be remembered in all this wheeling and dealing that if you can't use RMB to pay for larger travel expenses, the blackmarket isn't going to be a windfall. In Tibet you can use RMB for local transport, but not for rented vehicles. This is a rough guide for values in late-85 for the US$:

US$1 = HK$7.78 – official
US$1 = Y3.19 FECs – official
US$1 = Y5 RMB – black market, if FECs are swapped for RMB
US$1 = Nepal 18 Rps – official
US$1 = Nepal 23/25 Rps – black market, higher for large cash bills

Nepalese Currency Exchange

For some inexplicable reason, you can do a wonderful deal (legally) with Nepalese rupees at the Bank of China in either Lhasa or Zhangmu (Nepalese border). If you have changed your FECs into RMB, and then buy Nepalese rupees with the RMB at the Bank of China, you get a much better rate than you would trading hard currency on the streets of Kathmandu – check it out. It's apparently illegal to take Nepalese rupees into Nepal, but then it's also illegal to take RMB out of China – so between the two aspects, everyone seems to turn a blind eye. In late 1985 the Bank of China in Lhasa and Zhangmu was offering 100 Rps for Y14.9 RMB, or around 6.65 Rps for Y1 RMB. Once in Nepal you can use your rupees freely with the big exception that airlines in Kathmandu will only take travellers' cheques (in hard currencies). Going the reverse direction, from Kathmandu to Lhasa, the Bank of China gives Y1 RMB for 7.25 Rps, which isn't such a great deal since you wind up with RMB (not FECs). There is also a little wheeling and dealing by Nepalese merchants on the streets of Zhangmu in FECs and Nepalese rupees.

HEALTH

Most of Tibet is over 3500 metres. That being the case, it brings with it the pox of altitude sickness, and various respiratory problems – coughs, colds, sore throats – plus a catalogue of cracked lips, sore eyes, sunburn and sinus problems. The saving grace is that it eliminates mosquitoes and nasty parasites. The combination of the elements – fierce winds, strong sun, piercing cold and clouds of dust – often contributes to sheer exhaustion, multiplied by the fact that there is not a great amount of nutritious food around.

Altitude Sickness

Altitude Sickness, or Acute Mountain Sickness (AMS) is everything they say it is: dangerous. In extreme cases it can be fatal. Some travellers who have not quite adapted to the rarefied air after arriving by plane in Lhasa have been laid out for 10 days. In all probability, however, you will only be lightly affected. AMS is totally unpredictable – athletes have suffered from it, and those who've had no problems at high altitude before have suddenly come down with it. If you do have respiratory problems, a heart-condition or high blood-pressure, then a visit to Tibet is not a good idea. If you start to get *really* sick upon arrival in Lhasa, it's best to get the hell out of there and fly back to Chengdu. This may be a heart-wrenching thing to do, but it's better than having the heart wrenched right out of you. A traveller was hospitalised with AMS and the bill was Y500 for a few days.

Lhasa is at 3680 metres and AMS starts to become noticeable above 3000 metres. If you fly in from low-lying Chengdu (127 metres), you need to take it easy for about three to four days, possibly longer. You should, upon arrival, go straight to bed to allow your system to adjust. Lie low for the first few days, move around in slow motion, drink plenty of fluids, reduce or eliminate smoking, and do not drink alcohol. Going up the steep steps of the the Potala is probably the worst thing you can do in the first few days – it will knock you out. Limit yourself to easier projects for a while; like getting to the dining-room. Seriously though, your body has to undergo a physiological change to absorb more oxygen from the rarefied air. It has to build up more red blood-cells, and this takes time. Until this happens (a month or more is required for *full* adjustment), the heart and lungs must work harder – 50% or more – to compensate. Air-pressure is 40% less than it is at sea-level; in addition the air is very dry and the nights are cold.

The brain absorbs 40% of the blood's oxygen intake. Small wonder then that you get headaches if not enough oxygen is coming through. Mild symptoms to be expected on arrival in Lhasa are headaches and weakness; loss of appetite; shortage of breath; insomnia, often accompanied by irregular breathing; mild nausea; a dry cough; slight loss of co-ordination; and a puffy face or hands in the morning. If you experience a few of these symptoms you probably have a mild case of altitude sickness which should pass. You should rest until the symptoms subside but if the symptoms become more severe or do not improve you may have to descend to a lower altitude. Monitor your condition carefully and realistically.

Severe altitude sickness brought on by a rapid ascent to high altitudes can result in pulmonary oedema (the lungs fill with fluids), or a cerebral oedema (fluid collects on the brain) which is fatal within two days. Symptoms of severe altitude sickness include marked loss of co-ordination, dizziness, and walking as if intoxicated; severe headaches; serious shortness of breath with mild activity; severe nausea and vomiting, throwing up mucus and blood; extreme lassitude, loss of interest in food, conversation, and self-preservation; abnormal speech and behavior, progressing to delirium and coma; reduced urine output; bubbly breath, or persistent coughing spasms that produce watery or coloured sputum. The only cure for AMS is immediate descent to lower altitudes. When any combination of these severe symptoms occur, the afflicted person should descend 300 to 1000 metres *immediately*, the distance increasing with the severity of the symptoms. When trekking, such a descent may even have to take place at night (responding quickly is vital), and the disabled person should be accompanied by someone in good condition.

AMS is often a function of reduced fluid intake. Make sure you drink as much as you can, even if you have to force it down. Loss of appetite can wear down your resistance – so try and keep up food intake. Carbohydrates are supposed to be good for countering AMS (potatoes, bread). There's no cure for AMS except for descent to lower altitudes, but inhaling oxygen gives temporary relief. Neither of these options is readily available in Lhasa. Oxygen can be obtained at the Chinese Hospital there, and older group-tourists are supplied with plastic bottles of oxygen as well as oxygen-pillows with nasal tubes for the duration of their visit (these 'oxygen-cocktails' come from the medical clinic at No 3 Hotel in Lhasa). Oxygen has a largely psychological effect – it just delays the problem. In the Peruvian and Bolivian altiplano, the drug used for relief is Coca, usually drunk in tea. The drug Acetazolamide (Diamox) is supposed to be efficacious in relieving symptoms, but its use is controversial. You should, in any case, bring along some strong pain-killers, and some anti-nausea pills (Gravol is good for motion-sickness). Once again, these pills have a mostly psychological effect.

On a brighter note, once you have acclimatised and built up your red blood-cells, the altered blood-chemistry will stay with you for a few weeks. This means that if you descend to lower altitudes, such as dropping off the Tibetan Plateau into Kathmandu, you will feel like Superman or Wonder Woman. If you want to carry on trekking in Nepal (and it happens to be the right season) you're fully acclimatised and ready to go.

Higher Altitudes

AMS starts at around 3000 metres, becomes pronounced at 3700 metres, and then requires adjustments at each 500 metres of additional elevation after that. At 4300 metres, the body needs three to four litres of fluid a day. If you are venturing to, say, above 5000 metres, then you really have to undergo a second acclimatisation period. The first symptoms, conquered in Lhasa, may reappear. More red blood-cells are needed! If complications occur above 5000 metres, descend immediately to lower altitudes, and re-ascend in slow stages. Mountaineers will usually ascend, then return to a lower elevation to sleep the night (walk high, sleep low) to allow adjustment. The maximum ascent pace should be 300 to 400 metres a day.

Mountaineers who venture into the 6000 and 7000 metre zones have a peculiar problem to contend with: if they ascend too rapidly, they will come down with a severe case of AMS, but if they leave the acclimatisation period too long (at lower levels) their bodies will degenerate, and they will not be fit enough for the climb. Their timing must be perfect for this 'death-race'. After 7000 metres, acclimatisation is virtually impossible and 7600 metres is known as the 'death-zone'. Reinhold Messner, the pioneer oxygen-free climber was told that he would come back from the peak of Everest a raving madman, or at the very least, a brain-damaged automaton. He got his timing right, got to the top, and his brain is OK. Messner and other climbers have experienced strange encounters at high elevations – carrying on conversations with inanimate objects, hallucinations, talking to their feet. Messner claims that Tibetan monks may even obtain their visions this way.

Eric Shipton, who was with the 1930s British expeditions to Tibet, related how Captain Odell of the 1924 Everest expedition succumbed to the severe effects of high altitude. Odell, on Everest's upper slopes, had come across the first fossils ever from that region, and stuffed them into his pocket. Some time later, when he was hungry, he mistook the fossils for sandwiches, tried to take a bite, and thinking that the 'bread' had frozen solid, he threw the fossils away in disgust – they were lost to the world of science. Practical joker Shipton came up with a number of other tall tales and came back with a photograph of a yeti-footprint.

Coughs, Colds, & Sore Throats

Almost everyone seems to come off the Tibetan Plateau with a strange hack in their voice. Colds are to be avoided at all costs as they are very hard to shake off. Some unlucky people get cases of laryngitis, and on their return to China or the west are reduced to whispering urgently of their deeds in the Land of Snows. The best way to avoid this syndrome is to make sure you don't undergo drastic changes of body temperature. Make sure you have decent hot-weather and cold-weather clothing and that you can layer it on or off. This also applies to sleeping arrangements. There's not much heating in truckstops around Tibet. Bring your own medicines for coughs, colds and sore throats. Some stronger drugs (codeine compounds) can be multipurpose – for headache, pain, coughs, colds, and mild diarrhoea.

The Elements

Sunburn, windburn, chapped lips, lobster-

塔 牌

纸

共和國
造

DAGOBA BRAND

TOILET PAPER

MADE IN THE PEOPLE'S
REPUBLIC OF CHINA

face and red-eye are definite hazards in Tibet due to the (at times) ferocious effects of the sun, wind and cold. You should bring a good sun-block cream (preferably containing Paba) and chapstick (also with Paba). The use of some drugs such as Tetracycline (antibiotic) can result in your becoming sun-sensitised, and result in bad sunburn.

One of the greatest hazards is dust. It can get into your eyes, so contact lenses are not a great idea. A silk scarf, wrapped around your nose, throat and mouth, (bandito-style) will generally filter the dust out of your breathing apparatus, and the scarf can be used round your neck to keep you warm in a sudden change of temperature. In Lhasa you can buy gauze masks to counter dust; these are very cheap, so it might be an idea to get a supply. A good pair of Polaroid sunglasses or *dark* lenses are absolutely essential, preferably with the sides sealed off with leather or rubber. These shades will prevent Purple Haze (headache-inducing glare), and will keep the dust out of your eyes. A hat of some kind is useful. The

local remedy for sunburn and dryness is yak-butter, which is smeared over the skin. From an early age Tibetan urchins are smeared with yak-butter and left to wander around in the buff so as to build up resistance to the sun.

It can get *very* cold overnight in Tibet – and if you happen to be in the back of a truck, you may get frozen solid. Silk articles, favoured by western skiers, are especially useful for countering the cold – they're light and pack easily (balaclavas, long johns, socks, T-shirts, scarves, gloves). A woollen tuke or earmuff headgear will go a long way toward countering the cold.

Hygiene, Water & Toilets

Tibetan hygiene is atrocious. Were it not for the saving grace of altitude, the Tibetans would have been wiped out long ago by plague. Hygiene is up to you to organise and it mainly revolves around the getting of hot water. In Lhasa you can get the luxury of a solar-heated hot shower at the No 1 Hotel, but in the rest of Tibet it's mostly a case of tracking down hot water thermoses and metal basins. The thermos and basin are adequate for washing yourself in stages (hair one day, armpits the next . . .) or you can use a thin towel, soak that, and apply it Japanese style. There are hot-springs dotted around Tibet – which the Tibetans do, on occasion, use themselves. They are a real treat if you come across one. Otherwise, there are plenty of gushing rapids. You never seem to be too far from a running river in Tibet, or a crystal blue lake.

Although travellers haven't had too many problems with the runs, it's best to stick to a supply of boiled water for drinking and to steer clear of uncooked foods. Water boils at a lower temperature at high altitudes, so make sure it has 'boiled' for a while. A water bottle is absolutely essential – preferably a metal one since you can transfer hot water straight into it. Use boiled water for cleaning your teeth. Fluid intake can make the difference between being well and being sick in Tibet. As preventative measures some travellers carry their own enamel mug and eating utensils.

The trek to the toilet is an arduous one and you'd best come well-equipped for the ordeal. First, try not to look at the floor. Some of these toilets look like they've been backed up since the 1st century. Since the sanitation system is non-existent, the stuff just stays in the fly-infested pits below. A nose-peg and a set of horse-halters would be a good idea. A swig of whisky before the assault is recommended, and some are known to put a dab of Tiger Balm or Chanel No 5 on the upper lip to minimise the overpowering smells. Toilet paper is mandatory – carry your own supply (a little is available at Lhasa Friendship Store). You'll need a flashlight (torch) to make sure your don't fall into the back-up at night.

All Tibetan toilets are of the bomb-bay door design (squat and hope), and if you're off the track somewhere you'd be much better off creating your own toilet behind some boulders. In Lhasa, Tibetans often perform these rituals down side alleys. The pick of the budget toilets in Lhasa is the second floor, west end blockhouse at the Banak Shol Hotel, which has a view of the Potala through the bars! Takes your mind off the task at hand anyway. One of the few western toilets prior to tourism was the one belonging to the Dalai Lama's mother at the Norbulinka. Arguments raged amongst travellers as to the brand of this device. The sink in the same room is another piece of plumbing to drool at but it's now full of spare change from passing Tibetans. With the construction of new hotels in Lhasa and Shigatse there should be more places for western bottoms to sit on, but don't count on it.

Rabies

Tibetans believe that dogs are reincarnations of monks who didn't quite make the grade and have returned to their old haunts as punishment, and in the hope of being able to take part in the proceedings. Thus large numbers of medium-sized dogs rove around the monasteries and in the marketplaces in Tibet. Dogs, Gods, makes sense . . . Some are used as guard-dogs at temples, and they can and will attack. I had to fend off one pack of them with a swinging water-bottle. Picking up a stone sometimes has the right effect. If a dog draws blood, it's bad news. It's not known if Tibetan dogs have rabies, but if they do, and you're bitten (with blood drawn) then you could be in big trouble. The incubation-period for rabies is two months, depending on where the victim is bitten. If the victim is not given rabies shots within a certain time (there used to be 15 painful shots – now reduced to five), then the result is fatal.

Other

Around the end of 1984 a traveller came down with spinal meningitis. It's not known where he picked it up, although it could've been in Nepal. Travellers staying at Snowlands all raced off to get shots in

Lhasa. Malaria is not a problem in Tibet because it's too high for mosquitoes, and there are no leeches. The same, however, cannot be said of the south-west of China, nor of Kathmandu Valley (which is legendary for its abundance of stomach and other afflictions). If you're headed for Nepal, you should stock up on stomach-bug medicines (Flagyl is efficacious, as is Atabrine, also known as Quinacrine). The Nepalese lowlands require malaria tablets. Dysentery and the runs can lay you out in Nepal but they are not so prevalent in Tibet.

Malnutrition is a serious problem in Tibet. Take along vitamin pills, dried soup, and hot-water additives. If you're leaving Lhasa, take a big bag of food along. The Chinese neither have nor store Rh-negative blood for transfusions. You'd have to be evacuated to the nearest Rh-negative country. Type O is also rare, and if you're O and Rh-negative, try not to bleed.

Last but not least, there is a problem with bed-bugs and fleas in the ramshackle accommodation one finds in Tibet. Apart from spraying and powdering your humble bedding, or carrying anti-itch creams, there's little that can be done about it, and generally you will not be bothered. For some unfathomable reason, certain travellers seem to attract these bugs, and display their wounds to all and sundry the following morning.

I don't wish to heighten your paranoia about the health situation in Tibet, but you really have to think about the whole thing in terms of prevention and being your own doctor. Take along good medical supplies and a small medical kit.

FILM & PHOTOGRAPHY

In mid-85 there were absolutely no film stocks left in Chengdu, and don't expect to find anything in Lhasa. Travellers who had expected to load up in Chengdu suddenly found themselves filmless in Lhasa. Kodachrome became elevated to the status of solid gold and the filmless

would kill for it! Pick up your film in Hong Kong to be sure; it's fresher and cheaper anyway. Kathmandu stocks all kinds of film too. One traveller ordered a package of Kodachrome sent to Lhasa Poste Restante (express) and, amazing but true, it actually arrived (meanwhile his camera had decided to malfunction). Within China, slides and prints can be processed at major cities like Shanghai and Beijing, usually through the larger hotels. Film can also be posted out of the country if you care to run a gamut of doubts. Kodachrome cannot be processed in Hong Kong – or at least it must be forwarded to Japan or Australia first, ditto in Kathmandu. There's no real limit on the amount of film you can take into China.

The biggest technical problem with photography in Tibet is exposure. The sun can get very fierce and result in washed-out photos. Sun-flares, reflections ricocheting down your lens, are an added problem. Try and avoid the midday sun – only mad dogs and amateurs take pictures then. A lens-hood and a good polariser are essential. For readings, your camera light-meter can be relied upon, though it would be a good idea to adjust settings for underexposure. Take readings off the palm of your hand if you don't have a spot-meter. Readings of the sky can be *lower* than those of the ground – something to do with the thin atmosphere. Kodachrome 25 can be put to wonderful use in Tibet.

A peculiarly Tibetan hazard in the photography line is the ever-present yak-butter in the temple lamps. Sometimes you find yourself virtually skating over the stuff in temples – it gets on your hands somehow, and it isn't long before it makes its way to your camera lens, which is bad news. Make sure you take plenty of cleaning materials along for your lens, or you may just end up with a yak-butter fog on your pics.

Restrictions
There are strict controls over taking pictures within monasteries in Tibet.

Sometimes a fee will be demanded, either for individual photos, or for blanket permission for a group of photographers shooting in all directions. At the Jokhang Temple in Lhasa, the quote was Y20 for a single shot, or Y150 blanket permission for a group. Most individuals tend to ignore these guidelines and blaze away until they're stopped. It's not quite clear if the exorbitant charges are due to religious sensitivities, or are a plain money-making proposition for the Tibetan monks. Certainly in some temples you won't be allowed to take an interior shot no matter how much money you care to offer. Most temple-interiors require a strong flash-unit, which will immediately give you away if sneaking shots. Upon payment of a fee, a monk may turn on the lights making the flash less necessary. Apart from temples, a particularly sensitive area is the photography of sky burials – this is strictly taboo.

Amongst the Chinese, touchy or prohibited subjects are military installations, bridges and airports. You can probably take a picture from the plane if you're flying from Chengdu to Lhasa, although officially you're not supposed to do this.

People Photos

As in any country, including your own, sneak-shots of people will result in lousy pictures. Hang around, get to know people, ask permission. Sometimes a good exchange is a Dalai Lama picture – you take a picture, they get a picture. Or take down a person's name and address, and promise to send a copy. If they write it down in Tibetan script, you can later photocopy that, attach it to an envelope, add 'Tibet Autonomous Region, People's Republic of China' and post it. There's only one drawback – a lot of people don't *have* addresses. Nomads are nomads. If you do promise, follow up – it creates a bad name for other travellers if you don't. The worst thing you can possibly do is offer money for photos; you will turn the locals into a nation of beggars.

Unfortunately the Polaroid message has travelled far and wide. Apart from rampaging, group-tour, Polaroid artistes, the Chinese develop black and white portrait pictures in dirty buckets on the spot (at an outdoor 'studio' across from the Potala). If you photograph a Tibetan, he or she will probably wander up and demand an instant print. The best thing to do is to show another film from a spare canister in what will probably be a futile effort to explain it's not instant. Temporary distraction can be provided by allowing your subject a look through your camera view-screen. This is great fun for them, and will take the edge off their unfamiliarity with the camera.

Tibetan women are especially camera-shy, and don't pick on a nomad Khampa's girlfriend if you value your lenses! A startling piece of information – some Tibetans think that the photo you take of them may end up in a magazine, and then be used as toilet paper. I had never thought of it that way – aren't magazines a bit too glossy?

In 1979 a *National Geographic* photographer visited Lhasa and word got around that he was offering instant images – the disease travels quickly. At the Jokhang Temple, monks lined up, not for a Polaroid of themselves, but for pictures of the most sacred Buddhist statue – so that they could hold the developing picture in their own hands. The Tibetans are just as interested in photos of the Dalai Lama or the major temples of Tibet as they are in photos of themselves. If you are offering Dalai Lama pics, be very discreet about how you give them away. Producing these items can result in a large crowd homing in on you, and can even spark off a riot.

GENERAL INFORMATION
Post & Communications

Post offices are located in the major towns of Tibet – like Lhasa, Shigatse, Zêtang and Chamdo. Mail takes about 10 days to get from the outside world to Lhasa. Since most Tibetans are illiterate, there is not a great demand among them for postal service it's more for the benefit of the resident Chinese. There's a Poste Restante counter at the main post office in Lhasa. Make sure your correspondents address letters to the Tibetan Autonomous Region, People's Republic of China. You can also pick up mail care of the hotels in Lhasa (No 1 Hotel, or Snowlands). For Chengdu, send mail care of Jinjiang Hotel, 180 Renmin Nan Lu, Chengdu, Sichuan, People's Republic of China. For Xian, care of Renmin Hotel, 319 Dongxin Jie, Xian, Shaanxi, People's Republic of China.

When attempting to send any packages out of Tibet (or within China) do not seal the package – you'll only have to open it again for customs inspection. The best source of packaging materials is the Friendship Store. Large envelopes are unavailable so bring them with you or make them. Parcels are the most expensive postal category, with prices according to a formula of weight and country of destination. If you can call it a small packet (up to one kg) it's much cheaper. Postage to Hong Kong is dirt cheap, as Hong Kong is not regarded as 'overseas' but as an outpost of the motherland.

International phone-calls can be made from Lhasa – they are routed through Beijing with various degrees of success. Calls are placed at the Telegraph & Communications Office in Lhasa.

Banks

Banks? You want to go to the bank?! It's best to stock up where you can in Tibet, especially if you're heading off into the wilds. There are Bank of China branches in Lhasa, Shigatse, Zhangmu, Chamdo, Zêtang and a few other esoteric locations. They are usually a big town story, and even then the little buggers can be hard to find – they're well camouflaged. In theory banks are open 8.30 am to 12 noon and 3.30 to 6.30 pm.

Hospitals

Hospitals are few and far between. The larger towns have them, and there are clinics in some smaller places. Truckstops and army bases often have their own medical facilities. Chinese treatment for foreigners relies heavily on the use of antibiotics, which you can pack along with you anyway. There's a traditional Tibetan medicinal approach used at the Tibetan hospital in Lhasa and travellers have found the approach beneficial.

Electricity

There is enough electricity in places close to hydroelectric projects in Tibet (which are quite successful; there are lots of rapid rivers), but electricity is rarely used for heating devices. Supply is 220 volts, 50 cycles AC, and is often turned off (for lighting) around 10 pm. At best, electrical supply is unreliable so have battery devices as a back-up. In Lhasa you get to control the lights. In rural areas, there may be yak-butter lamps or fires to provide lighting. Solar-heating is still in the experimental stages and the potential has not yet been tapped.

Business Hours & Timekeeping

There are several time zones at work. The first is Chinese timekeeping, which sticks to Beijing's clock, even though Tibet is thousands of km to the west. There should actually be something like a two-hour time difference between Beijing and Lhasa (there *is* a two-hour difference between Beijing and Kathmandu, or Lhasa and Kathmandu). Thus, when it's 10 am in Beijing it should be 8 am in Lhasa, but it isn't – it's 10 am in Lhasa (and the same time in Hong Kong). If you add Greenwich Mean Time, and step back a few centuries, you've just about got the picture.

Chinese business hours are supposedly a morning session (roughly 9 to 11.30 am), then *xiuxi* the sacred siesta, and an afternoon session (roughly 3.30 to 6.30 pm). There is, however, considerable variation for services provided by the

Chinese. The non-working day is Sunday, although some shops may be open then. Hours are shortened in winter.

Tibetan timekeeping is erratic. Whether you're in the year of the Water-Hare or the New Moon of the Brass Monkey, life appears to function (in the markets anyway) from 9.30 am to 7 pm and nightlife, if it exists, can go on to 10 pm. Monastic timekeeping (ie when temples are open to tourists) varies considerably. Generally, the morning is a better time to visit. Sundays are bad all round – from the Tibetan point of view, and from the Chinese one.

For those who are superstitious, 1986 is the year of the Fire-Tiger, and the end of the 60-year cycle (XVI), which means that in February 1987 a new cycle of 60 years will begin (XVII). Tibetan New Year is in February, and the cycle uses the same zodiacal data base as the Chinese: Hare (1), Dragon (2), Serpent (3), Horse (4), Sheep (5), Monkey (6), Bird (7), Dog (8), Hog (9), Mouse (10), Ox (11) and Tiger (12). Added to these are the five elements: Fire, Earth, Iron, Water and Wood. The full 60-year cycle is computed by juxtaposing the Elements and the Animals.

1976	Fire-Dragon	(50th year in cycle XVI)
1977	Fire-Serpent	(51)
1978	Earth-Horse	(52)
1979	Earth-Sheep	(53)
1980	Iron-Monkey	(54)
1981	Iron-Bird	(55)
1982	Water-Dog	(56)
1983	Water-Hog	(57)
1984	Wood-Mouse	(58)
1985	Wood-Ox	(59)
1986	Fire-Tiger	(60)
1987	Fire-Hare	(1st in cycle XVII)
1988	Earth-Dragon	(2)
1989	Earth-Serpent	(3)
1990	Iron-Horse	(4)
1991	Iron-Sheep	(5)

Weights & Measures

The Chinese use the metric system, but they also use a more traditional system of measuring in the marketplace.

1 metre = 3 shichi
1 kilometre = 2 shili
1 hectare = 15 mu (2.47 acres)
1 litre = 1 sheng
1 kilogram = 2 jin (catty)

Tibetan weights and measures are now somewhat standardised by the Chinese system, but no doubt the older forms have survived to some degree. The old Tibetan system is highly complex and variable – standards were set, checked and tested by the local magistrate. A few snippets: yak-hair was weighed against yak-butter, which it equalled in value. Tea was sold by the brick (variable in size), and to complicate matters, Chinese black tea was used as currency. Distance could sometimes be given as the ground covered by a mule caravan in three hours (roughly 13 km). The Tibetans employed the rosary as a kind of abacus in the past. Rosaries have 108 beads, which is a holy measure. Thus the base of the chorten in Gyantse is supposed to measure 108 cubits, and if pilgrims do 108 circuits of holy Mt Kailas, they are assured entry into Nirvana.

Metric Conversion

1 metre= 3.28 ft
1 foot = 0.3048 metres
1 kilometre = 0.6215 miles
1 mile = 1.61 kilometres
1 kilogram = 2.2 pounds
1 pound = 0.453 kilograms

8800 metres = 28,872 ft
8600 metres = 28,216 ft
8400 metres = 27,560 ft
8200 metres = 26,903 ft
8000 metres = 26,247 ft
7800 metres = 25,591 ft
7600 metres = 24,935 ft
7400 metres = 24,279 ft
7200 metres = 23,662 ft
7000 metres = 22,966 ft
6800 metres = 22,310 ft
6600 metres = 21,654 ft
6400 metres = 20,998 ft
6200 metres = 20,342 ft
6000 metres = 19,685 ft
5800 metres = 19,029 ft
5600 metres = 18,373 ft
5400 metres = 17,717 ft
5200 metres = 17,061 ft
5000 metres = 16,404 ft
4800 metres = 15,748 ft
4600 metres = 15,092 ft
4400 metres = 14,436 ft
4200 metres = 13,780 ft
4000 metres = 13,124 ft
3800 metres = 12,467 ft
3600 metres = 11,811 ft
3400 metres = 11,155 ft
3200 metres = 10,498 ft
3000 metres = 9,843 ft
2000 metres = 6,562 ft
1000 metres = 3,281 ft

Beggars, Crime, Theft & Dope

There are a number of beggars around Lhasa, especially at festival times when the locals donate food and money as a way of earning merit. Beggars are more noticeable in Lhasa because people go there in large numbers on pilgrimage and often wind up broke. They can get aggressive. The double thumbs-up gesture, accompanied by *kuchi-kuchi* (please) is the mode of inquiry. Just about anything you have would be acceptable if you wish to encourage beggars. *Everyone* in Tibet wants Dalai Lama pics and they can be worth a lot of money in resale value. If you give one away, you will soon have a crowd around you asking for more, and you may have trouble extricating yourself.

Nomads are particularly keen on any empty tin cans you have which should be no problem for you. They apparently use them to manufacture other items like incense-holders. I had to give chase to a young Tibetan who had made off with my plastic water-canister – no ill feelings – he cheerfully gave it back with a winning smile. I'm not altogether sure if he intentionally stole it or thought he'd *found* it! However, there have been cases of theft. In Lhasa bicycles are stolen quite frequently. It remains to be seen how aggressive locals will be with the new influx of travellers. In Lhasa, the Tibetan hotel staff would inform me to be careful because there were Chinese in the next room, and then the Chinese would stroll in and inform me to be careful because of the Tibetans!

As yet, having dope is no problem. Up in Xinjiang, the Chinese refer to it as 'local tobacco', which the smiling minority peoples like to smoke (the minorities also like to smoke it in Yunnan and Qinghai). The situation may change, but the Chinese are not too keen on the upkeep of foreigners in their prisons, nor of any resulting publicity. As far as is known, there is only one case of a foreigner in a Chinese jail – up in Harbin, in north-east China. He left a cigarette burning, and the hotel he was staying in burnt down, killing 10 people. He got 18 months in jail (1985) and a fine of US$53,000. Usually, the worst the Chinese will do if there is any legal problem, will be to boot you out of the country and perhaps give you a fine. This is the 'soft glove' treatment and is far more lenient than that in any other Asian country. The Chinese reserve the third degree for their own kind. A bullet through the head is cheap enough, although the bill for that bullet is still sent to the executed victim's family. The Gulag of China is located in Qinghai Province, where large numbers of political and other prisoners are kept.

Media & Newspapers

Most media is in Chinese within Tibet, but there's little evidence of it. The Tibetan language has been reduced to a very low profile. A daily newspaper is issued in Lhasa and it offers a bland monotony of predictable non-events. It is printed in Chinese tabloid form, with a Tibetan facsimile. It's called the *Tibet Daily*. Maybe they'll bring out the *Daily Lama* in a few years for the tourist trade? Until then, you'll just have to content yourself with stray copies of *China Daily*, which is intended for foreigners, and when not pouring forth wonderful statistics, can be enlightening at times. There is a facsimile edition issued in Hong Kong, and a North American version is also published.

Radio Lhasa has been in operation since the 1950s. When it does broadcast in Tibetan, it is monitored by the Dalai Lama's government from a post in New Delhi. The Dalai Lama's government-in-exile is getting bigger on media and is now delving into movies and videotapes. If you want to get a more balanced view of things, they issue some news magazines which give current info on the state of things in Tibet. The *Tibetan Bulletin* (Dharamsala) is issued bi-monthly, and *Tibetan Review* (New Delhi) is issued monthly.

Tibetans were first able to tune into TV in 1979 when the Tibetan TV Station began broadcasting colour videos of Beijing CCTV programmes, which were delivered by air usually a week after they had been seen elsewhere in China. Reportedly, only one colour TV then existed in Tibet as opposed to several thousand now. The Tibetan TV Station can now receive programmes direct through a satellite receiving station completed in Lhasa in September 1985. A second channel has started to broadcast news bulletins, plays, dubbed films, and programmes made by the station in Tibetan. This will perhaps offset the problems caused by broadcasting in Chinese to speakers of Tibetan only.

Yin Hong, a film-maker with the Shanghai Popular Science Film Studio, has made several films on Tibet. His film *Tibet, Tibet* won first prize at an international film festival in France in 1985.

Maps

There is no decent separate map of Tibet. That being the case, you might be reduced to snipping off the piece you need from a larger all-China map. The best one around is a Chinese-Swedish production which has place names in English with Chinese characters next to them. Since most of the drivers around the place are Chinese, the Chinese characters come in handy. The map is quite a large one, titled *Map of the People's Republic of China* (Cartographic Publishing House, China, and Esselte Map Service, AB, Sweden, 1984), and it's all in pinyin.

In Kathmandu they were selling a large Tibet map based on 1919 topography! The Chinese certainly have the goods on Tibet mapping, but they're not about to release it, with the exception that you can get a fold-up map of Lhasa (either in Lhasa, or in Chengdu), which comes in two versions: one all-Chinese, the other all-Tibetan. At the CITS hideaway at No 3 Hotel in Lhasa, I spotted one mammoth two-sheet map of Tibet on the wall – I rubbed my eyes – this thing had elevations of hundreds of spots, exact road distances, great topographical data (all in Chinese, but still readable by features). No sooner had I started jotting down some details when a gentleman from CITS hauled me off and told me the map was not for western eyes. I walked downstairs, found the same map plastered on another wall there, and spent half an hour scrutinising it before I was hauled off by the collar again and thrown out the front door.

READING

For such a little-visited place, Tibet has generated an enormous amount of literature. Some of the general books that are easier to digest are briefly outlined here. The classic on modern Tibet, with a scathing news-style attack on the Chinese, is John F Avedon's *In Exile From the Land of Snows*, which covers the period 1933-84. A photographic record of the unique culture of Tibet is contained in *Tibet: The Sacred Realm, Photographs 1880-1950*, and in *A Portrait of Lost Tibet* (Rosemary Jones Tung, based on photos by Brooke Dolan and Ilya Tolstoy taken in 1942). You can compare the black and white photos to what now stands – or doesn't stand at all.

Amongst the spiritual guidebooks, of which there are a vast number, two worthy of mention are *Buddhism in the Tibetan Tradition*, by Geshe Kelsang Gyatso, and an intriguing account of the Shambhala legend in Edwin Bernbaum's *The Way to Shambhala*. The Dalai Lama has written a number of books on Tibetan Buddhism, as well as an autobiographical account titled *My Land & My People*, first published in 1962.

In the mountaineering line, Galen Rowell's *Mountains of the Middle Kingdom* stands out, and in *Everest: The Unclimbed Ridge* authors Chris Bonington and Charles Clarke provide a gripping account of an ill-fated expedition in Tibet. The adventures of travellers and others to the land of snows are chronicled in two paperbacks: Peter Hopkirk's *Trespassers on the Roof of the World* and Charles Allen's *A Mountain in Tibet*.

The travel classic of this century is Heinrich Harrer's *Seven Years in Tibet* (1953). At the ordinary traveller's level, Vikram Seth's *From Heaven Lake* (1983) is highly readable.

Educational comic from Gaurav Gatha, New Delhi, 1982, with some inflammatory frames

Best Fiction Award on Tibet goes to *The Third Eye* (1955), the autobiography of Lama T Lobsang Rampa. This bestseller was discovered to have been written by one Mr Hoskins, a plumber's son from Devonshire. His devotees, who eventually conceded that he wasn't a lama, nevertheless insisted that the soul of a Tibetan lama lived on within him. You could also try Lionel Davidson's *The Rose of Tibet* – his research is uncanny.

There will no doubt be a spate of coffeetable books covering the new travel in Tibet, and a few tomes in the guidebook line. In covering not only Tibet but the regions it borders on, the meat and potatoes Lonely Planet guides will modestly have to be recommended. In the series are *China, India, Nepal, Kashmir Ladakh & Zanskar, Pakistan, Thailand* and *Burma*, as well as separate trekking guides for the *Nepal* and *Indian* Himalaya, shoestring guides to help you all the way across Asia, and a number of phrasebooks, including the *China Phrasebook*.

TOURISM & INFORMATION

The China International Travel Service (CITS) is the official Chinese tourist body. There is a branch in Lhasa, and if you can actually track it down, it will prove quite useless for any information – either written or verbal. None of the 30 or so Chinese guides stabled at the newly formed Tibet Tourism Corporation (TTC) speak Tibetan, a curious lapse. A handful of Chinese-speaking Tibetan guides are kept on tap to give a spiel on aspects of Tibetan life, which the Han guide then translates into English, French, German or Italian. The whole role of tourism in Tibet is most peculiar – they want your money, but they don't wish to promote things Tibetan.

Group-tours are left with Han guides whose main object appears to be asserting China's claim over Tibet when it comes to a historical run-down. At the Norbulinka in Lhasa I came across a Tibetan caretaker who spoke perfect English (he learnt it in India), but he refused to answer any pointed questions, and would not be drawn into any opinions.

The Chinese have obviously decided that tourism in Tibet is a way of recouping some of the massive subsidies that have been poured in to buoy up the sagging Tibetan economy (and support Chinese troops). There is little infrastructure to support the projected influx of 40,000 tourists in 1986 (and double that number by 1988!). Ten new hotels are being constructed – four of them in Lhasa, but transport is especially weak, and food supplies are limited.

The sad thing about all this is that the Tibetans themselves have not been consulted about the projected tourist avalanche, which may result in foodshortages and skyrocketing prices for locals. The Dalai Lama himself has said in an interview that he approves of the new tourism, as it will help westerners to get a better idea of the situation in Tibet. The net effect of tourism will not benefit Tibetans economically because the big bucks go to the Chinese for hotels and transport. So while the TTC envisages a bright future of helicopter trips, boatrides down the rapids, and hunting parties over the Tibetan Plateau, the lot of the average Tibetan will probably remain unchanged – very poor. A fringe benefit is the restoration of a handful of Tibetan monasteries and temples, but this appears to be mainly for tourism, and not especially for the Tibetans themselves.

As for information, a 1985 *China Daily* article illustrates how misleading Chinese sources can be. The article says: 'Gadan Monastery, a gigantic array of temples rising from the mountains east of Lhasa, also reopened to pilgrims earlier this year'. Ganden is certainly to the east of Lhasa – but it doesn't rise. The place is a pile of rubble – it looks like it was dynamited. The same article makes the extraordinary claim that the Tibetan Buddhism College, opened in September 1985, 'is the first Buddhist College in the history of Tibet'. They have perhaps overlooked the fact that the Samye Monastery (a functioning Buddhist College) was founded 1200 years ago. In an effort to rewrite history (a favourite pastime in Beijing) there are a number of Chinese-authored books in English on Tibet. A corker is *Highlights of Tibetan History* (New World Press, Beijing, 1984), which finishes with a short and glorious chapter on the 1950 'Liberation'. Obviously there haven't been too many highlights since that date.

Pre-1950 Tibet, as written up by the Tibetans, appears to be nothing short of Shangri-La, and as written up by the Chinese, was nothing short of hell on earth. It is extremely difficult to get any accurate bearings on the situation in Tibet, past or present. However, due to the propaganda wars between the Chinese and the Dalai Lama's government-in-exile, there is more material available on the Tibetans than on any other minority group within China. It's a question of reliability – who do you believe? Given that the Chinese sources can often be an insult to one's intelligence, a clearer picture is to be had from the Tibetan sources, bearing in mind that they too can be exaggerated, and that they can overlook key aspects.

The Tibetan government-in-exile maintains a number of information sources. The major one is the Information Office, Central Tibetan Secretariat, Gangchen Kyishong, Dharamsala 176215, Himachal Pradesh, India, which distributes works printed by the Library of Tibetan Works & Archives. There are a number of interesting news magazines that you can subscribe to: *Tibetan Review*, monthly; and *Tibetan Bulletin*, bi-monthly. In Europe, the Information Office is the Office of H H the Dalai Lama, 3 Heathcock Court, Strand, London WC2R OPA, UK (tel 836 2237); in North America, it's the Office of Tibet, 801 Second Avenue, Suite 703, New York, NY 10017, USA (tel 876 8721); and in Australia, contact the Australian Tibet Society, PO Box 39, Gordon, NSW 2072, Australia (tel 449 2741).

The US office is also the home of Potala Publications, which specialises in material on Tibetan Buddhism, culture, language, medicine and other fields. Two other specialist publishers are Snow Lion Publications (Ithaca, NY), and Wisdom Publications (London, UK). There are additional representative offices of the Dalai Lama in New Delhi, Tokyo, Switzerland and Kathmandu.

In your own country, the best places to go hunting for books and information are the mystical-type bookstores, which as well as stocking a range on Tibetan Buddhism, often stock background material on Tibetan history and culture. Various Tibetan Buddhist associations can be tracked down as leads for information, and possibly for language classes. A major network is the Foundation for the Preservation of the Mahayana Tradition (FPMT), with links in Australia, the UK, France, Germany, Holland, Hong Kong, India, Italy, Nepal, New Zealand, Spain, and the USA. The FPMT publishes an annual magazine called *Wisdom*.

Your best source of travel information is other travellers, often encountered coming out of Tibet in places like Chengdu, Xian, Kathmandu and Hong Kong. Kathmandu is well-supplied with books on Tibet, including language materials, and you can easily get Tibetan language lessons there. Mountaineering books can be fruitful sources of the more practical kind of information, since mountaineers were amongst the first freelance travellers in Tibet.

TOURS & TREKKING

If writing cheques for six or seven thousand dollars doesn't faze you, then there are trekking, mountaineering and regular outfits who are quite willing to help you out. The fault does not lie entirely with them because charges stipulated by the Chinese are quite exorbitant. Group-tourists are expected to pay up to US$100 a day in Tibet (excluding airfare), and sometimes more. Trekking in Tibet comes under mountaineering rules, which are dictated by the Chinese Mountaineering Association (CMA). For more details on individual trekking and general trekking info, see the Trekking in the Everest Region chapter, the section on Yadong in the Gyantse & Chumbi Valley chapter, and the section on Mt Kailas in the Xinjiang Route chapter.

Within Tibet, organised trekking tours get to the following areas: Mt Everest base camp, Xixabangma base camp, Mt Namche Barwa, Lake Manasarovar & Mt Kailas, and the Makalu region. These trekking trips are generally of a month's duration.

A slightly cheaper option is to get a trekking tour or ordinary tour from the Nepal Travel Agent at the Yak & Yeti Hotel in Kathmandu. Many travellers have been very interested in Yak & Yeti's short three-day tour to the Tibetan border-town of Zhangmu, which works out to about US$200-300 a head, and it sure beats running all the way back to Hong Kong. If you're in Kathmandu and can't make it over the border by yourself, drop in and see the Nepal Travel Agent at Yak & Yeti – they may oblige (refer to Staging-point Kathmandu in the Nepal Route chapter for a clearer picture).

Straight tours from Yak & Yeti are 12 days to Lhasa and back to Kathmandu, costing US$1790 per person including transportation, accommodation, meals and guide-service. There is another 15-day itinerary which adds Samye and Zêtang, and a 15-day itinerary that continues after Lhasa to Chengdu, Xian, Kunming, Canton and Hong Kong. An eight-day itinerary costs around US$1500 per person.

Trekking tours include: 14-day Everest trek (six days actual trekking), 20-day Everest trek, 21-day Kailas trek (also 18 and 25-day versions), and 12-day Xixabangma trek. All of these are approached by way of Zhangmu, some include a run east to Lhasa and back, others don't. Costs vary from US$85 to US$185 per person per night, so you'd be looking at something like US$2000 for a 15-day trek, depending on the size of the group. Deposit is US$140, sometimes required 60 days in advance, with full payment 45 days in advance, and no refund after that date. If you roll up in Kathmandu, you can most likely just join a tour that's already been set up. Yak & Yeti will also arrange personalised itineraries if you form your own small group. They can be reached at GPO Box 1016, Durbar Marg, Kathmandu, Nepal, (tel 413999, Telex NP2237, Cable YAKNYETI).

For ordinary tours from Hong Kong, China Travel Service (CTS, an official Chinese tourist body) is offering eight-day itineraries, departing Hong Kong, visiting Lhasa and Shigatse, for around US$1700. The tour literature looks pretty boring (hum . . .) with a lightning visit of three days actually in Tibet. You might be able to take advantage of their direct charter flight from Hong Kong to Chengdu on an individual basis if you want to speed yourself through to Chengdu for the connecting flight to Lhasa. CTS or CITS is (blush) thinking of operating an office in Kathmandu in the future. More operators from Hong Kong and Kathmandu are jumping on the bandwagon and tours may be cheaper from these places in the future.

The Tibet Tourist Corporation, within Tibet itself (Lhasa), does organise trekking tours but stay well away. They're apparently a disorganised shambles – if the trek actually gets off the ground. Most trekking is done through the CMA, which has more experience. Something like 8000 mountaineers have passed through China under the auspices of the CMA, which must be getting pretty sharp at trimming the unwary by now.

ITINERARIES & TIMING

Can you cover Tibet in two weeks? The

answer is yes, but you're really pushing it – one month would be more reasonable. The shortest itinerary is to fly from Chengdu to Lhasa and return, which doesn't really give you much of an idea of Tibet. A better version would be to fly to Lhasa, branch out to Shigatse and Gyantse by rented transport, and then head back to Lhasa or complete an overland run to Kathmandu. It *may* be possible to do this trip in reverse – that is, Kathmandu to Lhasa overland, then fly to Chengdu for onward destinations in China and Hong Kong. Considering that you need at least a week to acclimatise in Tibet, and then allowing time for messing around with transport, you're really looking at a minimum of three weeks on the plateau. Getting to Lhasa, even by plane connections from Hong Kong, can chew up a lot of time, and planes (CAAC) suffer from delays.

If you want to do any overlanding by local transport (trucks) or get off the track, you need buckets of time. The only dependable itineraries are those by hired vehicle from Lhasa, and even these vehicles are prone to breakdowns. Two female travellers found themselves in a Beijing jeep which had a radiator that boiled, and a transmission that disintegrated near a washed-out bridge. They said they could deal with that, but they couldn't handle the fact that the jeep had a complete lack of braking power. Some travellers trying to hitch to Kathmandu from Lhasa have been holed up in obscure places for up to 10 days waiting for local transport (trucks). You should build a one-week leeway for transport problems into your proposed schedule.

Various combinations of Tibet and China proper are possible – particularly on the overland route from Lhasa to Golmud, and thence to Xining. From this area you can branch across China. Refer to the Getting There & Away and the Getting Around sections of this book for a better idea of routes, and refer to the detailed sections (which detail separate routes to and from Lhasa) at the rear of this book. If you want to take advantage of a hard-earned acclimatisation period in Tibet, plan on going for a month or more.

When to Go
Timing has plenty to do with the weather in Tibet. In the winter there will be more transport delays. Ice and freezing conditions finish off those poor old trucks (they're already gasping in the high altitudes). There is no heavy snowfall, but it can get very cold in winter. The best time for travel in Tibet is April to August (spring and summer). Everything thaws out, and besides, it's the picnic season! Tibet is in the Himalayan rain-shadow, and the place is quite dry and sunny year-round. Some monsoonal effects hit the southern border areas about July and August. You don't have to worry about the rainfall. Tibet sees about 25 to 50 cm of rain per year (up to 75 cm in the forested areas to the east and south-east borders). Drought is more of a problem for Tibetan farmers – and hail can be very damaging. From July and August onwards (autumn), the problem is not rainfall but flooding. The rivers coursing through Tibet get swollen from snowmelt in the autumn, and this can carve up the dirt-roads and play havoc with transport (mudslides, washed-out bridges). 'Flooded engine' takes on a new meaning.

PLACES TO STAY
For Tibetan nomads this poses no problem, since they trek around the highlands with their livestock and set up their tents wherever they wish. For foreigners, however, the choice of a place to stay is extremely limited (with the exception of Lhasa). In Lhasa and the few towns in Tibet you will usually be asked to fill out a registration form. Elsewhere, nobody really bothers with this formality – a point in your favour if you are travelling off the permitted track, since this is one way to attract the attention of the local PSB. If

there are no showers, ask for a basin and an extra thermos of hot water (*kai shui*). Accommodation in Tibet falls into four categories: guest houses, hotels, truck-stops and army camps.

Guest Houses and Hotels
Guest houses (Chinese: *ZhaoDaiSuo*) are found in scarce numbers in large towns and provide minimum standard accommodation for visiting officials. They usually have showers, flush toilets, a restaurant, a small shop and perhaps laundry facilities. Lhasa has several hotel projects aimed at providing western-style service for foreigners. The Lhasa Hotel and The Tibet Guest House, recently completed with all mod cons specially for foreign tourists, have taken over from Guest Houses No 3 and No 1. The management of the Yak & Yeti Hotel in Nepal has been invited to open a chain of hotels in different towns of Tibet. With the exception of Lhasa, hotels in Tibet are usually a cross between a hotel and a hostel (Chinese: *Lüshe*). They are usually found near bus stations and truckstops and offer a cheap bed, a scrawny dining room, outside toilet pits and little else. Expect to pay about Y2-5 per person.

Truckstops
These provide drivers with petrol, a safe place to park, a bed to snatch a few hours of sleep plus a canteen serving simple dishes. For a four-bed room, prices vary between Y2 and Y3 per person. Truck-stops are obviously the best place for hitchers to stay.

Army Camps
In some remote areas, army camps are the only place to stay. The commanding officers seem surprisingly unconcerned about taking in foreigners and try hard to please. Some camps try to charge extortionate prices but, depending on the rooms provided, prices usually vary between Y3 and Y6.

Other
In the weirder line of shelter, some have managed to stay with locals, and even at monasteries (along with pilgrims). Locals have mudbrick houses, or yak-hair tents, with a fire burning in the middle somewhere. They can get very smoky. Local accommodation can also get smelly – one trekker spent the night in a dried yak-dung storage section (the fuel pile).

Finally, a cautionary tale about a woman who was caught short in the freezing hours of early morning, in a room on the roof of a guest house, deep in the heart of Tibet. As the night was as cold as an iceberg, the need urgent and the toilet pit a long trek away, she decided to use the roof. Meanwhile, down in the room below, the Chinese cook was preparing to wash in a basin of hot water. Unfortunately, the roof of stamped earth was porous and the cook was dumbfounded by the deluge of what was quite clearly *not* rainwater. Within seconds, the enraged cook was demanding that the foreigner be thrown out, on the instant, by a sleepy, but secretly amused manager. Somehow the cook was placated and everyone went back to bed. By the morning, all trace of evidence had been absorbed by the roof.

FOOD & DRINK
Tibetan cuisine is not exactly the most varied in the world, but perhaps ingredients at this altitude are not easy to grow or catch. A couple of common Tibetan dishes are *momo* (a type of dumpling filled with meat) and *tukpa* (noodles with meat). The staple food of most Tibetans is *tsampa* (roasted barley flour), which they mix with yak-butter tea into doughy mouthfuls. The stuff will glue your insides together.

Outside of the main towns like Lhasa and Shigatse, there is very little food or drink around, unless you're fond of dried yak-meat. Yak-cheese, in its hard and dry state, can be eaten up to three years old, at which time it's bound to bust your teeth. It has to be chewed for several hours before it can be digested, and for this reason it is often given to Tibetan children as a kind of hard sweet.

Yak-butter tea is definitely an acquired taste. Some Tibetan women advised that it should not be drunk cold – otherwise those (rancid) globules of congealed fat may wreak havoc with your stomach. Given the choice, most travellers opt for a more familiar variety of tea (available in Lhasa and Shigatse) – sweet and milky. The Tibetans get their alcohol buzz by consuming large quantities of *chang*, which is a milky type of beer with a tangy taste, made from fermented barley.

Since the Chinese are present in Tibet in large numbers, it is hardly surprising to find their cuisine as well. The most common types are Sichuan-style and Muslim-style. Sichuan cooking is hot and spicy, but tell the cook *bu yao lade* if you don't want the hot stuff. *Chao cai* (fried vegetables) and *Hongchao Yu* (fish in a spicy sauce) are two common dishes. Some northern Chinese dishes such as *jiaozi* (similar to ravioli), *baozi* (dumplings filled with meat) and *mantou* (plain dumplings) are also served. Muslim restaurants serve *lamian* (noodles with meat and vegetables) and lotus-seed tea. Most of the Chinese restaurants serve hard-core spirits such as *maotai* and beer trucked into Tibet from Lanzhou, Chengdu, Kunming and even Qingdao.

In the '70s and early '80s the average Chinese needed coupons for many foodstuffs and goods. Now not much is rationed in China, and the 20 different kinds of coupons are no longer in evidence. A few things are still rationed: certain brands of cigarettes; high-quality bicycles from Shanghai and Tianjin; and gasoline, for which ration-coupons are required. In Tibet, even though there are no foodstuff coupons in evidence, it *feels* like there is rationing anyway, due to the limited food supplies.

THINGS TO BUY & TRADE

The Chinese, after dealing the Tibetan handicraft industry a deadly blow during the Cultural Revolution, are now attempting to stimulate it. Items for local consumption such as rugs, yak-saddles, and yak-butter churns are being produced. The tourist industry has no doubt stimulated demand for everything from turquoise ornaments to religious accessories. Not many can resist the temptation to take home a piece of Tibet and that's OK with the Chinese as long as it isn't an *old* piece. As in the rest of China, there are strict limitations on taking out anything that looks antique, even if it's a fake (an increasing number of items are). Customs will confiscate any antiques which are not certified for export. When foreigners first got to Tibet in 1979 there were lots of antiques on sale in Lhasa – prayer-wheels, old *dorjes*, daggers, gold and silver ornaments, woodcarvings, jewellery, copper teapots, ritual vessels – but there's not too much around these days (there's more in Kathmandu) and the prices have shot up.

Considering the number of exiled Tibetan craftsmen, Nepal is probably a more sensible place to shop for Tibetan curios, both newly-made, antique and fake – there is a booming trade in artificially-aged *thangkas* in Nepal. The prices for certain items will be higher in Kathmandu, but at least you have a selection. The once-famous Tibetan carpet output seems to have gone down the drain in Tibet although the Gyantse workshops have been revived. The carpet output in Tibet is so low that rumour has it the Chinese have to import carpets from Nepal, Qinghai or Xinjiang to sell to tourists in Tibet.

In Lhasa and Shigatse you can pick over the meagre offerings in the marketplace; you can get an old *dorje* for around Y30, a Tibetan leather belt for Y15, a pair of Tibetan boots for Y30 (readymade) or Y50 (custom-made), or have clothing tailor-made. Lots of Tibetans will approach you to sell personal items, rings, stones, portable shrines (prayer-boxes), or knives (it may not be clear at first that this item is being offered for sale!). They know the value of their goods well. Opinions on bargaining vary – some say the Tibetans love to bargain, others insist that the first price offered is *the* price and there's no backing off. In Lhasa itself, the Nepalese run shops, and give prices in rupees (meaning yuan). They undoubtedly have trade-links and import Tibetan handicraft items from Nepal.

Outside the main towns of Tibet, the locals live outside the cash economy and rely on barter. Whether or not you intend to trade, it's a good idea to bring along a few goodies to break the ice when it comes to hospitality. Disposable lighters, western clothing, western cosmetics – use your imagination. You will do great injury by handing out candy, balloons, or ball-point pens to Tibetan *children*. It will turn them into nasty beggars – think about it. The most barterable item or gift is, naturally, a Dalai Lama pic (which can be worth up to Y100 for a full colour glossy in Tibet). Most Tibetans possess pictures of the younger Dalai Lama, and are therefore after more recent pictures of him. The nicest Tibetan custom is the giving of the *khata*, the ceremonial white scarf, which in Lhasa is of the cheese-cloth looking variety and is cut off long rolls.

You will find (even if you don't care to haggle over things) that evaluating objects is an enduring pastime for the Tibetans, and you can bridge the language barrier by joining in. I spent an absolutely fascinating afternoon in a nomad tent in the middle of nowhere examining women's jewellery. The lady of the house showed off silver belt-clasps, conch-shell arm-bands, chunks of turquoise and talisman charm-boxes with the aplomb of a Parisian model (and with far less pretension). These items came from a wooden chest at the rear of the tent, which was obviously the portable bank. As we got down to fine details, the master of the tent engaged me in a hearty tugging match with my daypack as we disputed the merits of fastex buckles. He went into raptures over the structure of my runners – ah, the great and smelly mysteries of runners!

WHAT TO TAKE & HOW TO TAKE IT

Tibet has only a handful of towns, and even in Lhasa, the capital, you will be lucky to find anything more than essential items of food and clothing. Take as much as you can with you from home, Hong Kong, or neighbouring staging-points in China (such as Chengdu, Xining and Golmud).

Carrying Bags

If you are thinking of trekking or hitching, a backpack is essential. One system that works well is to take a backpack, a daypack and a food-bag. This means you can stash your backpack at the rear of the truck, bus (or yak) and still have essential items and valuables with you. Most of the hotels in Lhasa have luggage storage, so you can use them as a supply depot.

Clothing

Temperatures in Tibet can plummet with amazing speed from day to night and from sun to shade, so it's best to bring clothing you can wear in layers. Silk provides excellent insulation – it's light, strong, thin, and will absorb up to 30% of its weight in moisture and still feel dry, although it's not effective against wind or rain. Silk vests, T-shirts, socks, gloves and so on are excellent inner layers.

Down jackets with an attached hood offer good protection against cold and can be used as a cushion or pillow on bus rides. You need some kind of windproofing to cut down on the cold; a light anorak or gore-tex jacket is useful during the day when it can be worn over a thick sweater. Woollen long-johns worn under corduroys also keep out the cold. A wide-brimmed sun-hat (available in Lhasa) is good protection against the midday sun.

If you are hitching on the back of a truck,

it gets cold – really cold over the high passes – so it's useful to have a woollen balaclava or headgear with earmuffs, a woollen scarf and gloves. Rainpants and a rain poncho keep out rain and snow and help retain body heat. They also keep some of the dirt out if you are on the back of a coal truck!

Medicines & Toiletries
Take along toilet paper (available in Chengdu – there are flat packs in Lhasa, but no rolls), multivitamin tablets, diarrhoea and headache medicines, disposable face-wipes and cough or cold medicines. Sunglasses, lipsalve and suncream are absolutely essential at these altitudes, and it would be a good idea to take along a pocket-sized medical kit.

Food & Drink
Basically, anything that is brewed with hot water will be useful in Tibet. Instant coffee, drinking chocolate, tea(bags), soup cubes, drink powder and powdered milk can be a welcome addition to the diet after a few weeks in Tibet. Other food items worth considering are instant noodles, vegemite, nuts and raisins, chocolate and biscuits.

Accessories
A water-bottle is essential. Other handy items include a Swiss army knife, torch (flashlight) for temples and toilet expeditions, candles, umbrella (collapsible), zip-lock plastic bags (both large and small), and cloth stuff-sacks. Some travellers take their own enamel mug and chopsticks as preventative hygiene measures. Take large envelopes and sealing tape if you plan on sending bulky letters or parcels. If you bring a Walkman or a flash-unit, remember to load up on batteries. Stock up on film too – photographers in Lhasa who've forgotten to bring enough film can turn vicious in their hunt. A can-opener of some kind is essential if you wish to probe the mysteries of Chinese tinned foods (most travellers do). There are generally enough blankets around to insulate you in truckstop hotels, however, if you are passing the night in the back of a truck, a good down jacket (or a down sleeping-bag) could mean the difference between relative comfort and possible frostbite. Any kind of off-road travel needs careful thinking in terms of gear.

Getting There & Away

All loads lead to Lhasa. There is very little way round it at present since Lhasa is the only place open in Tibet. Whether you arrive by road or plane, that is your destination – at least that's what's on your ATP. In the process of arrival or departure, however, you can get to see half of Tibet along the way! For this reason, getting in or out of Lhasa is not just simple arrival or departure – it allows you a chance to view much more of the country than the Chinese showcase of Lhasa. Therefore you should think carefully about your route.

The one sanctioned road-route is Lhasa to Kathmandu and the Chinese will expect you to arrive in Lhasa by plane from Chengdu. Some travellers pretended to take the road exit to Kathmandu, then turned around before reaching the border and went back to Lhasa. This allowed them to get outside Lhasa. Travel from Kathmandu to Lhasa does not work so well. It is possible, but for a number of reasons – the visa situation, weak transport, the cost of jumping a tour and so on – it cannot be firmly recommended at this stage. For the moment, the most attractive proposition is to travel overland from Hong Kong or Peking and end up in Kathmandu. Travel is more reliable from east to west.

Overview of Land routes

Getting to Lhasa is a two or three part operation, depending on how you go about it. You have to get to Tibet, China or Nepal, then you have to get to a staging-point (usually Chengdu, Golmud or Kathmandu), and from there you dive into Tibet. The road-routes basically boil down to a Front Door entry/exit (from China – Peking or Hong Kong), and a Back Door entry/exit (Kathmandu, Nepal).

Individual chapters of this book are devoted to each of the five overland routes

(Nepal route, Sichuan route, Yunnan route, Qinghai routes and Xinjiang route), so refer to those chapters for more details. Included with the staging-points in those chapters (in particular Chengdu, Golmud, Xining and Kathmandu) are details that will give you further ideas on cross-China routes and onward travel. Although five routes are described, only two of them are used with any frequency or reliability. These are the Lhasa-Golmud run (Qinghai Route chapter) and the Lhasa-Kathmandu run (Nepal Route chapter). Travel-time on either of these routes is two to four days – and you may wish to stop along the way.

There is an odd situation with land travel to and from Lhasa – the routes go up and down like yo-yos when it comes to permission. In early 1985 Lhasa-Kathmandu was OK, and Kathmandu-Lhasa was OK, then Kathmandu-Lhasa closed to traffic, but Lhasa-Kathmandu was OK, and then a few travellers started to trickle through again in the latter half of 1985, coming from Kathmandu to Lhasa. Golmud-Lhasa by bus was OK in early 1985, but not Lhasa-Golmud by bus; then Golmud opened up with a permit, and in late 1985, it was OK to go from Lhasa to Golmud by bus. There is absolutely no way of predicting what the next trend in one-way traffic will be or why, so you're best advised to pick up the latest info from other travellers you meet along the way, and take your chances.

Train routes to Staging-points

In realistic terms, the places to aim for are Chengdu and Golmud. Trains are the fastest land transport within China – but in the western regions, it's a matter of getting on the train. They can be very overcrowded. Rail information is given with Staging-point Xining (Qinghai Route chapter) and with Staging-point Chengdu

Top: Yak herder, south-western Tibet (MB)
Left: Yak meat on sale in Barkhor Bazaar, Lhasa (MB)
Right: Yak-hide boat, Samye ferry-crossing (RS)

Top: Nomad herders in Anyemaqen Shan, Qinghai Province (RS)
Left: Exotic Chinese remedies on sale outside street clinic (RS)
Right: Roof detail from the golden temple, Taersi Monastery, Huangzhong County, Qinghai (RS)

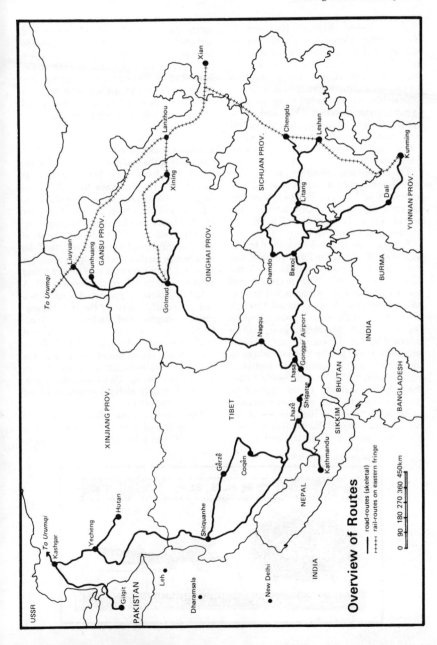

Overview of Routes

road-routes (skeletal)
+++++ rail-routes on eastern fringe

0 90 180 270 360 450km

(Sichuan Route chapter). Rail and air travel within China are surcharged for tourists; boats and buses are not. It's 75% extra for trains, and over 100% extra for planes. In addition, you must pay in FECs for planes, and increasingly so for trains. It is possible, but becoming more difficult, to pay for train tickets in RMB, and also to get the regular Chinese price. Travellers have used a range of strategies to do this. Chinese price is roughly Y3 per 100 km for a hard-sleeper.

The closest any rail line comes to Tibet is to Golmud (with a further possibility of approaching Golmud by road from the Liuyuan Station near Dunhuang to the north). Xining-Golmud by rail is 781 rail km and takes about 25 hours.

For years the Chinese have been toying with idea of a Qinghai-Tibet railway, but the only section completed thus far is the Xining-Golmud bit. The proposed rail route from Golmud to Lhasa will (eventually?) continue from Golmud through Nachitai, TuoTuoHe, Amdo, Nagqu, Damxung and Maizhokunggar before terminating at Lhasa. If the project succeeds, it will be the highest railway in the world and a formidable technical achievement. The route would pass through the Qaidam Basin (consisting mostly of deserts, salt lakes and areas of saline soil), cross the high ranges of the Kunlun and Tanggula mountains and pass over the Golmud, Tongtian and Lhasa rivers. Long stretches of the route would not only enter permafrost areas but also be exposed to the danger of massive earthquakes around Nagqu and Damxung. Now that the Qinghai-Tibet Highway has been widened and asphalted it appears that the railway is less of a priority and completion may be deferred until the year 2000.

Chengdu-Lhasa Flight

Chengdu is the main departure point for flights to Lhasa, with daily flights. It is possible to fly to Lhasa from Xian via Golmud (Wednesdays and Saturdays, both ways) but these flights are either overbooked, cancelled due to bad weather, or not available. CAAC (Civil Aviation Administration of China) will only fly if the weather is perfect, so be prepared for delays. Lhasa airport is notorious for bad weather and *any* flight can be delayed. A Tibetan airline is projected within two years, probably serving Beijing, Guangzhou, Shanghai and Sichuan Province. Until that time, you have to try and arrange connecting flights. If the planes from Xian via Golmud to Lhasa are delayed due to bad weather, the passengers are often re-routed Xian-Chengdu-Lhasa. As yet, flights from Kathmandu to Lhasa have not materialised.

The Chengdu-Lhasa flight costs Y322 one-way (about US$110) and takes two hours. It then takes about 90 minutes to

Russian turbo-prop on 2 fen note

get into Lhasa from Gonggar Airport on the CAAC bus. Gonggar Airport is about 95 km away from Lhasa. There are daily departures by plane on the Chengdu-Lhasa run (both directions), and sometimes two planes leaving every day. Try and take your luggage with you on the plane – it will arrive later if it's checked in. Usually it arrives the same afternoon at the CAAC office in Lhasa. CAAC buses to and from airports are free. If you want to get straight to Lhasa from either Hong Kong or Peking you would have to combine planes (Y226 from Peking to Chengdu one-way, and Y201 from Canton to Chengdu one-way). Chengdu is also connected to a number of other Chinese cities by air. If you combine planes from Hong Kong or Canton to Chengdu, then add the flight to Lhasa, it will work out at about US$220 one-way. For more details on the Chengdu-Lhasa flight, see the Getting There and Getting Away sections of the Lhasa chapter. For more details on the Hong Kong-Chengdu routes see Staging-Point Chengdu in the Sichuan Route chapter.

INTERNATIONAL EXIT/ENTRY POINTS FOR CHINA
Kathmandu
There is only one international exit/entry point for Tibet at present, and that is Zhangmu, between Kathmandu and Lhasa. In 1985, traffic was one-way: the exit was fine, but the entry was wildly unpredictable. Some travellers started to trickle into Tibet in the latter half of 1985. Earlier in the year, frustrated travellers either had to run all the way back to Hong Kong and enter China from there, or had to cadge their way across the border by jumping a tour from Kathmandu. The complicating factor here is that the Chinese Embassy in Kathmandu refuses to issue visas to individuals – it will only issue them to group tours. If a Chinese visa from Hong Kong suddenly appeared in Zhangmu, it was totally up to the border officials whether they would honour it or not – and

they could refuse entry if they wished. It is quite cheap to go overland from Kathmandu to Lhasa, but the Chinese, it would seem, would prefer you to work your way across China and shell out good foreign exchange. If you jump a tour going from Kathmandu to Lhasa you might be considered as having paid your dues, so they may let you go. For more details on tour-jumping, see Staging-point Kathmandu in the Nepal Route chapter.

You can make it from Kathmandu to Lhasa for US$40 by local transport *if* you have a Chinese visa, *if* you can make it through the border, *if* you can get an ATP in Zhangmu, and *if* there is any local transport on the Tibetan side to take you further inland. With rented transport on the Tibetan side, it might run to US$70 a head for the route (if there's any rented transport around). Added to the tour cost this might come to about US$270 to US$370.

Exiting from Lhasa to Kathmandu is no problem with visas or otherwise (you do need a Chinese exit permit). The problem is finding transport to get to the border (sparse after Shigatse). Hitch-hiking is possible but very difficult. If you're headed west from Kathmandu overland, you can pick up cheaper airfares in New Delhi. Kathmandu is not a bargain basement for airfares – it's not on the flight-path of major airlines. Kathmandu-Hong Kong is US$275, Kathmandu-Bangkok is US$190, Kathmandu-Rangoon is US$160 (all fares quoted are one-way).

Hong Kong
Hong Kong (HK) remains the most reliable entry and exit point for individual travellers to China. A further advantage is that you can pick up your visa and the latest info on the spot, and Hong Kong is hooked up with cheap airfares to Europe, the UK, the US, Canada, Australia and Asia. Usually, the cheaper the fare, the more restrictions – no refunds, advance-purchase, laborious routes, no stopovers,

low season, ad nauseam. Samples of outbound fares from Hong Kong in 1985 were HK$850 to Tokyo, HK$800 to Bangkok, HK$1500 to Rangoon, HK$2010 to Kathmandu, HK$850 to Manila, HK$2100 to San Francisco or LA, HK$2500 to Seattle, HK$3500 to Sydney or Melbourne, and HK$2450 to London (all fares quoted were one-way, with a minimal reduction for any return flights; exchange rate HK$7=US$1 at the time).

Numerous carriers fly into Hong Kong, one of the major crossroads for the internationals. Check around for the best carrier to get to Hong Kong – they swap and shuffle. In 1985, some good deals were available from the Canadian west coast on Korean Air, from the USA west coast on CP Air, and from the UK on British Caledonian.

From Hong Kong you can work your way by rail or air to Chengdu or Golmud for a run to Lhasa but it can be laborious getting to those staging-points. If you want to speed things up there are some direct CITS charter flights on CAAC (Hong Kong-Chengdu for HK$760, and Hong Kong-Xian for HK$1070) as well as direct flights from Canton. Otherwise, from Hong Kong, an armada of jetfoils, hydrofoils, ferries, slow trains, electric trains, buses and other wonders are waiting to get you into China, where your transport problems will begin in earnest. Try and avoid Canton and Guilin if possible. You can also hop across the border (literally, by bus) from the nearby colonial relic, Macau.

Beijing

Entry and exit points for China are now becoming quite diverse, especially with the option (?) of picking up your visa in places other than Hong Kong (see the Visa section in the Facts for the Visitor chapter). The most interesting overland possibility, in terms of Tibet, is arrival in Beijing by international air or train, and working your way toward Golmud, which is the staging-point for a truck-run to Lhasa. A lot of travellers pass through the transport centre of Xian en route to Xining and Golmud. Xian is at the junction of routes going south to Chengdu by rail, west to Xining, and north-west to the end of the line at Urumqi, where buses ply the Silk Road to Kashgar. Golmud is connected by rail and road to Xining, and by road to Dunhuang in the north (the nearest railway station is Liuyuan), and south to Lhasa. In theory there is a flight from Xian via Golmud to Lhasa, but it doesn't appear to run too often, if at all. If in a hurry, a direct flight from Peking to Chengdu (Y226 one-way) would do the trick.

International flights direct to Peking are expensive, no matter which direction you're coming from. International carriers coming into Peking include JAL, Aeroflot, Air France, British Airways, Lufthansa, Philippine Airlines, Qantas, Swissair, and PIA. Pakistan International Air (PIA) has cheap flights from Europe to Japan with a Beijing stopover. One of the cheapest carriers from the European end is Tarom Romanian Airlines. If arriving by air, and you already have a visa, no problems. If you want to risk picking one up at Peking Airport, then it seems to work.

A cheap and interesting route from Europe is the Trans-Siberian. Actually the trains you want are either the Trans-Mongolian (through Mongolia to Peking) or the Trans-Manchurian (through north-east China to Peking). These trains take about five or six days from Europe, and you can apparently pick up your Chinese visa at the border towns of Manzhouli (Manchuria) or Erenhot (Inner Mongolia). A nice loop can be done by coming in from Europe by rail to Peking, working overland to Lhasa, exiting to Kathmandu, and then carrying on westward back to Europe. Going the other way, from Peking to Europe, you can do all your paperwork, visas and ticketing in Peking – the process takes about a week.

Shanghai

Shanghai is connected by air to Japan and the US west coast (with both the Japanese and US Embassies being located in Shanghai as well as in Beijing). Shanghai is not strategically placed for link-up with trains or boats to the western regions of China. There is the possibility of getting a Yangtze boat, as far as Chongqing, but from the Shanghai direction it's upstream. Plane connections on CAAC to the west of China are, however, extensive enough. If headed east from Chengdu in the direction of Japan, Shanghai would make a decent exit (boat along Yangtze, then plane from Shanghai to Japan – there is also rumoured to be a boat to Japan, and there are liners running to Hong Kong from Shanghai).

Rangoon

Intriguing as an exit, but not particularly recommended as an entry, is the Kunming-Rangoon flight (Wednesdays). Kunming is nicely placed within reach of Chengdu, and the Burma 'side-door' would save a lot of backtracking to Hong Kong if you were headed in the general direction of Bangkok. The flight may get complicated unless your plane-scheduling and visas are in order. You cannot stop in Burma without a Burmese visa. These are not issued in Kunming, but are available in Peking, Calcutta, Kathmandu (same day), Bangkok (same day) and Hong Kong (same day or next day). Burma will only allow you a seven-day stay. and you have to show confirmed outward flights to enter Rangoon.

The cost of the flight Kunming-Rangoon is around US$170 one-way on CAAC, and flights are mostly empty. Since the CAAC flight runs in both directions on a Wednesday, you would have to schedule yourself out of Rangoon the following Wednesday by another carrier. A traveller who did not have a Burmese visa paid Y916 FECs for Kunming-Rangoon-Bangkok, with a confirmed flight from Rangoon-Bangkok. He had to sign a note absolving CAAC of all responsibility! A

visa for Thailand is not necessary for stays of less than two weeks (transit) but neither the Chinese nor the Burmese authorities seem to understand this, even though CAAC has an office in Bangkok. As for the other direction, Rangoon-Kunming flight, if you don't have a Chinese visa, then in theory you should be able to get one at Kunming Airport – if you can get through the rigmarole of Burmese officialdom first. Good luck! You'll need it.

ROUND-THE-WORLD TICKETS

With Hong Kong and New Delhi (or Bombay) along the flight-paths for major international carriers, you might consider the idea of a package flight deal; a round-the-world (RTW) ticket. By this method, you would arrive in Hong Kong, proceed at your own expense by land or air through China, Tibet, Nepal and India, and then pick up your round-the-world ticketing in New Delhi. A sample RTW ticket might run thus: Toronto (North America)-Tokyo-Hong Kong-New Delhi or Bombay-London (one stopover in European city allowed)-Toronto. This ticket worked out at Canadian $2100. RTW tickets may be valid for six months or one year, and generally for a limited number of carriers. Specifications are different depending on the agency you deal with. Generally no backtracking is allowed, and you might have to stick to a certain flight-path.

OVERLAND THROUGH ASIA

With the 'opening' of Tibet, the way from Peking or Hong Kong through to Istanbul is now possible by road, a grand concept when you think about it. Direction of travel is better from east to west. Coming through Tibet, you exit to Kathmandu, continue through India and Pakistan (skirting Afghanistan), then Iran and Turkey. The stumbling-block for visas is Iran – it may take up to two weeks to get one in New Delhi (if going west) or in Istanbul or Ankara (if going east). Visas are not normally issued to holders of US and Canadian passports so a plane might be needed to overfly Iran. Lonely Planet's *West Asia on a Shoestring* has full details.

In 1984-85 Nicholas Danzinger, a Briton backed by a fellowship from the Winston Churchill Memorial Fund, completed a 14-month journey from London to Beijing by local transport. His route was unusual – 13,000 km along old and disused caravan routes. The whole trip cost him £1000, about a third of his travel fellowship. An official letter from the Winston Churchill Fund went a long way – it got him across Iran, with the Iranian government being most co-operative. In Afghanistan, Danzinger entered on a convoy which included a truck with a Chinese rocket launcher – the most prized possession of Afghani fighters since it could bring down Russian MiGs and helicopters. Continuing in disguise, and dodging Russian bombing, Danzinger got a Mujahedeen stamp in his passport, and before he left the country the Mujahedeen offered to buy him a wife and make him a village commander.

Coming from Pakistan toward China, Danzinger travelled on a Pakistan government convoy of eight trucks, and entered along the Karakoram Highway at the Khunjerab Pass. Danzinger's passport was stamped 'No 1' by the Chinese, as no foreigner had gone through this pass for many years (there are rumours that the Karakoram Highway will open to foreigners in the future – the route leads from Rawalpindi to Kashgar). Danzinger spent over two months in Xinjiang, skirting the southern edge of the Taklamakan Desert on camels, with a Uighur guide. He managed to get permission to travel from outpost to outpost until he got to Lop Nor, China's nuclear testing site. There he was arrested and put on a bus out of town, but the next town didn't know what to do with him either. Eventually he took a three month detour to Tibet, hitched a ride with a truckload of pilgrims headed into Sichuan from Lhasa, and made his way to Beijing.

Getting Around

Transport infrastructure within Tibet is appalling. In pre-1950 Tibet, the wheel was spurned. It was thought that wheels would scar the sacred surface of the earth, releasing evil spirits – and the Tibetans may yet be proven correct. The only wheel in evidence was the prayer-wheel. Well, there were a few exceptions. The water-wheel was used, and wheels were used on pedal-worked lathes. In 1907 an eight horsepower Clement was carried over the Himalayas in sections and assembled as a gift to the Panchen Lama. This toy had novelty value only as gasoline was extremely expensive to import, and the primitive carburettor didn't work too well at this altitude. The 13th Dalai Lama had three cars imported in sections, the only ones to be seen in Lhasa at the time. They lie in a decayed state at the rear of the Norbulinka. Some wheeled carts existed in pre-1950 Tibet, on the plains of Lhasa. These were copied from the 1903-4 Younghusband expedition. On the eastern fringes of Tibet, horse-carts were used, introduced from contact with the Chinese, and Nepalese residents brought in bicycles with them. The majority of Tibetans used – and still do – donkeys, ponies and yaks for transport, or their own two feet.

Before the Chinese arrived, the only known landing of a plane was a forced landing by an American crew in WW II. The plane came down between Gyantse and Shigatse after being blown off course attempting to fly 'the Hump' (mountain ranges between China and Burma). Startled Tibetans held the crew captive for days before they were released by order of the Dalai Lama's office (Tibet remained neutral through both world wars). The story has passed into Tibetan folklore much the same way as an earlier story of Shangri-La (in James Hilton's *Lost Horizon*, 1933) passed into American folklore.

The Chinese, though they've been busy constructing roads, airfields and access to waterways in Tibet since 1950, have by no means solved the transport situation in Tibet. The construction of a railway from Golmud to Lhasa has been delayed to the end of the century and instead, efforts have been concentrated on upgrading roads into Tibet, particularly the Golmud-Lhasa road, which is paved. Air transport is also slated for an increase.

In the past, yak trains took a leisurely average of 10 months to complete the trip from Lhasa to Chengdu and back again. Pilgrims would prostrate – and some still do – thousands of km taking many months, even years, to complete pilgrimages. Today there is a much wider choice of transport but the soft options are in limited supply and you pay the price for luxury. The rough options are the most interesting, perhaps because they retain a whiff of danger and are utterly unpredictable.

HELICOPTER

In 1984, China purchased 24 F-70-CT helicopters (a variation of the Sikorsky Blackhawk) from the United States for military use in Tibet. These choppers are specially adapted for high altitude flying and can be used for troop transport. According to CITS in Lhasa, there are plans to use helicopters (perhaps these are the ones) for tourism. It looks like the vultures and hawks circling around sky burial sites may soon be sharing thermals with airborne tourists.

RENTED VEHICLES

Given the climatic conditions and the subsequent state of the roads in Tibet, it is hardly surprising that most of the vehicles and mini buses are of the rugged variety, and it is hardly surprising that they are prone to breakdowns. Off-road vehicles – Toyota Landcruisers, Beijing jeeps and

Land Rovers can be hired in Lhasa, and *might* also be arranged in other places like Zhangmu (usually returning from the Nepal border). Providing you can pack in enough people, the rates aren't too bad, but negotiation is called for. Rented vehicles are used with frequency by travellers to visit places around Lhasa, and for the run to the Nepalese border (there is little other transport along that route). Travellers seem to spend half their time in Lhasa trying to put one of these deals together – hastily arranging their group and trying to co-ordinate with the drivers. The vehicles available are over-worked and are in short supply (with great demand). Most of the drivers are Chinese with little interest in Tibet or the Tibetans and will react with horror if your route threatens to inconvenience them or their vehicles. For more details on pricing and dealing, refer to the front of the Nepal Route chapter.

BUS

Bus travel in Tibet is rough and erratic. When you are on the bus, the Tibetans do their best to ensure a safe journey by chanting prayers in the valleys and whooping at the top of high passes. The buses are antiquated, have poor brakes, cracked windows and next to no suspension.

Bus ticket stub from Qinghai

Avoid sitting at the back unless your skull and your backside are cast-iron. If you have to leave your luggage on the roof, make sure it is properly tied down and secure against dust, rain and snow. Large plastic bags are useful to pack your gear inside the backpack. As you can't normally climb onto the roof to extract items from your pack en route, it's essential to have a smaller bag (containing food, water, warm clothing, toilet bag, photo gear and valuables) with you inside the bus. Bus drivers will often go for hours without food or rest, so when they do stop, make the most of it.

TRUCKS & TRUCKING

Of all the forms of transport in Tibet, trucking is the one most travellers rave about. To ride over the high passes of the roof of the world, tucked in tight behind the cab, clutching its roof, watching an endless road disappear into a horizon of snowcaps and barren plateau is a rare experience – hitchhiker's heaven.

Beer from Kunming, building materials from Xining, videos from Chengdu – just about everything is trucked into Tibet. If you're lucky, you'll be in the back amongst the crates and boxes or, if you're luckier, you'll be up in the cab with one knee jammed in the glove-box and the other crippled by the gear lever.

Kinds of Trucks

There are three main types of truck used in Tibet. The *Jiefang* looks like a dinosaur, is usually painted green, has a long snout and can carry up to eight tons. A brand new Jiefang costs around Y15,000 and an updated model is due out soon. These are the slowest trucks on the road and the cab gets very cramped with two passengers.

The *Dongfeng* is a newer and more popular truck, often painted light brown, with a rounded front and a carrying capacity of 10 tons. The price for a new Dongfeng is around Y20,000. This is a faster truck with more space in the cab for two passengers. As the old Jiefang is

Jiefang truck on 1 fen note

phased out, this is becoming the commonest type of truck on the road in Tibet.

The Isuzu *WuShiLing* is a modern, Japanese-style truck with a sleek, rounded front and load capacity of 18 tons. A new Isuzu will set you back Y25,000. This is the fastest type of truck and the cab has plenty of room for two passengers. Other types of truck, such as Mercedes and Roman, have been imported and are in use in Qinghai and Tibet.

Most trucks have a stencilled sign on the front bumper which states in (10,000s) how many km the driver has driven. For the mileage of the vehicles, most drivers can only hazard a guess. Road conditions are atrocious in the winter and can also deteriorate rapidly at other times of the year. On the routes in and out of Tibet be prepared for landslides, rockfalls, mudslides, flooding, snowstorms and broken bridges. Bad weather, poor maintenance of vehicles, fatigue and drink cause frequent accidents and dramatic wreckage can often be seen littering the mountainsides. Drivers have a disconcerting love of coasting down from the high passes at top speed. Ailing carburettors, flat tyres and overheated engines are a common source of delay. After blowing a gasket on our truck I spent three hours with the driver carefully cutting a new gasket out of cardboard provided by a passing Tibetan!

Licence Plates

Many trucks have large logos painted in Chinese, Uighur or Tibetan on the cab doors which give an indication of their destinations, but the best clue is the licence plate. Each province in China is assigned a two-digit provincial number. After the provincial number, there is another number which denotes a specific area or county within the province (an example is 230-Lhasa, 2312-Shigatse, and 233-Chamdo). The following is a rough guide only, for provincial numbers commonly seen in Tibet:

Tibet	23
Gansu	25,55
Qinghai	27,26,86
Xinjiang	28,57,58
Shaanxi	24
Sichuan	20,50

Truck drivers

Truck drivers usually belong to one of three types: Han Chinese, Muslim Chinese and Tibetan. The Han and Muslim Chinese are mostly from Sichuan, Qinghai, Xinjiang and Gansu provinces. They have a hard and monotonous life. If you speak some Chinese (or Tibetan for Tibetan drivers) they will almost always go out of their way to help or please. Many drivers told me that they liked picking up foreigners, but they found it a strain to spend days (for some routes it could be

Truck convoy stamp

weeks) on the road with no way of talking to their passengers. Some drivers will even let you take the wheel.

China produces over 1000 billion cigarettes a year for its estimated 300 million smokers and these truck drivers must be among the heaviest smokers in China. Even if you don't smoke, take along cigarettes for the driver. No conversation is started, no deal clinched without the communion of tobacco. Etiquette demands that you offer cigarettes, beer, food or whatever at least three times. If you know the driver is refusing out of politeness, you can poke a cigarette into his top pocket. If you are a nonsmoker and want to stay that way your willpower will be sorely tried – just keep repeating *bu hui*, which means you don't

Gasoline ration coupon

smoke. Other ways to keep the driver amused include showing your family photos and playing Chinese chess at truck stops. Many drivers will pay for your meals, but you should at least make a show of refusing, and pay for the occasional beer.

For some truck rides you pay for an official ticket at the truck depot. For others, you make a private deal with the driver. It's best to reject demands for payment in FEC and hand over the cash only when you've arrived.

In parts of Tibet, traffic is rare and lifts even rarer (some hitchers have waited for days), so you can't afford to be choosy if the driver is only going part of the way to your destination. A good policy is to first name a point on your route that is close, then when you're on the truck, check out its destination. The driver will usually take you all the way if the destinations are identical or drop you off when he leaves your route.

Supplies

Make sure you are properly prepared with food, water and clothing for trucking. Keep a small bag with you containing warm clothes, valuables and photo gear, food and water. If you are in the back of the truck, useful items are gloves, rainpants, rain poncho, down jacket, down sleeping bag, sunglasses, wide-brimmed hat, suncream and lipcream.

Getting a Ride

Truck depots used to arrange rides and issue official tickets, although PSB offices have started to crack down on this. With persistent asking it is usually possible to arrange a private deal with drivers at truck depots, gas stations, truckstops/hotels and friendly checkpoints.

If all else fails, just grab your courage, station yourself visibly on the roadside, and show passing vehicles you are not yet another inert rock in the landscape by waving them down with a regal gesture. You might also like to try the system used by Tibetan ladies which is to put both hands in 'thumbs up' position vertically on top of each other and pump them up and down as if churning yak butter. The effect is heightened by shouting and dancing up and down at the same time. Extremists lie down or stand in the middle of the road but this is not recommended unless you are interested in sky burial.

Locals often show an avid interest in your progress of lack of it. After watching Landcruisers and minibuses packed with foreigners swirl past in clouds of dust, they are delighted to find a foreigner that has actually fallen to earth. Be prepared for wonderful, impromptu Tibetan lessons, long drinking sessions and hilarious group attempts to snare a ride. Tibetans are a rare breed.

OFFBEAT OPTIONS
Hitching
It follows, from the preceding, that hitch-hiking is eminently possible in Tibet, but done with varying degrees of success. Some travellers have the luck of the devil, and others get stuck for days in the middle of nowhere. Outside of Lhasa group tours or groups of travellers who have rented a vehicle may stop for you on the road, but they might also ask you to pay your share. You may well find yourself hitching on tractors, walking-tractors, horse-carts, dump-trucks and road-graders. Many tractors and walking-tractors cover huge distances – I followed one convoy all the way from Xining to Yushu. Dump-trucks are definitely a novel way to travel. One sighted near Gyantse was bouncing along with an entire Tibetan family singing, drinking and eating in the dumper part. Thumbs up! Keep on trucking . . . .

Bicycle
Lhasa has several places for bike rental. Models are of the black clunker variety – Phoenix, Forever, or else lesser breeds of Chinese lineage with no gears, heavy frames, solid tyres, unpredictable braking devices. Bicycling is a quick and con-venient way to cover Lhasa in the absence of a logical local bus system. Watch out for theft, and don't overdo the pedal power at this altitude.

Long-distance bikers have been sighted in Tibet. A Japanese brought his 10-speed into Lhasa by plane. In mid-1985 a Canadian and an Australian came across the Nepal-Tibet border at Gyirong over the high passes with mountain-bikes strapped to yaks. In Shigatse they were collared by the PSB, fined, dumped on the back of a truck and sent back to the Nepalese border. On the way, their truck broke down, so the intrepid duo grabbed their bikes and split north again! On reaching Lhasa, the police arrested them at their hotel. The bikes were confiscated and they were deported to Nepal. Here's the punch-line: the bikes remained in Lhasa and are now rented out to tourists at Y15 a day.

Chinese bicyclists have made inroads into Tibet. These amazing specimens are on round-China tours; A farmer from Sichuan, notched up 44,000 km around China (getting to all provincial capitals, including Lhasa) which is equivalent to a complete circuit of the globe – it just goes to show what can be done on a Chinese bike. If you have the lungs.

Boat
There are plans afoot to provide tourists with boating trips in Tibet on the Mekong, Salween and Brahmaputra rivers but CITS has not yet disclosed details. At the moment it is possible to hire yak-hide boats opposite Jarmalinka island in Lhasa for a short paddle. The ferry ride to reach Samye is another scenic boat trip lasting about an hour. In Lhasa some travellers were already excitedly talking about bringing kayaks and inflatable boats next time to have a crack at some of the wildest waters in the world.

Trekking
Yaks, horses and donkeys are all used extensively by Tibetans. If you are

trekking you can often hire a guide and animals at small villages. During harvest time farmers are unlikely to hire out animals needed for work in the fields. A yak can carry about three backpacks at a leisurely three kph.

A Japanese photographer tried twice to reach Mt Kailas from Lhasa on horseback. The first time was in the winter when he bought a horse for Y300 and resold it for Y250 when he had to abandon the attempt because of bad weather. The second time was in the summer when he bought a horse for Y450 and sold it for Y300 after successfully completing the trip.

Food, both for yourself and your animals, is not always plentiful so villagers en route may not be keen to sell you supplies. Take as much as you can with you. For more on trekking possibilities, see the Trekking in the Everest Region chapter.

Lhasa

Lhasa, once the national capital of Tibet, lies 3683 metres high in the Tibetan Himalaya beside the Kyichu (Happy River). For centuries it remained isolated from the outside world – a tantalising morsel for travellers, missionaries and explorers. In the heyday of the Asian trail many an overlander made a pilgrimage to the Nepalese border with Tibet to gaze wistfully and dream of Lhasa. Today, this city, described by Emanuel Freyre in 1716 as being the 'size of three parishes', has grown to 12 times that size and the Potala, no longer separated from the city by a stretch of greenery extending one mile, is hemmed in by the ugly paraphernalia of Chinese-style city planning. The population is estimated at 150,000 with the Han Chinese making up by far the highest percentage and, it is rumoured, the growing numbers of group tours may soon account for a creditable slice.

If you are disappointed with Lhasa, or feel cheated of the mystique you had expected, you won't be the first. The eccentric English traveller Manning delivered his verdict in 1812, and it still rings true: while he found the Potala extraordinary, he found the rest of the place a dump. In 1904, the invading English under Younghusband found their triumphal march into Lhasa impeded by piles of refuse, stagnant pools of water, open sewers, and various rabid animals foraging for putrid scraps of food. To add to the unreal air, when Brigadier-General Macdonald had trained his cannons on the Potala a salvo of fireworks went off as a greeting, at the Amban's residence. It was feared Macdonald might misconstrue this and open fire on the Potala, but all was well and the Amban passed around some Huntley & Palmer biscuits.

In 1949, Lowell Thomas Jr, on a rare visit to Tibet (at the invitation of the Dalai Lama) wrote:

Nothing is known of modern plumbing. Refuse piles up on all corners . . . once a year these offal heaps are transferred to the fields to stimulate crops. The odors are not entirely pleasant. The nobles hold scented handkerchiefs to their noses as they ride along . . . dead animals are tossed in refuse piles to be fought over and devoured by the city's scavengers – thousands of mangy dogs and ravens.

The Thomases bumped, inevitably, into Heinrich Harrer, an estranged German POW who had made Lhasa his home, and who had discovered why things didn't work so well under the ground in Lhasa. When, at the request of the Dalai Lama, Harrer set about building a dyke to stem the flooding of the Kyichu (which threatened the Norbulinka) his Tibetan work-squad had no idea how to dig, and were horrified to discover that worms dwelled in the soil. To cut one in half would have been a travesty of their religious sensibilities, so each worm that was uncovered had to be carefully put aside.

So much for the plumbing – these days there aren't even great numbers of Tibetans left in Lhasa. At first sight, Lhasa appears like a Chinese cake with the Potala as icing on top. But time spent around the Jokhang and Barkhor Bazaar should show that a distinctively Tibetan lifestyle still survives in Lhasa, despite all its outward Chinese trappings.

History

Lhasa became a centre of national power when King Songtsen Gampo moved his capital there from the Yarlung Valley during the 6th century AD. After the assassination of King Langdarma in 842, Lhasa lost political influence but later became the religious centre of Tibet. From the 17th century onwards Lhasa again became the seat of government until the Chinese occupation in 1951 which was followed by the final imposition of direct

Chinese administration after the uprising in 1959.

In 1965 the Tibetan Autonomous Region was founded and Lhasa designated its capital. In September 1985, Lhasa was chosen as the stage for celebrations of the 20th anniversary of this autonomy but the contrived and unconvincing show was marred by restrictions on Tibetans and foreigners.

Climate

The best time to visit Lhasa is between May and September. Once you are used to the altitude, it's an invigorating climate – low humidity, moderate rainfall and an average of eight hours of sunshine daily. In the summer, dust is a problem. In the winter, there is surprisingly little snow but be prepared for icicles on the ceiling if your room is unheated.

Lhasa Climate Chart

Month	Average °C	Highest °C	Lowest °C
Jan	0.3	12.2	-14.4
Feb	1.6	15.5	-11.6
Mar	5.5	18.3	-8.3
Apr	9.1	21.6	-4.4
May	13.0	25.0	-0.5
Jun	17.0	27.8	4.4
Jul	16.4	27.2	6.1
Aug	15.6	25.5	5.5
Sep	14.3	23.9	3.9
Oct	9.2	21.6	-5.0
Nov	3.9	16.6	-9.4
Dec	0.0	13.9	-13.3

Orientation

Traditionally, pilgrims who entered Lhasa performed three circuits in clockwise direction. The greater the number of circuits, the greater the merit acquired.

The *Lingkhor* (outer circuit – about eight km in length) went west, parallel to the road now called YanHe DongLu, and then branched off northwards in a long loop behind Chagpori (the 'iron mountain' on which the medicine college once stood) and continued behind the Potala before running eastwards, parallel to the road now called JianShe Lu. Pilgrims following the circuit then branched off southwards, parallel to the road now called LinKuo Lu, until they reached their point of departure. Much of the Lingkhor has been obliterated by barracks, offices and apartment blocks, but I did see prostrators following the first part of the route from Lhasa bridge and then continuing along YanHe DongLu – so perhaps it is still travelled, if only in part.

The *Barkhor* (inner circuit – about 800 metres in length) runs round the outer walls of the Jokhang and is still very much in use. The final circuit performed by pilgrims is that made within the Jokhang temple.

Although the Potala dominates the skyline, it is the Jokhang, the 'Cathedral of Buddhism',which remains the centre of Tibetan life in Lhasa. Roads fan out from the Barkhor, like a spider's web, linking up with LinKuo Lu and JieFang Lu which run north to south, and with XingFu Lu, RenMin Lu and YanHe Lu which run east to west.

Lhasa is speedily growing in size and with the same rapidity it is losing its Tibetan identity. In time for the 20th anniversary celebration, a large square with food and goods shops, was laid out in front of the Jokhang. The city can be divided into three types of neighbourhood: Tibetan, Muslim, and Chinese. The area around the Jokhang and the area which was once the village of Chö at the foot of the Potala are still traditionally Tibetan in style. There are a few hundred of the older Tibetan-style buildings left (or else replicas) in these two areas – they are two-storeyed, whitewashed, supported by colourful beams, and riddled with alleyways. The area east of the Jokhang, with a short radius around the mosque, has retained a strong Muslim atmosphere. The rest is Chinese. In the west, an ugly industrial zone sprawls from Doilungdêqên past the Norbulinka to the Potala. In the north, the residential blocks of New TuanJie Village vie with factories in a burst of concrete growth.

Information

CAAC (tel 22417) is next to the bus station. Opening hours in the winter are from 9.30 am to 12.30 pm, in the summer from 9 am to 12 noon.

CITS (tel 22980) is hidden away on the second floor at the back of No 3 Guest House. It is open Monday to Saturday 9 am to 12.30 pm and 3.30 to 6.30 pm; closed on Sundays. However, it is best to telephone before going because it will take almost half a day just to trek out there. One of the staff speaks excellent English. A piddling selection of pamphlets is on sale for Y2 apiece. On the wall is a huge military map of Tibet with magnificent detail . . . the only snag is that officials ask you not to look! A fleet of newly acquired Landcruisers and deluxe minibuses is available for hire (in theory). Landcruisers (maximum five passengers) cost Y1.5 per km and minibuses (maximum 15 passengers) cost Y2.5 per km. These are basic rates only, with additional charges payable depending on the type of tour which is organized. Don't expect unusual tours from CITS, they don't want to stray an inch from the straight and narrow.

Bank The Bank of China, guarded by a lone sentry outside the gate, is down an alley just past the truckstop on Yanhe Donglu. It is open from 8.30 am to 12 noon and 3.30 to 6.30 pm; closed on Sundays. Credit cards are not accepted at present. Nepalese rupees are sometimes available at the exchange counter.

Nepalese Consulate The consulate is just north of the Norbulinka. It is open from 11 am to 1 pm and from 3 to 6 pm. A one-month visa costs Y35 and is usually issued within an hour, but can take up to a day. Four photos are required and the application forms must be completed in quadruplicate.

Post Office The main post office, close to the Potala, is open in the summer from 9

am to 6.30 pm, in the winter from 10 am to 5 pm. Poste Restante is here – letters are kept in a cardboard box. Get your first day covers and the coveted Lhasa postmark here. Parcels are not always accepted on Saturdays and Mondays. Leave parcels unsealed for customs inspection at the counter. Sew up large parcels in cloth (available from the main department store) or use thick brown paper (*Niupi zhi* in Chinese), available from Xinhua Bookstore or other stores but only seal them after inspection.

The Telegraph & Communications Office is in the north-east of Lhasa, on Linkuo Lu. It is open in the winter from 7.30 to 9.30 am and from 10 am to 6 pm. In the summer opening hours are from 7 to 9 am and 9.30 am to 6 pm. There is also meant to be a night service from 6 to 11 pm. International calls are made via Beijing with varying degrees of success.

Public Security Bureau (tel 23170) is to the west of the Potala. It is closed on Thursday afternoon and on Sunday. On the other days it is open from 8.30 am to 12.30 pm and from 4 to 7 pm. The officials, one of whom speaks English, are strict with permits, so don't expect permission for closed places in Tibet. Visa extensions and exit permits for the Nepal route are available here. Some foreigners obtain the exit permit but change their minds en route and return via other places of interest. Get your visa extension, if required, first. Otherwise, you may be refused your extension on the grounds that you already have an exit permit. Once

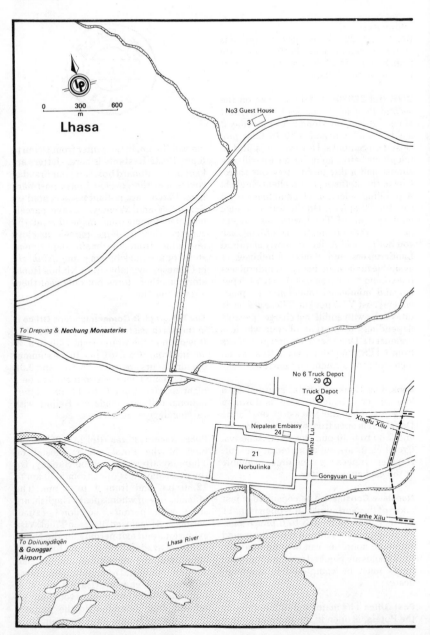

No3 Guest House
3

Lhasa

0   300   600
m

To Drepung & **Nechung Monasteries**

No 6 Truck Depot
29
Truck Depot

Xingfu Xilu

Nepalese Embassy
24

21
Norbulinka

Minzu Lu

Gongyuan Lu

Yanhe Xilu

To Doilungdêgên
& Gonggar
Airport

Lhasa River

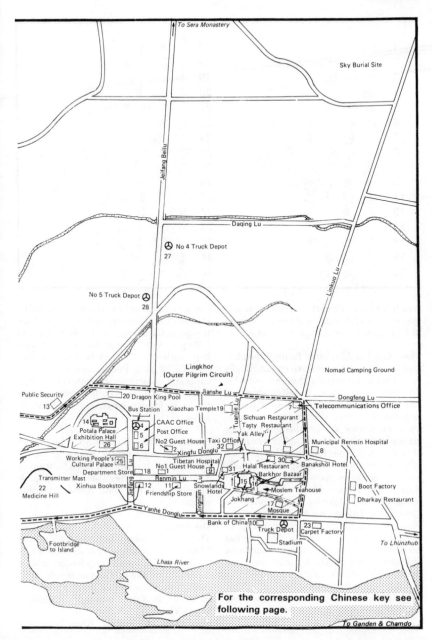

For the corresponding Chinese key see following page.

1	区一所	17	清真寺
2	区二所	18	百货商店
3	区三所	19	小昭寺
4	运站	20	龙王潭
5	民航局	21	罗布林卡
6	邮电局	22	药王山
7	邮电大楼	23	地毯厂
8	市人民医院	24	尼泊尔大使馆
9	藏医院	25	劳动人民文化宫
10	中国银行	26	展览馆
11	友谊商店	27	区汽车四队
12	新华书店	28	区汽车五队
13	公安局	29	区汽车六队
14	布达拉宫	30	八郎学旅社
15	大昭寺	31	雪域旅馆
16	八角街	32	城关区出租汽车公司

you have your exit permit, you may find it easier to buy a bus ticket at the bus station if PSB give you written authorisation.

Hospitals The *Municipal Renmin Hospital* (tel 23212) is at the eastern end of Xingfu Lu. This is reportedly the one used for foreigners who are usually admitted suffering from altitude sickness or resultant complications. Warnings about over-exertion before acclimatisation are not exaggerated. In 1985 an Englishman in his 30s died from heart failure in this hospital after attempting to hike up into the hills just a couple of days after arriving in Lhasa. The *Tibetan Hospital* (tel 24211), close to the Jokhang, specialises in traditional Tibetan medicine. One of the doctors speaks English. According to foreigners treated there, the herbal remedies for ailments such as diarrhoea are most effective. The hospital also has a room with various medical *thangkas* on display – quite interesting ones. The *No 3 Guest House* has limited medical facilities including oxygen bottles in the rooms.

Xinhua Bookstore is at the western end of Renmin Lu. Opening hours are from 9 am to 6 pm in the summer and from 9.30 am to 5.30 pm in the winter. Maps are on sale here, either in Chinese or Tibetan, and cost Y0.30 each. Potala tea-towels, post-cards and, sometimes, cassettes of Tibetan music are also on sale but there are no books in foreign languages on Tibet or Lhasa.

Friendship Store is on Renmin Lu, about halfway along, nearly opposite No 1 Guesthouse. It is roughly open 9.30 am to 4.30 pm daily. See the Shopping & Supplies section that follows in this chapter.

The Potala

The Potala Palace, perched high above Lhasa on the Marpori ('red mountain'), is a place of spiritual pilgrimage and a mammoth tribute to Tibetan architectural skills. The name Potala derives from the Sanskrit 'Bodala', meaning 'Buddha's Mountain'.

In the 7th century King Songtsen

Gampo first built a small meditation pavilion on this site, followed later by a palace. During the 9th century these buildings were destroyed after lightning set them on fire. On the orders of the 5th Dalai Lama construction was started in 1645, but he died before the Red Palace was started. However, before dying he asked his Prime Minister (Regent) to keep his death secret lest construction work be discontinued. The Prime Minister found a monk who resembled the deceased and thus was able to conceal the death until all 13 storeys had been completed. From the time of the 5th Dalai Lama onwards, the Potala became the official winter residence of the successive Dalai Lamas.

During the 1959 uprising, the PLA shelled the Potala. It is rumoured that the wholesale destruction of the Potala during the Cultural Revolution was averted by Zhou Enlai, who pledged his own troops for its protection. In June 1984 an electrical fault caused a massive fire which destroyed the Hall of the Buddha Maitreya. Large water tanks and extensive plumbing were then installed as part of a fire-control plan. The authorities are now planning an assault on what may prove to be the deadliest threat yet – wood-boring insects!

Built of wood, earth and stone, the Potala has 13 storeys rising over 117-metres high. The whole structure is a maze of rooms – over 1000 of them, with 10,000 shrines and some 200,000 statues. The storeys are not continuous, and access to particular halls may be hidden behind pillars. The walls, varying in thickness between two and five metres were strengthened against earthquakes by pouring in molten copper. No steel frame was used, and no nails were used in the woodwork. Since the wheel had not been introduced to Tibet at the time of building (17th century), stones were lugged in on donkey-back, or on the backs of humans. Simple equipment was used to fashion a skyscraper – an achievement on a par with the building of the pyramids.

Seen from the front, the Potala consists of the Red Palace in the centre flanked, on both sides, by the White Palace. The White Palace was completed in 1653, and construction on the Red Palace started in 1690 (completed in 1694).

The **Red Palace** contains assembly-halls, shrines, 35 chapels, four meditation halls and seven mausoleums. These mausoleums contain the remains of all the Dalai Lamas from the 5th to the 13th, (with the exception of the 6th) with their salt-dried bodies placed in individual chortens which are covered with stupendous amounts of gold plating, and inlaid with diamonds, pearls, turquoise, agate and coral. The 5th Dalai Lama's chorten is covered with 3700 kg of gold! His chorten is 20-metres high, rising through three storeys. Nearby is the tomb of the 13th Dalai Lama, 22-metres high and made of solid silver, covered with gold leaf and precious stones.

The Dalai Lamas from the 8th to the 12th inclusive perished at an early age, and in mysterious circumstances. Power was held by the Regents. The 6th Dalai Lama was, according to most sources, killed in Litang. One of the reasons that the Dalai Lama was housed in the Potala high above Lhasa was to preserve the incarnation in isolation from the riff-raff. The 6th Dalai Lama was a somewhat unconventional incarnation. Because the death of the 5th Dalai Lama was concealed (he was said to be 'meditating'), the 6th took over as a grown boy (not an infant like many of his predecessors) did not take celibacy vows, and was never fully ordained as a Lama. He was a prolific rake – no woman in Lhasa was said to be safe from his indulgences – and he was one of Tibet's greatest poets:

I dwell apart in Potala
A God on earth am I
But in the town the chief of rogues
And boisterous revelry

Despite his behaviour, the 6th was revered by the people, who came to the conclusion that the living Buddha had two bodies – one which stayed in the Potala and meditated, and the other that got rotten drunk and chased Lhasa women. The 6th Dalai Lama disappeared at the age of 23 in Litang, and his reincarnation was found in Litang and brought to Lhasa.

The western section of the Potala used to house a community of over 150 monks, whilst the eastern section contained government offices, a school for monk officials, and the meeting halls of the National Assembly. The Potala also served as a storehouse for thousands of ancient scrolls, illuminated volumes of scriptures, armour and armaments from ancient times, gifts and treasures. The myriad storehouses and cellars in the base of the building contained government stocks of provisions for officials, monasteries, and the army. The torture-chambers, reserved for high-ranking offenders, were once standard fare on the tour group menu, but appear to be out of bounds again.

At the base of the Potala is a collection of buildings. This was once a separate village, called **Chö**, which contained government offices, the Tibetan Army Headquarters and a printing works once famous for its wood blocks of the *Kanjur*. The area has now lost much of its character to infringing Han architecture.

The Roof The top section of the Potala, though you may not be able to get up there, consists of the former private apartments of the Dalai Lama, left in the condition they were in when the clock stopped in 1959 with the flight of the 14th Dalai Lama. There are prayer-halls, reception-rooms, and bedrooms of the Dalai Lama, with some rather curious decorations. A couch side-table bears an inverted skull with a silver jaw and eyeballs, which once held ritual offerings of sacred tea or beer. Next to that is a small drum made from skin stretched over two skulls. The skull symbolises the impermanence of the human body in its endless rounds of reincarnation.

At the very top of the Potala is the Sutra Hall where the Dalai Lama would sit on an ornate, soft throne and read scriptures. From the roof-top, lamas would blow their four-metre-long brass horns to call the kingdom to prayer. It is difficult to get access to the roof, which has stupendous views of Lhasa, and ornate decorations. The monks are not keen on allowing foreigners access. One American gleefully scrambled up though a side door. When he tried to come down again, a grim-faced monk locked the door and told him he would only be allowed down on a payment of Y10.

Opening & Closing The Potala is open on Wednesdays and Saturdays from 10 am to 4 pm, but check beforehand. The Potala phone number is 22896 if you care to test your language skills to the limit. Rooms are constantly being closed and re-opened, so it pays to make several visits, and it's best to steer clear of the place until you're acclimatised to the altitude – the steps up can be heavy going (group tours are often driven up a road at the back). It seems that groups can visit almost any day, so you might be able to tag along. If you go on your own, it's worthwhile just to follow the pilgrims as they present offerings, recite prayers and prostrate in a long procession up and down stairs, through countless halls, past frescoes, images, shrines and relics.

Visitors enter the Potala through the

East Gate which is reached by climbing a long series of stone steps, designed wide and low enough for riders on horse, or for palanquin-bearers. Inside the East Gate there is a ticket office on your left; tickets cost Y0.30. Once through the East Gate, you enter the Deyangshar (East Terrace) where Cham dances and religious rituals were once held. A small shop on the right sells postcards (Y1.20) and a brochure in Chinese about the Potala. Remember to take a torch/flashlight (most rooms are dimly lit), a water bottle and, perhaps, some Dalai Lama pics. Always walk in a clockwise direction around shrines and sacred images, otherwise you will offend the monks and the pilgrims. Most visitors exit from the north side of the Potala, down steps and along a path which leads to the Dragon King Pool (LongWangZe).

Surprisingly, some monks in the Potala speak a little English and show a keen interest in worldly affairs. I was a bit taken aback when, after casually discussing a statue with a friendly monk, he promptly offered the best rate in town if I needed to exchange money. Other monks will be gasping for Dalai Lama pics. Photography is officially forbidden in the Potala and the same applies to smoking and shouting. However, it is possible on payment of horrendously high fees which can vary between Y10 and Y50 *per photo*. You may find Dalai Lama pics are a cheaper alternative, for gaining permission. An American lady talked to a monk who showed interest in her camera and offered, of his own accord, to take a picture of her. Just before he clicked the shutter, he dangled a handwritten request for Y20 (FEC) in front of her nose. This was too much for the lady who firmly asked for her camera back. The monk refused and backed off until the exasperated American, temporarily lost for suitable words, shouted 'You, you *monk* you!' and snatched back her camera.

As part of a drive to make the Potala more palatable to tourists, the Tibet Tourist Corporation plans to reduce the butter lamps, install bright lighting and provide modern toilets. These measures may please tourists who, inevitably, consider the Potala as something lifeless, a desiccated museum. But, from the Tibetan point of view, no amount of tinkering with the Potala can disguise the eerie absence of the force within – the Dalai Lama.

The Dragon King Pool

This pool is said to have appeared when workers dug clods of earth behind the Potala to make cement for the walls during reconstruction work in 1645. Later, the Dragon King Temple (Lukhang) was erected on an island in the lake. According to one legend, an evil dragon which required a male human sacrifice once a year used to live here. After many years of sacrifices, one boy chosen for sacrifice decided to fight the dragon. The fight lasted seven days and seven nights before the dragon was killed. To celebrate this victory, Tibetans come here every year on April 15 for a festival. The pool is inside a pleasant park which is a favourite spot for Tibetans to have picnics.

Opposite the bus station entrance, at the foot of Marpori, there is a small temple with prayer wheels outside. An old Tibetan lady is often found nearby, carefully carving inscriptions on small stones. For a few *mao* she will carve a stone for you.

Chagpori

Chagpori ('iron mountain') is opposite the Potala and easily identified by the radio mast on the top. This was the site of a famous college of medicine razed during the Cultural Revolution, but now being rebuilt. Lower down the hill, partially set into a cave, is a small temple with prayer-wheels and friendly monks. There are excellent views from here and plenty of fine spots to photograph the Potala. The climb up this hill is best done after you have acclimatised to the altitude for a few days.

Norbulinka (Summer Palace)

Construction of the Norbulinka ('precious jewel island') was started by the 7th Dalai Lama in 1755. This is a large complex of small palaces and chapels within a walled garden, about four km north of the Potala. The earliest building in the park is the Gesang Pozhang Palace built by the 7th Dalai Lama. In 1954 the present Dalai Lama started construction of the New Palace which was completed by 1956. The PLA inflicted heavy casualties and immense damage during the uprising in 1959 when the Norbulinka was shelled the day after the Dalai Lama had slipped away in disguise on his flight to India. During the Cultural Revolution further damage was done. Many of the frescoes on the walls are still daubed with crude slogans and pictures of Mao.

The New Palace is tiny, compared to the Potala, but it contains fascinating murals in excellent condition. A guide who speaks some English will first take you round the South Hall and North Hall. The tour then continues through the Dalai Lama's meditation room, bedroom (notice the Russian radio), sitting room (complete with Philips radiogram), bathroom (plumbing by courtesy of a British company), reception room and throne room (superb mandala and fresco depicting the Dalai Lama with foreign heads of state). The New Palace is open from 9 to 11.30 am and from 3.30 to 5 pm (closed on Sundays – tel 22644). Admission costs Y2 for foreigners and Y0.30 for locals. Photography is not allowed. Take your shoes off at the entrance and leave them with the exotic pile left by pilgrims.

The gardens are a favourite picnic spot. Performances of Tibetan dances and opera are held here during the 'Xuedun Festival' which falls on the last day of the 6th lunar month (end of July). Behind the New Palace is a depressing zoo where sad-eyed lynxes, deer, Himalayan brown bears, monkeys and seagulls endure baiting with cigarettes and dream of feeding time when they receive – what else

in Tibet – *tsampa*! In one of the courtyards behind the New Palace is the orange, rusting hulk of a 1931 Dodge. Nearby, is the almost indistinguishable wreckage of two 1927 Baby Austins: one blue, the other red and yellow. These were presented to the 13th Dalai Lama, carried by yaks over the Himalayas in pieces and then reassembled. On the death of the 13th Dalai Lama, these cars, the only ones in Lhasa, were not used until, in the 1950s, the present Dalai Lama succeeded in putting them into working order with the help of a Tibetan trained as a driver in India.

Jokhang Temple

The Jokhang is the religious and geographical centre of Lhasa. From morning to night an astounding display of chanting, prostrating pilgrims revolves around Barkhor Bazaar and the Jokhang. Hundreds of faces, dialects, ornaments, clothes and colours swirl round in a gigantic whirlpool of religious fervour.

In contrast to other Tibetan monasteries, the Jokhang is used by people from all the different sects of Buddhism, and does not have a large monastic community attached to it. The temple was founded in 650 by Songtsen Gampo on the site of what was once a great underground lake in which visions of the future could be seen. According to one version (favoured by the Chinese), Songtsen Gampo built this temple to house the statue of Sakyamuni presented to him by Princess Wen Cheng. Other sources indicate that the temple already existed before the arrival of the Princess. Tsong Khapa introduced the Monlam Qinbo (Great Prayer Festival) in 1409 and designated the Jokhang as the principal venue for religious celebrations of the Yellow Hat sect which he founded.

The square in front of the Jokhang has been 'modernised'. The incongruous result looks like a cross between a western shopping mall and a Chinese square. Perhaps as a result of the construction work, my attempts to find the famous willow tree planted by Princess Wen Cheng were unsuccessful. Two stone buildings opposite the Jokhang entrance house two stone *stele* (tablets). If you hang around long enough, you will notice the Tibetans gouging little bits out of one of the tablets, which was erected in 1794 by the Chinese and tells the procedure for dealing with smallpox. The superstitious believed that the 'smallpox pillar' had curative powers, and they have, for decades, gouged out bits to make into powder for medicine.

The flagstones at the entrance to the Jokhang have been polished smooth by thousands of pilgrims. Pilgrims crowd around, constantly praying and prostrating. Follow the pilgrims inside, past rows of prayer-wheels and then continue (clockwise) on a grand tour of the main hall surrounded by chapels dedicated to Avalokitesvara, Amitabha ... Within the central hall is the famous sitting statue of the 12-year-old Sakyamuni (one of only three made during his lifetime) which was a gift from Princess Wen Cheng to her husband Songtsen Gampo. There is a vague rumour that zealous Red Guards erroneously smashed the statue of Wen Cheng herself, and what you're now looking at is a duplicate (?).

Tibetan legend has it that a sure-footed goat carried soil and rocks for the filling of the lake over which the Jokhang was supposedly built. A statue, known as Ramo Gyalmo (Queen of the Goats) was erected to honour this quadruped, but it seems that the present statue is a duplicate. Deep in the bowels of the place is also, according to legend, a waterdragon to which offerings were made. The four-storey Jokhang was enlarged numerous times between the 7th and 17th centuries, with particularly rich additions by Tsongkhapa in the 15th century, and by the 5th Dalai Lama in the 17th century. The Great Fifth wrote a guidebook to the temple – by which time a book must have been sorely needed to find one's way to the upper floors (I wish I had a translation).

If you don't, or can't, make it to the top (which offers splendid views of the Potala, and has intricate exterior decoration), try indulging in the good old sport of rooftop hopping. The Jokhang is surrounded by a ramshackle selection of housing grafted onto its sides so that it's difficult to tell where the temple ends and the housing begins – I even found a nomad and his tent up in the vicinity of the roof-top!

The ground floor of the Jokhang alone has some 20 chapels dedicated to Buddhist deities, Indian saints and Tibetan kings (and queens) – if you peer into the darker corners with a flashlight you may stray across murals relating to the bliss of Nirvana, or the horrors of hell. There were 18 hells impressed upon the plebs by Lamaism – eight scorching ones, eight frosty ones, and a few reserved for specialist tortures. One of the greater hells was called The Forest of Razors.

There are supposed to be over 250 statues within the Jokhang, though you most likely won't be allowed past the ground floor (by vigilant monks) to view the treasures up above. The 4th floor was apparently cleaned out during the Cultural Revolution, during which time (1966) the Jokhang was called Guesthouse Number 5, a temporary headquarters for Red Guard factions. The yard was used to keep pigs, and in an orgy of destruction mobs burned scriptures and destroyed or defaced large numbers of statues and frescoes. During the 1959 uprising, the Jokhang became a temporary sanctuary for Tibetan fighters and pilgrims who thought the Chinese would not attack it. The Chinese did attack it – they shelled it, and rammed down the front gate with tanks.

If you find the lighting of the Jokhang interior to be gloomy, it's certainly much brighter than it used to be – and cleaner. In 1904 English historian L A Waddell saw lots of rodents running around one devilish, holy image:

Tame mice ran unmolested over the floor, feeding on the cake and grain offerings, under the altar and amongst the dress of the image (the she-devil Palden Lhamo) and up and down the bodies of the monks who were chanting their litany, and were said to be transmigrating nuns and monks.

The white mice were holy – in Deshnoke, Rajasthan, there is a temple where rats are worshipped as reincarnations, which goes back to a legend connected with Yama, the God of Death (also worshipped in Tibet). Anyhow, there are few if any mice to be seen at the Jokhang now, but there is plenty of yak-butter being burned, as there always was. Landon, special correspondent for *The Times* with the Younghusband expedition, wrote:

Everything one touches drips with grease. The fumes of the burning butter have in the course of many generations filmed over the surfaces and clogged the carving of doors and walls alike.

The following article and the sketchplan opposite indicate some of the problems involved in identifying the jumble of fake, restored and original objects within present-day Tibetan monasteries.

Those who value their camera-lenses should heed this description! Behind the rows of butter lamps are rows of golden offering bowls.

The Jokhang is worth visiting as often as possible. Strictly speaking, the Jokhang is only open in the morning, but many of the monks are pleased to see foreigners and sometimes take you on an impromptu tour in the afternoon. The telephone number is 23129. Take a torch (flashlight) and Dalai Lama pics (which could help relax the rules against photography).

Barkhor

This is Lhasa's inner pilgrim circuit, shaped roughly like an octagon, which runs round the Jokhang. The circuit is lined with markets, shops, stalls and street vendors providing every conceivable item a Tibetan could need. The best place

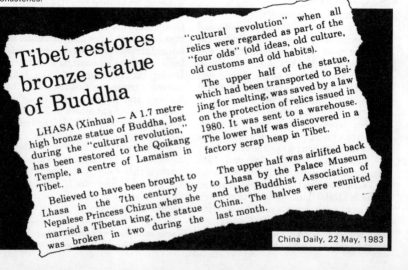

Tibet restores bronze statue of Buddha

LHASA (Xinhua) — A 1.7 metre-high bronze statue of Buddha, lost during the "cultural revolution," has been restored to the Qoikang Temple, a centre of Lamaism in Tibet.

Believed to have been brought to Lhasa in the 7th century by Nepalese Princess Chizun when she married a Tibetan king, the statue was broken in two during the "cultural revolution" when all relics were regarded as part of the "four olds" (old ideas, old culture, old customs and old habits).

The upper half of the statue, which had been transported to Beijing for melting, was saved by a law on the protection of relics issued in 1980. It was sent to a warehouse. The lower half was discovered in a factory scrap heap in Tibet.

The upper half was airlifted back to Lhasa by the Palace Museum and the Buddhist Association of China. The halves were reunited last month.

China Daily, 22 May, 1983

Jokhang Temple (Tsugla Khang)

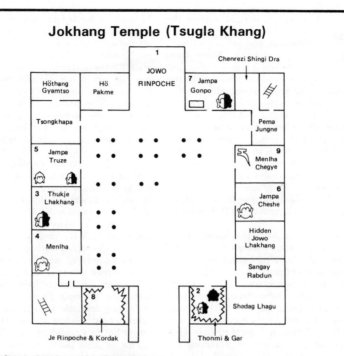

1. Jowo Rinpoche chapel (statue of Sakyamuni Buddha, said to have been brought to Tibet by Princess Wen Cheng).
2. Choegyal chapel (first floor) with the chapel of Thonmi and Gar (ministers of King Songsten Gampo) below. The image of King Trisong Detsan is a fake. The image of Songsten Gampo is slightly damaged. The walls have been damaged and later repaired.
3. Thurje Lhakhang or Avalokitesvara with 11 heads. Some original parts of the image were smuggled into India by Tibetans and are now in Dharamsala.
4. Deshek Gyal chapel, with a fake Medicine Buddha image.
5. Jampa Truze chapel.
6. Jampa Cheshe chapel. The original image of Jampa (or Champa, Buddha of the Future), which used to be taken in procession around the Barkhor during the Great Prayer Festival, is no longer here. In its place is another image originally belonging to Drepung Monastery.
7. Jampa Gonpo chapel.
8. Chapel of Je Rinpoche (Tsongkhapa) and eight Khordag Namgyal deities.
9. Menlha Chegye chapel with a Medicine Buddha fresco. Images of King Songsten Gampo and his two queens. The bust of Ramo Gyamo (the goat, in the left corner, on the wall) is a fake.

Selective Restoration

The Chinese decided against restoring the tantric murals and scenes of hell, now found in dark corners of the Jokhang. Some tantric murals show many-headed beasts in sexual union with women half their size. Some images relate to earlier Bon rites. A statue of Palden Lhamo, a wild she-devil given to eating brains from a human skull, was moved from a prominent place to a coy hideout within the temple.

	Images faked
	Defaced but restored
	Images completely destroyed
	Ache Gyasa'i Thab (fireplace of Princess Wen Cheng), now replaced by a bust of Jowo (Buddha) of Ramoche (temple to the north of Lhasa)
	Walls destroyed
	Bust of Ramo Gyamo
● ● ●	Pillars
	Passage

Sketchplan of the Jokhang Temple ground-floor chapels, from a Dharamsala Report, 1976-78.

to start your circuit is right outside the Jokhang, but remember to walk in a clockwise direction and mind you don't step on the prostrators. Apart from numerous alleys (too tiny to describe, but great to explore – just keep heading for the Jokhang and you'll eventually hit the circuit), there are two other ways to enter: one is via a street running past the mosque, the other is via a street running south off XingFu DongLu, just before the Banak Shol Hotel. If you enter off XingFu DongLu, you'll cross *Yak Alley* which is a gory sight with tables of meat and yak carcasses on the ground and packs of dogs. There's a small open market here as well as stalls selling *chang* (Tibetan barley beer).

Just past Yak Alley you reach a large square with a monument used for burning incense. The building behind reportedly housed a government prison where unfortunate transgressors could suffer tortures such as being dropped into vats of leeches, being skinned alive, having their tongues cut off, their eyes torn out or the muscles ripped from their legs. One corner of this square is reserved for carpets which are not necessarily Tibetan and rarely of good quality. However, the carpet lads from Xinjiang know about the merits of foreign currency. Tibetans, especially the tough-looking Khampas, will be keen to sell or barter earrings, purses, tinder boxes, coral, turquoise, old coins, daggers and ornaments. Bargaining is a 'must' since prices are usually steep, and it's worth remembering that the export of antiques is prohibited by law.

Prayer-flag sellers have bunches at Y1 each. Yoghurt is usually available in the early morning at Y0.6 per jar. It's best to have your own jar (use an empty fruit jar) otherwise you may be refused, or have to pay Y0.10 deposit. Enterprising yoghurt merchants have been performing an early morning circuit of the Snowlands and Banak Shol hotels where their wares are pounced on by droves of sleepy foreigners. If you feel thirsty or hungry, try one of the Muslim teahouses for *lamian* (noodles with meat) and lotus-seed tea with rock crystal sugar at Y0.4. Some of the traders are Nepalese, speak excellent English and are willing to chat or help, even if you don't buy any Nepalese glucose biscuits or Indian snuff. Some stalls sell skins of rare animals. The quality is dubious and, anyway, who wants to encourage the extinction of rare species. Other stalls sell ceremonial scarves (*khata*); felt Stetson hats made in Tianjin at Y20 each; gaudy, embroidered hats with ear-flaps at Y7.60 each and rolls of attractive, striped cloth. Street vendors sell bunches of juniper for incense, and incense holders (made out of soldered tin cans) at Y1.50 each.

Pilgrims who have travelled vast distances and lack the money to return, sit against walls selling clothes and jewellery or reciting prayers. Another strange sight on the circuit is a troupe of scantily clad prostrators (foreigners have nicknamed them 'the Olympic Prostrating Team') performing dramatic rituals. In the evening, monks hold recitation sessions with prayer books, ritual drums and bells.

This is one place in Lhasa where Tibetans rule, in numbers and in spirit – any Han Chinese who venture here keep a low profile. Knife fights are not uncommon – a Chinese was knifed by a Khampa after an argument in early 1985. If on arrival in Lhasa you feel depressed at its dismal, Chinese appearance, the best cure is to plunge straight into the Barkhor. After a couple of circuits it really should feel like Tibet!

Ramoche Temple
This temple is in the north of town, just off TuanJie Lu. It is not yet officially open as it is still under renovation. If you are lucky, an old couple living there may show you around. No doubt, once renovation gets under way, an image of Buddha will replace the two portraits of Mao on the altar!

Lhasa River (KyiChu)

A pleasant place on the river with superb views of the Potala, is Jarmalinka island, connected to YanHe XiLu by a bridge which is festooned with prayer-flags. You pay the bridge-keeper a fee of Y0.10 to cross. If you arrive early in the morning, yak-hide boats can sometimes be hired for about Y1 per person for a return trip across the river. Water burials take place a short distance downstream. Jarmalinka island is a popular picnic spot for Tibetans on Sundays. During the *Washing Festival*, which usually lasts for seven days during September, the whole area is crowded with bathing Tibetans.

AROUND LHASA

Drepung Monastery

This Gelukpa monastery, once the largest in the world, was founded by Jianyang Qujie, a disciple of Tsong Khapa, in 1416. It stands about six km west of Lhasa at the foot of a mountain, with fine views across the Lhasa valley. The buildings were extended in the first half of the 17th century during the time of the 5th Dalai Lama. This was a monastic university – one of the 'three seats of state'. The other two were Ganden and Sera monasteries.

Various paths lead up from the road past store rooms and monks' quarters which once housed 10,000 monks. Monks were usually housed according to the area they had come from. Thus there were quarters for monks from Sichuan, Qinghai, Chamdo and Mongolia. Above these quarters are the large Dukhang (assembly halls) with courtyards in front. Four colleges here taught different aspects of Buddhism. In the 'Great Sutra Chanting Hall' is a white conch with a counter-clockwise spiral, believed to have been discovered by Tsong Khapa, and a gold statue of Buddha (Jianbatongzhenma). A Vajra statue in the Ngabazhacang temple has the remains of the great translator Duojita inside its belly.

The name Drepung means 'Rice Heap', perhaps a reference to its general

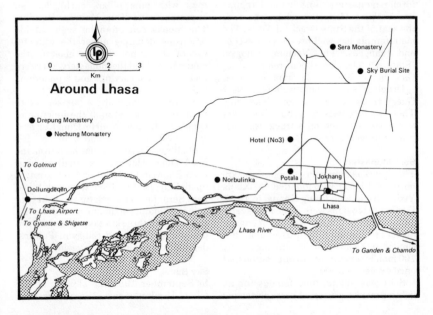

appearance, but in fact named after a Tantric temple in India. The fact that the monastery once controlled a vast manorial estate, as well as subsidiary monasteries, means it would have had plenty to do with rice, as did the monastery's vast granaries. During the uprising in 1959, many monks from Drepung abandoned their vows and took up arms against the Chinese. Spent cartridges can still be found away from the paths. The few monks left here are not eager to admit foreigners to the temples but you can ramble round, taking a look at whatever happens to be open. The kitchens are gigantic. You can also walk up to see carvings and paintings on the mountainside or just sit and absorb the atmosphere in ghostly silence.

Drepung has one population that *is* thriving – dogs. Most monasteries have resident packs of dogs which are believed to be reincarnations of past monks who failed to return in a higher form. Apparently the dogs are still interested in religion and lope around seeking admission to their former monastery. Just below Drepung lies *Nechung Monastery* which was once the seat of the State Oracle of Tibet. The main temple has well preserved frescoes and thangkas. The Nechung Chogyal (State Oracle) has been relocated at Gangchen Kyishong in Dharamsala, India.

Drepung is a two-hour walk from No 1 Guest House or a half-hour bike ride. There is a bus twice daily, but it's quicker and easier to hitch on a truck, walking-tractor or whatever.

Sera Monastery

This Gelukpa monastery (about three km north of Lhasa) was founded by Xiajia Yixi, a disciple of Tsong Khapa, in 1419. Further extensions were made in the early 18th century. Sera was a monastic university, smaller than Drepung, but similar in the layout of its buildings. Only 100 monks remain out of a population that once exceeded 5000.

Sera was at one time famous for its fighting monks, who spent years perfecting

the martial arts. They were hired out as bodyguards to the wealthy. They even took on the Tibetan army, as in a minor coup d'etat in 1947 in Lhasa when government troops shelled Sera. Sera means 'hail' – a name said to derive from the fact that Sera was in continual competition with Drepung, and the 'hail' of Sera scattered the 'rice' of Drepung. Once a year, in December, the fighting monks of Sera used to race starkers along a river bank for several km to toughen up.

Here, as at Drepung, many monks renounced their vows to take up arms during the uprising in 1959. Restoration work is still in progress to repair immense damage inflicted during the Cultural Revolution. It's best just to wander around and see which of the temples are open. There are four main temples with numerous chapels dedicated to Tsong Khapa, Sakyamuni, Dharmapala, Amitabha, Yamantaka, and other deities. One of the temples, constructed with 108 pillars (12 rows with nine pillars each), has an imposing statue of the Maitreya Buddha. The monks can often be seen outside practising debating under the watchful eye of the abbot. If you hike up the mountain behind the monastery, there are rock paintings, carvings and a panorama of Lhasa.

There is, reportedly, a bus service to Sera (try the bus stop at the junction of QingNian Lu and YanHe DongLu) at 8 am, 11.30 am, 3 pm and 6.30 pm. It's probably easier to walk (one hour from the No 1 Guest House), bike (half an hour from Snowlands Hotel) or hitch straight up JieFang BeiLu. Some travellers hiked past Sera, further north up the valley, to another temple, a nunnery and hermit caves. About three km east of Sera are two prisons: Drapchi and Sangyip. Political detainees are said to be in residence.

Sky Burial

In September 1985 the sky burial site (about 15 minutes east of Sera monastery, at the foot of the mountain) was officially closed to tourists. Unless this decision is reversed you would be unwise to visit as this will incur the wrath of the Chinese authorities and the Tibetan burial squad. Enterprising tourism officials are now toying with idea of erecting coin operated telescopes to give a vulture's-eye view of this ritual.

Of the five types of burial practised in Tibet (sky burial, water burial, earth burial, fire burial and embalming), sky burial is the commonest. Bodies are laid out in the open, and are carefully skinned and dissected. The bones are crushed and mixed with tsampa. At the end of this procedure, huge flocks of vultures, hawks and ravens descend and polish everything off with great zest. Although it might be thought a strange way to leave this earth, sky burial is a necessity in a country like Tibet, where fuel is scarce and the ground is usually far too rocky to be dug. Tibetans believe that the sky burial offers the deceased the chance to gain merit by offering his corpse for the benefit of sentient beings.

Unfortunately, this site became a magnet for large numbers of tourists who sat around looking – except for their photo gear – remarkably like the vultures perched in rows on the mountain behind. At first, the Tibetans performing the burials welcomed the tourists who, for the most part, did not abuse the privilege. Later, the families of the deceased objected to photography and warned the burial team that payment for burial would only be made if photography was stopped. As the driver of the corpse truck said to me: 'How would you like it if swarms of people came to photograph your dead mother?'

It was then only a matter of time before serious confrontations took place. An Australian tried to hide up the mountain and take tele-photo pics. Whilst hopping around on the skyline, he scared the birds away – an exceptionally evil omen. The irate burial squad gave chase brandishing knives and showered him with rocks. A three-day ban on tourists followed, but the scene did not improve. Hong Kongers and Han Chinese were chased off by the burial squad who tried to club them with bloody bones. Then a new approach was tried. Photo bags were collected at the beginning of the ceremony and then handed back at the end when photos were allowed. This didn't work either. As the crowds of camera toting sightseers grew larger and more inquisitive, not a day passed without Landcruisers, PLA soldiers or surreptitious photographers being bombarded with rocks, chased with knives or threatened with meaty leg-bones ripped straight off the corpse. Closure of the site was the result.

Now, presumably early in the morning each day, on the flat rock near Sera, sky burials are performed as usual. No tourists, no photos – just the corpse, the relatives, the burial squad ... and the vultures.

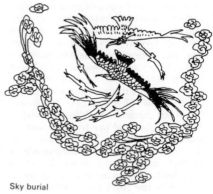

Sky burial

Places to Stay – bottom end

The *Snowlands Hotel* and *Banak Shol Hotel*, near the Jokhang, are very popular with budget travellers. Unlike the other hotels, they are Tibetan: Tibetan architecture, Tibetan management and a whole lot of crazy, anarchic, Tibetan fun.

Snowlands has a few doubles, but mostly four-bed or five-bed rooms (Y5 RMB per bed). The hotel is constructed on three floors around a courtyard, so life is communal. Most people go to No 1 Guest House for showers. A bathhouse is under construction, but at the moment water comes from a pump in the yard. There are plenty of thermoses of hot water (*kai shui*) and bowls for washing. It's impossible not to like the Tibetan women who run the place with laughter and water-fights. The odoriferous toilets are a standing joke – put a clothes-peg over your nose, enter, take aim, fire and exit as fast as your legs permit!

The restaurant downstairs serves food, Sichuan style. Bikes are available for hire at Y6 per day. Check your bike *before* departure. Although the bikes arrived new (in knock-down form), their assembly wasn't exactly perfect and I had a close shave when the brakes failed at a busy crossroads. The shop next door sells stationery, sweets, Nepalese biscuits and excellent sets of thangka posters at Y10. In the winter the place is an ice-box, so try and get a room on the sunny side. A room next to reception is used for storing baggage. Reception will help to organise a taxi. There's an impromptu noticeboard on the second floor for seats on hired buses, hitching partners and so on.

The Banak Shol has three-bed rooms (Y5 RMB per bed), doubles and singles. Walls are thin and one traveller said he was kept up all night by the couple next door bemoaning the breathtaking problems of high altitude copulation. Water is supplied from a tap in the yard – or take a shower at the No 1 Guest House. The hotel is run by a Tibetan co-operative which also markets tsampa and runs the restaurant/tea-house downstairs. The restaurant now has a dining-room for foreigners which is a favourite meeting-place. You choose your own ingredients from bowls in the kitchen, put them on a plate and have them cooked. Depending on the food selected, a serving costs Y2.

Sweet, milky tea costs Y0.25. Bikes are for hire here at Y6 per day. Postcards are on sale at reception where they can also help you organise a taxi or a tour.

Across the street from No 1 Guest House is the *Public Bathhouse*, usually open from 9 am to 5 pm, including Sundays. I've no idea if they've cleaned up their act yet – in 1985 if a traveller rolled up for a bath, the staff would take him or her, complete with platform wooden shoes (Japanese style) to keep off the slimy floor, to one of the best stalls. It's best not to get too close to the walls either. 'Green things dripping from the ceiling' was how one traveller put it. For showers, it's Y1.50 for men, and it's Y2 for women (perhaps because only the wealthier ones are welcome, or is it that they take longer?). This bathhouse also has rooms for Y10 a night.

No 2 Guest House (tel 22185) is 100 metres east of the Potala on XingFu DongLu. It's for Chinese guests (local or overseas) but some foreigners have stayed – for Y30 a double.

Places to Stay – middle

The one redeeming feature of the *No 1 Guest House* (tel 22184) is its position in the centre of town. The atmosphere is strongly Chinese – not a trace of Tibet. There are four doubles; 30 triples; 30 four-bed rooms; four seven-bed rooms and one 10-bed room. A bed in a four-bed room costs Y10 FEC; Y6 FEC in a dormitory. Reception has a sign asking for FECs for all payments. Baggage can be stored in a room opposite reception. Ask at reception about bikes for rent at Y5 per day and be prepared to put down a deposit of Y50 and an ID card or similar. Reception also arranges taxis and tours.

Showers (solar-heated) are available daily from 4 to 6 pm (except on Sundays) on the 3rd floor of a building at the rear of the compound. You don't have to stay here to use them. Buy shower tickets (*xizao piao*) for Y1.50 FEC at reception. The shower is a great meeting-place for travellers to exchange the latest news or brag about reaching places in Tibet no-one has heard about. The laundry service here is not cheap but it is efficient. Each time I came back from a trip out of town, I'd take a shower, dump an evil-smelling bag of sweat-soaked, dust-encrusted washing and stay elsewhere. In the winter, higher room prices include a heating supplement and, reportedly, the shower closes down. The restaurant serves plain, Chinese food. Buy meal tickets (fan piao) for Y2 at reception.

Places to Stay – top end

The *Lhasa Hotel* is the flagship hotel, Lhasa's lap of luxury, strategically placed between the Norbulinka and the Potala. US$8 million in foreign currency reserves were used to purchase the latest in foreign plumbing gadgetry. Nearly 2000 workers and technicians from Jiangsu province toiled to complete this three-building complex in the nick of time for the autonomy celebrations in September 1985. Every single item required for construction was lugged overland from China. The hotel boasts over 400 rooms and 1000 beds. All bedrooms have air-con, closed-circuit TV, telephone and, of course, oxygen supplies. There is an assortment of Chinese and western restaurants, bars, coffee shops, teahouses, ballrooms, a bank and a post office. If a yak messenger thunders into Lhasa bearing news of your fabulous inheritance, you might care to take up residence in one of the two-storey 'presidential villas', specially reserved for heads of state or visiting dignitaries.

Despite token bows to Tibetan architecture this remains a stolidly Chinese edifice and when the first foreign tourists occupy their rooms, they can expect no less than US$100-a-day price tags.

The Tibet Guest House right next to the Lhasa Hotel, scheduled for completion at the end of 1985, will have 220 beds.

No 3 Guest House (tel 22225) is still the domain of tour groups. It is a ridiculous six km out of town and grossly overpriced at US$100 per day for bed and board. Inside the dreary compound is a shop, the local CITS office and a clubhouse with a bar. Tour groups are shown videos of the Panchen Lama. Limited medical facilities are available (tel 24037).

Places to Eat

The food situation in Lhasa has improved. A year or so ago there were just a couple of restaurants – now hardly a month goes by without the opening of another eatery. Since most of the food in Lhasa is trucked in from China, it's not surprising that meals are relatively expensive, and that the cuisine available is not madly exciting. All restaurants serve either Sichuan or Muslim dishes.

There are no restaurants specialising in Tibetan food which is restricted to a few dishes like *momo* (dumplings) and *tukpa* (noodles with meat). Nobody seems to mind if you bring your own bottles of beer, plastic containers of *chang* (Tibetan beer) or cans of food (tinned fruit is pleasant as a dessert).

No 1 Guest House has a restaurant serving standard fare suited to the taste of Lhasa's Chinese ex-pats. *Snowlands Hotel* and the *Banak Shol Hotel* both have more imaginative restaurants where you choose your own ingredients and the way in which you want them cooked. The dining-rooms are popular meeting-places which stay open until late. Some westerners have put together an unusual creation here – yakburgers! This is a yak-meat and onion mix with bread, but no ketchup.

The Tasty Restaurant (on the left hand side of XingFu DongLu, about 200 metres before the Banak Shol Hotel) is a lively place with the usual system where you go into the kitchen to choose ingredients from bowls of scallions, garlic, peanuts, green beans, tinned bamboo slices, eggs, diced yak meat, tinned mushrooms and greens. A large meal will cost about Y3. The dumplings are good if they are fresh. Tea is brought round to the tables.

The one problem with this place (as opposed to the other places mentioned) is that you eat your meal amidst what can only be described as a circus. Beggars scrounge the scraps which are scraped into bowls – some of them are obviously pilgrims from remote places who have made it to Lhasa but run out of funds. Kids beg for pens by making a scribbling motion in their palm which becomes obnoxious when thrust between your chopsticks and your face. Meanwhile cripples will hunch over your table intent on swiping an empty beer bottle to get the deposit back, whilst beneath the table, snapping away between your feet, are dogs of all shapes and sizes. Once you've finished though, you can have fun watching how the others react under attack!

The Halal Restaurant (next to the cinema, diagonally across the street from the Tasty Restaurant) is a Muslim outfit with excellent noodles (*lamian*) and lotus-seed tea.

The Sichuan Restaurant (opposite the Banak Shol Hotel) has a menu and the food, particularly the dumplings, is good. If you don't want it too hot, say *bu tai la*.

The Dharkay Restaurant (turn right outside the Banak Shol Hotel, then right again at the T-junction and it's on your left 100 metres down the road) is run by an old Chinaman who came to Lhasa over 30 years ago, married a Tibetan and stayed. Travellers feed the cassette recorder with their tapes and create an atmosphere reminiscent of Kathmandu as it was many aeons ago. An excellent dish here is the local fish done in a sweet and sour sauce. Pork and peanuts (*gong bao rou ding*) is also good. A kettle of *chang* is Y2.

Try Barkhor Bazaar and the area around the mosque (look for blue flags with red Chinese characters) for Muslim teahouses and restaurants where you can have noodles, lotus-seed tea or even mint tea. Street stalls and small places tucked down alleys are always interesting spots to meet the locals over a bowl of noodles and a container or two of *chang*.

Night Life & Entertainment

Night life in Lhasa is low-key and impromptu. Videos are the latest rage and films (mostly kung-fu) are usually advertised on boards outside houses on the streets near the Banak Shol Hotel and Snowlands Hotel. There's a cinema close to the Banak Shol Hotel and another opposite the Tibetan Hospital. Discos and dances take place on Saturday and Sunday nights at various locations around the Barkhor area. Ask at the Banak Shol Hotel or Snowlands Hotel for the precise time and location of the weekly bop.

The night of a full moon sees packs of dogs and restless travellers roaming around Lhasa. Others spend the evening sampling *chang* at stalls and stumbling round the Barkhor in slow and erratic circles. Street lighting is just a glimmer, so watch out for fast-moving Khampas on bikes. Keep an eye open for packs of dogs in the shadows: if someone treads on a dog it will probably shoot off like a rocket and sink its fangs into the nearest person – not always the perpetrator!

Tibetans love picnics. At weekends and on public holidays, they head out for the nearest park, lake or river armed with plastic containers of *chang*, thermoses of butter tea, *tsampa*, biscuits and a make-shift tent to enjoy themselves singing and dancing. I lost count of the number of times I was beckoned to join a group for non-stop hospitality and laughter.

Photo studios in Lhasa offer cheap amusement too. You can have your picture taken sitting behind a cardboard cut-out of a MiG fighter, a Shanghai sedan or even the Potala. Try the photo stalls in front of the Potala or the studios on JieFang Lu and RenMin Lu. Film development costs Y1.5 plus Y0.30 per print (black and white with frilly edges).

Shopping & Supplies

Lhasa does not have the facilities of large Chinese cities, so don't expect to be able to buy vital items of food, clothing, medicine and photo equipment. Bring

Top: Potala Palace, Lhasa (MB)
Bottom: Yak cheese and yak butter in Barkhor Bazaar, Lhasa (MB)

Top: Jokhang Temple, Lhasa (MB)
Left: Dalai Lama's residence, Summer Palace (Norbulinka) (MB)
Right: Nomad women, Barkhor Bazaar, Lhasa (MB)

everything with you. If you plan to make Lhasa a base for long trips, use your hotel baggage room as a supply depot.

The Friendship Store is a large building on RenMin Lu, about 100 metres past the No 1 Guest House, in the direction of the Jokhang. Opening hours vary, but the core time is from 9.30 am to 4.30 pm, including Sundays. The selection is sparse and prices are relatively high. The first floor has cosmetics, stationery and canned foods. The *FangFang* lip salve sold here in small, pink sticks is good to stop your lips cracking and you can get gauze facemasks for the dust. Packs of instant noodles, tins of pineapple slices, bars of chocolate and peanut nougat are useful items for trips out of Lhasa. The second floor has clothing. The third floor is the pricey part for foreigners and sells T-shirts (Yak, Everest and Potala), sweets, canned drinks, jam, peanuts, glucose biscuits, foreign smokes, slides and postcards. To the right of the entrance to the Friendship Store is another shop which has a selection of fruit, fish and meat in tins.

There are several bakeries in Lhasa. One is in Barkhor Bazaar, another is diagonally across the street from the Friendship Store and yet another is next to Snowlands Hotel. The main department store is Lhasa is on RenMin Lu, opposite XinHua Bookstore. Water bottles are sold here for Y1.90. The carpet factory in the east of town, on YanHe DongLu, sells unexceptional carpets. Some are not Tibetan, but Chinese in style. Tibetan dragons have four claws, Chinese have five. There are at least two boot factories in Lhasa. One is near the mosque, the other is right next to the Dharkay Restaurant. Leather boots take a week to make and, depending on the style, cost between Y30 and Y50. Colourful Tibetan boots with curled toes can be bought made-to-measure or in Barkhor Bazaar. Some visitors also buy local cloth and ask a tailor to make a *chuba* (a wonderfully warm, wrap-around, Tibetan coat). Total cost for cloth and tailoring is about Y80.

Barkhor Bazaar is the main hunting ground for shoppers. Tibetan handicrafts include rolls of striped cloth, daggers, religious ornaments, tinder boxes, tsampa bowls, bracelets, carpets, boots, rosaries, purses, rings, prayer-flags and prayer-wheels. Old coins, turquoise, amber Tibetan stone-eye (stones with circular patterns) and coral are also offered here. Local food items sold here include puffed rice, wheat, barley, tsampa, yak butter, corn, dried apples, pears and nuts. Bargain for everything or, even better, try bartering with Dalai Lama pics, foreign coins, badges or clothing.

Getting There

Air Although there are supposed to be flights from Xian via Golmud to Lhasa, not many arrive from this direction. Most travellers arrive from Chengdu, where flights are more frequent. Official policy encourages the use of air routes and discourages land routes. Chengdu-Lhasa planes (one or two daily) leave Chengdu around 6.45 to 7.30 am, and get to Gonggar Airport around 9.30 am if there are no delays. The turbo-props take longer to get there and fly at lower altitudes. Jets used on the run are Boeing 707s, or the old Ilyushin 18s (Russian planes designed in the 1950s). Being tested on the run, to carry goods to Tibet, are Chinese-made Yun-8s, produced in Xian, and copied from western jets.

It is 1300 km non-stop from Taipingsi Airport in Chengdu to Gonggar Airport. The highest peak the jets fly over is 7756 metres (Mt Namche Barwa, in eastern Tibet). The cost of the flight is Y322 one-way, payable in FECs. Travellers, surcharged in FECs will find some solace in examining the geology of the Himalayan ranges of eastern Tibet – hundreds of km of snowy peaks and jagged granite outcrops, with sharply sculpted glaciers. Pilots flying the 'Hump' in WW II (from China to Burma) were given to reporting peaks in this range to be higher than Everest, and looking out the window will perhaps confirm how these misunderstandings came about (some sightings were hoaxes). The nearest that any traveller has got to beating the FEC payment for plane tickets was a student in China who paid half in FECs and half in RMB. The CAAC office is across the street from the Jinjiang Hotel in Chengdu.

CAAC buses to and from airports are free if you show your air ticket. The elevation change from Chengdu to Lhasa is around 3500 metres – a sharp difference, and you are likely to suffer from it.

Gonggar Airport Lhasa airport is *not* in Lhasa, but 96 km away at Gonggar. On arrival at the airport there will be buses waiting to take you on the 90 minute ride to Lhasa. Don't wait around at the airport for your baggage. It will be delivered separately, at least three hours later, to the CAAC office in Lhasa where you collect it.

Mercifully, asphalting of the road to the airport was completed in June 1985 as a special project for the autonomy celebration in September. If this had not been done, some of the first impressions made on visiting dignitaries would have been dents in their heads after being bounced into the roof of the bus. Prior to asphalting unsuspecting tourists fresh off the plane, eager to be enchanted by Tibet, were treated to a long and atrociously bumpy ride. Numerous foreign heads were launched against the bus roof. One lanky German cracked his neck and spent the rest of his painful time in Lhasa walking with a stoop!

Truck The major routes for trucking into Lhasa are as follows:

Sichuan-Tibet Highway (Chengdu-Chamdo-Lhasa)
Yunnan-Tibet Highway (Kunming-Dali-Markam-Lhasa)
Qinghai-Tibet Highway (Xining-Golmud-Lhasa)
Xinjiang-Tibet Highway (Kashgar-Shiquanhe-Lhasa)
Nepal-Tibet Highway (Zhangmu-Shigatse-Lhasa)

For details of these routes see separate sections in this book. Strictly speaking, foreigners are only officially tolerated on the Nepal-Tibet Highway and the Qinghai-Tibet Highway.

Bus Buses run on the Qinghai-Tibet and Qinghai-Sichuan highways. In 1985 the situation with buses was in a state of flux. In mid-1985 travellers could go to Lhasa, but were not permitted to leave from Lhasa, on the Qinghai-Tibet highway. In Lhasa, mid-1985, a traveller found a local to buy his ticket, however, no sooner had he boarded the bus than the driver shot off to Lhasa public security and unceremoniously dumped him there. Come September 1985, happy travellers were merrily buying their tickets in Lhasa and proceeding to Golmud with no problems. Perhaps the fact that Golmud had opened (to permit-holders) had something to do with it, since earlier, travellers had been turned back coming into Tibet by road. The situation got so confusing that some travellers left Lhasa in late 1985 not even knowing Golmud was open – and no-one asked for their permits anyway!

Yup, some strange things happen out there on the Golmud route. A Scandinavian was bouncing along on the back of the Golmud bus, headed for Lhasa, trying to keep his toes warm (the route is freezing) and trying not to throw up from the effects of altitude sickness. He decided to risk raising his bilious eyes, and there, in the dead centre of absolutely nowhere, was a mirage enveloped in a cloud of dust – a Fiat racing car bombing past the bus. Realising that he must have contracted some rare form of altitude sickness that included hallucinations, he wisely dropped his head again only to hear the shattering sound of another Fiat speeding by. Feverishly fumbling for his camera to try and prove possession of his mental faculties he was too late to capture the third and final mechanical monster roaring past.

Golmud-Lhasa or Lhasa-Golmud costs around Y60 on a bus; depending on the condition of the bus, it could take 30 to 50 hours straight through.

Getting Around

Bus Buses materialise at stops so infrequently that they are not a dependable means of transport in Lhasa.

Taxis & Rented Vehicles Taxis are expensive and in short supply. Apart from No 1 and No 3 Guest Houses which mainly organise tours, the only specialist taxi service in town is the *ChengGuanQu ChuZu QiChe GongCi*, about a five minute walk from Snowlands Hotel. This company has a notoriously battered vehicle pool including Shanghai and Warszawa limousines, Beijing jeeps (Chinese: *Beijing Jipu*), minibuses (Chinese: *Mianbao Che*), and an antique Austin Gypsy.

A Shanghai ride to Drepung Monastery costs Y32 return (Y16 one way) plus Y20 per hour of waiting time. Prices vary, but the basic rate per km for a minibus is Y1.80; for a Beijing jeep, Y1.20. It's best to book vehicles in advance. Additional charges are made for the number of passengers, the number of days travelled and for the return section of a one-way trip. For more info on vehicle rental options and pricing, refer to the Lhasa to Kathmandu section in the Nepal Route chapter. A second taxi service outfit was said to have opened in late 1985.

Bicycle This is really the best way to move, but take it very slowly until you have become accustomed to the altitude. The following places rent bikes:

No 3 Guest House,
No 1 Guest House (deposit Y50; bikes in reasonable condition at Y5 per day),
Snowlands Hotel (bikes in suicidal state at Y6 per day),

Banak Shol Hotel (bikes for Y6 per day).

Go early to have a good choice of bikes. Check your bike thoroughly *before* you leave, otherwise you are likely to end up in a tangle of metal with Chinese and Tibetan cyclists at the first crossroads. If left in the sun, over-inflated tyres are quick to explode at this altitude. Bike theft has reached epidemic proportions in Lhasa, so if you are out at night, wheel your bike inside the restaurant, hotel, or wherever you can keep an eye on it and, preferably, use a lock of your own as well as the fitted lock. I had a meal in a restaurant opposite the Banak Shol Hotel with a friend who had locked and parked his bike outside, about four metres behind our table. Within half an hour the lock had been picked, the bike stolen and the next day my friend had to forfeit his Y50 deposit.

On Sundays there is a bike market outside the main mosque – maybe this is where some of the stolen ones resurface. A bike in reasonable condition should cost about Y70. Make sure you get the licence and check its number with the number on the bike. When you leave Lhasa you can resell to a foreigner or a local. You can make a big saving on rental charges if you're staying a reasonable length of time.

Hitching This is an excellent way to travel a long distance across town or even further. A smile, a determined signal and you are off on a walking-tractor, riding on the back of a truck, riding pillion on a bike (hop off discreetly if 'cops' are around – it's sort of illegal) or bouncing along with a tractor and trailer.

Getting Away

Air There are flights to Chengdu, and in theory, to Xian (via Golmud). Tickets are sold at the CAAC office. Since Gonggar (Lhasa Airport) is 96 km out of Lhasa, and flights leave in the morning, passengers are usually required to stay overnight at the airport. The airport bus leaves from the CAAC office between 4 and 5 pm. On arrival at the airport hotel, a ramshackle collection of barracks, there is a long bout of queuing for bed tickets, bath tickets, food tickets ... the paper never ends. Beds cost Y4.50 each. Last minute packing comes to an abrupt halt at 10.30 pm, when the generator packs up for the night. No need to set your alarm – hotel staff and loudspeakers will turf you out of bed at 6.30 am. The electrical supply is totally at the discretion of hotel staff. Planes leave around 10 or 10.30 am and arrive in Chengdu about 2½ hours later.

Rented Vehicle For rentals to the Nepalese border, see the Lhasa to Kathmandu section of the Nepal Route chapter.

Truck Until recently it was quite easy to truck out of Lhasa, but the authorities have now advised depots not to take foreign guests. Checkpoints inside and outside Lhasa check whether you have an official ticket and will fine the driver if he has done a private deal. There is also now, apparently, a permit checkpoint on the road to the airport.

However, some trucks leave in the middle of the night when officialdom is tucked up in bed, and once you are out of Lhasa, there are less complications. Zêtang, Shigatse and Gyantse (to name a few) all have depots with trucks doing long distance runs. If you walk out very early over the Lhasa River Bridge (for the Sichuan Highway) or pass the checkpoint at Doilungdêqên (for the Qinghai Highway or Shigatse), you should be able to hitch a ride.

There are plenty of truck depots or departure points dotted around Lhasa. Some depots specialise, others serve several destinations. The following list is a rough guide only:

To Golmud The No 1, 2, 4 and 5 truck depots; truck depot in front of Potala;

truck depot at junction of XingFu XiLu and MinZu Lu; truck depot on YanHe DongLu just past Bank of China. Some Golmud trucks leave from Zêtang (No 1 Truck depot) and there are plenty from Shigatse which go via Yangbajain. Some Lhasa trucks leave in the afternoon, spend the night at Yangbajain and then do a straight run to Golmud.

To Sichuan Most of the trucks only run as far as Chamdo. From there you find another ride to Chengdu. The No 6 truck depot has trucks running in this direction. In Zêtang, the No 2 truck depot has trucks running the Chamdo route.

To Xinjiang There are very few trucks running this route direct from Lhasa. Look for large, new Isuzu trucks with Uighur (looks like Arabic) writing on the cab doors. Try the truck depot at the junction of XingFu XiLu and MinZu Lu or the area around the mosque. There is a hotel, just past the mosque, with a courtyard used as a truckstop by Muslim drivers. Trucks also run to Xinjiang from Shigatse.

To Shannan area, Shigatse and Gyantse Try the No 2 Guest House – go through the entrance gate and turn left into the small, parking area. Trucks for these destinations also leave from the truck depot just past the Bank of China, on YanHe DongLu.

Bus The main bus station (tel 22757) operates buses to destinations within Tibet and to Sichuan and Qinghai provinces. The ticket clerks are not always keen to sell tickets to foreigners but will yield under pressure. Get to the ticket office before 9 am. The following is a rough timetable for selected destinations (check with the ticket clerk for changes in departure days or additional buses):

destination	departure	price	distance
Chengdu	Friday	120.80	2416
Chamdo	Saturday	56.40	1127
Nyingchi	Friday	21.20	424
Liuyuan	Wednesday	91.00	1820
Zêtang	Tuesday & Saturday	9.80	195
Shigatse	Friday & Tuesday	17.80	355

All prices are in RMB and tickets are sold the day before departure.

Apparently, the ticket office also sells tickets for truck passengers (slightly cheaper than the bus) but they are not keen to sell to foreigners. Ask at the office in front of the waiting hall if you want to rent an entire bus (mostly vintage bone-shakers carrying a maximum of 25 passengers) with a driver. Several groups of foreigners have done this to make trips to the Nepalese border via Gyantse, Shigatse, Sakya, Lhazê, and Xêgar. Rental charges are calculated at Y0.025 per km, Y1 per hour and Y1 per day per seat. This works out at about Y2500 RMB for six days.

The airport bus is intended for CAAC passengers but you might wriggle on and spend the night at the airport hotel before continuing to Samye or Zêtang the next morning. Perhaps you are seeing off/meeting a friend ... The pilgrim bus to Ganden which leaves daily at 6.30 am from Barkhor Bazaar (opposite carpet corner) is also a possible method to get out for some serious hitching on the Sichuan route. Get off the bus on the main road before it turns off to the left and starts to climb up to Ganden.

Yarlung Valley & Monasteries & Sites

GANDEN MONASTERY

Tsong Khapa founded this, the first Gelukpa monastery, in 1409 on one of the most spectacular sites in Tibet, about 40 km east of Lhasa near Dagzê. Here too, work has begun to restore the damage wreaked by the Cultural Revolution. So extensive is the damage, one might easily think Ganden had been subjected to saturation aerial bombardment. The four main temples now house about 200 monks who are the remnants of a population that once exceeded 4000. The views from Ganden, down into the Kyichu Valley and across to the distant snowcaps, are quite exceptional. When I went, I hiked around the mountain tops and saw several sky burials.

There is no official accommodation, although you might be able to arrange some with the monks or use one of the ruined buildings (if you can stand the cold). Take food and water.

To reach Ganden you can take a pilgrim bus, pilgrim truck or hitch. If you hitch, you should be out early on the road, just past the bridge outside Lhasa. From Dagzê it's a long climb up the mountain (at least two hours). Pilgrim trucks for Ganden leave at about 6.30 am from the nomad encampments in the north of Lhasa and from the square outside the Jokhang – days and times of departures are flexible, so check beforehand. Trucks usually return around 3 pm. A pilgrim bus leaves daily at 6.30 am from Barkhor Bazaar (opposite carpet corner and the monument). Be there early and sit on the left; it costs Y7 return. The bus takes two hours and returns around 3 pm. If you want to stay longer at Ganden, you can climb down the mountain and hitch back.

MINDOLIN MONASTERY

Mindolin, one of the most important Nyingmapa (Red Hat Sect) monasteries, was founded in 1671 by Dieda Linba. The four main temples, one of which houses a fine statue of Sakyamuni, are being restored. The monastery is approximately mid-way between Zhanang and Samye ferry. Ask the bus driver for Mindolin Gompa and be fully prepared with food, water and clothing as it is a long trek away from the road.

SAMYE MONASTERY

Samye was built between 763 and 775 by Padmasambhava (also known by Tibetans as Lopon Rinpoche), during the reign of King Trisong Detsen. It is said that Samye was modeled on the university of Otantapuri in India and planned as a representation of the universe. The main temple in the centre corresponded to Mount Rirab (the centre of the cosmos), whilst four pagodas (white, blue, green and red) represented the four worlds to the north, south, east and west. Smaller temples represented the islands between the worlds and two temples to the north and south of the main temple represented the moon and sun respectively. The main temple, dedicated to Chenrezig, has three storeys which each have a different architectural style. The lower storey is Tibetan, the middle storey is Chinese and the top storey is Indian. Once reputed to be a forest of 108 temples, Samye is still one of the most imposing sights in Tibet. Reconstruction is now in progress to repair damage done during the Cultural Revolution and some temples still function as granaries – you literally have to wade through the grain to look at the frescoes.

The chief monk is not always willing to open up the higher storeys of the main temple to individual visitors and you may be told that *each photo* taken inside the temple will cost Y10. In contrast, the Tibetans renovating other temples are

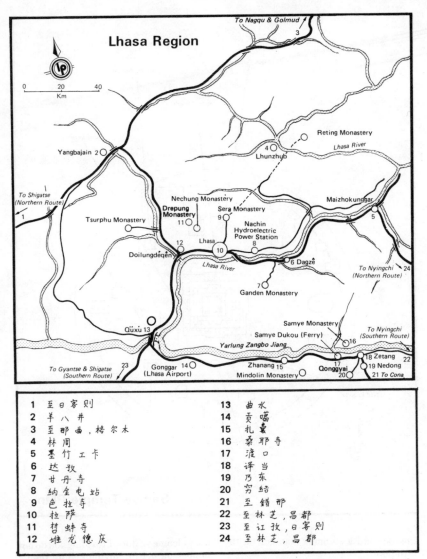

Lhasa Region

To Nagqu & Golmud
3

0   20   40
Km

Reting Monastery

Lhasa River

Yangbajain 2

4
Lhunzhub

To Shigatse
(Northern Route)
1

Maizhokunggar

Nechung Monastery

Drepung Monastery
11

Sera Monastery
9

Nachin
Hydroelectric
Power Station

5

Tsurphu Monastery

12

Lhasa
10

8

To Nyingchi
(Northern Route)
24

Doilungdeqen

Lhasa River

6 Dagzê

7

Ganden Monastery

Samye Monastery

To Nyingchi
(Southern Route)

Samye Dukou (Ferry)
16

Qüxü 13

Yarlung Zangbo Jiang

18 Zetang
22
19 Nedong

17

To Gyantse & Shigatse
(Southern Route)
23

Gonggar 14
(Lhasa Airport)

Zhanang 15

Mindolin Monastery

Qonggyai
20

21 To Cona

1	至日喀则	13	曲水
2	羊八井	14	贡嘎
3	至那曲,格尔木	15	扎囊
4	林周	16	桑那寺
5	墨竹工卡	17	渡口
6	达孜	18	泽当
7	甘丹寺	19	乃东
8	纳金电站	20	穷结
9	色拉寺	21	至错那
10	拉萨	22	至林芝,昌都
11	哲蚌寺	23	至江孜,日喀则
12	堆龙德庆	24	至林芝,昌都

very friendly and will usually let you wander around and give you butter tea. In the valley to the north behind Samye there are said to be more temples and the view of Samye from the top of the mountains to the east (follow the pilgrim tracks up to the chortens) is spectacular. South of the main temple in Samye is another large temple – this temple (*Khumsum Sankalin*) is still full of grain but it contains superb

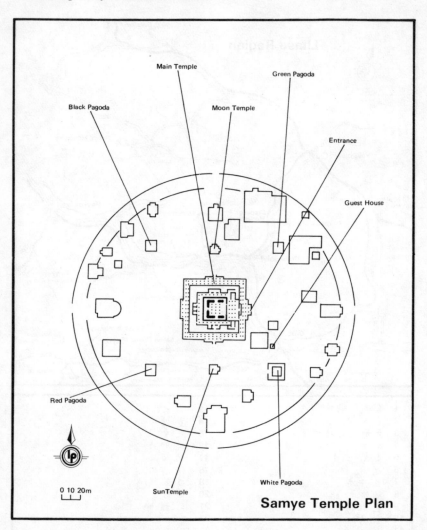

Black Pagoda

Main Temple

Moon Temple

Green Pagoda

Entrance

Guest House

Red Pagoda

Sun Temple

White Pagoda

0 10 20m

Samye Temple Plan

frescoes and a stunning mandala on the fifth floor.

The Only Place to Stay

The only accommodation at Samye is in a small courtyard near the entrance to the main temple. The old lady in charge does not welcome visitors. Providing you do not impose on her for anything more than a roof over your head, she will grudgingly give you a bare, four-bed room (Y2 per bed). If she asks for a letter of introduction ... well, your passport is near enough. No light (take candles) or food is available here. Hot water may be forthcoming if you can get the old girl to smile.

Getting There & Away

Getting to Samye is quite an experience and is not advisable for those averse to the fun of rough travel. There are sometimes pilgrim buses from Lhasa to Samye which leave in the afternoon, overnight near the ferry and then wait to pick you up from the ferry next day in the late afternoon. You can also take the bus from Lhasa in the direction of Zêtang and ask to get off at the ferry (Samye Dukou) which is between km markers 89 and 90 (distance marked from Qüxü Bridge). Another possibility is to take the airport bus from Lhasa to the airport, stay overnight at the airport hotel and then get out early to hitch.

The ferry is a makeshift affair, using small boats with outboard motors, which takes you across the Yarlung Zangbo (Brahmaputra). In theory, there are crossings at 9 am, 12 noon, 3 pm and 6 pm but ... engines break down, important cadres keep the boats waiting for hours and, sometimes, boats get stuck on sandbanks in mid-stream. The crossing fee appears to be Y0.50 for locals and Y1 for foreigners and Chinese cadres. Be prepared to wade to get into the boat.

The trip – what a trip – takes about an hour and you can lie back on sacks of flour gazing at the sky and the mountains or watch their reflections in the water. On the other side you may have to wade ashore. Everybody has fun. The Tibetan women laugh themselves silly if you give them a piggyback to the shore. Onward travel to Samye (there is no road, just a track) takes about 45 minutes, costs Y1 and is provided by a horse and cart or a tractor and trailer. The cart is a peaceful ride but tends to get stuck in sand. The tractor also gets stuck occasionally but it is quicker, unless a tyre blows ... in which case you have a long walk ahead.

South of the main temple in Samye is another large temple, **Khumsum Sankalin** – about 10 minutes on foot. A tractor or

Guru Padmasambhava

horse-cart usually leaves from here at 10 am to catch the noon ferry back to the other side where you can hitch back to Lhasa or continue to Zêtang (about 30 km). A combination of blown tyres and broken engines left me waiting on the riverside for five hours. Apart from getting my feet badly sunburnt, I had a great time with a whole squadron of girls and grannies from Nêdong drinking butter tea, munching tsampa, getting drunk on chang and paddling with the local dogs. On foot, Samye to Lhasa is about a three or four-day trek.

ZÊTANG & NÊDONG

These two towns are about 195 km from Lhasa in the Yarlung Valley which is considered the cradle of Tibetan culture. Zêtang, the capital of Shannan prefecture, has merged with Nêdong into a sprawl of Tibetan and Chinese buildings. There are various sights to see around these two places and they can be used as a base for trips to Qonggyai, Samye, Cona and further towards Chamdo.

Technically, you need a permit (there are rumours that this area will be open

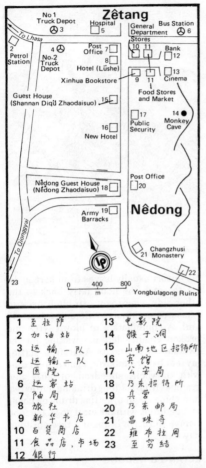

Map Legend (Zêtang / Nêdong)

1	至拉薩	13	电影院
2	加油站	14	猴子洞
3	运输一队	15	山南地区招待所
4	运输二队	16	宾馆
5	医院	17	公安局
6	运客站	18	乃东招待所
7	邮局	19	兵营
8	旅社	20	乃东邮局
9	新华书店	21	昌珠寺
10	百货商店	22	雍布拉岗
11	食品店，市场	23	至穷结
12	银行		

soon but Lhasa PSB still tends to refuse permission) but if you stay away from officials and official places, nobody seems concerned.

Things to See

In Zêtang itself, the market is worth a visit since all sorts of Tibetans trek in from outlying areas. Behind the hospital there is the **First Field in Tibet**. According to legend, this field was planted by Chenrezig's monkey incarnation, Trehu. Tibetan

farmers make an annual pilgrimage here before the planting season, to take back a handful of earth which they sprinkle on their own fields to increase fertility.

Monkey Cave This cave is one of three in the mountainside east of the town. Allow three hours for the stiff climb and follow the piles of stones left by pilgrims or ask a local to guide you.

For Tibetans this cave has great importance as it is connected with the legend of their origin. According to this legend, before humans came to Tibet, it was a land peopled by spirits. Then Chenrezig and his consort Dolma decided to send incarnations. Chenrezig's incarnation was a chaste monkey, Trehu Changchub Sempa. Dolma's incarnation was Tag-senmo, a beautiful ogress with a taste for cannibalism. Trehu was quite content to sit and meditate in his cave. But, one day, when he heard Senmo weeping he felt pity and went to investigate. Senmo explained that she was lonely and needed Trehu as a husband. Trehu was not keen on the idea but Chenrezig advised him that it was time for Tibet to have children so he should live with Senmo. Senmo and Trehu then married and had six children. According to one form of the legend, the children grew up to found the six different types of people found in Tibet today. In Tibetan, Zêtang means 'playground', a reference to the place where the six children played.

Changzhusi Monastery This monastery is about five km south of Zêtang. It was founded during the reign of Songtsen Gampo. According to legend, many years ago this area was a vast expanse of water, inhabited by a deadly dragon. Songtsen Gampo decided to reclaim the land beneath the water, in order to found a city. He enlisted the help of two magicians who asked a roc (a mythical bird) to slay the dragon. The roc then beat the dragon over the head with its wings and killed it. Seven days later the waters dried up and a

Yongbulagong before destruction

grateful Songtsen Gampo built the monastery.

In the 14th and 18th centuries the monastery was enlarged. At present all the buildings are under repair. The main temple, three-storeys high, has a large Sutra Chanting Hall in the centre of the ground floor. A small temple at the rear of the walled compound has some interesting thangkas.

Yongbulagong According to legend, this was the first building in Tibet, constructed as a palace for the first king, Nyatri Tsanpo. Yongbulagong is on a mountaintop about 10 km past Changzhusi monastery. If you hitch, get out on the road early as traffic is infrequent. This tiny palace must have been an imposing sight once, but most of it is now in ruins.

Other I was told about, but was unable to visit, two other monasteries near Nêdong: **Zecuobasi** monastery built by a king of Nêdong in 1356; **Zantangsi** monastery (also called **Yuyi Lhakhang**), three km south-west of Nêdong, in the village of Zantang.

Places to Stay

A new hotel (still under construction) next to the Zêtang Guest House will certainly be the plushest pad in town. At present it looks remarkably like a two-funnelled ship stranded behind steel railings – a fine example of the incongruity of modern Chinese architecture in Tibet.

The *Zêtang Guest House* has no character but clean rooms. It's Y4 FEC for a bed in a four-bed room. The manager is meticulous about checking your credentials. Buy meal tickets at reception; breakfast from 8 to 8.30 am, lunch from 12 noon to 12.30 pm, dinner from 7 to 7.30 pm. The shop in the foyer is well stocked with beer, sweets etc (opening hours: 1 to 3.30 pm and 7 to 8 pm). There is a large truck park in front which is a good place to find lifts to Lhasa, Golmud, Gyantse, Nyingchi ... Ask the man in the office next to the gate if he can connect you with a driver. It may also be possible to hire a Landcruiser here for a visit to Samye, Qonggyai or Mindolin. Watch out for flooding! One night when I was there, a massive thunderstorm followed by a catastrophic downpour left the truck park under a metre of water. The desperate management smashed a hole through the outside wall to pull the plug on their problem. As a result, the Tibetan construction workers who had been living next door in makeshift tents literally floated off down the road.

There are various hotels near the market which are primarily intended for construction workers from China. You get a bed for Y2 in a no frills 10-bed dormitory. *Nêdong Guest House* is a Tibetan-style building opposite Nêdong Post Office. This place is essentially a restaurant but the friendly Tibetan family in charge will fix a bed with a mattress in a room upstairs for Y1.50 – once they get over the shock that you actually want to stay there. Admittedly it is very basic and fly-blown, but it has what the Chinese concrete hutches lack – character. In the evening, giggling Tibetan girls from the construction sites drop in for a cup of tea whilst horsemen (tough looking dudes from the Wild East) hitch their horses to the doorpost and order plates of *tukpa* (meat and noodles). Meanwhile, across the street, hordes of Tibetans cluster round a TV to watch a video about the Gestapo. Where am I?

Getting There

From Lhasa main bus station there are buses to Zêtang or you can hitch on trucks. Some travellers were able to hire a Landrover from the Taxi Company in Lhasa for a four-day trip to Samye, Zêtang and Qonggyai. Not a bad idea, since transport in this area can be a real pain if you are dependent on local buses and trucks.

Getting Away

Buses to Lhasa leave most days at 8.30 am from the bus station. I only took the bus as far as Samye ferry, but the decrepit old banger took four hours and as many breakdowns to cover 30 km! If you want to hitch to Lhasa, try asking drivers at the Zêtang Guest House or at the petrol station about three km out of town on the road to Lhasa. The No 1 Truck Depot has trucks to Lhasa and Golmud. The No 2 Truck Depot has trucks to Nyingchi and Chamdo.

QONGGYAI

Qonggyai, about 28 km south west of Zêtang, was the ancient capital of the Tubo dynasty. When King Songtsen Gampo moved the capital to Lhasa, Qonggyai lost influence as a centre for government, culture and trade. Apart from a ruined palace (Qingwa Dazegong) with Tibet's much smaller equivalent of the Great Wall, the main attractions here are the tombs of the Tibetan kings.

The Tombs of the Tibetan Kings

The Tibetans did not give their kings a sky burial but chose interment in tombs instead. Experts differ in their explanations: some believe this was due to the cultural influence of the Tang dynasty in China, others consider this was a result of Buddhist influence. Both of these explanations have been undermined by an archeological survey of Tibet, started in 1984, which has discovered over 1000 graves in 20 groups near Nêdong. Since these graves belong to a neolithic culture which flourished over 3000 years ago, it appears that burial in the ground was a common practice long before the Tibetan kings were interred in tombs.

Historical records speak of 13 tombs at Qonggyai, but only nine have been found. The easiest tomb to identify (if you can find a guide, then so much the better) is that of Songtsen Gampo which has a small temple on top containing, amongst others, images of Songtsen Gampo, Princess Wen Cheng and Princess Bhrikuti.

Getting There

To reach Qonggyai, you can hitch out on the road, organise a Landcruiser from the Guest House in Zêtang or ask truck drivers at Zêtang market. It may be possible to stay in Qonggyai but take food and water.

DESTINATIONS WITH TOUGH ACCESS

Cona

Cona lies in a mountain valley close to the Bhutanese border, about 211 km south of Zêtang. Travellers reported that the lush scenery is similar to that around Yadong. Try hitching a ride with the trucks parked near the market or station yourself on the road from Nêdong to Qungdogyang. Be prepared for a long wait – traffic is sparse on this road.

Reting

Reting, about 150 km north-east of Lhasa (near Lhünzhub), was a famous monastery of the Kadampa sect and was founded in 1056 by Dronton. To reach Reting you might be able to hire a jeep, take the bus to Lhünzhub (and then trek the rest) or trek the whole way.

Tsurphu

Tsurphu (also called Tulung Churbu Gompa) lies about 70 km north-east of Lhasa. It was a famous monastery of the Kagyupa sect. To reach Tsurphu you might be able to hire a jeep, hitch along the main road towards Yangbajain then trek the rest, or trek the lot.

Gyantse & Chumbi Valley

GYANTSE

Gyantse (Gyangzê) is the fourth largest city in Tibet (after Shigatse and Chamdo). It is small as cities go (population perhaps 10,000) and largely Tibetan in character – for a change. Strategically sited at a junction between Shigatse and Lhasa, and lying along the caravan routes from Sikkim and Bhutan to the south, Gyantse assumed an important role as a military centre, and as a market-town – particularly for wool and handicrafts. In the 1870s the British dispatched a pundit for Tibetan reconnaissance – he was designated by the codename A K (real name Kishen Singh). Here's his description (1878):

Giangche, a small town on the right bank of the Pena Nang Chu river. The town is situated about two small hills which lie east and west, and are united by a saddle; the western hill is further connected with a chain of mountains to the north. On the eastern hill, which is about 600 feet above the surrounding plain, is a large fort ... and on the western hill is a Gomba inhabited by five hundred Dabas. In this Gomba there is a Chiorten, called Pangon Chiorten, which is considered by the Tibetans a most holy place. Besides the fort and temple, there are about one thousand dwelling houses on three sides of the double hill. Woollen cloth called Nhambu is manufactured. There is a large market; and traders from Nepal and India reside here.

A K's compass points are a bit off, but if you realign those, the description is still a feasible orientation to Gyantse. The town used to be under control of the monastery, which owned the marketplace and collected

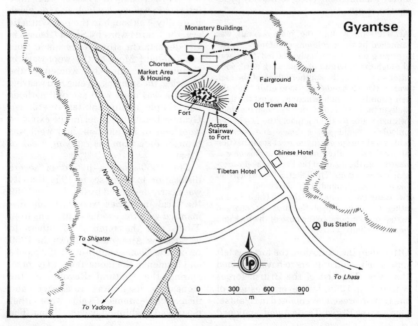

Gyantse

- Monastery Buildings
- Chorten Market Area & Housing
- Fort
- Access Stairway to Fort
- Fairground
- Old Town Area
- Chinese Hotel
- Tibetan Hotel
- Bus Station
- Nyang Chu River
- To Shigatse
- To Yadong
- To Lhasa

0   300   600   900
m

rents from merchants. At one time there were up to 3000 monks in Gyantse.

There is a large area under cultivation around Gyantse and dominating the town and countryside for miles is the great fort. This Dzong was built in the 14th century and the whole town used to be surrounded by a wall about three km in length. The Tibetans maintained a garrison of 500 soldiers in Gyantse. The fort guarded the main Lhasa road, and the Younghusband expedition of 1904 found the fort a formidable obstacle. One of the British officers described it as 'the strongest fort in Central Asia'. After several weeks of siege, the British decided to storm the fort. It was estimated there were some 5000 Tibetans guarding it, although their technology for warfare was somewhat limited. Earlier the Tibetans had showered the British at Chang Lo (below Gyantse) with small cannon-fire – when the Tibetans ran out of lead, they used copper balls. Peter Fleming (*Bayonets to Lhasa*) picks up the story:

At 0400 on 6 July the main assault was launched by three columns of infantry ... the storming-parties gradually blasted their way through the labyrinth of stonework until, soon after sunrise ... the southern flank of the rock was in British hands ... Soon after 1500 the ten-pounders went into action against the thick walls of the Fort ... and soon, through the cloud of dust made by their impact, the fascinated onlookers could see a black and steadily widening hole appear in the great stone bastion above them ... Presently, a dull explosion was heard from the inside of the Fort as the powder-magazine went up. The Tibetan fire, which had been furious, immediately slackened off, and two companies – one from the 8th Gurkhas, the other from the Royal Fusiliers ... charged across open ground to the base of the rock and began to climb ...

Other than the explosion, the fort was left untouched – and appears to have remained that way. The last of the British forces withdrew in 1908, but several vestiges of the British presence remained in Gyantse. One was the British Trade Agent, stationed

with an Indian guard in a small fort just south of Gyantse (there were other trade-agents at Yadong and Gartok). Another was the telegraph line through to India from Gyantse, which remained the property of the Indian Government (the line from Gyantse to Lhasa became Tibetan property). The Tibetans at first did not understand the purpose of the telegraph line, which came with the British Field Office in 1903-4. When questioned as to what it was, the British engineers said it was a device to enable them to find their way back to India when they withdrew, as they had no decent maps. Also established in Gyantse was a British post office (1906), a British school for upper-crust Tibetan children (1921), and a British wool-agent station.

By the 1940s a great deal of Gyantse's (and Tibet's) sheep-wool production was slated for export to British India (where it was eventually woven into warm socks for the British navy?). There was little interest in yak-wool, which was too harsh in quality – although in the pre-synthetic era, the beards worn by Santa Clauses in US department stores were made from yak tail-hair! Most of the wool-work in Gyantse was done by women – the shearing, the spinning, dyeing and weaving – and it was done with age-old methods and simple equipment (as it still is). Gyantse became a funnel for the export of wool due to its location, and wool was brought here from the outlying areas of Tibet.

The 1950s saw a period of severe dislocation in Gyantse. In 1954 the city was nearly destroyed by flooding; in 1959 the local industries were virtually dismantled with the exodus of artisans from Tibet, and the removal of others to workcamps. After putting down the 1959 revolt, the Chinese imprisoned 400 monks and laymen in the monastery at Gyantse. During the Cultural Revolution, the monastery itself was ransacked and dismantled – items of value were either destroyed or shipped back to China. The chorten, however, was spared. In recent years, or more particularly since 1980, the Chinese have attempted to stimulate handicraft production, for which Gyantse is, or was, famous. So the centuries old carpet centre at Gyantse has been revived, with weavers exempt from taxes.

On the agricultural score, the Chinese have had less success. Or have they? According to a *China Daily* story, farmers in Gyantse County jettisoned or buried fertiliser and insecticides donated by the state (killing of any life, including insects, is sacrilegious in Tibet). The *China Daily* goes on to say that this all happened before 1979, when farmers planted only on auspicious dates and paid lamas for incantations to drive out pests. To induce rain in times of drought (or if threatened with a smallpox epidemic) a huge volume of the *Kanjur* used to be lugged around the city. It took at least two men to carry the sacred volume around. Then, magically, in 1980, the Chinese turned the Gyantse County farmers onto science and modern agricultural techniques! The *China Daily* story ends with a typical got-rich farmer story. This one reaped a bumper harvest under the responsibility system and translated it into a truck, several tractors and other items to add to his collection of cassette players, bikes and TV set.

Information

There is a medical clinic at the north-east end of Gyantse, at the edge of the old town. Dust can be a severe problem. Sometimes clouds of it sweep across the plains and you can barely make out a metre ahead. Get yourself a snorkel and mask. You don't really need flippers. Gyantse sees about 30 mm of rain a year and most of that falls in July and August.

Pango Chörten

The main sight of Gyantse is the immense chorten, or *Kumbum* (outsized chorten, or pagoda of 100,000 images). It was built by Rapten Kunsang Phapa (1389-1442).

Chortens are receptacles of worship, similar to the stupas of India, with many sacred objects within: statues, books, frescoes, and items of gold and silver. The Gyantse chorten is a deluxe model, and is quite innovative in its architecture – it has about 70 interlocking chapels that you see as you spiral your way to the golden plume at the top. Each chapel is richly, often grotesquely, decorated with thousands of frescoes, statues and artifacts, and lined with Buddhist texts inscribed in Sanskrit.

It is not possible here, unfortunately, to identify the demonic gods that lurk within the chapels. To consolidate their hold over the population the ruling lamas of Tibet devised a fearsome array of wrathful deities, demons and monsters, which they threatened to let loose on any Tibetan foolish enough to wander from the path laid down by the ruling class. It was a kind of rule of the ignorant by terror, and perambulating through the chapels you will get a good idea of the demonic forces at work – some deities seem to like collecting human skulls. Under the top section, eyes are painted on four sides of an exterior rectangular section – they represent those of Buddha.

In aerial perspective, the chorten is supposedly shaped like a Mandala, the embodiment of the Lamaist universe. Pilgrims circumambulate this giant wedding-cake; the inner spiralling circuit of the chorten is a meditational aid to enlightenment, with the top canopied section representing the highest plane of wisdom. As you wind your dizzy way through to the top, you begin to appreciate this principle. Our small group, however, had a rather different experience than enlightenment – we carried on a running battle with the caretaker monk to get to the top. At each level (there are 9 of them), he would blackmail us for a Dalai Lama picture. This was in addition to an entry-fee. By the 5th floor we were outraged and refused to cough up any more pictures. In the dark, however, the entrance to the next staircase could not be found without the monk (some entrances are hidden James-Bond-style behind statues!) and the monk had the relevant keys to the padlocks anyway. A few Dalai Lamas later, we finally set foot on the rooftop patio, with a grand view of Gyantse town. In parting, the monk shot us a splendid smile as he conferred with a colleague, and pored over his new collection of pictures.

The chorten is closed on Sundays and open mornings otherwise. If you roll up in the afternoon the deal is that you pay Y2 entry and take an escorted tour (with a monk). Most of the chapels are locked and you need someone to open them. It is pretty dark in most sections within the chorten and its chapels so a flashlight (torch) is absolutely essential. Nothing less than a powerful flash-unit will capture the interiors.

Palkhor Choide Lamasery

The area around the chorten – Palkhor Lamasery – lies in ruins. Pictures taken by Leslie Weir on a visit in 1930 show a complete town within the monastery walls (Weir was British Trade Agent at Gyantse from 1909 to 1915). The main monastery walls are still there, but the town within the walls has been razed, with the exception of a few of the larger buildings. Pilgrims coming to pay homage to the chorten camp out in the area, giving the place the flavour of an inhabited ghost-town. One or two families have set up home in the monastic ruins toward the rear of the hill. Monastery buildings that are left standing – those near the chorten – are being restored, and contain demonic statuary and battered frescoes. It's dark inside these buildings, and you have trouble making things out.

In November 1942, Ilya Tolstoy and Brooke Dolan, two US Army officers on a mission to Lhasa, stumbled through Gyantse, and timed it just right to witness *Cham* dances performed by monks as part of religious festivities. At Palkhor Choide Lamasery (a Gelukpa monastery) they were treated to a variety of masked figures from Buddhist and Bon mythology, including the Snow Lion, and dancers wearing heavy stag-head masks. In the *Yama Dance*, figures were made to resemble fearsome skeletons. The *Black Hat Dance* re-enacted the story of the 9th century king, Langdarma, who suppressed Buddhism. The dance followed the legend of a monk called Lhalung who wore a black and white reversible robe and a white horse coated with charcoal. Having assassinated Langdarma, the monk rode his horse into a river – and since he now had a white horse and a white cloak (reversed), he made an easy getaway. Accompanying the *Cham* dance were monk musicians with long telescopic horns designed to sound long, clear notes that echoed from one mountain to another.

The Fort

The thick walls and the building-shells of this fort are much better preserved than other forts around Tibet, but it is very difficult to get to see this 500-year-old colossus. You have to somehow try and get hold of a key from a white house at the base, toward the south-eastern side. Ingeniously, for times of siege, the fort had its own wells dug within the walls. It's not known if they are still in place.

The Old Town

The section immediately to the south of the chorten is where buying and selling is done and most of the buildings here are fairly new. The older part of town is to the south-east of the monastery ruins. You can get there by taking a pathway at the east gate of the monastery. The older section is full of dusty alleys and densely packed housing festooned with dried yak-dung.

Other

There is a rug factory near the fort. Weaving is done by hand, using Tibetan wool and vegetable dyes. At various times of the year there are fairs in Gyantse: yak-racing, archery, dancing and merriment in

Top: Female temple repair squad at Samye (RS)
Bottom: Canoes on Yarlung Zangbo (river) near Quxu (RS)

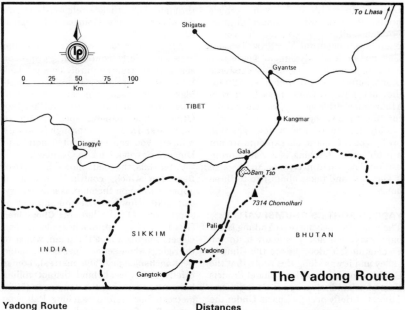

The Yadong Route

Yadong Route	Distances	
	intermediate	*cumulative*
Gyantse 江孜		
Kangmar 康马	47 km	47 km
Gala	47 km	94 km
Pali	70 km	164 km
Yadong 亚东	46 km	210 km

an impromptu tent city to the east of the monastery.

Places to Stay & Eat

There are two hotels you can stay at – both near the bus station. The Tibetan one is preferable and is Y2 a head for a spartan dorm. This hotel also doubles as the truckstop, so you could arrange lifts to Shigatse or Lhasa from there. Food is whatever you can scrounge, which ain't much. There are a few little teahouses in the section south of the monastery. It's about two km from the hotel to the chorten.

Getting There & Away

Gyantse is approachable by bus from either Shigatse (Y5) or Lhasa (Y15). Trucks are faster and slightly cheaper. You can get advance tickets for the Lhasa-Gyantse run from the main bus station east of the Potala. Buses generally include Gyantse on a route to Shigatse, and some stop overnight in Gyantse. Therefore, if you get off in Gyantse, you shouldn't have too much trouble getting another bus later to continue to Shigatse. There are several buses a week running from either direction.

If there are no breakdowns, the bus should take about 10 to 12 hours to get to

Gyantse from Lhasa. If your vehicle breaks down, or suffers from respiratory problems, all the more chance for you to photograph beautiful Yamdrok Tso – it may not be a disadvantage. There is a more comfortable variety of bus (Japanese coach, softer seats) that charges Y20 for the run to Gyantse from Lhasa. If you're in a four-wheel drive vehicle, you can cut the run to a mere six hours.

Although there are a few guarded bridges out of Lhasa, checkpoints are not a problem, so hitching is a viable proposition. The run from Gyantse to Shigatse is very fast and takes about two to three hours.

YADONG ROUTE & CHUMBI VALLEY

The route from Gyantse to Yadong is not only scenic but also has many historical associations. Yadong lies in the Chumbi valley and it was along this route that the British expedition under Colonel Francis Younghusband advanced from India into Tibet, to briefly occupy Lhasa. Under the terms of the agreement reached in 1904, foreign traders were granted the right to use this route as far as Gyantse. The Dalai Lama stayed in Yadong in 1950 to avoid the invading Chinese and again in 1956 when he visited India for Buddhist celebrations.

Try the truckstops in Gyantse for a ride to Yadong. Walk out to the road junction just outside Gyantse early in the morning if you want to thumb. A fully laden truck takes a day, an empty truck about nine hours.

Gyantse to Yadong

About two km out of Gyantse the road branches: left to Yadong, right to Shigatse. On the way to Kangmar you pass a ruined Dzong and Gompa, a hydroelectric power station and rock paintings.

Gala is approached across a huge, barren plain. The checkpoint at Gala is a small office in front of two mud walls which jut into the road leaving an opening just large enough for trucks to squeeze through. The officials religiously record details of anybody, Chinese or foreigner, who passes.

Access to Yadong, which is in a border area, is strictly controlled. Permission seems to be granted purely on a pot luck basis. Some foreigners are refused point-blank; some receive permission just to take a peep round the corner at Bam Tso. Others show papers, speak a bit of Chinese and are waved through (if you are refused, you can either hitch across to Dinggyê or truck back to Gyantse).

After Gala, the road follows the shore of **Bam Tso** which, contrary to what it appears to be on the map, is a huge, dry, salt lake. However, disappointment is short-lived. On the left, **Mt Chomolhari** (7314 metres) approaches closer and closer, soaring above the plain, whilst to the right, a whole series of peaks dominated by **Kanchenjunga** (8585 metres), comes briefly into view behind distant rolling hills. After crossing the **Tang pass** (5060 metres), just before reaching Pali, you reach **Pali Gompa** which was once inhabited by hundreds of monks but now, reportedly, only has 30. Although currently under restoration, an army unit is still stationed there.

The tiny settlement of **Pali** presents a strange sight. The road cleaves it like an apple, into two distinct architectural segments: Tibetan stone and mud buildings on one side, Chinese prefabs on the other. Pali, or Phari as it was formerly called, was noted by European visitors to the region earlier this century as a town of epic filth. Spencer-Chapman wrote in the 1930s that the streets were 'so choked with the accumulated garbage of centuries that they are many feet higher than formerly and in most cases actually obscure the ground-floor windows'. Others commented on the filth, stench, dead dogs, bones and foulness, and remarked on the contrasting squalour of Phari as compared to the splendour of its setting.

As the road leaves the desolate plain and starts to descend into Yadong, vegetation slowly starts to reappear, becoming lusher and lusher. Most of the trucks on this route run empty down to Yadong and return with timber. There is a timber checkpoint (permits are required for the timber) about an hour after Pali. The houses lower down the valley resemble Swiss chalets and, in contrast to the barren plain, the rest of the route to Yadong is a riot of flowers, fields, streams and forests.

YADONG
Yadong is right next to Sikkim and Bhutan. One traveller obtained a visa at the Bhutanese border, providing he left his camera behind. Bhutanese and Sikkimese traders amble in and out of town shouldering huge bags of goods. Most of them simply appear out of or disappear into surrounding forests where they climb mountain trails to avoid border posts. Apparently, some traders are also looking for a different commodity – marriageable ladies. The borders seem porous. One Tibetan I met had left for India via Bhutan, spent four years in New Delhi,

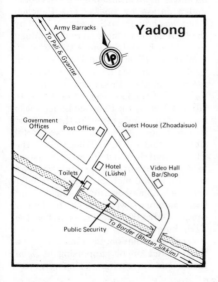

Dharamsala and elsewhere before returning to Tibet via Nepal.

According to a newspaper report, 'wild men' or 'snowmen' also roam the forests – so keep your eyes peeled. Locals were keen to report another mysterious occurrence called the 'Thumbs-up American'. This was a rare hitchhiker who had arrived on the back of a truck. He spoke no Chinese other than the word for America and restricted communication to his vertically raised, right thumb.

The forests around Yadong provide splendid hiking with mountain strawberries, hemp, irises, azaleas and rhododendrons in abundance but watch out for voracious midges. Accept at once if a driver offers to take you to a logging camp near the border – it's a great trip.

Places to Stay & Eat
The best hostel in Yadong is the one close to the bridge. Most of the trucks stop here, so it is easy to arrange a ride. A bed in a five-bed room costs Y2.50. The rooms are on the 2nd floor. The toilets are outside, just in front of the bridge. You can eat in the kitchen or join everyone else in the restaurant. The food here was some of the best I had in Tibet: momo, mutton with potatoes, chapatis, vegetables in batter and gallons of hot, milky tea. Ask the manager if you want a shower. The shower is in a building across the bridge, under a waterfall.

Getting There & Away
There is, reportedly, a bus from Lhasa to Yadong on Tuesdays; from Yadong to Lhasa on Thursdays. It is unlikely that you will be sold a ticket at the bus station in Lhasa. An easier way to return is on one of the many trucks heading back to Gyantse with timber. I had a bumpy, but magic ride, travelling through the night, stretched out on the timber in the back of the truck, gazing up at an unbelievable number of stars.

Shigatse

Shigatse (Xigazê) with a population of around 40,000, is the second largest city in Tibet, and the traditional seat of the Panchen Lama. Tsong Khapa, the originator of the Yellow Hat Sect (Gelukpa, 14th century), advocated strict celibacy and discipline – the idea of reincarnation of Grand Lamas was one way of 'continuing the line'. The principle was well established by the 16th century. The highest incarnation became the Dalai Lama, and the second highest incarnation became the Panchen Lama. The official Panchen Lama's residence is Tashilhunpo Monastery, built in 1447, although it did not really become the seat of the Panchen till almost 200 years later.

Stories of the origins of the Panchen Lama vary – some say he is a reincarnation of Tsong Khapa's second disciple, some claim he was Tsong Khapa's brother, others that he was the Dalai Lama's tutor. There is considerable confusion in Tibetan records as to how many Panchen Lamas there have been, depending on how authentic the incarnation was reckoned to be. The first recognised reincarnation was Lobzang Chokyi Gyaltsen (1570-1662). The Panchen Lama was sometimes referred to as the *Tashi Lama* and also as *Panchen Erteni* (Precious Scholar). The 5th Dalai Lama recognised the Panchen Lama as a reincarnation of Amitabha, the Buddha of Limitless Light.

With the establishment of Chinese overlordship in Tibet after 1720 came the beginning of a long policy of playing off one high incarnation against the other. From the 17th century on, the elder of either the Panchen Lama or Dalai Lama served as tutor for the other. In 1728, the Manchus removed the 7th Dalai Lama; he was invited to Peking, but got no further than Litang, where he remained in exile for seven years. In his place, the Manchus offered the Panchen Lama control over wide areas of Tibet. The Panchen declined the offer, but did extend his control over the districts around Tashilhunpo Monastery. The Tibetan people have never recognised the Panchen Lama's authority to rule over the country; his rule was always restricted to the Shigatse area. The Chinese, however, have seen fit to promote the rivalry between the Panchen and Dalai Lamas.

In 1923 there was a rift – the 6th Panchen Lama fled Shigatse for Peking, sure that the 13th Dalai Lama was persecuting him for helping the Chinese during the 1910 invasion. The Panchen died in Qinghai in 1937. The present Panchen Lama, thought to be the 7th incarnation, was born in 1938, in the Koko Nor region, Qinghai. His selection was influenced by the Chinese Nationalists.

He was certified in Xining (1949) without the approval of Lhasa. He then fell into Communist hands. His 'qualifications' as an incarnation were accepted under duress by Lhasa. The Panchen Lama was brought to Shigatse in 1952 by the PLA as the Chinese were determined to belittle the Dalai Lama's authority.

With the flight of the Dalai Lama in 1959, the Panchen Lama was appointed as Chairman of the Preparatory Committee for the Autonomous Region of Tibet. In late 1960, while the Panchen Lama was in Peking delivering a report to the National People's Congress about 'the wonderful situation that exists in Tibet today', the PLA surrounded Tashilhunpo Monastery (which had hitherto escaped reforms) and seized all 4000 monks. Some were later executed, some committed suicide, and large numbers were taken to labour camps. Only 200 monks remained at the Tashilhunpo.

From this point on, the Panchen Lama changed tack, openly supporting the Dalai Lama, and increasingly refusing to co-operate with the Chinese. In 1961 the Panchen Lama's Council was dissolved – it was the last vestige of Tibetan rule. The Panchen Lama was asked to move into the Potala to replace the Dalai Lama, and was asked to condemn his fellow incarnation. He flatly refused to do so, dropped out of public view, and was forbidden to speak in public. In 1964 he was again asked to denounce the Dalai Lama, at the height of a prayer-festival in Lhasa. A crowd of 40,000 gathered outside the Jokhang and the Panchen Lama delivered a stunning speech of solidarity with the Dalai Lama, and in favour of Tibetan independence. He was promptly placed under house-arrest, denounced as a reactionary by Zhou En-Lai, and brought to trial. After being beaten to induce confessions, the Panchen Lama disappeared together with his parents and entourage.

By 1969 the Panchen Lama was rumoured to have died in a Chinese prison. Then, in 1978, he miraculously surfaced in Peking, announcing that – guided by Mao's thoughts – he was a new man. He had undoubtedly been tortured, but he was still alive. The Panchen Lama is known in Peking as Bainqen Erdini Qoigyi Gyaincain. He is married, lives in Peking, and holds the post of Honorary President of the Buddhist Association of China. He also holds a post as one of the numerous Vice-Chairmen of the National People's Congress Standing Committee (China's rubber-stamp parliament), an honour he shares with Ngapo Ngawang Jigme (who is a leading Tibetan collaborator with the Chinese). The Chinese have made it clear that were the Dalai Lama to return, he would hold a similar post – a desk-job in Beijing – with limited privileges to visit Tibet.

Despite his compromises with the Chinese the Panchen Lama is still revered. Inside Tashilhunpo Monastery

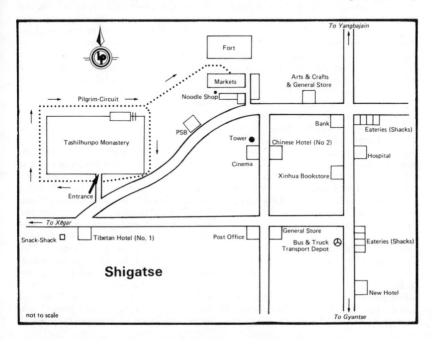

there are innumerable photos of him. His two month inspection tour in 1982 almost unleashed riots. Tens of thousands poured out to greet him. In a speech to local cadres, the Panchen said: 'We must safeguard the unification of the motherland as carefully as we protect our eyeballs ... ' He went on to extend an invitation to the Dalai Lama to return and join his 'good Buddhist brother', as the successors to the venerable Tsong Khapa.

In September 1985, the Panchen Lama popped up again in Lhasa and Shigatse with a 16-strong entourage, timed for the 20th Post-Mortem of the TAR. If the Chinese couldn't get the right numbers of Tibetans for 'celebrations', the Panchen Lama certainly had no trouble (or perhaps this was the intention in allowing him to visit?). A crowd of 10,000 Tibetans flocked to the Jokhang for a blessing by the Panchen Lama – and broke through ranks of police wielding electric batons. In Shigatse, thousands lined the dirt roads for his visit there.

Orientation & Information
Shigatse always had a floating population of worshippers and traders. The Tibetan end of town is now around the entrance to the Tashilhunpo. The rest of Shigatse is a remarkably ugly Chinese town of drab concrete blocks. It has a number of facilities that you won't find elsewhere in Tibet (except in Lhasa and Chamdo). It boasts a post office, bank, hospital, cinema, and even a few shops! The PSB office is quite helpful: office-hours are 9.30 am to 12.30 pm and 3.30 to 6.30 pm. In theory it's only open two days a week, but in practice it's open most of the week; good for visa extensions.

Tashilhunpo Monastery
The Grand Monastery of Tashilhunpo is a town by itself – a vast spread of buildings faced in cream, brown and ochre. This theopolis was built 1447 by the first Dalai Lama. The monk population has dwindled from around 4000 (1950s) to some 700.

Most of these monks are not actually at the Tashilhunpo on any given day as they have to help earn their keep by operating a farm about 20 km east of the temple (barley cultivation, several hundred yaks and goats). The monks living at the Tashilhunpo, as elsewhere in Tibet, are on Peking's payroll. There are few younger initiates; admission is screened by the Chinese Religious Bureau, which allocates funds for restoration. This raises the essential question: Can you be a practising Buddhist and a devout Communist at the same time? No, says DeChin, a living Buddha and one of the most revered monks in Tibet: 'I am a lama. How can I be a member of the party?' DeChin leads the chanting of the sutras by night, and shepherds tourists around by day. He is Vice-Chairman of the Tibetan Buddhist Association.

Though you may not get to see all the activities, Tashilhunpo is a fairly active monastery. The monks get up at 7 am and spend most of the day reciting scriptures or doing chores, then go to sleep at 11.30 pm. The monastery runs a one year course in Tibetan language for young initiates wishing to become lamas. Wandering the narrow alleys of Tashilhunpo, you can stray across snippets of monkish life: lama musicians blowing on decorated conch-shell horns or long trumpets, costumed mask-dancing, chanting of the sutras, debating, printing in progress ...

The centre-piece of Tashilhunpo Monastery is the **Hall of the Maitreya** which is housed in the fortress-looking building toward the west side (the largest building on that side). This block looks out of place, it's taller and more solid-looking than the others and it was built 1914-18. The Maitreya is the Buddha of the Future, known in Tibetan as *Champa*. The Tibetans believe that Champa will return to preside over the world when all human beings have earned deliverance from suffering. Champa is almost 27-metres high, a gold-plated, bronze image on a lotus seat. The Buddha bears the mark of divine wisdom on its forehead, and the hand gesture indicates the giving of the gift of religion. It is possible to climb to the head of the Buddha (3rd storey) but you will most likely be waylaid by monks before you get that far. The Buddha's ears are almost three metres in length.

Nearby is the **Great Hall** which contains funerary pagodas of former Panchen Lamas. There are frescoes and statues depicting the life of Tsong Khapa and his disciples. Largest among the funerary pagodas is that of the 4th Panchen Lama (17th century). It is 11 metres high, plated with gold and silver, and encrusted with precious stones. It was built in 1662.

Scattered around the Tashilhunpo are scores of halls. Though buildings at the monastery were dismantled during the Cultural Revolution, the main halls were spared. The greatest loss was the burning of the sutras. Some of the halls were previously used as colleges, assembly-halls, chapels, and palaces. Like other great monasteries in Tibet, the Tashilhunpo had its own squad of artisans: woodblock printers, sculptors, stonemasons, tailors, and metalworkers. The artisans are slowly returning to restore the monastery. To the east side of the Tashilhunpo is a large rust-and-black complex with a gilded roof, which houses a maze of courtyards and halls. If you wander around you'll find a huge enclosed courtyard that once held thousands of monks during special ceremonies. There's a small printing-works nearby, and some beautiful hand-embroidered thangkas – very large ones – arrayed round a massive Buddha statue. In the same complex is a hell's kitchen: mammoth copper cauldrons, giant implements, and fires burning away on a scale that would've had Macbeth's witches cackling.

At the back of the Tashilhunpo, at the north-east end near the outer walls, is a huge fortress-like structure. It was built in remembrance of the Buddha Sakyamuni, and on special occasions gigantic thangkas would be unfurled from the west end of the tower. On 1 July 1985, an ancient three-day festival was revived for the first time in over 20 years. It drew a crowd of tens of thousands of worshippers (and a number of tourists), and a satin weaving 40-metres long hung from the tower. The tower was also used in previous times for grain-storage. There is a gate in this area that leads outside the walls to the mountain-side.

The Tashilhunpo is closed on Sundays. The rest of the week it's open 9.30 to 12.30 mornings only (you can try afternoons, but there's no guarantee you'll get in). Entry is Y3 for foreigners. Photo-fees are supposedly Y20 per room, but you shouldn't have problems taking pictures, except that you need a flash for interiors, and the large assembly courtyard to the east side bears a notice forbidding photography.

Outside the Walls

To the south-west of the entrance, and near the Tibetan hotel, is the small summer palace of the Panchen Lama, but it's not of great interest. To the west of the Tashilhunpo is a sky-burial site. Apparently the style here is very different from that of Lhasa; the body, still dressed, is placed seated on the ground in a Buddha pose. The relatives gather round to watch the dissection, and the master of ceremonies hands around goblets of wine.

Pilgrim Circuit

Just as interesting as the monastery is the cross-section of pilgrims who come from far and wide to pay homage. Whilst not present in the great numbers that flock to the Jokhang in Lhasa, there are never-theless some 300 worshippers daily at the Tashilhunpo, and up to 3000 on holy days. Opposite the gates in the early morning are the 'break-dancers' – doing their prostrations. There is a rather gruelling prostration circuit of the monastery walls (outside). Gruelling because half the terrain is not flat and is therefore not conducive to inchworming. I saw one cheerful chap with the latest in prostrating gear: thick rubber apron, reinforced wooden handgrips, and rubber kneepads. He needed every bit of his equipment to make it around without skinning himself. Most Tibetans prefer the walk.

If you follow the clockwise circuit of the outer walls (or start from the north-east gate of Tashilhunpo), you'll arrive at a fixed prayer-wheel section at the north-east end, which is a good spot to observe the pilgrims' progress, and it offers a fine view over Shigatse. With each spin of the large prayer-wheels, the wielder gains merit. From here you can continue to the east along a ridge and arrive at Shigatse Dzong – what's left of it. Traffic along this ridge is from west to east. Start the Tashilhunpo shuffle from the monastery end, and finish at the Dzong, by a path which then leads down to the markets.

Samdup-tse Dzong

This once mighty fort goes back several centuries; some say to the 15th century. It was used by the Tsangpa rulers as their main centre (this dynasty once ruled parts of Tibet). The fort was the site of the formal installation of the 5th Dalai Lama as spiritual and temporal head of Tibet, and was later used as the headquarters of the local government, and the seat of the Magistrate of Shigatse, along with his court. The Dzong was dismantled stone by stone during the Cultural Revolution, apparently by hundreds of Tibetans, some from a commune outside Shigatse, at the instigation of the Chinese. Whatever happened, the Dzong is gone (the memory lingers on?), shaved off the mountainside where it once dominated the whole town. Only a few ramparts are left.

Markets

Below the ruins of Shigatse Dzong there are corrugated tin roofs sheltering the markets. The markets actually stretch further than that, lining the roads into the area. They are open from roughly 9.30 am to 7 pm and mostly sell housewares, yak butter and meat, and vegetables. There are a few stalls of the antique and curio variety. Occasionally livestock is sold near here – it's just the place to get your yak! The markets are the best place to get your food. You can find bread and yoghurt, and there's a noodle-shack open to 10 pm that sells hearty beef-noodle soup for 50 fen, and milk-tea for 10 fen.

Places to Stay & Eat

For the present, the choice is limited to the Tibetan hotel opposite the Tashilhunpo (also called *No 1 Hotel*), and the Chinese hotel across town (*No 2 Hotel*). A large new construction was in progress to the south-east of Shigatse; probably svelte stuff for breathless group-tourers. The Tibetan hotel is far preferable in terms of location and ambience than the Chinese hotel. The Tibetan hotel is, however, often packed out with pilgrims, and you may have trouble getting in there. It is also the truckstop hotel – regardless of whether you stay there go and visit if you want to line up a lift to, say, Sakya. Beds at the Tibetan hotel are Y5 in dorms. Next door is a small snack-shack which is a little expensive (Y3 for rice and eggs).

The Chinese hotel (No 2) is about a 20-minute walk from the Tashilhunpo. The Chinese hotel looks like an army barracks, and the staff act like its officers. This is a group tour and expedition hotel, with those visitors paying exponentially more than you do. There is a restaurant within the hotel with good food for *groups* (recycled expedition goodies?). Possibilities exist for hot water to wash with (not a shower) from 8 to 8.30 am and from 6 to 6.30 pm. Beds go for around Y5.

Around the town (see map) there are tiny shacks selling tiny snacks (momos, jiaozi, tea). The Arts & Crafts/General Store (see map) has some interesting tins. It is a modified version of a Friendship Store, and apart from items being sold to locals, such as hardware, it has some nice thangkas, Tibetan headgear and carpets for sale.

Getting There & Away

Getting to Shigatse takes a whole day on a bus from Lhasa, possibly with an overnight stop in Gyantse. It costs Y20 and you catch it at the station just east of the Potala. Frequency is three times weekly or more and it takes between 10 and 15 hours. Minibuses and Landcruisers can make it to Shigatse the same day from Lhasa, in about eight hours or so if the going's good.

In Shigatse, bus and truck transport is lumped together in the same compound (see map). You should also check the Tibetan hotel for rides. It is worth remembering that buses can originate in Shigatse, meaning that you *may* be able to get a bus to Nyalam or Zhangmu, and the same goes for trucks. It may be possible to get trucks for the Qinghai and Xinjiang routes from here.

Sakya

Sakya (Sag'ya, 'Grey Earth'), off the main Shigatse to Tingri route, was once the base of the Sakyapa Sect (Red Hats) which rose to power in the 13th century. The sect has numerous followers in Tibet, so Sakya is naturally the object of their pilgrimage. The founder of the Sakyapa was Drokmi, who set up a monastery in Sakya as early as the 11th century. The term 'Red Hats' applies generally to the 'unreformed' sects (such as the earlier Nyingmapa and Kagyupa schools). The Sakyapa were strong on magic and sorcery, and permitted their abbots to marry and to drink intoxicating beverages. This led to hereditary rank; it also led to a rather unsavoury reputation for worldliness among the monks. Although rank is hereditary, it is traditionally believed that seven incarnations of the Buddha of Wisdom (Manjusri) have appeared in the lineage of the Sakyapa.

Under Mongol overlordship, the Sakyapa ruled Tibet from roughly 1200 to 1350 AD, and their power declined from 1350 to 1400. The Mongols, in charge of China at the time, considered Tibet a vassal state but largely left it alone. Sakya Pandita (1182-1253), otherwise known as Kunga Gyaltsen, established strong diplomatic relations with Genghis Khan, and visited his court at Khanbaliq (Peking) in 1244. It was through Sakya Pandita's diplomacy that Buddhism was established as a force in Mongolia itself.

Phakpa (1235-1280), nephew of Sakya Pandita, widened the control of the sect over large areas of Tibet, and cemented this deal with Kublai Khan. It was the Sakya Grand Lamas who established the idea of a hierarchy of monks – an idea that the Yellow Hats later adopted with great success. In this theocracy, the Red Hats would use force if a rival sect became disruptive. From the 14th century on, they came into increasing conflict with the stricter Yellow Hat Sect (Gelukpa), which was later supported by the Mongols. The Mongols had lost control of China by the mid-14th century, and Genghis Khan's successors fell back on their old Shamanist religions. In the late 16th century, the regrouped Mongols adopted Yellow Hat Lamaism as the official Mongol religion, following a visit by the 3rd Dalai Lama. In 1641-2, the Khoshot Mongols (under Gushri Khan) interceded in the struggle between sects in Tibet and squashed the Red Hats. The Mongols then set up the 5th Dalai Lama (Yellow Hat) as leader.

The present heir to the Sakya lineage, Sakya Dagtri Rinpoche, was born in 1945. He is also known as Sakya Trizin (the Throne-holder) and by several other titles. Since rank is hereditary with the Sakyapa, there are no oracles, signs or prophecies that lead to obtaining the title. The post alternates between two families: Dolma Phodrang and Phuntsok Phodrang, with, sometimes, a nephew inheriting. The present Sakya heir is from the Dolma Phodrang, and the next heir will be from the Phuntsok Phodrang (if the candidate wishes to take the position).

In 1959, at the age of 14, Sakya Dagtri Rinpoche was enthroned at Sakya Monastery, becoming the 41st Patriarch. Almost immediately after the event, he and his entourage of teachers and personal staff fled to India. It took Chinese soldiers several months to get to Sakya after the 1959 uprising in Lhasa. The Chinese told the 500 monks at Sakya Gompa that they had supported the Khampa rebels, the monastery was seized, the grain-stocks confiscated, and monks and nuns were submitted to thamzing (struggle-session). Sakya Dagtri Rinpoche, meanwhile, had set up his new base in Dehra Dun, in Uttar Pradesh, with a Sakya centre and a Sakya college established in the 1960s. Today there are Sakya centres all over the world,

The Sakya next in line for succession is the cousin of the present Sakya Lama's son who lives in the United States in Seattle. On a recent visit to Dehra Dun, where he was accorded the honour and respect which his position decreed, the young man appeared reluctant to change his residence from the United States to India, or to assume the mantle or the 42nd patriarch when the time comes.

For the 14-year-old Sakya leader crossing into India twenty-five years ago, everything was strange and bewildering. Plunged from the lonely vastness of the Sakya monastery, where the only purpose of his life was to study, meditate and train for his high position, he suddenly found himself in a noisy, densely, populated environment where people appeared strangely different. He saw cars, trucks, aircraft, trains and other forms of transport for the first time.

He was taken at first to Mussoorie where the Dalai Lama and his

Sunday Observer, Bombay, 20 January 1985

including the US, the UK, France, Canada, Switzerland, Italy, Holland, Greece, Singapore and Malaysia. Sakya Dagtri Rinpoche has many disciples and followers around the world and apart from receiving foreign visitors in Dehra Dun, he has toured extensively, teaching in Europe, America and Asia.

While he can spread the 'lamp of the dharma' in a way that was never before possible, Sakya Dagtri Rinpoche views with great concern the fact that there is now a generation of Tibetans in exile who are weaned on television, pizzas, hot-dogs and jeans, and who are no longer fixated

with religion. He has two sons who, although raised in the tradition of Tibetan Buddhism, are also exposed to a great many western influences. A visit to Sakya will perhaps illuminate the present throneholder's concerns about changing lifestyles. Life in Sakya seems unchanged by the centuries.

Orientation

Sakya is a sleepy Tibetan hamlet with a beautiful location on a valley-floor. The town is bisected by a river, with a hilly section to the north, and a plain to the south. Rising out of the plain is a monolithic walled structure that at first appears to be a fort – Sakya Monastery, one of the best-preserved in Tibet. Somehow it seems to have escaped the ravages of time and Chinese vandalism.

The same cannot be said for the tiered group of monasteries that once stood on the northern hillside, and pre-dated Sakya Monastery by several centuries. The whole structure was intact in pictures taken 50 years ago. All that's left in the aftermath of a Chinese run-amok session are some patchy ruins and a crumbling brick stupa.

Sakya Monastery

Sakya Monastery contains possibly the finest artwork in all Tibet. Nothing appears to be tampered with and it is all in pristine condition. The monastery is thought to date to the days of Phakpa (13th century), and the project of building was continued by successive Patriarchs. It seems that the basic architecture has changed little to this day, although there has obviously been some reconstruction and repair. The walls within the monastery carry some frescoes relating to the building of the monastery, and to later repairs.

One of the monastery's most precious parchments is an appointment letter with an official gold seal, sent by Kublai Khan, and authorising the Sakyapa to rule over Tibet. By the mid-13th century, the Sakyapa were powerful enough to import

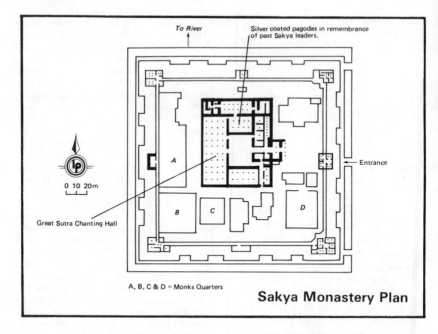

To River

Silver coated pagodas in remembrance of past Sakya leaders.

Entrance

A

B C D

Great Sutra Chanting Hall

0 10 20m

A, B, C & D = Monks Quarters

Sakya Monastery Plan

not only large numbers of Tibetan workers and artisans, but also artists from India, Nepal and central China, to decorate the monastery. In addition, this treasure-house shows some Mongolian influences in its architecture.

The monastery is bounded by a high wall with corner-turrets and watchtowers. The grounds of the Gompa cover an area of over 18,000 square metres, with the main hall sprawling over an area of 6000 square metres. Inside the main Sutra Chanting Hall are four rows of roof-supporting pillars – 10 in a row. At the base of the massive tree-trunk pillars are lotus-patterned stone pedestals, and between the pillars are low carpeted benches with seating for some 400 monks. The four pillars toward the middle of the hall are especially grand; one of them has a diameter of 1.2 metres. Glancing down from the ceiling are rows of small wooden gargoyles.

The main focus of the hall are the massive, gilded Buddha statues strung in a row along the back. These statues are surrounded by thousands of artefacts, particularly Chinese vases donated in centuries past. Statuary, seals, ceremonial props, ritual vessels, and books were amassed from all over Tibet. They are presented in no particular order, and are rarely identified, although undoubtedly the collection would be the envy of any museum in the west. It's a bit like fossicking around in a giant antique store. Occasionally you spot something familiar like a Dalai Lama picture. The collection of safety-pins (donated by pilgrims) is definitely on the junkyard side of the offerings! Pilgrims believe that adorning statues with pins sharpens their mental powers.

To the front of the hall is a huge bookshelf, about 60-metres long, 10-metres high, and one-metre deep. It is

Sakya Pandita

laden with Buddhist scriptures – many thousands of them. The sutras were hand-copied by Tibetan calligraphers, and illuminated with gold or silver ink.

Other parts of the monastery are not so accessible. There is a side-room with a remarkable collection of statuettes; on the floor above the main hall is a library housing rare books; and there are dining rooms for monks. It is possible to get onto the roof, but difficult to do so. The gompa is open 9 am to 4 pm and charges Y3 entry for foreigners. For that you get into two halls – count yourself lucky if you get any further. At least three monks are assigned to your case if you are spotted with an SLR at the ready and it is their mission to make sure you take no photos within the halls of the monastery. They do a damn good job. The monastery is quite active, and it is prudent to observe protocol if there is chanting of sutras in progress. Walk clockwise within the main temple.

Around the Town

A scramble to the hillside north of the river is well worth it. There are squat rooftops covered in fuel (yak-dung patties and brushwood), crumbling ruins, dust, and snot-nosed kids. There is some cottage industry (weaving), and the tinkle of donkey-bells in the narrow alleys. Some of the battered buildings are undoubtedly used for corralling cattle in the winter.

Places to Stay & Eat

There are two Tibetan hotels you can stay at. Directly in front of the monastery and toward the river is a Tibetan truckstop hotel. Not far away, to the north-east corner of the monastery, is another hotel arranged round a courtyard. A bed is Y2 to Y3 in a simple dorm. Both hotels are pretty basic (filthy, reeking of yak butter), but some rooms have windows that allow you to air yourself out. The manager of the latter hotel at first refused to give me a room, partly because she must have thought them below par for a foreigner, but finally she conceded.

The eating area, if it can be called that, is in the same place as the two hotels.

Attached to the hotel at the north-east corner of the monastery is a small noodle-shop, where you can get a cup of tea. There's a small market close by, and you may be able to scrounge a few sweets or a tin of pork, but that's about it.

Getting There & Away

There is no regular transport but you can try and get a pilgrim truck or bus leaving early in the morning from the Tashilhunpo area (Shigatse) and returning the same day (some buses stop overnight). You may also be able to hitchhike and pick up a pilgrim bus along the way. One foreign hitchhiker got to Sakya and got a place to stay with a Tibetan household – but hitching is difficult. Sakya is 150 km south-west from Shigatse. You go down the main road toward Lhazê, but turn off before reaching Lhazê. The turn-off is 125 km from Shigatse or 25 km from Lhazê. From the turn-off it's 26 km along a dusty, dirt road into Sakya. The trip from Shigatse to Sakya takes three to five hours; from the turn-off into Sakya it's about one and a half hours. There's very little motorised traffic going in and out of Sakya from the turn-off; horses and donkeys are more likely. Therefore, if you're hitching, you may get stranded at the crossroads on the way in.

Trekking in the Everest Region

Tibet has the greatest trekking country on earth. For starters there are the mighty mountains that form Tibet's natural borders – a trekker's paradise. The borders cut right over the summits of major ranges; a climber attempting Everest fell from the Nepalese side and ended up in Tibet (he lived but had some concussion). In China, trekking comes under mountaineering rules which are supervised by the Chinese Mountaineering Association (CMA). Some of the peaks open to climbers are:

in Tibet, Everest – 8848 metres, Xixabangma – 8012 metres;
in Qinghai, Anyêmaqên – 6282 metres;
in Sichuan, Gongga Shan – 7556 metres, Siguniang – 6250 metres;
and in Xinjiang, Bogda – 5445 metres, Mustagh Ata – 7549 metres, Kongur – 7719 metres, and Kongur Tiube – 7595 metres.

Generally speaking, you can drive straight up to these mountains' base camps – that's why they're open. Group-tour trekkers are honing in on the newly opened mountain zones in Tibet (for trekking alone – no summit attempts are permitted). These include the Makalu area, Mt Kailas (West Tibet) and Mt Namche Barwa (East Tibet). Namche Barwa (7756 metres) is the world's highest unclimbed peak and the Chinese are not about to let anyone else take the prize. A 1984 Chinese expedition failed to reach the summit. A runner-up for high unclimbed peaks, Gurla Mandhata (7694 metres), at the other end of the country (west Tibet) – was scaled for the first time in 1985 by a combined Chinese/Japanese expedition.

The CMA rules for group treks are that they must be accompanied by a liason officer, an interpreter and a cook. Porters are generally hired as an extra expense. The food offered by the Chinese is insufficient nourishment, and has to be supplemented by the tour operator. Transport in chartered trucks, jeeps, buses, or with animals, is priced very high, and so is hotel accommodation. In addition, the tour operator must first send a leader to China to work out arrangements with the CMA. The upshot of all this is that trekking in China with a group becomes a very expensive business. The more remote the location, the higher the fees; Tibet is classed as very remote, so the fees become astronomical.

Although an agreement has been signed between the Nepal Ministry of Tourism and the Tibet Tourist Corporation to open the border to tourism (Lhasa-Kathmandu), trekking over borders is a different story. The Nepalese Government has not opened its restricted areas – but there has been discussion about opening routes through to Manasarovar and Gyirong, as well as a direct route to Shigatse. Sikkim and Bhutan are extremely sensitive about any border-crossings.

If you think that as an individual you can get permission to mount a trek in Tibet, think again. Until such time as China starts handing out trek permits (as in Nepal) you'll end up strangling yourself in red-tape, not to mention what will happen to your bank account. There's only one way to do it: don't ask questions, and when in doubt – split! Individual trekking is possible, but not easy. There's very little (if any) food in the areas you go to; you have to lug your own around. There's no equipment for hire; you have to bring it with you. There's no medical rescue squad if you get into trouble. Worst of all, there are no maps; you have to bone up on obscure mountaineering manuals. Still, that's half the thrill, and the achievement – to get away with it against all odds.

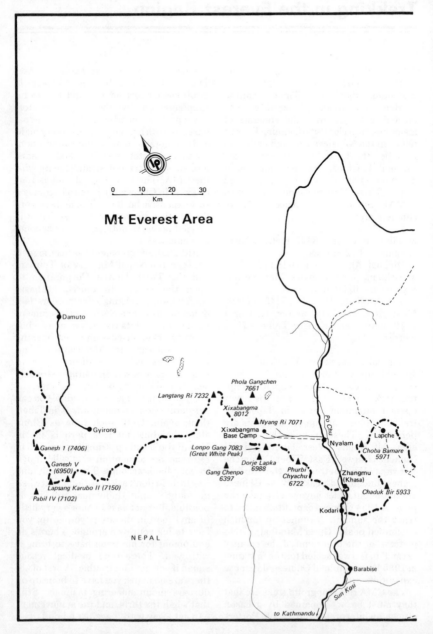

0   10   20   30
Km

Mt Everest Area

Damuto

Gyirong

Ganesh 1 (7406)

Ganesh V (6950)

Lapsang Karubo II (7150)

Pabil IV (7102)

Langtang Ri 7232

Phola Gangchen 7661

Xixabangma 8012

Nyang Ri 7071

Xixabangma Base Camp

Lonpo Gang 7083 (Great White Peak)

Dorje Lapka 6988

Gang Chenpo 6397

Phurbi Chyachu 6722

Nyalam

Po Chu

Lapche

Choba Bamare 5971

Zhangmu (Khasa)

Chaduk Bir 5933

Kodari

NEPAL

Barabise

Sun Kosi

to Kathmandu

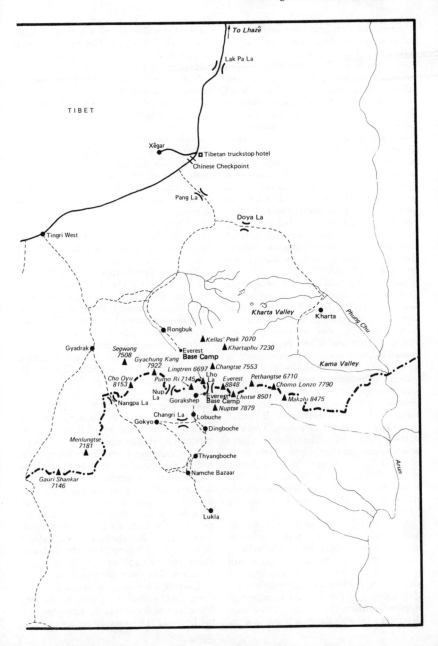

Some travellers have been very successful at mounting their own expeditions in Tibet. They have managed to sleep in local hamlets along trekking routes, although even then you need a good down-filled sleeping-bag, or a down-filled jacket, or both. Trekking is expeditionary in Tibet – you need a strong heart, an even stronger will, a devious mind, and the best food and equipment you can muster. Group-trekkers use goggles, crampons – the whole works. Warm windproof and waterproof clothing, thermal underwear, gloves, jacket, medical supplies and so on, are essential. Dehydration can be a severe problem, so you need water bottles. Something light to carry but sustaining would also be essential: vegetable extract, high-glucose tablets, vitamin tablets, natural cleansers such as garlic, and freeze-dried foodstuffs.

Getting to a trailhead can be a major task in itself, and might wear you out before the actual trek. This is the luck of the road; if you manage to hitch, or arrive some other way, you can conserve your energy. Since four-wheel drive vehicles rented in Lhasa are often requisitioned by group tours, the drivers know the way, and you might be able to assemble your own small group, persuading the driver that your destination is 'just a short way off the highway'. Do not go by yourself. If you fall sick, there will be no-one to help. Trekking at these elevations can be serious business when it comes to your health – so do not go about it lightly. If you do start getting above 5000 metres, allow sufficient time to acclimatise to the new heights (refer to the Health section in the Facts for the Visitor chapter).

A yak will take three packs (50 to 80 kg), and travel 15 to 25 km a day, a handy mantra. They apparently can be ridden, but hate the idea – and it takes great skill to control a mounted yak. You can set about hiring yaks from villagers for around Y10 a day, and the Tibetan handler will require another Y10 a day. Prices vary depending on who the deal is made with,

and where. Bargaining is essential. Yaks love high altitudes, in fact they're so well adapted that they can't survive at lower altitudes. These gracious animals have accompanied organised trekking expeditions up to 6500 metres.

Only a few areas for trekkers are mentioned in this section. If you use your imagination, there are hundreds of possibilities. There are the large lakes in Tibet, there are the holy sites (eg Mt Kailas – see Xinjiang Route chapter for a rundown) and there are all kinds of passes over into India, Ladakh, Sikkim and Bhutan, and Nepal – which will get you into a lot of trouble. Some description of the Chumbi Valley area around Yadong (near the Bhutan/Sikkim border) is contained in the Gyantse & Chumbi Valley chapter of this book.

The best time to trek is spring (April to June) when it's not too hot. Winter can be freezing. Rain is not really a problem as it is in Nepal, although flooding can occur from swollen rivers in autumn. There is a short period of rain in July and August, when monsoon rains manage to cross the Himalaya from the south. Apart from this, the areas bordering the Himalaya on the Tibetan side are quite dry.

Approaches to Everest

There are two approaches to the Everest region – from Xêgar (which is where most mountaineering groups start from) and a second approach from Tingri West. Both routes converge later (see map), and the Xêgar route is preferable. Getting to Everest will be a major expedition in itself, unless you can persuade the driver of a four-wheel drive vehicle to go on safari. In a vehicle it's about seven hours from Xêgar to Rongbuk; on foot it's about three days of hiking from the Chinese checkpoint (to the west of Xêgar) into Rongbuk. The total distance from Xêgar to Everest base camp is about 110 km. From the checkpoint it's roughly 100 km. If you hike in, it will take the better part of the first day (12 hours) to get up to Pang

La, then a further two days down the valley.

There are a few villages along the route where you can stay and travellers have managed to do this. There's very little food in the villages; you might be offered some tsampa and that's about it. The villagers haven't got anything else to offer. Traffic is *very* slim: there may be the odd tractor or road-grader, and you might be lucky enough to be picked up by an expedition truck (you're better off trying your luck in Xêgar). The combination of hitching and walking will get you there in the end, if your lungs don't pack in (the average elevation is 5000 metres). At such high elevations, the sun becomes a real problem – even some of the Tibetans at Rongbuk carry dark goggles (left over by expeditions). Rongbuk is the last inhabited place before the Everest base camp. Expeditions sometimes hire yaks to carry gear from the Rongbuk area and you might be able to do likewise.

As for rented vehicles – if you can talk the driver into it, well and good. Most Chinese drivers, however, don't want to risk their vehicles, or themselves, down this rough road. There is a series of rivers to ford at one spot and come hell and high water you'll have real problems getting through.

XÊGAR ROUTE & PANG LA

Coming from the Lhazê direction, there is a Tibetan truckstop hotel at the turn-off to Xêgar. It's Y3 a head in a dark dorm. From the truckstop hotel it's two km to the Chinese checkpoint (open 24 hours, just bang on the door). The officer may or may not wish to check your Nepalese exit permit as in theory you need one to go beyond here if you're coming from Lhasa. Exactly 11 km from the checkpoint to the west is the turn-off that runs to Everest. It is not marked and is easy to miss. The roads in the area are little more than tracks, and you can get lost trying to follow them. Just keep screaming 'Chomolongma' to the locals and they'll point the way.

From the turn-off the road goes up to the **Pang La** at 5200 metres. From here you get a magnificent view of the Himalayan Range: from left to right, Makalu, Lhotse, Everest, Nuptse and Cho Oyu. If there are clouds none of them may be visible. It's hard to distinguish which one is Everest. The mountain is deceptive from afar and it may not look like the biggest. The view from Pang La far surpasses any from the plains of Tingri West, so even if you can persuade a driver to go this far (about 20 km from the Lhasa-Kathmandu highway), it will be worth the trip.

. After the pass, the road forks: one track goes to Kharta, about another 110 km away, and the other goes to Everest base camp. At a point between Pang La and Rongbuk (about 35 km from Pang La, or 25 km from Rongbuk) there is a fast-flowing river, Dzakar Chu, which is formed from Everest meltwater. If there is flooding or ice, the river will vary from dangerous to impossible to cross. The best time of year is May or June. The river runs over a plain that is filled with stones and boulders. You can wade across the river, but there are rapids and it may take some time to find a good spot. It's not just one river you have to cross because several tributaries charge across the boulders at this place. The road continues through very rugged terrain to Rongbuk Monastery – or the ruins of it. It is about 60 km from Pang La to Rongbuk.

Everest disappears after Pang La, and will not reappear until you're almost on top of Rongbuk – but what a sight! The mountain fills the whole Rongbuk Valley. The big E will blow you away; literally. Gale-force winds come whipping down the valley. They are often quite fierce, bringing with them a biting cold. Amazingly, little urchins wander round Rongbuk in the buff and seem not in the least bit concerned. I don't know whether it was my eyesight or what, but those children looked almost black. Wind-gusts of up to 120 kph blast snow off the north face of Everest.

Rongbuk Monastery

Though its heyday was short, Rongbuk Monastery has a powerful presence. It lies in ruins at a bend in the valley facing Everest. It was destroyed by villagers during the Cultural Revolution. The villagers had been given 'political education' and were told that the monastery was exploiting and oppressing them, so they smashed it. Wooden parts were used for firewood. Rongbuk, the world's highest monastery, is now being repaired by some of the same villagers, financed by the Tibetan regional government, and by believers. The monastery is one of the most romantic sights anywhere, although only a handful of Tibetans live sheltered among the ruins in impromptu housing and lean-to tents. Two monks and five nuns have returned to help the restoration, but since there were no photographs of the original murals, most of the repainting must be done from memory.

Rongbuk Valley is the 'Sanctuary of the Birds'. There was a strict ban on killing any animal in the area. Domestic animals could be eaten as long as they were slaughtered outside the valley. The British Everest reconnaissance party, arriving in Rongbuk in 1921, found the animals of the valley extraordinarily tame; wild blue sheep would come down to the monastery. There were hundreds of lamas and pilgrims engaged in meditation in a cluster of brightly coloured buildings. The British did not meet the Head Lama as he was off doing a year's 'time' in a cave.

Pilgrims used to travel thousands of km to pay their respects to this most sacred spot. Each major peak in Tibet is the home of some deity; Everest is believed to be the abode of the Five Sister Goddesses. In order to escape the terrible cycle of reincarnation, hermits would lock themselves up in caves and cells around the valley. Some lived out their lives subsisting on water and barley passed through a slit in their cell-wall.

Not a stone or plant was allowed to be removed from Rongbuk Valley and, as the British expedition discovered, this even extended to geological specimens. The monks and nuns were separated; there is a ruined nunnery about one km further up the valley.

The history of Rongbuk is sketchy: It is believed to have been built sometime early this century, and was most likely destroyed between 1965 and 1975. The last abbot of the monastery fled to Nepal. In the late 1960s there was heavy military and scientific activity in the area. The PLA dug into caves and hills around Rongbuk in 1968, camouflaged from aerial reconnaissance, and in 1970 radar-dishes popped up along ridges in the area.

No building was left unscathed at Rongbuk – only the shells remain. The stupa, which was split in two and ransacked of its treasures, has been resurrected and patched together. In the early 1980s several expeditions into the Everest area reported that Rongbuk had been turned into a rubbish dump and lavatory – by westerners. Some climbing teams were disgusted to find the ruins filled with cans and toilet-paper that could only have come from the west. The place has been cleaned up, and an odd assortment of Tibetan herders call the ruins home. A high home at that – the monastery rests at 5000 metres.

Some have cited Rongbuk as the model for the piece of fiction about Shangri-La (*Lost Horizon*, by James Hilton, 1933). At Shangri-La the monastery was backed by a spectacular mountain called Karakal, which was supposed to be over 28,000 feet (Everest is 29,028 feet, or 8848 metres). In Hilton's novel, however, the mountain was in the Kunlun Range, not in the Himalaya. It's possible that Hilton may have have drawn material from the 1920s British expeditions and transposed it. In any case, there is a rugged pass between Everest and Cho Oyu (Nepalese side) called Changri La. On the Tibetan side, there's a pass called Chang La

(North Col), although several passes up and down the range bear this name (there's another near Leh). As a point of trivia, Conway is the main character in Hilton's novel, and Conway also happens to be the name of a mountaineer who set a new height record (around 6900 metres) in a climb in the Karakoram Range (1892). That particular climb posed the question: 'Can Everest be conquered?'

THE NORTH FACE

Everest was not 'discovered' by the west until 1852, during a survey of India. In that year, after triangulation, Peak XV was found to be the highest on earth. Its height was estimated at 8840 metres, or 29,000 feet. The surveyors thought no-one would believe the round figures, so they made it 29,002 feet. A hundred years later this was adjusted to 8848 metres (29,028 feet). The Chinese now insist that it is 8848.13 metres, in the interests of purists.

The mountain was named after Sir George Everest, who was the Surveyor-General of India. The name has stuck, though the Tibetan name *Jolmo Lungma* (Goddess Mother of the World) is centuries older. Both Tibet and Nepal were off-limits to foreigners, and it was not until

1921 that the British managed to get permission for a reconnaissance from the Tibetan side. The British expedition's first job was to *find* the mountain as they had no maps of the area. Neither did they have any idea of the prolonged effects of high altitude, or how high a climber could survive without oxygen. George Leigh-Mallory describes the first view of Everest:

We saw the great mountain sides and glaciers and ridges, now another through the floating drifts, until far higher in the sky than imagination dared to suggest, a prodigious white fang – an excrescence from the jaw of the world – the summit of Everest appeared.

The British were viewed suspiciously by the lamas of Rongbuk Monastery, and had to feign they were on a religious pilgrimage. The first expedition added, as did later expeditions, to the lore of the Yeti – that elusive, big-footed, cattle-eating creature. At Rongbuk the ice-clad monster was known in Tibetan as *Migyu* and was given to carting off defenceless women for supper. Sherpas found large tracks, which expedition members attributed to melted-out fox tracks. The Tibetan blue bear may account for another sighting of a dark figure moving across the snow.

In 1922 the first attempt on the summit of Everest took place, with the British team wearing woollens, thick tweeds, Norfolk jackets and studded leather boots. The only hardware was ice axes and primitive crampons, but the team was lugging oxygen tanks for the first time. In the attempt, seven porters were killed in an avalanche. The lamas at Rongbuk forecast that the demons of Everest would cast down any man who dared tread the slopes and a fresco to this effect shortly appeared on the monastery walls. The man being cast down was European. Undaunted, climber George Mallory was back with the third British foray in 1924. George Mallory and Andrew Irvine were last seen making good time for the summit (they were estimated to be at the 8500 metre level) when they were enveloped in cloud and not seen again.

The two must have died in a fall. Whether they succeeded in gaining the summit is one of mountaineering's greatest mysteries. In all probability the mystery will never be solved, as the vital evidence — both Mallory and Irvine carried cameras — has never surfaced. In 1933 another British expedition found an ice axe, which could only have belonged to Mallory or Irvine, on the 'second step' (20 metres of vertical terror and frostbite high up on the North Face). Later Chinese expeditions found objects which belonged to the pair, and a climber on the 1975 Chinese expedition claimed he'd come across the body of a westerner at 8100 metres, below the 'second step'. Official sources in China denied the claim.

The British enjoyed a monopoly of Tibetan access to the mountain between the two world wars (although the Tibetans imposed a nine year ban on expedition attempts after the disastrous 1924 climb). From 1933 to 1938 there were four more British expeditions from the Tibetan side and though they failed on Everest, they did conquer a few other peaks in the area (Khartaphu – 7320 metres, and Kharta Changri – 7055 metres, were climbed in 1935). In 1934 there was an unofficial solo attempt on Everest. Ex-army officer Maurice Wilson (British) announced to the world that he was going to crash-land a Tiger Moth on the slopes of the mountain, and hike up from there to plant the Union Jack on the summit. The Indian Government promptly seized his light plane, but Wilson did not give up, he saw himself as the world's guru, a man with a mission.

Disguised as a deaf and dumb monk, he found his way through to Rongbuk where he got on famously with the head lama. Wilson had no mountaineering experience, no warm clothing, and little equipment. He thought he could pray his way to the top. He died at advance base camp, probably of exhaustion.

In 1947 the Dalai Lama banned issue of travel permits to Tibet. With the 1950 Chinese takeover, Tibet was firmly closed off. By this time, however, Nepal had opened its doors, and climbers from several nations vied for the summit on that side. On 29 May 1953, New Zealander Edmund Hillary and Sherpa Tenzing Norgay 'knocked the bastard off' (as Hillary put it) in the course of a British expedition.

In Tibet, in 1959, the Chinese and Russians undertook a joint reconnaissance on Everest. China's first mountaineering teams had gone to Russia for training. With the rift between the Chinese and the Russians in 1960, China carried on the work alone, and then stepped into the Everest spotlight in a big way. In March 1960 the Chinese claimed that all of Everest, as well as an eight km stretch south to Namche Bazaar, belonged to China. At this time China was busy testing the limits of Indian and Nepalese patience in border disputes. The Everest claim did not sit well with the Nepalese Prime Minister, who made a counterclaim that all of Everest belonged to Nepal, including parts of Rongbuk glacier.

The same month (March) a 214-man Chinese expedition arrived at Rongbuk base camp for a summit attempt. In April,

Chinese Premier Zhou Enlai flew to Kathmandu for a visit. The Nepalis may not have understood political football, but they did understand the theft of a holy mountain. Gurkhas with fixed bayonets were posted every two metres along the route from the airport into Kathmandu centre to protect Zhou Enlai. In May 1960, in an outright display of nationalism, the Chinese expedition claimed victory in the name of Mao. Three climbers had plonked a bust of Mao, a Chinese flag, and some notes at the summit, and collected geological specimens as gifts for Mao Zedong. The climb was disputed, perhaps unfairly, by cynics in the west, as there were no pictures taken on the summit (the final ascent was made at night).

In 1975 (by which time the border between Nepal and Tibet had been firmly delineated as running across the summit), the Chinese mounted another huge expedition. One Chinese (Hou Sheng-fu), and eight Tibetans (one a woman) gained the summit and left a tripod there, which became something of a landmark – an undisputed one.

There have been more than 70 expedition attempts on Everest to date. Over 150 climbers have gained the summit (more than 20 of them Sherpas), and over 60 climbers have died in the attempt. From 1950 to 1980 most of these expeditions took place from the Nepalese side. From the Tibetan side, there was rumoured to be a disastrous Russian attempt in 1952 (the summit party of six is said to have died but the Russians have neither confirmed nor denied the report). Then there were the Chinese attempts and scientific expeditions (1960, 1966-68, and the confirmed summit climb of 1975).

In addition to these, there were a few illegal climbs from the Tibetan side. In 1947, Earl Denman, a Canadian, sneaked through to Rongbuk with two Sherpas, Tenzing Norgay and Ang Dawa. They were forced to turn back above the North Col, at around 7100 metres. In 1951, a Dane, Klaus Becker-Larsen, crossed Nangpa La with four Sherpas, and made his way to East Rongbuk Glacier. This attempt failed near the North Col, and Larsen returned to Namche Bazaar undetected by the Chinese. In 1962, three Americans and a Swiss obtained permission from the Nepalese side to climb Gyachung Kang (7922 metres). The team changed tack, headed over Nup La (5985 metres), traversed the West Rongbuk Glacier and reached the North Col, attaining a height of 7600 metres on the North Ridge. The attempt was then abandoned and the climbers made their dangerous way back to the Nepalese side. This illegal foray was undetected by the Chinese, but the Nepalese closed the Himalaya to expeditions from 1964-1969 as a reprisal.

By 1980, the Chinese, satisfied that they were the first to conquer the North Face, opened up the Tibetan side to foreign climbers again. An invitation had been extended to the Iranians to try the summit, and when political turmoil in Iran cut them out, the Chinese invited the Japanese instead (late 1970s). With the waiting list rumoured to be up to 10 years on the Nepalese side, Tibet suddenly became very attractive. The drawback was the exorbitant fee-structure for Everest attempts on the Tibetan side. One Japanese expedition cost around US$1 million. Expeditions were mounted by the British, Swiss, Japanese, Chileans, Italians . . .

Early in the piece in 1980, the Japanese climber Yasuo Kato, who had previously gained the summit from the Nepalese side, went back for a second helping on the north side. He succeeded, though several expedition members died. Hot on his tail came the Italian climber Reinhold Messner. Like Kato, Messner had already been to the top once – but without oxygen. In 1980 he wanted to attempt Everest from the north side, solo, and without oxygen. With his girlfriend waiting at advance base camp at 6500 metres, Messner made a superhuman, alpine-style dash for the summit. The trip started off on the wrong foot when he tumbled down a crevasse just after leaving his base camp, but he painstakingly extricated himself and ploughed on. His only climbing hardware was ski-poles, an ice axe, and an ice screw and rock piton to anchor himself overnight. Along the way, suffering from the bizarre effects of high altitude, he shared food with an imaginary partner, held conversations with his backpack and treated his ice axe as a friend.

Messner gained the summit on the third day of climbing but, due to cloudy weather, missed the views for a second time! Not content with this feat, he set up several self-timer photos on the summit to prove it (the effort of arranging a camera at this altitude is calculated to be a near-impossible task). Messner's ultimate project is to conquer all 14 of the world's peaks over 8000 metres – without oxygen. He has 12 under his belt.

An interesting variation on double-ascents was a 1983 Japanese expedition; Kazuyuki Takahashi led a southern assault from Nepal, while his wife led another team from Tibet. They had hoped to meet on the summit, but it was not to be. Is there no end to the Kingdom of Adventure?! In a spectacular 1983 climb, six Americans scaled the sheer Kangshung or East Face from the Tibetan side. The Kangshung Face has long been considered totally impossible. Not only did the Americans conquer it but they got most of their team up there. A small Australian expedition pulled off a major feat the following year (October 1984) when two climbers gained the summit on the north side by a new route, without oxygen.

For every success on Everest, there are at least three failures, and the inevitable deaths or casualties. For Everest climbers, the odds are 50-50 that they will not return. Attempting the north-east ridge from the Tibetan side in 1982, British mountaineers Pete Boardman and Joe Tasker were last sighted at 8250 metres.

Their deaths paralleled the Mallory-Irvine legend as their bodies were never found. And why do climbers continue to scale Everest? As Mallory casually told a *Times* reporter before the ill-fated 1924 climb: 'Because it is there'.

EVEREST BASE CAMP

Unlike the highly dangerous Khumbu icefall approach to Everest on the Nepalese side, the way to Everest from the north is straightforward. There is a road right up to base camp. The road (all the way in from Xêgar) was scoured out by the Chinese for their 1960 attempt on Everest.

Base camp is 12 km beyond Rongbuk Monastery at 5200 metres. At the moraine where the base camp is, there are little piles of trash from previous (foreign) expeditions and group-tours: brand names from the USA, England, Germany, France, and discarded medical junk in six European languages.

From here on, you need proper mountaineering equipment. You would be most unwise to proceed any further unless you're in tip-top shape, have mountaineering experience, and know what you're getting into. Without a guide or a medic, you could get into serious trouble, and no-one is about to rescue you. Yaks can be hired from the Rongbuk Monastery area; say Y10 a day for the yak, and a similar amount for the Tibetan handler. Beyond base camp there is different terminology for camp I, camp II and so on. It depends which expedition is referred to. The old British camp I was at around 5400 metres, and camp II at 6000 metres. There is roughly an 'intermediate' camp at around 5700 to 6000 metres, and an 'advance' camp at around 6500 metres on the East Rongbuk Glacier. There is a miracle 'ice highway' through the pinnacles of glacial ice on the way to advance base on the East Rongbuk Glacier, which makes the mountaineer's progress somewhat easier. This trek to the 6500 metre level, on a trail winding through giant seracs of ice, is the world's highest possible trek not involving actual climbing. Crampons are needed to get up to this old British camp III, as the ice-path can be quite hard and slippery.

Everest is in the shape of a pyramid, with three wide faces (the North, the East, and the South-west Faces), and three major ridges (North-east, West, and South-east). Hanging off the slopes on the Tibetan side are massive glaciers: the West Rongbuk Glacier, the East Rongbuk Glacier, and the Kangshung Glacier. Everest base camp is near the junction of the East and West Rongbuk Glaciers (base camp is at 5200 metres, and the actual glacier junction is at 5500 metres). The Dzakar Chu (river) dribbles out here. The moraines (scree) at base camp were formed from glacial debris.

One hundred million years ago the whole zone was under the sea. About 50 million years ago, the collision of the Indian and Asian plates caused the massive upheaval that is known as the Himalaya (one of the youngest mountain chains around). This would explain the fragments of fossil marine creatures, billions of them, found near the summit of Everest. Essentially Everest is a rock peak, with strata on the North Face. The most prominent is a layer of marine limestone called the Yellow Band.

NANGPA LA

Approaching by direct 'road' (track) from Tingri West is an unusual method of entering Nepal. Nangpa La (or Khumbu La – 5716 metres) is nothing unusual for the locals, however. It has been a trading route for centuries. It links the Tibetan Everest area with Namche Bazaar (the starting point for Everest treks from the Nepalese side). There is an air-link from Lukla to Kathmandu. It should also be possible to get to Nangpa La from the Rongbuk area. Nangpa Pass cuts through a parting of the Great Himalaya, with Cho Oyu to the east (8153 metres). The pass is used for summit attempts on Cho Oyu. The first ascent of Cho Oyu was done on this route by an Austrian expedition of three members and seven Sherpas (1954). The Cho Oyu base camp is in fact on the Tibetan side, just north-east of Nangpa La, at 5560 metres.

Cutting east and west of Nangpa La are two peaks: one 6470 metres, the other 6600 metres. The route in from Tingri West traverses the Gyabrag Glacier on the Tibetan side, and runs along the east rim of Nangpa Glacier on the Nepalese side. The route down through Nepal is mainly above 4000 metres, with Namche Bazaar itself at 3440 metres. The trek from Tingri West to Namche Bazaar will take at least six days. You would have to be well equipped for sleeping out, and obviously you will have some trouble if you're spotted by Chinese border-patrols (the Nepalese won't be too thrilled either). You're heading into uncharted territory when it comes to Chinese patrols. They may be tight to stop Tibetans crossing into Nepal, although the policy changes from time to time. A hired Tibetan with a yak would be a useful adjunct. Perhaps you could train the yak to sleep on top of you at night. It can get really frozen up there, and frostbite should not be ruled out.

KHARTA

Kharta is the trailhead for treks toward Everest East Face (Kangshung Face), and gateway to the Kama Valley below Makalu. Kharta itself is set in green surroundings near the Arun River which is a sharp contrast to the desolate moonscape at Rongbuk. Getting to Kharta is a major trek in itself, unless you can somehow requisition transport. The track to Kharta goes over two passes of 5200 metres: Pang La and Doya La. You may find shelter in the hamlet of Kharta. It is about 140 km from the Lhasa highway turn-off to Kharta.

MAKALU & EVEREST EAST FACE

From Kharta there are two valleys: the Kharta Valley, which runs along the Kharta River due west of Kharta; and the

Kama Valley, which runs along the Kama River to the south-west of Kharta. The Kama Valley is the one you want if you're seeking to get closer to the Kangshung or East Face of Everest. The valley offers views of such giants as Makalu, Chomo Lonzo, Pethangtse and Lhotse, as well as Everest itself. This is approaching the highest trekking territory in the world, with passes getting up to 6000 metres.

Back in the heady days when Tibet had just opened up to individuals, travellers got to some pretty strange spots – like the Kama Valley. A bizarre encounter took place in this rugged valley. A high-tech tour-group with a train of a dozen trekkers, two dozen Tibetans and two dozen yaks came across a ragged trio of individuals (plus two yaks and two Tibetans). They swapped information; the individuals asked for food, warm clothing, bearings (which way is bloody Everest then ?!) and medical assistance (the Australian of the trio had severe altitude sickness and was coughing up blood). The tour-group trekkers were a bit shaken because the valley no longer appeared to be the pristine exotica they'd invested in. The tour-group leader departed, scratching his head. How the hell did those travellers get there? Well, it seems that they'd picked up the relevant tour brochure, and though it contained no map, they had discovered enough of the route to beat the group to the location. The three had hitched and walked into Kharta, picked up their yaks and handlers, and managed a 10 day trek in this area. This was done with winter approaching – in October.

The next-door neighbour to Everest, Makalu, derives its name from the Tibetan *Mahakala* or the 'Great Black Deva' – a reference both to the mountain's dark granite formations, and to the deity lurking within the granite. The four-armed protector Mahakala is often depicted in thangkas as a demonic figure holding a chopper, sword, trident and blood-filled skull-cap, and wearing a crown of skulls.

The first ascent of Makalu was achieved by the French, coming from the Nepalese side, in 1955.

XIXABANGMA BASE CAMP
Xixabangma (Shishapangma or Gosainthan) was the last of the 8000 metre giants to fall. It fell to the Chinese in 1964. Ten of them gained the summit in the course of a 205-man expedition which included many scientists. The mountain received a second ascent by a West German team in 1980, and has fallen half a dozen times to foreign climbing groups since then. In Tibetan, *Shisha Pangma* means 'Crest above the Grassy Plain'. *Gosainthan* is the Sanskrit name for the mountain, meaning 'Abode of the God'. The mountain, as with all major peaks in Tibet, is holy. To the south, in Nepal, is Gosainkund, a large holy lake that is associated with Shiva (whose celestial home is Mt Kailas).

Xixabangma is the only 8000 metre peak totally within Tibet. For a long time it was not a question of climbing it, but getting to see it. It was not until 1951 that Peter Aufschnaiter (the Austrian who escaped with Heinrich Harrer to Tibet, and stayed on) was able to get within 10 km of Xixabangma to photograph it. This was only the second photograph taken of the mountain, the first being an aerial one taken in 1950. Aufschnaiter returned to draw sketch-maps of the Xixabangma area and the area has still not been properly surveyed. The elevation of Xixabangma is given at 8012 metres by the Chinese, but a 1975 survey in India placed its height at 8046 metres.

Ironically, with the improved road from Lhasa to Kathmandu, Xixabangma is now one of the most accessible of the Himalayan mountains. You can drive straight up to Xixabangma base camp from Nyalam, as group-tours are prone to do (four-wheel drive vehicle). The distance from Nyalam to Xixabangma base camp is around 25 km – it should take about two or three days to walk in from Nyalam. The route in follows a river to the west, and slightly

north of, Nyalam. Base camp is at 5000
metres, and advance base camp is around
5700 metres.

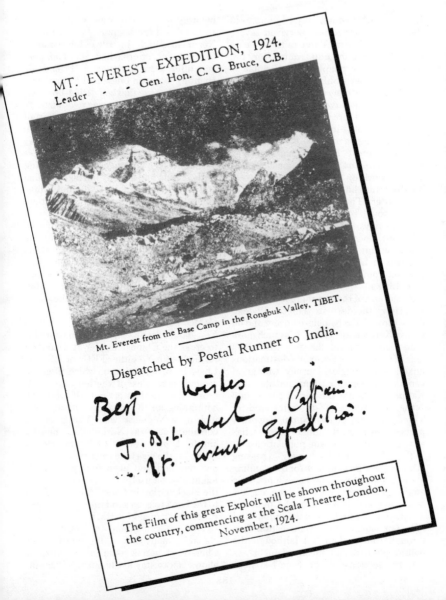

MT. EVEREST EXPEDITION, 1924.
Leader - - - Gen. Hon. C. G. Bruce, C.B.

Mt. Everest from the Base Camp in the Rongbuk Valley, TIBET.

Dispatched by Postal Runner to India.

Best wishes -
J. B. L. Noel
Captain.
Mt. Everest Expedition.

The Film of this great Exploit will be shown throughout
the country, commencing at the Scala Theatre, London,
November, 1924.

Nepal Route

By the Tibetan count, only 13 temples in the whole of Tibet have survived severe Chinese vandalism. Three of those lie on the Lhasa-Kathmandu route (for full details see the chapters on Gyantse & Chumbi Valley, Shigatse, and Sakya). The Nepal route permits a majestic rear-view of the Himalayan Range, and, if you can manage it, there's magnificent trekking among the giants in the Everest, Makalu and Xixabangma areas (see the Trekking in the Everest Region chapter). The scenery along the way is a moonscape and a graveyard of civilisations. Up to a hundred ruins line the dirt road through to the border. The whole ancient trading route through to Kathmandu can be done in three days if you have the transport arranged. Local transport is sparse after Shigatse, but vehicles can be rented for the trip in Lhasa. Food is largely non-existent from Shigatse to Zhangmu – BYO from Lhasa.

At the end of the trip there is a startling drop from the desolate Tibetan Plateau down through the Nepalese border and on to lush Kathmandu Valley. It's much more than a geographical change – this is the king of routes – it's two exotic destinations linked in one magical journey, with great variation in peoples, customs and lifestyles. Kathmandu is not the end of Tibet. In a sense, it's where a different kind of Tibetan journey begins. Nepal, like other parts strung along the Indian borders, has sizeable Tibetan refugee populations.

The Tibet-Nepal border crossing provides new possibilities for overlanding – ones that travellers have long been awaiting. From Beijing or Hong Kong it is now possible to travel through China and Tibet, on through Nepal, India, and Pakistan, skirt around Afghanistan, then through Iran to Istanbul (although the political climate can quickly change).

Early sections of the Sino-Nepalese highway to Shigatse were completed in 1955-56 and the highway snaked toward Xêgar in 1958. In 1961 the Chinese Government approached the Nepalese and offered to construct a 'Friendship Highway' between Lhasa and Kathmandu. The road was finished 1964-66. The purpose of the highway was to open trade between the two countries, and permit pilgrims to travel, but the world watched in consternation as work on the highway progressed. It was seen as a nasty Chinese preparation for an advance into Nepal and India (China had already infringed Indian and other borders in the 1950s and 1960s, and had talked of the peaceful 'liberation' of Sikkim and Bhutan).

With Lhasa much more accessible by land from Kathmandu than Chengdu, the highway is going to see a lot of travellers now that it has opened up (one way definite, the other undecided as yet). Get there before they turn it into the Indy 500. You take the low road and I'll take –

LHASA TO KATHMANDU

You should get an exit stamp on your visa to cross the Chinese border at Zhangmu (available for Y5 either FECs or RMB at Lhasa PSB, depending on which official is around), regardless of whether you wish to cross the border or not. If you are continuing on to Nepal you should also pick up a Nepalese visa (Y35 from the consulate near the Norbulinka, open 11 am to 1 pm, and 3 to 6 pm, closed Sundays; the visa takes either one hour or one day and you need four photos) It might also be useful to buy and trade on the blackmarket in Lhasa, then run down to the bank to get a good rate on Nepalese rupees exchanged for RMB.

That's if you intend to continue into Nepal – many don't. In theory, your Chinese exit permit stamp in your passport allows you to stay in Shigatse, Xêgar and

Zhangmu along the route, and to cross the checkpoint west of Xêgar. Those three towns are eventually slated for full opening. If you're not going further than Xêgar – say, doing a round-trip through Shigatse – then don't bother with the exit permit. If you are going beyond the checkpoint west of Xêgar, you show the exit permit and then when you come back, you say you've changed your mind about Nepal, and they'll understand! There's only one flaw with all this, and that is once you have an exit permit stamped in your passport, your original visa, in theory, cannot be extended (although it has been done by travellers – they get the exit permit cancelled somehow). In any case, if you intend doing a round-trip, you should make sure that you get your original visa extended *first* (say one month), and then ask for the exit permit, which is valid until the end of the extension. PSB in Lhasa is reluctant to extend your original visa until it has almost run out but it depends on who's around. They certainly won't extend it after you get an exit-permit – that would have to be done elsewhere.

This all sounds horribly complicated; you have to make up your mind if you really want to exit, and whether you want to go west of Xêgar. To solve that one, a few travellers have slipped around the Xêgar checkpoint, but this is not recommended. It's better to slip *through* the checkpoint – just confuse the officials there.

Local Transport & Hitching

Public transport is OK as far as Shigatse, but then you might be stranded till you work up a group for a truck of pilgrims headed to Nepal. Public bus is Y20 to Shigatse, then a truck to the border is about Y45 to Y60 (22 hours straight, pilgrim truck, 25 people; you sit in the back and pay a different price to the locals, bargaining is necessary). Some have managed to get a ride for Y30.

You may be able to jump a pilgrim bus from the Tashilhunpo in Shigatse, and get

to Sakya Monastery, and try to arrange a hitch from there. Some travellers have hitched the whole route on trucks, but this is not easy as there is very little traffic after Shigatse, and army trucks will most likely not pick you up. You *may* be able to get a direct truck from Lhasa to Zhangmu (from No 6 depot, Y80, up to 45 hours straight run, no stops). Once a month there is the mythical Lhasa-Zhangmu direct bus, intended for the locals, not you. It's Y60 to the border, and a gruelling 36 to 48 hours with no stops.

Hired Vehicles

These are your best bet if you don't wish to get stranded. Another advantage is that you get to see the scenery (you won't see much from the back of a truck!) and you can stop for photographs. You have to negotiate firmly on vehicle hire, but you don't have a great choice to negotiate with. Negotiating points are the length of the journey, price, number of passengers, and itinerary. Establish whether the passengers are returning to Lhasa, or being dropped off at the border because the price is different. Few of the negotiating committees speak English so you should dredge up a translator (Chinese/English). You are not responsible for the driver's food and accommodation.

Bus Depot This is just east of the Potala: a group of travellers arranged, with some translation help, for a freak-bus to run to the border. This cost Y1880 RMB and the bus had space for 25 passengers, but the group decided to leave with 15, which came to Y125 RMB per head for a three day run to the border, with some passengers returning. This must have been a crazy bus ride, with passengers getting off left right and centre along the way. One guy got off in Lhazê to continue along the road to Xinjiang, others jumped ship in Tingri to hike off to Everest! A second group of travellers using the same depot paid Y2500 RMB for 25 people on a six-day trip, which is Y100 each.

Taxi Co, Lhasa This possibility consists of a variety of beaten-up vehicles that may or may not make the trip. There have been strange reports on the vehicles. One jeep is notorious for its lack of brakes, another is famous for its engine that blows up on the high passes, and the drivers sometimes try to get extra money by loading up on Tibetan riders for the return run. Make it clear that if you hire, it's your vehicle. To cut a long story short, there are two minibuses available, and several Beijing jeeps. The following prices were quoted for the 894 km journey to the border:

Minibus (eight passengers); one-way (two days), Y1.80 per km x 894 km = Y1610; return (four days), Y2.40 per km x 894 km = Y2145;
Beijing jeep (four passengers); one-way (two days), Y1.20 per km x 894 km = Y1070; return (four days), Y1.60 per km x 894 km = Y1430.
Extra days cost Y80 a day in minibus or a jeep (after the second day on a one-way trip, or after the fourth day on a return trip). Example: Minibus (eight passengers); return (eight days), Y2.40 per km x 894 km = Y2145 (for standard four day trip) + Y80 per extra day x four extra days = Y320; the total for an eight-day day trip = Y2465.

All of this should be taken with a grain of salt. Travellers have bargained and arranged a six-day minibus itinerary (four days out, two back) for Y1860, which works out around Y232 a head. One group got a Beijing jeep and a four-day itinerary for Y1000, or Y250 a head. Expect to pay Y150 to Y250 a head for a four-day itinerary (eight passengers in a minibus, round-trip from Lhasa). The usual deal is that half the money is payable in RMB and half in FEC. If you can dredge up a Hong Konger, prices will drop dramatically (Y1 per km for the minibus).

Landcruisers Toyota four-wheel drive Landcruisers can be arranged through the desk at No 1 Guesthouse. There is a government car-pool at the west end of Renmin Lu, but you can't deal directly with the work-unit involved. Landcruisers are ideal for the terrain you cross – very comfortable, reliable, fast – but not cheap. You will need an excellent Mandarin speaker to arrange the deal, as reception at No 1 Guest house is stroppy. The maximum number of passengers is four, but you can squeeze a fifth in the back with the luggage if you push when negotiating. It's Y1500 to Y1800 for the trip to the border and return, and they don't seem to care if it's four days or six days or eight days (after eight days they do care – it's Y200 a day extra). Since they claim to be a government work-unit, they want all the funds in FECs, and will not bend (one traveller said he'd changed all his money into RMB coming in from Kathmandu, so he didn't have FECs! He got away with paying RMB for his share of the Landcruiser trip). There are a number of Landcruisers at the car-pool but whether they're available or not is a different story.

CITS & TTC vehicles Official tourism, hiding out at No 3 Hotel, says it has vehicles for hire. This is probably baloney – most of their pool is overworked for group tours, and it's best to steer clear of this lot if you value your sanity. Prices quoted were Y2.50 per km for a deluxe minibus (15 passengers) and Y1.50 per km for a jeep. On top of those fees there was a surcharge of Y60 a day for the driver's food and accommodation.

Warning
Numerous travellers have had their skulls banged on the interior roof of minibuses and Landcruisers. There are no seatbelts, and you can end up with a very nasty neck problem. Brace yourself somehow, especially if you're sitting at the rear of the vehicle. In general, the Chinese drivers originating from Lhasa are quite bent. Unlike the veteran truck-drivers who have

learned to control their DTs and Dong-
fengs at high altitude, the minibus, bus
and Landcruiser drivers are out to lunch.
Useful phrases to memorise (in Chinese)
are 'slow down!' and 'Watch out – we're
going off the edge of the mountain!'

Drivers tend to want to take over the
itinerary and rush you through it as fast as
they can. They are not in the least bit
interested in the Tibetans, nor in the
sights along the way. All they want to do is
get it over with, and get back to Lhasa
where it's more civilised. Don't let the
driver take command of the itinerary. If
you hired the vehicle, then you run the
show. Learn how to stay 'Stop – I want to
take a photo' in Chinese – otherwise the
driver won't stop. If you want to stop for a
picnic somewhere, likewise. It's best to
make it quite clear *before* you set out
where you want to stay for the night, map
out each day – and get it written on paper
as a receipt. You can always vary things
once you get started (add a day or
whatever) but you need a firm basis to
start with. If you are setting out on a longer
itinerary, and you have rented a vehicle,
load up on as much food and water as you
can manage.

Sample Itinerary
Avoid including a Sunday in the schedule
if possible as the Tashilhunpo in Shigatse
is closed then (so are some of the other
temples). Large hotels are located in
Shigatse, Xêgar and Zhangmu, meaning
rip-off stuff, but that's where your driver
will prefer to hang out. The driver can do
up to 12 hours a day on the road. The
following itinerary is for a four day trip to
the border, one-way:

Day 1 depart early from Lhasa, reach
Gyantse by afternoon, visit chorten,
continue same day to Shigatse, sleep
Shigatse.
Day 2 Tashilhunpo Monastery in the
morning, plus pilgrim-circuit out to back
of fort and down to markets, sleep
Shigatse.

Day 3 Drive to Sakya, spend half a day
there, continue to Lhazê, Xêgar or Tingri
West for overnight stop.
Day 4 Drive to Tingri West (Himalayan
view-spot), depart lunch-time for border
at Zhangmu. The same day you can get to
the bank, carry on to Nepal and overnight
in Tatopani, ready for a next-day truck to
Kathmandu.

THE HIGH ROAD
There are two routes through to Shigatse
from Lhasa – the more direct road to the
north, and the more interesting southern
road via Gyantse. The north road goes
through two high passes (both over 5000
metres). It is 78 km from Lhasa to
Yangbajain, and 250 km from there to
Shigatse. The scenery varies from snowcaps to rocky desert and grassland. You
cross the Tsangpo River by ferry.

On the south route, leaving Lhasa,
watch out for rock-sculptures and ruins.
About 20 km from Lhasa there is a large
rock-sculpture of Buddha off the side of
the road. It seems Tibetans would carve
and paint images on any open stone
surfaces along a road or mountain pass, a
religious reminder to those drifting through.
After you cross the Tsangpo River there is
the **Khamba La** pass at 4900 metres, with a
great view of **Yamdrok Tso** (Yamzho
Yumco or the Turquoise Lake). Beyond
the lake, on a clear day, you get a sneak
preview of the Himalayan mountains
floating out of the Bhutan border.

Yamdrok Tso is a lake of a glowing blue
that radiates a near-mystical charm and
there was once a monastery here for
contemplating it. This was Samding, the
'Hill of Deep Meditation', to the north end
of Yamdrok Tso. In the early 18th
century, legend has it, the Abbess of the
Monastery (venerated as the 'Thunderbolt
Sow', and the only female incarnation in
Tibet) transformed herself and her cohorts
into pigs to save themselves from a Tartar
attack. The Tartars left the monastery in
disgust, finding nothing in the grounds but
a bunch of pigs, whereupon the denizens

resumed their ordinary appearances. Not much is known about the present state of Samding – whether it still exists, and if so, in what condition. It followed the Bodong School of Tibetan Buddhism, whatever that school may be. Neither is much known about the female incarnation, other than the fact that records go back to 1717, and that the lineage is still continued . . . well, sort of.

The Thunderbolt Sow is a terrible translation of *Dorjee Phagmo* (believed to be a reincarnation of Dolma Tara, the spiritual consort of Chenrezig). In 1937, the acting Regent of Tibet announced that the 6th Dorjee Phagmo had been recognised in a young girl, even though the 5th was still at large. He argued that the transferral of souls actually took place in this case *before* death. The 5th Dorjee Phagmo died the following year, but the Tibetans would not accept the 6th as a true incarnation, and three other candidates were put forward. The matter was hotly disputed by the 6th's father (versus the inmates of Samding?) and a costly legal battle drained the funds of Samding and tore its monks and nuns apart with internal strife. The 6th Dorjee Phagmo, it appears, hardly took up residence at Samding, since the legal wrangle carried over into the 1950s. In 1959, she fled for India, but the same year decided to return to Tibet by way of China. It seems that she then sided with the Chinese in her loyalties and made it clear that she did not wish to be a Living Buddha anymore and, furthermore, that she thought Living Buddhas were false. She is married, has three children, and when last heard of (1980), was living in Lhasa, and held the position of vice-chairman of the Tibetan branch of the Chinese People's Political Consultative Committee.

Yamdrok Tso is about 240 km in circumference and is more like an inland sea. There are yak-herders around, and the lake itself supports a population of scaleless fish in its non-saline waters. There are one or two fishing villages along the way, plus a sprinkling of chortens and ruined forts. If you glance at the map, you can make out the shape of the lake as a scorpion with pincers – which is what the Tibetans believe it to be. Further on is the 5200 metre **Karo La** pass (75 km from Gyantse, or 175 km from Lhasa) which has the dubious distinction of being the site of the highest battle in history. In 1904, 3000 Tibetans massed at a large fortification guarding the pass and showered down boulders and small-arms fire on the invading British. The British were forced to turn their hand to mountaineering to dislodge the Tibetans, climbing to a height of 5800 metres to attack their position.

From Karo La the road goes steadily down to Gyantse, at a mere 4000 metres. By four-wheel drive vehicle, the trip from Lhasa to Gyantse takes about six hours, on a bus, about 12 hours. From Gyantse to Shigatse at 3900 metres is an easy drive of less than three hours.

SHIGATSE TO LHAZÊ & SAKYA

The direct distance from Shigatse to Lhazê is about 150 km. Along the way there is a turn-off to Sakya, which is a boomerang trip of 50 km. The turn-off is 125 km from Shigatse, or 25 km from Lhazê. There is one pass of 4500 metres (Po La) between Shigatse and Lhazê. Lhazê (around 4000 metres in elevation) is a boring place, with the major sights being dust and grit. It does, however, have a hotel and a theatre! About five km to the west of Lhazê the road forks: south-west to Nepal, and directly west for the run to Mt Kailas and Xinjiang. It takes between three and five hours to get from Shigatse to Lhazê. There is very little transport after Shigatse, mostly army trucks going to the border. Travellers have managed to hitch this stretch, and got holed up in places along the way. Take a book. You're better off with a hired vehicle, if you can afford it.

Top: Ruins of Rongbuk Monastery with Mt Everest in background (MB)
Left: View of Yadong valley, close to Sikkim border (RS)
Right: Yadong bus passing Chomolhari (RS)

Top: Caravan on road to Gyantse (MB)
Left: Yamdok Tso, the Turquoise Lake (MB)
Right: Villagers on road to Gyantse (MB)

THE TINGRIS

From Lhazê, directly south-west, the road continues over the Lak Pa La pass of 5220 metres to Xêgar, otherwise known as Tingri. This run from Lhazê to Xêgar takes about three to five hours. There are two places vying for the honour of being called Mr and Mrs Tingri. One is Xêgar, otherwise known as Big Tingri, or New Tingri (Xin Tingri), which is the Chinese side of things as they now stand. To the west is Little Tingri, Old Tingri (Lao Tingri), which is designated in this book as Tingri West to save confusion. Tingri West is the Tibetan village. The Chinese characters for big, new, Chinese Tingri and little, old, Tibetan Tingri look identical – so you won't be the only one who's confused. One set of characters is bigger than the other! There is another place not too far off with a similar-sounding name: Dinggyê.

XÊGAR

Most group-tours and climbing expeditions are diverted to Xêgar (4300 metres), which is seven km back off the main road. The reason for this is simply that Xêgar has a large compound-style Chinese hotel with a restaurant, and exorbitant prices. The hotel charges Y15 a head, and refuses to back off, although some travellers have managed to get a bed for Y5. The restaurant wanted a similar deal; Y15 a head. I jumped into the queue, noticed that the man ahead of me was forking out less than Y2, demanded a similar deal, and got it. There is a large ruined fort at Xêgar, up a hillside overlooking the town. Xêgar Dzong and 'Shining Crystal Monastery' once housed 400 monks and dominated the village below. In 1924 a member of the British Everest expedition marvelled at the fantastic dream-castle, perched on the 5300 metre mountain-top, a fusion of rock and architecture. Today barely a single piece stands upright – it was demolished during the Cultural Revolution.

XÊGAR TO TINGRI WEST

There are a number of things to see en route. Where the Xêgar turn-off joins the main Lhasa-Kathmandu highway, there is a Tibetan truckstop hotel, where a bed is Y3 a head which is much more reasonable than at Xêgar, and there's nicer management too. There's no electricity, but you do get blankets, in a large dorm. Two km down the road is the Chinese checkpoint; open 24 hours, bang on the door. It's no big deal – they're not that interested in you. To make sure they don't get stopped, some travellers have by-passed the checkpoint in the wee hours of the morning, and have been chased up and down the hillsides in the dark by rabid dogs. In theory you need a Nepalese exit permit in your passport if proceeding west through the checkpoint. That's the theory – if you jumble up a bunch of passports they probably won't even notice. Exactly 11 km beyond the checkpoint, to the west, is the turn-off to Rongbuk Monastery (see the Trekking in the Everest Region chapter).

TINGRI WEST

This is a Tibetan village arrayed over a hillside (elevation around 4300 metres). It was once a trading centre (Tibetan-Nepali) for grain, goods, wool and livestock – a trade that died out after 1959. There are signs that this trade might be revived. Right near the main road there is an army garrison. You can wrangle your way in there for Y2 a head; failing that, try the Tibetan village around the corner (some travellers have got into homes there). If you have a tent, there are plenty of nice spots to camp out (as nomads do). A meeting with local Tibetans will prove entertainment enough for both parties. The village, though poverty stricken, is charming enough. Food is scant – a BYO situation. *Top Ramen* (noodles) is about all you can get.

Tingri West lies at the edge of a vast plain. There are great views of the Himalayan giants to the south, assuming

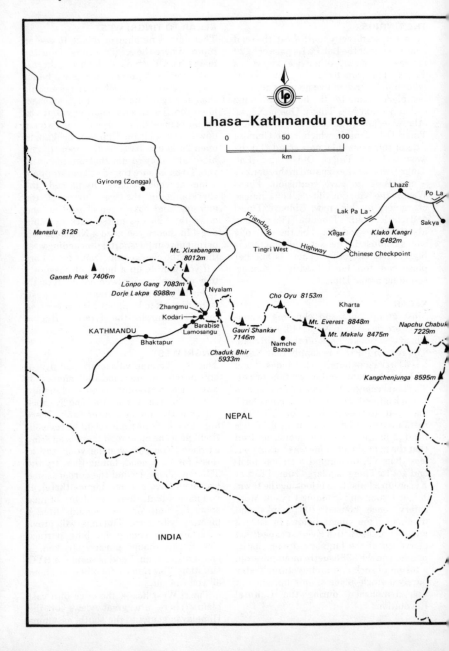

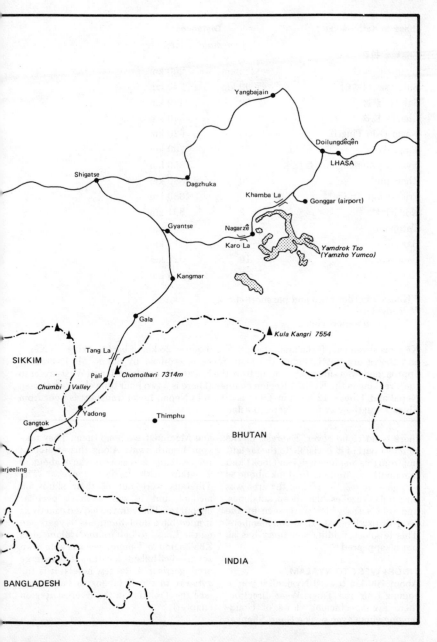

Lhasa to Kathmandu	Distances	
	intermediate	*cumulative*
Lhasa 拉萨		
Gyantse 江孜	250 km	250 km
Shigatse 日喀则	90 km	340 km
Sakya 萨迦	150	490 km
Lhazê 拉孜	50	540 km
Xêgar (Xin Tingri)	90	630 km
Tingri West	70	700 km
Nyalam (Zhalangmu) 聂拉木	150	850 km
Zhangmu*	30	880 km
Friendship Bridge**	9	889 km
Kodari***	2	891 km
Tatopani	2	893 km
Barabise	24	917 km
Lamosangu	10	927 km
Kathmandu	77	1004 km

* Khasa – border town and passport check
** Youyi Qiao
*** Nepal passport check

Xêgar is seven km off the main road; Sakya requires 26 km of backtracking – if Xêgar and Sakya are not included the main route is reduced by 66km. Mt Everest is approached from side roads leading from the Xêgar area and from Tingri West – refer to the Trekking in the Everest Region chapter. There is a two hour time change between Nepal and Tibet – 12 noon in Tibet is 10 am in Nepal. Local transport is poor from Shigatse all the way to the Nepal border.

there is no cloud-cover. Everest, or the topmost part of it, is visible to the far left, but from this distance it doesn't look like a mammoth. Something to think about as you gaze across the plains: the area was once full of gazelles, blue sheep, antelopes, and wild asses which were seen by the 1921 British Everest expedition members. This fabulous wildlife sanctuary has all but disappeared.

TINGRI WEST TO NYALAM
About 100 km toward Nyalam, if you're coming from the Tingri West direction, there are spectacular views of cloud-busting Himalayan peaks: Gauri Shankar and Menlungtse among them. They take your breath away. Along this stretch of road we came across a caravan of about 50 Tibetans with loaded donkeys. The Tibetans were out of their skulls on alcohol and it was a most peculiar encounter. This caravan looked exactly as it must have done hundreds of years ago on the Lhasa to Leh route. Nyalam, alias Zhalangmu or Tammu, is a sizeable town set in a nice hillside location. It has a large army garrison and a few hotels. It is the gateway to the Xixabangma base camp (see the Trekking in the Everest Region chapter).

NYALAM TO ZHANGMU

From Nyalam there is an incredible drop from the Tibetan Plateau through every shade of green imaginable. The switchback road from Nyalam cuts past waterfalls, rocks, jungle, evergreen forest, shrub, and canyons. If you consult your satellite readout, you can see what happens here. The Landsat two-section map of Nepal (computer corrected and colour-enhanced) shows the road running through a cleft in the mighty Himalaya. North of Nyalam is an alpine steppe area (3500 to 5500 metres) with dry northern Himalayan vegetation (rhododendron shrub, juniper, grassland and desert). Nyalam itself lies at the edge of a wetter southern Himalayan zone where miraculous alpine forest appears (conifers and rhododendron). This zone is from 2000 to 4000 metres, with Nyalam at 4000 metres, and Zhangmu just above 2000 metres. Headed toward Zhangmu there is another zone of sub-tropical monsoon forest from 1000 to 2500 metres (oak, pine and chestnut). Straight across the map, cutting east and west of Nyalam, are large splotches of mountain terrain over 5000 metres high, with the perennial snowcover and glaciers of the Himalaya. From Tingri West down to Zhangmu is a fast drive – about three to six hours. In the reverse direction, it takes longer as it's all uphill.

ZHANGMU

Zhangmu (Khasa or Dram) is the border town, which is arranged along a series of sharp switchbacks. About 300 Chinese troops are stationed here – to 'stop infiltrators'. Meanwhile, there are scores of Nepalese running in and out of the town – some operate shops in Zhangmu. Back in the 1970s and early '80s Zhangmu was the small town that travellers would squint at from the Nepalese side, proud to have glimpsed what they thought was Tibet. Now Zhangmu has suddenly leapt onto practical traveller's maps and minds. The town is a centre for the booming

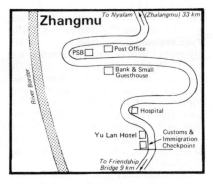

Tibetan-Nepalese trade. It's much easier for the Tibetans to obtain goods from Nepal than it is from the Chinese provinces. At various junctures along the Tibetan-Nepali borders there is apparently all sorts of unofficial trading going on, with the Tibetans selling fleeces, hides, butter and meat to the Nepalese, and the Nepalese trading in commodities and consumer goods. In 1980, Lhasa authorities slashed tariffs on Nepalese goods, including some from India. Twenty-seven trading centres have been set up along the Sino-Nepalese border. Nepali vendors trudge up to Zhangmu with massive loads of bananas and cloth, and reload with bedcovers and Chinese thermoses. In Zhangmu shops you can find Indian coffee, and Nepalese biscuits, beer and hair-oil.

The major thing of interest in Zhangmu is the bank, a bright green building with no English sign (see map). The bank is open 9 am to 12.30 pm, and 4 to 6 pm, and is closed Sundays. Bear in mind that there is a two hour time difference between Nepal and Tibet (ie between Kodari and Zhangmu), and that the non-working day in Nepal is Saturday. This means that if you try to depart Nepal on a Saturday and arrive in Zhangmu on a Sunday, you're sunk when it comes to banking. You can still use rupees in Zhangmu. If you are leaving Tibet, you should get rid of your RMB – it's illegal to take RMB out but

FECs are OK. The Zhangmu bank deals in both RMB and FEC, but mostly RMB. If you're coming from Lhasa, change RMB to rupees (there is a nice premium – see the Money & Costs section in the Facts for the Visitor chapter). Coming from Nepal, you may just have to take what you're offered – and though FECs would be preferable, you may be given RMB by the bank as the Zhangmu economy is based on RMB. There is a minor blackmarket in Zhangmu; one dealer was changing Nepalese rupees for FECs.

Zhangmu has a Public Security Bureau (not too far from the bank) where travellers coming from Nepal have managed to get an ATP with Lhasa on it, giving them a few days to roll off to Shigatse to get a visa extension. There is a brand-new 100-bed high-rise hotel plonked right next to the customs crossbar. It is called the *Yu Lan* (Rhododendron), and is a great introduction to Chinese tourist methodology if you're coming in. Go to the bank first – this one will cost you Y25 a night! It is Y5 a person for a meal and there are hot showers. There is another cheaper hotel near the bank.

Customs

The Chinese are more interested in what you take out than what you bring in. As you leave they will look for precious items bought in Tibet and no matter how much you protest that these items are blatant fakes, they will confiscate them unless you have an official receipt of purchase (ie from a Friendship Store). You will be asked for your ATP, the exit permit in your passport, and your customs declaration form (watch, camera, etc). You will also be asked if you're taking RMB out of the country and the correct answer to this is no (it's illegal to take RMB out). If you are found with RMB, it's no sweat – you'll just have to go back to the bank and change it. Customs will ask you for a money-exchange voucher showing that you've changed your last bit of RMB back into Nepalese currency (it's illegal to take

rupees into Nepal, but the Nepalese don't care!). FECs can be taken out. If you're coming from Nepal, you'll get a declaration form from customs with a space for declaring your total cash assets (it's not serious – there's no follow-up), and you should be able to get an ATP with Lhasa on it from the PSB up the hill.

Generally, there are no paperwork problems leaving Tibet. One woman, however, overstayed her visa by three weeks, and was told she would be stopped from exiting at the Zhangmu border post. She sat down at the customs checkpoint and fasted for ten days, which was enough to breach any border-guard's heart – so they let her go. The border is open 24 hours (same in Nepal).

FRIENDSHIP BRIDGE

From Zhangmu down into Nepal things get decidedly hotter, stickier, more humid and monsoonal. From the Chinese customs checkpoint it's a nine km walk down to the Friendship Bridge – you either walk or pick up a Nepalese truck going back to the bridge (5 Rps for the ride). In mid-85 the 65 metre, arch-span bridge was still undergoing reconstruction. It had been washed away in flash-flooding in 1981, along with a section of highway at the border. The bridge was scheduled for re-opening in 1986. There are other places to cross the fast-flowing river gorge, usually in the form of precarious wooden and rope bridges. Technically, the river is the border. In practice, the Chinese customs checkpoint is the border, with a kind of no-man's land down to the river which is inhabited by all sorts of wayward Nepalese.

KODARI

After you cross over to Nepal you have to walk a further two km to Kodari, where Nepalese Immigration is situated. The road here is rough and there are constant landslides and mudslides in the area. For 10 Rps a pint-sized Nepali will sling three backpacks over his forehead and march off for Kodari. Kodari (1660 metres) is really just a formality; there's no baggage search just a one-man shack for immigration. You don't even need a visa. The immigration officer will issue one on the spot, good for seven days, renewable for another 23 days in Kathmandu, and costing 181 rupees exactly (no change given).

TATOPANI

A further two km walk brings you to Tatopani Hot Springs, where there are at least three rickety lodges with restaurants attached. There is no electricity, no running water, no toilets, but there are hot spring-water showers down by the river. *Prem Lodge*, straight across from the police checkpoint in Tatopani, charges 7 Rps for a bed, and 15 Rps for a full meal. From Tatopani you should be able to pick up a converted Mercedes truck for the run all the way into Kathmandu (about six hours, 30 Rps a person, leaving around 10 am, arriving in Kathmandu at Ratna Park). If this doesn't work, you'll have to try and get to Barabise, and get regular bus transport from there.

TATOPANI TO KATHMANDU

The highway is mostly sealed and is very smooth – one of the best roads in Nepal, constructed with Chinese help. It passes through hamlets, rolling rust-and-green terraced mountains, and intensive farming areas, on past the larger towns of Barabise and Lamosangu, and the ancient city of Bhaktapur. On the Landsat map, Kathmandu shows up as a large, orange and yellow, built-up blob, set in the midst of the larger, green, Kathmandu Valley blob – which just about sums the situation up. From barren Tibet into the fertile Kathmandu Valley; from no food to an abundance of consumer goods, movies, western music; and from thin dry air to moist tropical heat.

It's a four to six hour haul to Kathmandu, where the excruciating luxury of the nearest budget hotel awaits you. Hot showers, clean white sheets, Swedish massage, change money, apple pie, your own pet western toilet – whatever your fetish is. Beware of the sudden change of diet on arrival from Tibet (what diet?!) because steaks and dairy foods can wreak havoc on your system. Ice-cream cones come in a profusion of flavours: malaria, dysentery, hepatitis, worm, meningitis, giardia . . .

Staging-point Kathmandu

Just as Hong Kong is the best place to get the goods on China, Kathmandu is the best place to load up on current information on Tibet. It hasn't taken the Nepalese merchants very long to wake up to the fact that they are now selling Tibet as well as Nepal to tourists. Unfortunately, Kathmandu is placed at the wrong end of things. In Hong Kong, you can get your supplies and information and truck off into China; in Kathmandu you may not be so lucky. For the moment, it appears to be one-way traffic; Lhasa to Kathmandu. This situation may change as Kathmandu is certainly much handier than Chengdu for access to Tibet by road.

Budget-travellers hang around the Thamel District of Kathmandu (northwest corner). This area is riddled with hotels, guesthouses, bookstores, ritzy restaurants and bars. *Kathmandu Guesthouse*, with its pleasant garden, has a good reputation among travellers. In the Thamel District you can get brown bread, quiche, pizza, and anything else you want. There are loads of places to rent trekking equipment, boots, packs, and sleepingbags. Some of it is high quality stuff left by expedition members. You can buy 'Free Tibet' T-shirts (emblazoned with a Tibetan flag), pictures of the Dalai Lama, Tibet flag postcards, sets of Tibetan stamps made up for Dharamsala, books about Tibet and mountaineering in Tibet, and a small Tibetan/English phrasebook produced in Nepal (*Tibetan for Travellers & Beginners*, Melvyn Goldstein, 1982).

It's legal for Tibetans to have Dalai Lama pictures, but you will have problems taking them in. They can be seized by Chinese customs. Anything to do with an independent Tibet will not go down well at customs. This includes the Tibetan flag. One traveller openly wore his 'Free Tibet' T-shirt within Tibet, even when lounging around PSB offices! He also had embroidered, on the back of a jacket (in a Nepalese shop), a large colour portrait of Chairman Mao, which he placed on the top of his pack when entering Tibet. The customs man opened the rucksack, saw the Mao jacket, snapped the pack shut and immediately waved him on. How disgusting! A Mao jacket!

Although it's more expensive, Nepal has a much greater selection of Tibetan goods than you will find in Tibet itself. This is explained by the exodus of refugee artisans to India and Nepal. As there is now a shortage of handicraft artists in Tibet, Nepalese-made carpets and other items are trucked back into Lhasa for sale there. If you want a Tibetan antique, a Tibetan carpet or otherwise, you're more likely to find what you want in Kathmandu. A number of Tibetan artefact and curio shops are concentrated around Bodhnath Stupa, to the north-east side of Kathmandu. You can get such items as Tibetan boots (180-200 Rps). If you are seriously interested in Tibetan-style carpets, you'd be better going direct to the weaving factories around Kathmandu.

Near Bodhnath Stupa (on the road in from Kathmandu centre) is the specialised *Indo-Tibetan Bookstore*, which mainly stocks books of the Buddhist mystical variety, as well as books written in Tibetan. It has some fat dictionaries and grammar-manuals, and some artefacts. Kathmandu is the best place to try and bone up on your Tibetan language skills, although Chinese (Mandarin) might be more useful when it comes to getting truck-rides in Tibet. There are enough

Tibetans around Kathmandu, and enough teaching outlets, for you to have intensive Tibetan lessons.

The best way of getting around Kathmandu is by bicycle. There are numerous places to rent clunkers made in India (Hero, Atlas) around the Thamel District, and at Freak Street downtown by the main square. You can get a bike for less than 10 Rps a day, but usually in bad shape, with the brakes falling off.

ONWARD FROM KATHMANDU

From Kathmandu there are extensive connections overland and by air. You can proceed to the Tibetan communities in exile at Dehra Dun, Dharamsala and Leh in northern India. If you have come off the Tibetan Plateau, the altered blood-chemistry stays with you for a few weeks, so you can go back to higher altitudes without major adjustments. Some travellers have arrived in Kathmandu and headed out trekking in Nepal with no side effects. The trekking season is roughly October to March in Nepal. The rest of the year sees fewer tourists and is low season, so it's cheaper. The monsoon is roughly from June to September and is a bad time to trek.

There are hundreds of cut-throat travel agents operating in Kathmandu who will fix you up with anything from a Delhi bus to a Calcutta trishaw. Shop around, or buy your tickets direct from the bus stations. Buying airfares is a shifty business. You cannot buy airfares with Nepalese rupees; payment must be made in hard currencies. It's best to shop around for a deal on airfares. Some operators will give you the price for air tickets that is supposed to be the official one, and will then give you a 'refund' (an under the table wad of rupees, say 250 Rps). That way it appears that you paid the US$200 or whatever for your ticket, but you actually didn't pay that much if the 'refund' is taken into account. Bear in mind that your travellers' cheques used for buying tickets are readily negotiable by travel-agents on the blackmarket. Air tickets are non-refundable in hard currencies. If you want to get a refund for a cancelled ticket, it will come back in Nepalese rupees, for which you can thank the greedy Nepalese bureaucracy. You can only exchange 15% of your rupees back into hard currency upon departure at Kathmandu airport.

Kathmandu to Hong Kong is around US$275 one-way. Burma Airways and Royal Nepal Airlines fly to Rangoon for about US$160 one-way and Rangoon to Bangkok is US$110 one-way. If you want to link with a flight from Rangoon to Kunming, telexes have to be sent to Rangoon to confirm your flight on CAAC (about US$185 one-way from Rangoon to Kunming) and your visas must be in order.

KATHMANDU TO LHASA

Step one is to get a Chinese visa. In early 1985 travellers were mailing their passports to Kong Kong for a Chinese visa stamp, *but* there is no obligation on the Zhangmu customs to honour it, unless perhaps the visa itself *specifies Zhangmu as an entry-point*.

It's pretty useless trying to get an individual Chinese visa in Kathmandu, the embassy there is only interested in issuing them to group tours, as operated by the Nepal Travel Agent. There were rumours that CITS would start up operations in Kathmandu, which may make a difference in the future. The border officially opened in April 1985 but traffic for individuals was suddenly closed down from Kathmandu to Lhasa in May 1985 (the other way is no problem). What happened between the opening in April, and the semi-closure in May was that some enterprising asshole in Kathmandu posted notices all over the city saying that he would arrange for a courier to fly down to Hong Kong with a load of passports to pick up Chinese visas. A Chinese official from the embassy spotted a poster, ripped it down, sent it to Beijing, and Beijing said stop the traffic going east.

In July 1985 a few travellers were trickling through again – by themselves – but the situation was very much at the whim of the officials in Zhangmu. In case the situation does turn for the better, and travellers are going through, you can get to the border by local transport. There doesn't seem to be any direct public transport from Kathmandu to Tatopani. A regular bus to Barabise is 15 Rps, and then a truck to Tatopani is 10 Rps. There are frequent buses to Barabise from a large bus station at the lower east side of Ratna Park, near City Hall. You might also arrange a taxi for a group of five, and ride in style to the border – and at some expense.

Being in Kathmandu and not knowing if you can make it across the border can be a very demoralising experience, since all your travel plans will be thrown out if you don't make it across. To give an example (a success story) an American traveller got to Kathmandu (in late 1985) having previously picked up his visa in Hong Kong. He showed the visa to the Chinese Embassy in Kathmandu and they told him there was no way he'd get across. With eight days left on the visa, he set off for Zhangmu, got through, and not knowing about PSBs and ATPs, he jumped a truck immediately to Sakya for Y20 and was in Shigatse within four days. He was lucky, because other travellers (some Hong Kongers) had been waiting three days in Zhangmu for a ride. To get to Shigatse, he had sailed straight through the checkpoint to the west of Xêgar, with no questions asked. In Shigatse he went to see the PSB since his visa had almost expired, and they extended it. 'Er, by the way, do you have an Alien Travel Permit?' the kind PSB man asked. 'What's that ?' asked the American. They issued him an ATP with Lhasa on it, and he continued on his way.

Tour-jumping

This is a favourite sport among those eager to get in from the Nepalese side.

The package that attracts is the three-day wonder to the Tibetan border-zone, as organised by the Nepal Travel Agent, which has offices in the Yak & Yeti Hotel and also on Ram Shah Path. Included in the package is a seven-day visa for China, which is extendable once you are safely across the border. The visa comes from the Chinese Embassy in Kathmandu, which is located on luxurious grounds at the north-east end of the city, but is largely unapproachable by individuals. The actual visa cost is 120 Rps, but the price varies slightly according to the passport-holder's nationality. Visa issuing hours at the embassy (tel 11289), are Mondays and Thursdays only, from 1.30 to 4.30 pm and the office hours are from 9 am to noon, and 1.30 to 4.30 pm, Monday to Friday.

Nepal Travel Agent (tel 413999), from its office in the Yak & Yeti hotel, will arrange the three-day tour from US$170 to $300 a head, depending on the size of the group (minimum of 11 or more people for the lowest rate; the highest rate is for two people). This is for three days, and two nights. They take you to the border-town Zhangmu, and then further into Tibet to an Everest view-point along the Friendship Highway. There is another tour of four days and three nights to the Zhangmu area. Visas cost extra and all arrangements can be made within two days if the visa office is open within that time (it might take longer) and you can depart after getting the visa.

After getting over the border at Zhangmu, the idea is to approach Zhangmu Public Security Bureau for an Alien Travel Permit (ATP) with a Lhasa stamp on it. If you get one of those, you can race along toward Lhasa, and get your initial seven-day entry visa extended in Shigatse or Lhasa. If your visa is extended, then your ATP is also extended. One group of travellers, arriving on the Yak & Yeti short-tour, got their ATPs in Zhangmu, told Yak & Yeti to shove it, and through CITS in Zhangmu they were able to arrange a 15-seat minibus (at Y140 a head) for the run to Shigatse, where they extended their visas for one month at the PSB. The trick is that you have to extend your initial seven day-visa, and you have to get an ATP with Lhasa on it somehow. After getting through the Chinese border you may be able to jump a four-wheel drive or some other vehicle which is unloading travellers coming from the opposite direction. Zhangmu is your best bet for onward transport, so hang around.

The Nepal Travel Agent has a number of longer tours, as well as trekking tours – the longer, the more expensive. Costs vary between US$85 and $185 per person per night, depending on the tour and the number of participants. For more details, see the Tours and Trekking section in the Facts for the Visitor chapter. Costs include transportation, accommodation, meals, sightseeing and guide service in Tibet. Other operators are bound to follow the lead of the Nepal Travel Agent if they can procure the correct contracts and permission. Some travellers in Kathmandu have been approached by operators guaranteeing to get them across the border for US$100. You'd better check the operator's credentials before proceeding – that could be a scam.

Unbelievably, a couple of wily Australian travellers did manage to get a re-entry visa from the Chinese Embassy in Kathmandu. The pair of female travellers turned on the waterworks, and spun a tale about left-luggage in Lhasa (from whence they had come), stolen cheques that could only be replaced in Kathmandu – it must have been quite a story. Instead of turning back from the Zhangmu border (from the Lhasa side, on the popular round-trip) they had continued straight through to Kathmandu – and, yes, they made it back to the plateau too. They were last heard of hitchhiking east of Chengdu, presumably with the left-luggage in tow, and a couple of things to chuckle about.

Sichuan Routes

If you imagine Tibet to be a high, barren plateau, the impression will be confirmed on the Golmud-Lhasa run. But you're in for an astonishing geography lesson on the Chengdu-Lhasa run. The variation of landscape with the change of altitude places this route on a par with any national park in North America – all 2400 km of it. Ethnically, the western approaches from Sichuan to Tibet *are* Tibet. After 1950 the Chinese reduced the entire Tibetan area, donating chunks to neighbouring provinces. In 1953-54 part of the former Kham district of Tibet came under the jurisdiction of Sichuan Province; it actually doubled the area of Sichuan. Three zones were set up: Garzê Tibetan Autonomous Prefecture to the west, Aba Tibetan Autonomous Prefecture to the north, and Dêqên Tibetan Autonomous County (Yunnan) to the south.

The Sichuan-Tibet road, both north and south routes, is a military road, constructed in 1954-55. It was along both these routes that the Chinese People's Liberation Army (PLA) mounted its attack on Chamdo in 1950, then continued on to Lhasa. The Chinese encountered no real opposition except for the rugged terrain, and you will soon find out what is meant by 'rugged terrain' – it is absolutely spectacular. A lingering legacy of the PLA is Chinese army compounds planted every 100 km or so; the settlements along much of the route are Han-dominated.

Due to landslides, mudslides, snow, washouts and even glacial blockages, the route is best not attempted in winter (September to February) although the scenery is supposed to be quite dramatic. You may not, however, enjoy the feeling of having icicles hanging out of your nose. If there is flooding from torrential rain or snowmelts (July-August) then the road will be impassable in sections. In August 1985 there was a massive mudslide that wiped out a section of the highway in Linzhi County between Tangmai and Nyingchi. This cut all communication until the mess could be cleared up. Trucks do go through in the months mentioned, and drivers also get killed. Snowfall starts sometime in September and you can get deep-frozen by October. The best time to attempt the trip is from April to June.

You need at least seven days for the run, and possibly up to three weeks if there are delays. Ten days should do it if you don't strike mechanical problems. A full day's run is about 350 km by truck. Accommodation along the way is mainly in truckstop compounds or army garrisons – just tag along with your driver. Truckstops need not be in towns. Charges are Y1 to Y3 a person for a bed, and Y1 to Y2 a head for a meal if you are sharing. The compounds usually have their own restaurant and often have their own medical facilities.

Supplies: you're best off loading up with a 'nose-bag' of oats and other goodies in Chengdu: tinned fruit, fruit-juice, chocolate – anything you can lay your greedy hands on. You should also bring your own chopsticks and tea-mug (usable for cleaning teeth). Food in towns along the way is mainly of the spicy Sichuan variety, and you can easily get bored with it, or lose your appetite altogether. Drivers like cigarettes so take along a carton even if you don't smoke. 555s or any foreign brand are in demand, and so are exclusive Chinese brands like *Golden Monkey*. Since you can get alternately frozen or roasted due to elevation changes, clothing becomes important. Nights can get very cold, although truckstops furnish blankets. Hydro-electricity is common enough in the villages along the route but a flashlight (torch) is essential. You don't want to step in the wrong thing (toilets are disgusting)! For cleaning up, well, let's see, um, oh yes . . . there's the Yangtze, and there's the Mekong, and the odd hotspring bubbling out of the grasslands.

Getting started is the most difficult thing of all. It takes that extra touch of ingenuity to get over the initial hurdles, but there are few permit-hassles once you're in the thick of things. Checkpoints are mainly interested in the driver, not you (see this chapter for Chengdu to Lhasa and Lhasa to Chengdu sections). The description given here goes from Chengdu via Chamdo to Lhasa, but it can be read in reverse by following key sites.

Staging-point Chengdu

Chengdu is one of China's megalopolises – it has a population above four million, with 1.5 million living within the city proper. It's a pleasant enough place as Chinese cities go. With an elevation of 126 metres, it's a long drop down from Lhasa (3680 metres).

Information

The selection of foodstuffs in the stores located on the Jinjiang Hotel ground floor is far greater and more varied than you'll find at the so-called Friendship Store downtown. If you're heading off for Tibet, the Jinjiang has the best range of exotic foods and other hardware. In 1985 there was no Kodachrome, or any slide-film, in stock in the hotel (periodically they run out). There's not much else in the way of film around Chengdu itself. Within the hotel you can use RMB or FECs, it depends on who you're dealing with and why. Try the RMB first. You'll find in the food-sections that the prices are not the same for RMB and FEC, which in general applies to the rest of black market Chengdu. Don't worry about finding the black market – it will find you, outside the gates of the Jinjiang. The rate is around Y160 RMB for Y100 FECs.

CAAC is across the street from the Jinjiang Hotel. For more information on

flights to and from Lhasa, see the Getting There section in the Lhasa chapter.

Chengdu Climate Chart			
Month	Average °C	Highest °C	Lowest °C
Jan	6.7	18	-4
Feb	8.1	21	-3
Mar	12.7	30	-1
Apr	17.7	32	3
May	22.3	36	9
Jun	24.1	36	15
Jul	26.5	36	17
Aug	25.8	38	16
Sept	22.0	35	12
Oct	17.6	30	6
Nov	12.5	24	1
Dec	7.7	21	-3

The Place to Stay

The *Jinjiang Hotel* is Chengdu's pleasure-dome of creature comforts after the high-altitude rigours of Tibet. If you're headed the other way, the Jinjiang has the last clean toilets you'll see. Stock up on toilet paper here! The Jinjiang costs Y10 a bed in a three-bed dorm (no bath, but good facilities down the hallways), or Y44 – Y70 for a whole double room with bath. Breakfast in the second floor dining-hall is Y3 regular, or Y2 student-rate (minus the eggs!). Lunch or dinner is Y6 (less for students, but less food too). The information exchange point is the rooftop bar, which is open till around midnight – get the latest on Lhasa from those returning. On the rooftop area there are several discos, with the odd wild brawl. Next the Chinese will have disco-police. The discos are intended for the Chinese; one ballroom on a lower floor carries a sign saying 'Chinese Only'.

The Jinjiang is a mini-state type of hotel; you need never leave the gates of this 1000-room fortress. You can get mail delivered to the desk (the address is care of Jinjiang Hotel, 180 Renmin Nan Lu, Chengdu, Sichuan, PRC) – this in effect is Poste Restante for Chengdu. You can have your washing done here, do all your eating within the confines of the hotel if you so desire, and do all your banking. You don't even have to leave the hotel to get an ATP, either. Travellers have picked up their ATPs, with Lhasa on them, right at the front desk at the Jinjiang. You may find that the Jinjiang is packed out, periodically, with all kinds of long-term and short-term dignitaries – in which case you may be re-routed to another hotel across town.

Places to Eat

Chengdu has some great snackbars and eateries – eating out is a real adventure here. There are not many main course restaurants. Try some of the places indicated on the map. The following are recommended: *Chengdu Restaurant* and *Rong Le Yuan* restaurant for main courses; for fiery snacks try *Chen Mapo Dofu* or *Lai's Rice-balls*.

If you prefer your own raw materials, Chengdu is alive with street-markets with fresh food for sale. Although not sustaining, Chengdu's numerous tea-houses are relaxing places to sit around. Some newer ones (operating at night) feature traditional instruments (*pipa, erhu*) being used to play upbeat tango, disco and waltz numbers! Ask reception at the Jinjiang for directions, and expect, as a 'western expert', to be dragged onto the dance-floor.

Getting Around

The best way to get around Chengdu is by rented bicycle. The buses are hopelessly overcrowded and muggy. Attached to the Jinjiang, at the outer wall, is a bike-rental place for Y6 a day or Y0.28 per hour. Around the corner from the Jinjiang (go north, then west to No 31 on Jiangxi Jie) is another place renting for Y3 a day or Y0.30 per hour. The best navigation mark in Chengdu is the giant Mao statue on Renmin Nan Lu.

Watch out for exorbitant taxi-charges. The buses disappear around 9.30 pm, and rip-offs in taxis are rife. A taxi to Chengdu

Airport should cost around Y16. Much cheaper than the taxis are the little three-wheelers that bomb around.

CHENGDU TO LHASA – OVERLAND

Lots of travellers have tried – and failed – to get started from Chengdu. The correct mix is; be fast, have good language assistance, keep a low profile, reduce your 'group' to two people, don't ask too many questions, and have your papers in order ('Car' not struck off ATP). One method is to work your way up to Kangding via Ya'an from the Emei Shan area. Kangding is the place you have to get past to get on the road to Tibet, and if you are on the southern route, watch out for Markam (foreigners coming from the Dali direction have been nailed in Markam and sent back).

Bus

The direct Lhasa bus is a very rare animal indeed – once a week from Chengdu if you're lucky. Anyhow, there is a place in northern Chengdu where you can go hunting. The bus depot is at the back of a large compound (see Chengdu map), at No 58 Yihuan Lu. The bus takes two weeks, costs Y127, and probably breaks down frequently. There's a chalkboard at the compound that announces in Chinese if the bus is in, and whether it's still alive, and when the next zoo tickets will be sold (usually one or two days in advance, very busy). There's no particular schedule, the bus comes in, fills up, goes out. I only heard of one foreigner who ever got on the bus and the condition the traveller arrived in is unknown. Apparently the Chinese are reluctant to sell the bus tickets to big-noses. There are a few other buses parked down at the Chamdo Transport Co (see under Trucks below for directions). They run to Chamdo, intermittently, and cost Y66.

Another tack is the 'leapfrog technique'. Take a bus to Ya'an, another to Kangding, and just keep jumping. You can get the first bus ride from the Xinanmen Station

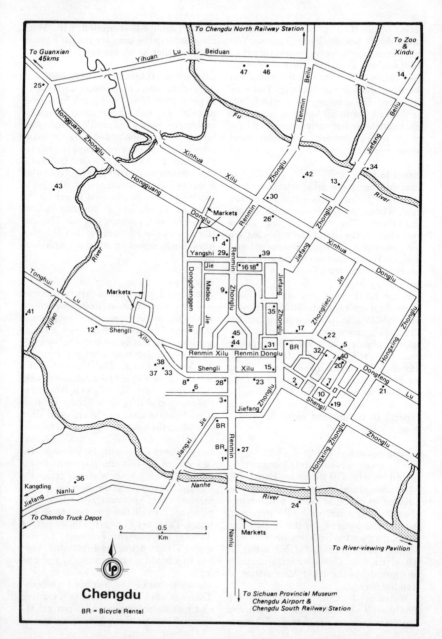

To Chengdu North Railway Station

To Guanxian 45kms

To Zoo & Xindu

Yihuan Lu Beiduan

Renmin Beilu

Hongguang Zhonglu

Fu

Xinhua Xilu

Renmin Zhonglu

Jiefang Beilu

River

Hongguang

River

Donglu

Markets

Renmin Zhonglu

Jiefang

Xinhua

Donglu

Tonghui Lu

Dongchenggen Jie

Madao Jie

Zhonglu

Jiefang Zhonglu

Zhongjieci Jie

Hongxing Zhonglu

Markets

Xiliao

Shengli Xilu

Zhonglu

Renmin Xilu

Renmin Donglu

Shengli

Xilu

BR

Dongteng Lu

Jianxi Jie

Jiefang Zhonglu

Renmin Nanlu

Shengli

Hongxing Zhonglu

BR

BR

Kangding

Jiefang Nanlu

Nanhe River

To Chamdo Truck Depot

0   0.5   1
Km

To River-viewing Pavilion

Markets

Nanlu

Chengdu

BR = Bicycle Rental

To Sichuan Provincial Museum
Chengdu Airport &
Chengdu South Railway Station

1	Jinjiang Hotel / CITS	1 錦江宾馆
2	Chengdu Restaurant	2 成都餐厅
3	Furong Restaurant	3 芙蓉饭店
4	Rongleyuan Restaurant	4 荣乐园饭店
5	Dongfeng Restaurant	5 东风饭店
6	Rongcheng Restaurant	6 蓉城饭店
7	Yao Chua Restaurant	7 耀华饭店
8	Wang Pang Duck Restaurant	8 王胖鸭店
9	Waisolo Cold Duck Restaurant	9 烤鸭店
10	Friendship Store	10 友谊商店
11	Drum & Cymbal Shop	11 鼓店
12	Lacquer Ware Factory	12 漆器厂
13	Sichuan Embroidery Factory	13 蜀绣厂
14	Bamboo Weaving Factory	14 竹编工艺厂
15	Renmin Market	15 人民市场
16	Soda Bar	16 冷饮柜台
17	Fuqi Feipian (Husband & Wife Lungs) Snackshop	17 夫妻肺片
18	Chen Mapo (Granny's Beancurd) Snackshop	18 陈麻婆豆腐
19	Long Chaoshou Soup Dumplings	19 龙抄手饭店
20	Lai Tangyuan Rice-ball Restaurant	20 赖汤元饭店
21	Snackshop (Sweets)	21 小吃（东风路）
22	Zhong Shuijiao Ravioli Restaurant	22 钟水饺饭店
23	Advance Rail Ticket Office	23 火车售票处
24	Chengdu Bus Terminal (Xinanmen Station)	24 成都汽车站
25	Ximen Bus Station (Buses for Guanxian)	25 西门汽车站
26	Public Security Bureau	26 公安局
27	CAAC	27 中国民用航空总局
28	Xinhua Bookstore	28 新华书店
29	Foriegn Languages Bookstore	29 外文书店
30	Chengdu Theatre	30 成都剧院
31	Telecommunications Building	31 电讯大楼
32	Bank of China	32 银行
33	Renmin Park	33 人民茶馆
34	Teahouse	34 解放北路茶馆
35	Xiao Yuan Teahouse & Bar	35 晓园茶馆
36	Temple of Wuhou	36 武侯祠
37	Renmin Park	37 人民公园
38	Monument to the Martyrs of the Railway Protecting Movement 1911	38 烈士纪念碑
39	Blind Peoples Massage Parlour	39 按摩院
40	Acrobat Theatre	40 杂技场
41	Cultural Park & Qingyang Palace	41 文化公园
42	Wenshu Monastery	42 文殊院
43	Tomb of Wang Jiang	43 王建墓
44	Mao Statue	44 毛泽东碑
45	Sichuan Exhibition Centre	45 展览馆
46	Lhasa Truck Depot	46 拉萨运输站
47	Lhasa Bus Compound	47 拉萨汽车客运组

in Chengdu (south-east of Jinjiang Hotel). It's Y5.7 coach, Y4.2 ordinary bus, to Ya'an (150 km); Y12.7 coach, Y6.3 ordinary bus, to Luding (320 km); and Y14.7 coach, Y7.3 ordinary bus, to Kangding (370 km). From Kangding to Batang is around Y18 on a two-day run, and from Batang you'd probably have to resort to hitching.

Hitching
Hitching has been done, though you may end up paying for some of the rides, which won't be much anyway. The best places to hang out are the trucker's rest-compounds en route. The road out of town from Chengdu is in the same direction as the Chamdo Transport Company (south-west).

Truck
There are at least two truck depots in Chengdu, and these are your best chance. To the north part of the city (see map) there is one from where drivers will probably take the south route via Markam. They will charge Y130 for a passenger. It's best not to approach the office. Go in there after office hours, or drag one of the drivers away and discuss a deal with him. Lhasa licence plates are 230, and Chamdo 233.

To the south-west of Chengdu is the Chamdo Trucking Co. (*Chamdo Yun Lian Gong Ci*) which is about half an hour by bicycle from the Jinjiang Hotel (seven km; you can also get there, or close, by No 10 bus). Go past Wuci Temple, continue till you go over a set of railway tracks, look for the depot on your left. It is closed on Sundays. Book and register one day before. It's Y50 in the cabin to Chamdo, but you might have trouble getting your message across, and there's no guarantee they'll take you. The compound also has a few jeeps and Landrovers lying around.

Other Transport
There's one hell of a lot of free enterprise going on in Sichuan Province (Deng Xiaoping's home province). This is especially true around Chengdu. Many people imagine that peasants get rich from diligent farming – that's true, but they also get rich from running transport businesses. A peculiar phenomenon that has surfaced over the last few years is that more and more Chinese now have transport that virtually amounts to a private vehicle, or comes from a vehicle pool. Therefore, you may be able to gate-crash a buy-and-sell trip toward Tibet. One group of foreigners, frustrated in their attempts to get away from Chengdu, came up with the brilliant idea of *hiring* Landcruisers (still cheaper than the plane, and payable in black market RMB). They set everything up with a local vehicle pool, paid for it, and were all set to leave when the fatal phone-call came through: 'Meiyou!' Yes, it was Meiyou County where they were finally headed – nowhere. They gave up and took the plane. It appears that Hong Kongers can avail themselves of these rental services with no problems – so if you tag along, who knows. One Hong Konger took a motorcycle along part of the route. You could also try to rent a vehicle to get further afield from Chengdu, and then jump ship.

CHENGDU TO CHINA
If you're leaving Chengdu, and heading into China, onward transport from Chengdu can be arranged through the CITS desk at the Jinjiang Hotel, and flights can be arranged through CAAC across the street. You need to book at least three days in advance for train tickets with CITS, and you may or may not be able to get Chinese prices (they may also demand payment in FECs). You can also try the advance rail ticket office on Shengli Xilu (see map). Chinese prices are Y3.40 hard-seat to Emei Shan (three hours); Y31 hard-sleeper to Kunming (25 hours); Y26 hard-sleeper to Xian (20 hours); while Chengdu to Beijing is Y55 hard-sleeper (37 hours, 2048 rail km).

Trains proceed from the North Station

(the No 16 bus goes past the Jinjiang Hotel to the North Station). It's easier to get to Leshan and Emei Shan by bus. The bus station selling tickets for those destinations is the Xinanmen Terminal to the south-east of the Jinjiang Hotel, across the river.

LHASA TO CHENGDU – OVERLAND

Similar strategies to those already described apply to getting away from Lhasa. The trick is to get sufficiently removed from Lhasa, and then you're off and running. Since Ganden Monastery lies on the way out, you have a good excuse to be out on the road early in the morning for a hitch. You can also get a kick-start from a bus at the station just east of the Potala. They occur infrequently and the cost to Bayi/Nyingchi (420 km approx) is around Y22. Again, the mythical bombs run all the way to Chamdo and beyond, but your chances of getting on them are not so good. The cost to Chamdo is around Y58, and to Litang, around Y80.

Trucks, the better alternative to go for, leave from No 6 Depot (see Lhasa map) in the direction of Chamdo. You may have to get your tickets from the *bus* station in Lhasa, even though they're for the truck. Sichuan licence-plates are 20, 50 and 80. If Lhasa fails, you might consider an excursion to Zêtang for a kick-start toward Nyingchi.

In the bad old days of Tibet travel, an American managed to get to Lhasa (he played around with his ATP), and then decided to hitch back to Chengdu. He wrote himself out permission to hitchhike the road back (in Chinese) and set off, no hassles. The authorities along the way were not in the least concerned, because he had an official-looking piece of paper. Leave it to your imagination how he came by that piece of paper (clue: the ink on the original document was water-based). This was in 1982 when Tibet was firmly shut. Now that Tibet's open, it's easier to justify yourself running along these roads. Don't try and hide – there's nothing to be paranoid about. Act as if you have permission. Nobody, after all, says you *haven't*. You have Lhasa on your ATP, you're allowed to go to Chengdu, but no-one in authority has told you *how* to get there. Ergo, if you do not have 'Car' struck off your ATP, you theoretically have the permission. The first thing that Chengdu PSB will do if they hear the word 'overland' will be to cross 'Car' off your ATP.

HONG KONG TO CHENGDU

Chengdu is connected by rail and air with the rest of China, but the rail services are heavily overloaded, as is the case with the South-Western Provinces (Guangxi, Guizhou and Yunnan) leading into Sichuan from Hong Kong (HK). There is a charter flight sometimes available from Hong Kong direct to Chengdu – commandeered by CITS clients, but they may have some seats. The flight leaves Hong Kong on Saturdays, costs HK$760 one-way, and takes two hours (there is a flight the same day from Chengdu to Hong Kong). Other flights worthy of consideration are Hong Kong-Kunming, HK$976 one-way (departs Sundays); and Hong Kong-Xian, HK$1070 one-way (departs Sundays).

There are a number of planes on the Chengdu-Guangzhou (Canton) run; cost is Y201 one-way, departures daily. If you really want to speed things up getting to Chengdu from Hong Kong, you have to throw a plane in there somewhere. Some sample flights are Canton-Guilin Y60 one-way; Guilin-Chengdu Y141 one-way; and from Guiyang or Kunming to Chengdu works out to around Y85 one-way. There are other plane connections from Chengdu to Beijing, Changsha, Chongqing, Nanning, Shanghai, Xian, Wuhan and other points.

High tourist pricing (over 100% surcharge in FECs) is unavoidable on CAAC, the Chinese airline. On trains, if you want to battle it out, you might be able to get Chinese price (tourists are surcharged 75% for train tickets, and might also have to pay in FECs). The entire distance from

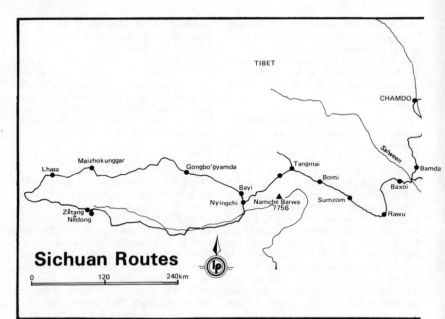

Sichuan Routes

0   120   240km

North Route via Chamdo	Distances	
	intermediate	*cumulative*
Chengdu 成都		
Luding 泸定	320 km	320 km
Kangding 康定	50 km	370 km
Luhuo 炉霍	270 km	640 km
Garzê 甘孜	110 km	750 km
Dêgê 德格	200 km	950 km
Tibetan border	30 km	980 km
Chamdo 昌都	305 km	1285 km
Bamda	165 km	1450 km
Baxoi 八宿	100 km	1550 km
Rawu	90 km	1640 km
Bomi (Zhamo) 波密	120 km	1760 km
Tangmai	90 km	1850 km
Nyingchi (Linzhi) 林芝	130 km	1980 km
Bayi	20 km	2000 km
Gongbo'gyamda 工布江达	120 km	2120 km
Lhasa 拉萨	285 km	2405 km

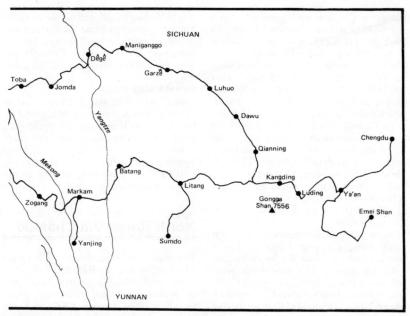

South Route via Markam

Distances

	intermediate	*cumulative*
Chengdu 成都		
Luding 泸定	320 km	320 km
Kangding 康定	50 km	370 km
Litang 理塘	250 km	620 km
Batang 巴塘	170 km	790 km
Markam 芒康	105 km	895 km
Zogang 左贡	160 km	1055 km
Baxoi 八宿	175 km	1230 km
Rawu	90 km	1320 km
Bomi	120 km	1440 km
Tangmai	90 km	1530 km
Nyingchi	130 km	1660 km
Bayi	20 km	1680 km
Gongbo'gyamda 工布江达	120 km	1800 km
Lhasa 拉萨	285 km	2085 km

The north and south routes converge near Baxoi for the run to Lhasa. There is a particularly bad section of road between Tangmai and Nyingchi – this 40 km section will probably be impassable if there is autumn flooding or winter ice.

Canton to Chengdu via Kunming by rail is over 3300 km. You can expect to spend a long time getting there by rail. A shortcut is to get up to Guilin by air (Y60 from Canton), or jump a jetfoil from Hong Kong to Wuzhou (10 hours, leaves every other day, HK$250, proceed to Guilin by bus). Guilin is a stumbling-block for trains, which take the long route. It's 24 hours from Canton, and Canton itself can hold you up for ages (trying to get out of it, that is). From Guilin you can try and battle your way through to Kunming (Y20, hard-sleeper, Chinese price, 15 hours by fastest train). The Guilin to Kunming flight is Y109. From Kunming it's 35 hours by rail to Chengdu (1100 km, Y30, hard-sleeper, Chinese price).

Since Guilin is a prime tourist spot (for both foreigners *and* Chinese) you're warned that the place is very difficult to get out of by rail and you may end up being stranded. Planes and trains out of Guilin can be booked out for a week – or weeks – ahead. CITS is a waste of time for getting your tickets; try the black marketeers who deal in tickets and FECs at the same time! If you really want out, try and get to Nanning instead of Kunming (from Nanning you can fly to Kunming), or get to Liuzhou where you'll have more success getting onward tickets.

You can skip Guilin altogether as part of the route to Chengdu and if your time is limited, this would be the best option. Other routes to Kunming and Chengdu exist. You could get a ferry from Hong Kong to Haikou (five times a month, 18 hours, HK$400 approx), or a ferry from Hong Kong to Zhanjiang (three times a month, 16 hours, HK$350 approx), and from either of these points work your way up to Nanning. From Nanning to Kunming by plane is Y88 one-way (four flights weekly). An alternate rail route through the south-west is to get to Guiyang from Hong Kong, change for a run to Chongqing, and then get another train to Chengdu (both of these trains take 11 hours each). Yet another game-plan is to make your way to Wuhan by rail, and cruise along the Yangtze to Chongqing (unfortunately, heading west, this takes five days; if you're going east, it's three days). From Chongqing you can take the train to Chengdu.

BURMA SIDE-DOOR

A very interesting shortcut in and out of China, and along the route to Chengdu is the flight from Rangoon to Kunming. You need to have your papers and airlines in order to do it, and it's not cheap. More details on this exit/entry are given in the Getting There and Away section in the Facts for the Visitor chapter.

North Route Via Chamdo

The route to Kangding is Chengdu-Shuangliu-Xinjin-Baizhang-Ya'an-Tianquan-Luding-Kangding. There are other roads that lead in through Ya'an from Emei Shan/Leshan; Y3.6 from Emei to Ya'an by bus. Ya'an has several bus stations, and a hotel near one of the stations is Y7 a double. From Ya'an to Kangding costs Y8.6 by bus (around nine hours). On the road to Luding there is a pass of over 3000 metres, as the ribbon of road heads straight for the Tibetan Plateau.

At **Luding** (around 3400 metres), you enter Garzê Zang Autonomous Prefecture, and this marks a kind of invisible border-line where Tibetan peoples start to appear. It's not quite clear how this prefecture is administered, but it certainly appears lax. The truckstop compound at Luding is Y7.50 for three people (Y2.50 each). You will probably not be asked for an ATP, but the Chinese registration form asks you to fill in your work-unit (just put down 'English'!).

Nestled at around 2900 metres is **Kangding** (Dardo) which was once a Han-Tibetan trading town and Tibetan doorway into China. The Chinese bought silver, furs, and herbs from the Tibetans, and the

Tibetans purchased items like tea. The route from Kangding to Chamdo became known as the 'Tea Road', or the Tibetan Silk Road. Early in this century, Kangding fell exclusively under Chinese domination.

Today Kangding is a sprawling mixture of the old, the cobbled, the concrete, and the hydro-electric. The population is around 30,000. The fast-flowing Zheduo river provides heating and electricity for the town and is deployed for dumping corpses, in what is known as 'water burial' (sky, fire and earth burials are also practiced in Kangding). One of the reasons Tibetans prefer not to eat fish is that they claim the fish eat the bodies dumped in rivers like the Zheduo, and are thus contaminated (others believe the fish are reincarnations).

To the south of Kangding, and reached from it, is the mighty peak of Gongga Shan (Minya Konka, 7556 metres) which is one of the mountains open to foreign climbers. To behold the peak is worth 10 years of meditation, or so says an inscription in a ruined monastery at the base of the mountain. The peak was scaled in 1932 by two Americans, and in 1957 by six Chinese Trade Unionists (who were members of the All-China Federation of Trade Unions, and got their training in Russia in 1955 – China's first mountaineers).

KANGDING TO DÊGÊ

After Kangding, the road climbs through a pass of 4050 metres (Zheduo Shankou) to alpine tundra with distant snowcaps and a shifting mirage of yaks and hardy herders. There are some tiny outposts with distinctly Tibetan-style architecture; low squat buildings, ornate windows, and fluttering prayer-flags. With the exceptions of Dêgê and Chamdo there are no sizeable Tibetan towns along the route to Lhasa. The Tibetans are mainly nomadic herders who camp out. It's the Han who are the 'settlers'. It really amounts to a Wild West situation, with the Han forts, garrisons, compounds, whatever, and the Tibetans

roving around like Apaches. They drift into town reeking of alcohol, in search of rides (or perhaps it's plastic containers?). The towns that have reasonable Tibetan populations, Dêgê and Chamdo, have large monasteries. The Tibetans are easily distinguished by their brightly coloured clothing, thick leather belts, daggers, and outrageous jewellery and headgear.

Paving continues, at intervals, through the pleasant village of **Qianning** (Gartar), and the scenery shifts from alpine back to coniferous forest with pines, birches and poplars. Logging and the hauling of logs by truck are common industries in the region. You can use the vegetation and the treeline as an altimeter; the treeline stops at 4000 metres, and the snowline begins at around 5000 metres. Blue and yellow poppies prefer the higher elevations, and juniper and rhododendron scrub appear above 4000 metres. Altitude-sickness strikes before Kangding – stay with it for a few days and it should clear up. Some days I had a three hour struggle with the stomach over saving lunch!

Most of the road to Lhasa follows a river of some kind – brooding white water flowing out of clefts in rock, bubbling through boulders, and on occasion, running across the road. This causes muddy stretches, so the road is dug up and reinforced with slabs of stone. Stationed at intervals along the road are crews who camp out. It is their job to try and keep the road half decent, and this dirty work appears to fall mainly to the Tibetans. In winter some snow-ploughing is done by modified tractors, and trucks use chains on their tyres.

After **Luhuo** (Zhaggo) you cross a grassland plateau with sheep, goats, yaks, and stray Tibetans on horseback. I lost count of the different varieties of goat and sheep – so many monstrous permutations of horns seem impossible, but there they are. This whole route is really a feast for the botanist and the naturalist. For large animals, this refers to the domesticated variety as the Chinese settlers and PLA machine-gunners have destroyed a large amount of Tibetan wildlife, particularly wild yaks and ducks. The wildlife had previously been strictly protected but some species have now been hunted to the point of extinction. With the codes broken, Tibetans themselves have joined the hunt. One of the sickening sights along the way was a Tibetan offering a snow-leopard skin for sale. For the ornithologist there is ample to observe, not in numbers, but in variety. I spotted about 20 varieties of bird-life and could not identify them all. Apart from the more obvious hill pigeons and hawks, there are some residents native to Tibet, like the Tibetan Snow Finch.

From **Garzê**, a nice stockaded village with a small monastery, the road runs over grassland dotted with nomad tents and the smoke from their yak-dung fires. Halfway between Garzê and Dêgê is **Maniganggo**, where a fork of the road branches off toward Qinghai Province. The road then climbs sharply and you chug up – radiator willing – through **Cho La**, a pass of 4600 metres.

Snowcaps and glacial tongues abound here. After the dirty, crowded cities of China it looks so clean, fresh and open in this region. The locals, true, are dressed in rags, but half the time you have the grasslands to yourself. Trucks can go for miles without any sign of human habitation. It is a delicious luxury after China. The crystal blue lakes formed from glacial meltwater are a tonic; there's no pollution and no rubbish.

DÊGÊ

Dêgê is the first sizeable town after Kangding on this route, and if you manage it, try and stop here. Drivers may not want to stop, and it may be difficult to get onward transport. There are no particular truckstop hotels but there are some smaller regular places; Y4 for a whole room.

Dêgê is the home of a famous printing-

works monastery, an operation which is spread up a hillside overlooking the town. The monastery is capped with the familiar Tibetan Wheel of the Law, flanked with gazelles. The printing lamasery has a 260 year old tradition. With a vast collection of ancient Tibetan scriptures from the five Lamaist sects, it is revered by followers the world over, with visitors coming from Sikkim, Bhutan, Japan, and further afield. The monastery apparently does not do any printing in the winter as it's too cold.

Tibetan pilgrims do a circuit of the main monastery building. Dangling from one side of the monastery walls is a blackened mop where ink drips down to the ground. The pilgrims prostrate themselves at this spot and either rub the dripping ink into their hair, or wash in it – or drink it. Yum! The books printed at Dêgê, though mostly read or chanted by monks, are sacred. Seventy-five percent of Tibetans are illiterate, but the ink is still holy, and so is the paper.

Woodblock print of Sakyamuni
from Dêgê Monastery

The oblong Tibetan book is composed of unbound leaves, which are pressed together and kept in order with outside hardcovers and a ribbon. All the printing is done with woodblocks, with characters first copied from a master-calligrapher, and then carved in relief (and reverse) onto hard wood. At one time there were large printing works in Narthang (near Shigatse), and Kumbum (Taersi Lamasery near Xining) – and the one at Dêgê, which still functions much the same way it must have done in centuries past. Dêgê possesses the only brass printing plates in Tibet. These are more durable than the wooden ones.

Inside the monastery are hundreds of thousands of woodblocks and you can see the printers working away in a trance. They sit opposite one another, bobbing up and down at an incredible pace; one inking the block, the other rolling the strip of paper over the woodblock. It is an enormously complicated operation to assemble one of these books. Some of the looseleaf books run to several hundred plates and someone has to co-ordinate all those bits of paper. The *Kanjur*, or *Canon of Buddhist Law*, runs to 108 volumes, and the *Tenjur*, or *Commentary on the Canon of Buddhist Law*, is 225 volumes, with 25,000 double-sided leaves. Both of these have been translated from Sanskrit.

The printing done at Dêgê is done in a surprisingly small space. Printing is done to order and the orders come from within Tibet, Mongolia, Qinghai and Gansu Provinces. Export is not in the scheme of things. Texts include ancient works on astronomy, music, geography, medicine, and Buddhist classics. A history of Indian Buddhism, comprising 555 plates, is the only surviving copy in the world (written in Hindi, Sanskrit, and Tibetan).

The Abbot of Dêgê, after some arranging, will take you on a guided tour of the printing-works (nobody speaks English). Out the back, further up the hill, is the place where logs are chopped into blocks and carved up with painstaking attention

(and gradual loss of eyesight) by a crew of many workers. It takes about three months and five pairs of glasses to finish a large thangka woodblock. Lighting in the work-area is dim, for some inexplicable reason. Other parts of the operation are calligraphy, printing, cutting, and binding. There are two chapels within the complex but they are locked up. With a bit of coaxing, however, the Abbot will escort you through them. There's lots of demonic statuary, a few snow-leopard skins, and protecting the monastery from fire and earthquake is a guardian goddess, a Green Tara. Since everything is made of wood, her vigilance is needed.

BORDER BRIDGE

Thirty km from Dêgê brings you to the Tibet border; a bridge, manned by a sentry, with Tibet carved in script on a cliffside. The bridge spans a river that is better known (by the time it gets to China) as the Yangtze. From here you venture into the ancient province of Kham, where two other mighty rivers – the Mekong and the Salween – flow parallel with the Yangtze. A further 75 km from the bridge brings you to the army base at Jomda, and just before Chamdo there is a pass of 4350 metres.

CHAMDO

Chamdo (elevation around 3200 metres) is Tibet's third largest city. At the turn of the century it had a population of around 12,000 with a quarter of that being monks. It was a sutra-printing centre, site of an ancient market, and it served as the regional capital of the old Tibetan province of Kham. Today, in an expanded (mostly Chinese) population version, it seems that a quarter of the population is involved in the trucking industry, supplying eastern Tibet with goods originating in Sichuan. As the regional seat of the Chinese Prefecture of Qamdo, the city functions as a major communications link, and is slated for industrial development. In this Chinese build-a-block city, there are at least four truck company compounds, and there is a variety of facilities: post-office, hospital, bookstore, and bank.

The city and the area around it was once home-base for the fierce tribesmen known as Khampas. The men are easily identifiable by the tassels of red yarn in their braided hair. Long feared and respected throughout Tibet, the Khampas have posed a great problem for the invading Chinese. Historically, the area of Kham

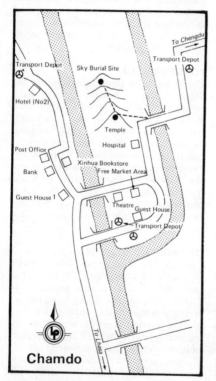

Chamdo

was beset by feuding Khampa tribes. If the Chinese tried to intervene in the area, the tribes united to fight them. There were confrontations with Khampas in 1918, 1928, and 1932. In 1933 the Khampas even attempted to shake off the Lhasa

administration. In the 1930s the Khampas took on the Chinese Nationalists, as well as Mao's forces which retreated through Kham on the Long March. Chamdo was still under Lhasa's administration, but the rest of Kham came under the control of local warlords: the Abbot of Litang, the Chief of Batang, and the Prince of Dêgê.

In 1950, the Chinese captured Chamdo without firing a shot. They set off a huge fireworks display near Chamdo the night before, and the Tibetan general fled, leaving angry Khampa troops behind. This was not the end of the Khampas, however. In central and eastern Tibet, Khampa guerrilla warfare has been a constant headache for the PLA. CIA-trained Khampas, operating out of a base in Mustang (Nepal) harassed Chinese troops for over a decade before the Mustang base was destroyed. Chairman Mao personally threatened the Nepalese king with reprisals if he didn't shut down the operation somehow. King Birendra complied, and in the mid-70s, in secret co-ordination with the PLA, launched an assault to wipe out the Khampa base.

There is little to see in Chamdo that you haven't seen in China already. The most interesting part is wandering around the grubby back-alleys, and going to the free-market. The religious (here synonymous with the Tibetan) end of town is a hilltop monastery with a pilgrim circuit around various parts of the hill. The temple is approached by a trail near a bridge (see map) – it's small, active, and has a courtyard full of dogs. Behind that is a sky-burial site. The monastery dates back to the 15th century. Although Tsongkhapa visited Chamdo in 1373 and suggested a monastery be built, it was not until 1473 that one of his disciples started the construction of the Changbalin Monastery, which later housed a community of 2500 monks, with five main temples. Only the main hall and two other buildings now remain. The rest were destroyed by the Chinese (the main hall was used as a prison) – some restoration has begun.

Sichuan Routes 217

Places to Stay & Eat

There are several guesthouses in Chamdo which function as truckstops, although the trucking companies have their own compounds. *No 2 Guesthouse* is a cut above the rest (Y2 to Y5 a head). Outhouses are basic (nosepeg recommended). Food is dismal but there are stores where you can procure canned food.

CHAMDO TO NYINGCHI

After Chamdo, it's shake, rattle and roll towards Bamda with a pass of over 4600 metres just west of Chamdo. We got a ride with some wheeler-dealers from Sichuan who had a small truck with two rows of seats in the cabin, and a rear section stuffed full of contraband video equipment. The 'crew' set up a travelling cinema at army depots where they wished to stay the night and showed violent Hong Kong kung fu epics. We ate in army messes from then on, and got pretty sick of looking at green army-ration tins by the time we got to Lhasa.

Tired of the same rugged outdoor adventure stuff? In late 1985 the PLA (Luofu Shan Military Barracks near Canton) offered visitors three days in a military camp; cot, meals, uniform and ammunition inclusive, for US$75. You can get the same thing in Tibet for next to free – and basketball to boot.

The road to Nyingchi crosses high, windswept plains with dusty horsemen, lichen, mosslands, boulders and snowcaps. It is a desolate landscape of great majesty, with the occasional yak-herder with matted hair and layers of rags. The road runs along the upper reaches of the Mekong. There is a lot of military activity in the area, with frequent army convoys on the road.

Bamda (4400 metres) is an army garrison, roughly 1000 km from Lhasa. There is a small Tibetan village tucked around the corner. After Bamda the road joins the southern highway coming in at Markam. About 70 km from Bamda, between Bamda and Baxoi, is a rough stretch of road known as the '72 Bends', a series of hairpin switchbacks that descend into a long canyon with a muddy fast-flowing river. You'll need your crash-helmet for this ride! Landslides are frequent in the area and the dust is legendary.

Baxoi is a one street town of little consequence, simply an army base and truckstop hotel. Further down the line is **Rawu**, which has an absolutely splendid backdrop of snowcaps. The main industry is Rawu logging and there is a truckstop hotel there. The scenery here is very reminiscent of the Canadian Rockies, or the Swiss Alps if you prefer (Alaska and Afghanistan might qualify!). There are waterfalls, forests, deep green rapids, and a lake large enough to have its own sandy beach.

From Rawu onward, the road deteriorates – landslides are common, and the road is gouged by streams. Landslides are sometimes cleared by bulldozer, but more often it's heave-ho – you and the driver have to do it. At one spot we saw a 'dig' going on, a road-crew obviously at work, then three men came rushing out to flag us down. Shortly after, a loud explosion rocked the cabin. Precautions for blasting are few in these regions ... Further ahead, another unusual obstacle was a number of prostrating pilgrims. They could only be headed for Lhasa, which was a good 600 km away. It is a difficult concept to grasp, but they would be doing 'push-ups' all the way to Lhasa; no walking, no food, no luggage. People along the way would assist them in their once-in-a-lifetime journey.

At **Bomi** (Zhamo, or Bowo), there is an army garrison where they'll put you up for Y6 a head, foreign rate. It's a nice receipt to hang onto if you want to impress hotel managers back in China. There are several cheaper truckstop hotels in town. Bomi, at around 2800 metres in elevation, is the market-town for the region.

Tangmai is, surprise, set in lush jungle

vegetation – the road dips down to around 1700 metres. There are ferns and rain forest, even monkeys here. Although there's no electricity, and no actual town of Tangmai as such, there is a truckstop hotel. Just after Tangmai, an already muddy track parallels a *very* fast river and at times dips perilously close to it. It is dangerous to negotiate and a local claims that over 70 drivers have lost their lives on this stretch over the last 30 years. Under conditions of heavy rain, or solid ice, it's very slippery. Considering there is such a bad stretch here, it's odd that the drivers don't take the northern road from Chamdo (through Dêngqên, Baqên, Nagqu and Damxung to Lhasa). When questioned, our driver mentioned something about getting shot on that route and didn't care to elaborate. Maybe there aren't enough army bases around.

Though you may not get to see it, there is a major mountain off the Tangmai to Nyingchi route. This is Namche Barwa (Namjagbarwa Feng, 7756 metres), the highest unclimbed mountain in the world. The peak has not been opened to foreign climbers yet (some Americans reportedly offered $150,000 for the peak, but were politely turned down by the Chinese). Some trek-groups go to the base area, where the vegetation is subtropical. A Chinese scientific expedition dispatched to the area in 1983 came to the conclusion that the whole eastern Himalayan range has moved 60 km in the last 30 million years, or an average of two cm a year. There is an advancing glacier on the north-western slope of the mountain – watch out!

After the jungle interlude from Tangmai, the road rises again, over a pass of 4600 metres, and coils back down into the valley that contains Nyingchi.

NYINGCHI TO LHASA

Nyingchi (Linzhi) is a predominantly Han town. It's quite large (it has more than one street), and is set in a fertile, cultivated valley. Apart from being an industrial centre, Nyingchi is a major transport centre. There are buses from here, running a few times a week to Lhasa (they cost around Y22). There are several places to stay in Nyingchi. Traffic picks up from here on. It must be the road from Tangmai to Nyingchi that stops the truckers from going any further. There is also traffic going to and from Zêtang, which is then connected to Lhasa.

At **Bayi** (Bayizhen), which is in the same jurisdiction area, and is considered an offshoot of Nyingchi, there is a textile and carpet factory employing about 1300 workers – half of them Han. It was started in 1966 by Shanghai entrepreneurs, with personnel sent in from China. The dilapidated factory produces about 50 kinds of woollen fabrics, including woollen Panda blankets, and many thousands of km of knitting yarn (if Chinese sources are correct). The production is rather uninspiring for prospective western buyers. The factory reeks of chemicals. Holy Mao! What's this?! A large painting of the heroic younger Helmsman surveys the workers on the factory floor. At the height of the Cultural Revolution, some 40,000 Mao posters were put up around Lhasa – they've all been removed, but this piece of history is still in Bayi. Factories in the Bayi-Nyingchi area produce, apart from woollen goods, batteries, paper and matches. Bayi has an army garrison where you can stay.

Another day of being banged around will put you very close to Lhasa. Hang onto your fillings, and shut down your lungs – the road is a dustbowl. At **Gongbo'gyamda**, Tibetan architecture becomes more pronounced, and past **Maizhokunggar** (about 70 km from Lhasa), the build-up for the Holy City begins.

South Route via Markam

This can be done a couple of days faster than the north route and the scenery is very similar. The south route splits after **Kangding**, where it heads for Litang. **Litang**, at about 4700 metres, is 1000 metres higher than Lhasa, and just a few hundred metres short of the world record for high towns (Wenchuan, on the Qinghai-Tibet Plateau). It rests at the edge of a vast grassland, and a trading-fair and festival lasting 10 days is held there annually. The meet is sponsored by the Grand Living Buddha of the Kangba Plateau, and Tibetan horsemen come to show their skills. You can get a bus from Kangding through Litang to Batang (Y19, two days). There are cheap hotels and places to eat in both Litang and Batang.

The travellers's favourite is **Batang**, at around 2700 metres. It is a pleasant town surrounded by barley fields. There's a hotel at the bus station (Y2 a head). **Markam** is not a traveller's favourite –

some people have been stopped there, coming from Dali. If you come from the Batang side, the road goes straight past Markam, which may be a good idea under the circumstances. In any case, Markam is not a truckstop town. The one sight of interest would be the annual horse-racing fair. Markam is the first town inside Tibet proper. There is a guarded bridge over the Yangtze marking the border, between Batang and Markam. No buses ply this gap.

To the west of Markam you cross the Mekong, and continue through to **Zogang** (Wangda), an ugly hole of a place (nice mountains!). It has a truckstop hotel on the main street, er, wait a minute – on *the* street. The road then zeroes in for **Bamda** where you can stay at the army barracks, and joins the north route road for Lhasa (see north route section for details).

Yunnan Route

The Yunnan-Tibet Highway offers an alternative to entering Tibet via the Sichuan-Tibet Highway but it is conspicuously 'off the paperwork trails'. Not surprisingly, only a few foreigners who attempt this route actually complete it. Various checkpoints (Jianchuan, Zhongdian and Markam, to name a few) are now on the alert and diligently turn back those without permits. Hitching on trucks is preferable to public transport. Security officials will usually send you back to your starting point, although they prefer to return you to Yunnan, rather than Tibet. If you are in the middle of the route and are questioned while overnighting, you might say you have come from your destination. The best policy is to keep moving, arrive late, leave early. If you have no luck in town, walk out of town to hitch. Make sure you take food and warm clothing.

In the winter of '84 two female travellers made it through to Lhasa from Dali. They were dressed in heavy Tibetan coats, and apparently drove their truck-driver crazy by demanding that he keep to schedule, despite awesome winter conditions. They were Swiss and they kept looking at their watches.

Yunnan – Tibet Highway	Distances	
	intermediate	*cumulative*
Kunming 昆明		
Xiaguan 下关	398 km	398 km
Dali 大理	14 km	412 km
Jianchuan 剑川	112 km	524 km
Baihanchang	29 km	553 km
Zhongdian 中甸	152 km	705 km
Dêqên 德钦	184 km	989 km
Gejiehe 隔界河	103 km	1092 km
Yanjing 盐井	8 km	1100 km
Markam 芒康	112 km	1212 km

You might also find your ride takes the route via Lijiang (main town of the Naxi minority) in which case your route would be:

Dali 大理		
Dengchuan 邓川	37 km	37 km
Lijiang 丽江	107 km	144 km
Baihanchang	46 km	190 km

Thereafter the route to Markam is detailed above. Markam to Lhasa is 1114 km.

The Yunnan-Tibet Highway

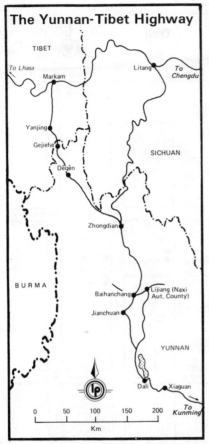

Staging-point Dali

Dali lies just off the old Burma road, and was the centre of the Bai Nanzhao Kingdom. Six small Bai kingdoms amalgamated to establish the Nanzhao Kingdom by the mid-700s AD and this conglomerate beat imperial Tang forces in two battles. In one battle a whole Chinese army was virtually wiped out. In the 13th century the Mongols captured the kingdom and moved the capital back to Kunming. Yunnan has always been a trouble spot for the Chinese because of its mix of minority peoples – among them Yi, Miao, Tibetan, Dai, Bai, Naxi, Hui – the most of any province in China. Serious rebellions, particularly those of the Muslims in the 19th century, were put down. Slowly the number of Chinese settlers increased to reduce the region's autonomy.

Most of the million-odd Bai minority live in the Dali Bai Autonomous Prefecture. In the face of socialist transformation, they cling to their old customs and beliefs (which were severely attacked during the Cultural Revolution). The Third Moon Street Fair, held annually in April, is a stunningly colourful event which attracts huge crowds from the local Bai minority and many other minorities who trek in from miles around. There are festivals and trading-fairs at other times of the year, including a Torch Festival and Dragon-Boat Racing. Minority clothing is more evident among the women and is used for market days or special occasions (making the clothing was discouraged by the Chinese since it reduced time in the fields; some materials are now factory-made in Shanghai).

The name Dali actually means 'marble'. Dali has long been famous for this 'white jade', which is quarried in the area. Marble from Dali is highly prized and has been used in temples and palaces throughout China. One of the customers (long ago) was the Forbidden City in Peking.

KUNMING TO DALI

Buses leave every other day from the Western Bus Station (the building with the large clock) – 10 minutes up the street from the railway station, and it's on your left. Minibuses take nine hours and cost Y24; standard buses take 11 hours and cost Y14. On the days when there are no bus departures from the Western Bus Station, take a bus from behind Kunming Hotel (*Kunming Fandian*); buy your ticket from the hotel.

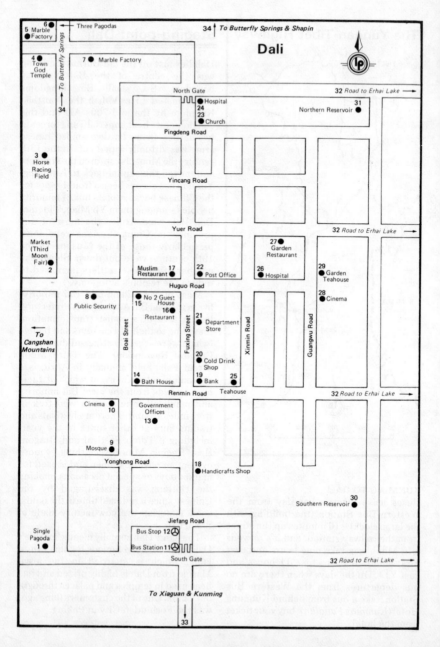

Dali

6 ● 5 ● Marble Factory

← Three Pagodas

34 ↑ To Butterfly Springs & Shapin

4 ● Town God Temple

7 ● Marble Factory

To Butterfly Springs

34

North Gate

32 Road to Erhai Lake →

● Hospital
24 23 ● Church

31 ● Northern Reservoir

Pingdeng Road

3 ● Horse Racing Field

Yincang Road

Yuer Road

32 Road to Erhai Lake →

Market (Third Moon Fair) ● 2

27 ● Garden Restaurant

29 ● Garden Teahouse

Muslim 17 Restaurant ●

22 ● Post Office

26 ● Hospital

Huguo Road

28 ● Cinema

To Cangshan Mountains ←

8 ● Public Security

● No 2 Guest House 15
16 ● Restaurant

21 ● Department Store

Boai Street

Fuxing Street

20 ● Cold Drink Shop

Xinmin Road

Guangwu Road

14 ● Bath House

19 ● Bank

25 ●

Renmin Road

Teahouse

32 Road to Erhai Lake →

Cinema ● 10

Government Offices

13 ●

9 ● Mosque

Yonghong Road

18 ● Handicrafts Shop

30 ● Southern Reservoir

Single Pagoda

1 ●

Jiefang Road

Bus Stop 12 ◉

Bus Station 11 ◉

South Gate

32 Road to Erhai Lake →

To Xiaguan & Kunming

↓ 33

Places to Stay & Eat

Dali opened officially to individuals in June 1984 and has become popular as a rest-stop for battered China travellers. *No 2 Guesthouse* is at present the best place to stay (preferable to the hotel in Xiaguan). *No 2 Guesthouse* is a 15½-minute walk from the bus-stop into town, and prices vary from Y2 to Y4 in a dormitory with three or four beds (the lower price is the student rate), with Y12 a double at normal rates. Facilities are basic; there are no showers, a communal wash-room, and fair to disgusting toilets. Maps of the town are available at the hotel, and bikes can be hired for Y2 a day from the Happy Bike Shop next door. Marble Bath-house, not far from the hotel, is 60 fen a bath, with additional massage available; open 8 am to 7 pm.

Dali has several teahouses and restaurants: the *Moslem Restaurant*, the *Garden Teahouse* and the *Garden Restaurant* (open 8 am to 11 pm). The *Garden Restaurant* has good fare and friendly people; every backpacker seems to eat there.

Around Dali

Hiking is very popular in the Cangshan Mountain Range, which backs Dali, and around Erhai Lake, the 40 km stretch of water that complements the town. The three large white Buddhist pagodas at the foot of the Cangshan Mountains date back to the Tang Dynasty, with later Ming renovations. Other sights worthy of your attention are the tea factory in nearby Xiaguan, and the fascinating houses that once belonged to wealthy tea merchants in Xizhou. Not to be missed is the Monday market in Shapin, about 25 km north of Dali, at the end of the lake. Regular buses leave Dali on market day. The market is full of Bai and other minority peoples in full regalia and is a riot of local colour – live animals, baskets and mats, fruits and potions, haircutting and teeth-filling.

DALI TO MARKAM

The route from Dali skirts Erhai Lake, runs northwards to Jianchuan and on to Baihanchang where it is joined by a road from Lijiang. After Baihanchang you continue past Mt Yulongxue (5596 metres),

1	一塔	18	工艺美术店
2	三月街	19	银行
3	赛马场	20	冷饮店
4	城隍庙	21	百货公司
5	大理石厂	22	邮局
6	三塔	23	教堂
7	大理石厂	24	中医院
8	公安局	25	茶馆
9	清真寺	26	中医院
10	电影院	27	杏花村饭馆
11	长途汽车站	28	东门电影院
12	公共车站	29	花园茶社
13	人民政府	30	南水库
14	沐浴旅社	31	北水库
15	招待所	32	至洱海
16	饭馆	33	至下关
17	清真饭馆	34	至蝴蝶泉

across the Jinsha (Yangtze) river to Zhongdian, a small town where the Tibetans dress in a distinctive red turban. From Zhongdian there is also a road branching off to Litang (426 km) on the Sichuan-Tibet Highway. Leaving Zhongdian the road recrosses the Jinsha river and heads over Hengduan Shan to Dêqên which is still in Yunnan. From Dêqên the route goes over a pass at Gejiehe and drops down into Yanjing (Salt Well) which is in Tibet. After Yanjing the road briefly follows the Lancang (Mekong) river before veering off to Markam, a small town on the Sichuan-Tibet Highway. For onward travel refer to the South Route Via Markam section in the Sichuan Routes chapter.

In July 1985 a slew of new places opened up in Yunnan Province. Amongst them was the 'Autonomous County of Naxi nationality' which presumably means Lijiang, to the north of Dali (the base of the matriarchal Naxi nationality, although they are distributed in Sichuan and Yunnan, is Lijiang). If this is so, then Lijiang could become an interesting stepping-stone on the route northward toward Tibet. Try for a permit.

Top: Valley and village near Chamdo, Tibet (MB)
Left: Village on Tibetan plateau, along Sichuan-Tibet Highway (MB)
Right: Lake near Rawu, Tibet (MB)

Top: Pilgrims circumambulating Tashilhunpo Monastery, Shigatse (MB)
Left: Pango Chorten, Gyantse (MB)
Right: Pilgrims pause at prayer-wheel 'stop' behind the Tashilhunpo Monastery (MB)

Qinghai Routes

QINGHAI PROVINCE

Qinghai (Tsinghai) formerly known as Amdo (the north-east province of Tibet) or Koko Nor, is now a west-central province of China bordered by Xinjiang and the Tibetan Autonomous Region on the west, Sichuan province in the south and Gansu province in the east and north. Qinghai province covers an area of 720,000 sq km, is mostly grassland, and has a total population of approximately four million.

History

Historically, Qinghai province was a part of Tibet, a remote region lying west of China proper until it was passed to the Mongol overlords in China in the 14th century. It then became part of Gansu and after 1724 it was administered from Xining as the Koko Nor territory. In 1928 Qinghai became a province of China.

Population

The population is composed mainly of Han, Tibetan, Hui, Mongolian, Tu, Salar, Kazakh and other nationalities. Since the 1950s there has been a huge influx of Han Chinese as part of a drive to develop the west. Although it is the third largest political unit, it is sparsely populated with only nine persons per square km. The capital is Xining, with an area of 350 square km and a population of 550,000; compared with 1949 when the area was three square km and the population only 50,000. Xining has become a focus of development in west China.

The rest of the province is divided into national areas: Yushu Tibetan Autonomous Prefecture; Hainan Tibetan Autonomous Prefecture; Huangnan Tibetan Autonomous Prefecture; Haibei Tibetan Autonomous Prefecture; Golog Tibetan Autonomous Prefecture; Haixi Tibetan-Mongol-Kazakh Autonomous Prefecture.

Unaccounted for are the numbers of prisoners in labour camps in Qinghai. Gansu and Qinghai were dubbed a 'black hole' – for an inestimable number of prisoners. The camps go back to 1949, when Qinghai was closed off to the rest of the world. It remained that way until the early 1980s when the first group tours were allowed through to the 'spirit mountain' of Anyêmaqên.

Geography & Climate

The province is made up almost entirely of mountains and high plateaux at an average of 4000 metres in elevation. To the north are the Qilian mountains; through the central part of the plateau run the Kunlun mountains which extend into the Bayan Har mountains (which form the watershed for the headwaters of both the Yangtze and Yellow rivers). In the south, the Tanggula mountains run parallel to the border with the Tibetan Autonomous Region. In the south-east, the Anyêmaqên mountains (with peaks over 7000 metres) run along the Qinghai-Sichuan border. In the north-west lies the Qaidam basin (Qaidam is Mongolian for salt marshes), a vast lowland irrigated by the Qaidam river. There are hundreds of lakes; the largest is Koko Nor (English: blue sea, Chinese: Qinghai Hu) which is also the largest salt lake in China with an area of 4,100 square km and lying at an altitude of about 3200 metres.

The climate varies considerably with the terrain. Rainfall averages about 20 cm annually and falls mostly during the hot summers. Winters are bitterly cold, dry and windy.

Economy

The Riyue mountains divide Qinghai into two parts: the eastern side is mostly farmed by the Han Chinese who grow barley, wheat, potatoes, beans and hemp;

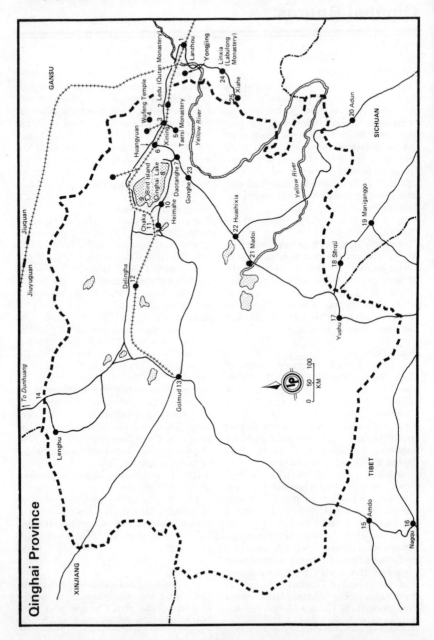

Qinghai Province

the western side is where Tibetans and Mongolians engage in animal husbandry (yak, cattle, goats, sheep and horses) with some mixed farming. The forests around the Kunlun and Qilian mountains have fruit orchards (pear, apricot, walnut and pear) and timber products such as fir, spruce and birch. Special local products in Qinghai include pilose antler, musk, black moss, Chinese caterpillar fungus (*Aweto*), Xining wool, hides, carpets, furs and jewellery. The horses from this area are the subject of a Tibetan saying: 'the best religion from U-Tsang (Central Tibet), the best men from Kham (Eastern Tibet) and the best horses from Amdo (Northern Tibet)'. Huge petroleum resources are now being tapped in the Qaidam basin. Coal, iron ore and other minerals are also extracted near Xining which has a thriving industrial base concentrating on dairy products and textiles.

Getting There

The Xining-Golmud railway was opened recently for civilian use. Roads have been expanded since the initial burst of road construction by the PLA during the 1950s. The major routes are from Xining to Tibet (via Golmud); Xining to Sichuan (via Maniganggo or Aba); Xining to Xinjiang; and Xining to Lanzhou. Truck transport has increased at a tremendous rate – Golmud now has a nickname, 'the city of vehicles'. Air communications are limited to flights from Xining to Golmud, Xian, Lanzhou and Beijing.

QINGHAI-TIBET HIGHWAY

The Qinghai-Tibet Highway is the world's highest road, passing through the Qaidam Basin, the Kunlun, Tanggula and Nyainqêntanglha mountain ranges at altitudes between 4000 and 5000 metres. The People's Liberation Army (PLA) completed the Qinghai section in 1952 and the Tibet section from 1953-4. The route is a long succession of desolate runs through uninhabited high plateaux, broken only occasionally by mountain passes.

Until recently, this route was one of the roughest rides in the world. In July 1985 an 11 year, 770 million yuan scheme to straighten, widen and asphalt the road was completed. To offset road-bed deformation caused by asphalting, those parts of the road which crossed permafrost

1	兰州	14	至敦煌
2	乐都 (瞿昙寺)	15	安多
3	西宁市	16	那曲
4	五峰寺 (互助)	17	玉树
5	塔尔寺 (湟中)	18	石渠
6	湟源	19	马尼干戈
7	倒淌河	20	阿坝
8	青海湖	21	花石峡
9	鸟岛	22	玛多
10	黑马河	23	共和
11	茶卡	24	监夏词
12	德令哈	25	夏词
13	格尔木		

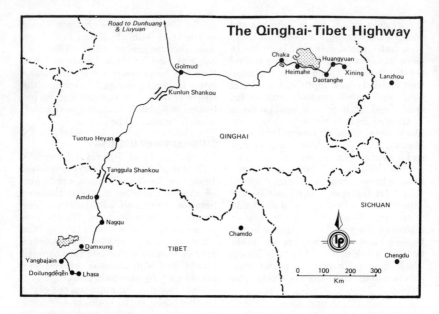

The Qinghai-Tibet Highway

areas (earth perennially frozen to a depth of up to 120 metres) were resurfaced with polypropylene. Most of the work was done by PLA recruits who received about Y14 monthly, local Tibetan and Hui road gangs and, it is murmured, members of the penal labour camps. Formerly, the sand and stone highway quickly disintegrated in the extremely harsh weather conditions. Drivers would leave the road to churn hundreds of individual tracks on massive detours. Heavily-laden trucks sank into a quagmire and were often left stranded in a sea of mud for weeks. This gives you some idea of the weather conditions out there. If you're travelling in winter, or even late spring and early autumn, you're inviting frostbite if you don't dress for the occasion.

Since deferment of the Qinghai-Tibet railway project, the Qinghai-Tibet highway has become the most important transport artery and the fastest road route into Tibet with a huge volume of truck traffic. Average time for a fully laden truck from

Golmud to Lhasa is two to three days. From Lhasa to Golmud, when trucks are usually empty, the run averages two days. For details of transport on this route from Lhasa, refer to the Getting Away section in the Lhasa chapter. If you're coming from Golmud to Lhasa, bus and truck information is in the Staging-point Golmud section of this chapter.

LHASA TO GOLMUD
Immediately after leaving Lhasa you reach **Doilungdêqên** where the road branches north for the Qinghai route and south for Lhasa airport (Gonggar) and Shigatse (southern route). At Doilungdêqên there is a small hotel, army barracks, petrol stations and, of course, a checkpoint. If you are hitching from here, try moving a short distance further on.

At **Yangbajain**, noted for its hot springs and geothermal power unit, the road branches again: north for the Qinghai route, south for Shigatse (northern route). About two hours out of Yangbajain you

Qinghai-Tibet Highway	Distances	
	intermediate	*cumulative*
Lhasa 拉萨		
Doilungdêqên 堆龙德庆	2 km	2 km
Yangbajain 羊八井	76 km	78 km
Damxung 当雄	75 km	153 km
Nagqu 那曲	164 km	317 km
Amdo 安多	136 km	453 km
Tanggula Shankou 唐古拉山口	89 km	542 km
Tuotuo Heyan 沱沱河沿	155 km	697 km
Kunlun Shankou 昆仑山口	324 km	1021 km
Golmud 格尔木	106 km	1127 km
Chaka 茶卡	484 km	1611 km
Heimahe 黑马河	80 km	1691 km
Daotanghe 倒淌河	116 km	1807 km
Huangyuan 湟源	51 km	1858 km
Xining 西宁	52 km	1910 km

Most travellers take the train between Xining and Golmud but the road route has been included here for those interested in variety or a direct connection with the Qinghai-Sichuan Highway.

Approximate distances for towns on or connected with this route:

Lhasa-Golmud	1166 km
Amdo-Xining	1482 km
Golmud-Dunhuang	520 km
Golmud-Liuyuan	654 km
Golmud-Xining	783 km
Lhasa-Xining	1937 km

pass Damxung which is close to **Nam Co**, at 4678 metres the world's highest named lake and, with a surface area of 1959 square km, Tibet's largest. It is also called Tengri Nor.

After crossing the pass over Nyainqên Tanglha Shan the road approaches **Nagqu**, the capital of Nagqu prefecture. Just outside Nagqu (Tibetan – black river) is a checkpoint. Foreigners are not usually of primary interest, but if your ride is a private deal and no ticket has been issued,

the driver may suggest you step out for a short, circuitous walk and meet up further down the road. Since the other side of town has a similar set-up, your truck may make a similar detour. At the centre of Nagqu is a crossroads. The road west leads to the Ali region; the road east is the northern route to Chamdo (764 km) which is disliked by drivers because of bad road conditions, lack of truckstop facilities and, so it is rumoured, attacks by marauding bandits.

The route continues through **Amdo**, a scruffy, semi-Chinese town where another road branches west to Shiquanhe (1336 km) on the Xinjiang route. After Amdo you cross the Tanggula mountains at **Tanggula Shankou** (5180 metres), a pass which is snowbound virtually all the year round.

A short distance to the west lies Mt Geladaintong (6621 metres) where the Tuotuo river rises as the source of the Yangtze; the world's third longest river, with a total length of 6380 km. Another record goes to Wenquan, just north of Tanggula Pass, which at 5100 metres is the world's highest town. It was built by the Chinese in 1955. At Tuotuo Heyan the road crosses the Tuotuo and continues in a flat run over the steppes. You may be lucky and see large herds of Tibetan gazelles down from the hills grazing by the roadside, until you reach the pass over the Kunlun mountains at **Kunlun Shankou** (4837 metres). The rest of the route is downhill to **Golmud**.

About an hour before Golmud there is a checkpoint for skins and furs and little interest is shown in passengers. Drivers caught smuggling face fines of up to Y300. After running through dramatic scenery with eroded gorges and rock caves (a Sakyamuni statue found in one of these long-deserted caves in 1918 is now in a museum in the United States), you descend into the flat Qaidam Basin. About three km out of Golmud there is another checkpoint. This *is* for passengers, and drivers who are carrying passengers on a private deal will be fined. Understandably, some drivers disagree with this – so hang on to your fillings if they take evasive action and turn a dried riverbed into a racetrack detour.

Staging-point Golmud

Golmud is a newly developed town with a population of about 90,000. Its ugly sprawl has no attractions worth noting, so most travellers speed through, spending only the time it takes to arrange onward transport.

As of June 1985, Golmud is open to foreigners with a permit. Prior to this date officialdom was already turning a blind but benevolent eye on considerable numbers of travellers passing through. Tremulous backpackers entered a candy-shop atmosphere at the PSB where nervously proffered wishes were granted by the Fairy Godmother. Two Swedes received a note for the truck depot which stated simply: 'Help these boys'. An Irishman, unsure of onward transport, fearful of the notorious bus trip or even the dreaded refusal, asked for advice. 'Why don't you ... ?', the PSB lady murmured, lost in thought. 'Yes, yes ...', stammered the Irishman with terrible trepidation. 'Why don't you ... *take a truck*?', continued the lady. And so it was that one insanely happy Irishman finally reached Lhasa by truck, where, for all I know, he lived happily ever after.

Places to Stay

The *Municipal Guest House* is the best place in town but it is a long, long way from the truck depots. A bed in a seven-bed room costs Y4: a double with attached bath costs Y12. Within the building there is a coffee room, a dining room serving reasonable food, a small shop and a ticket office. With a little persuasion it should be possible to rent a bike, it saves time when checking out truck depots – ask at the desk or at the gate. A bus leaves from the door at 10 am for the station, but check at the gate first. The station is a 20 minute walk from here. Take special care of valuables, particularly if you have just arrived after an exhausting ride and your room is invaded by curious locals. One traveller lost his camera equipment that way.

The *Golmud Guest House* (*Golmud Banshichu Zhaodaisuo*) is located closer to the truck depots but foreigners are not

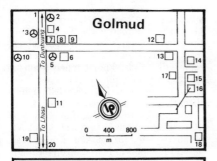

Golmud

```
0    400    800
         m
```

1 To Dunhuang
2 No 3 Truck Depot (Lhasa Yunshu San Dui)
3 Guest House (Golmud Banshichu Zhaodaisuo)
4 No 2 Truck Depot (Lhasa Yunshu Er Dui)
5 Bus Stop for Station
6 Hotel (Lushe)
7 Shop
8 Restaurant
9 Hotel (Lushe)
10 No 1 Truck Depot (Lhasa Yunshu Yi Dui)
11 Lhasa Transport Company
     (Xizang Lhasa Yunshu Gongci)
12 Public Security
13 Bookstore
14 Market
15 Restaurant
16 Municipal Guest House (Shi Zhaodaisuo)
17 Department Stores
18 Train Station
19 Checkpoint (Diancha Zhan)
20 To Lhasa

1 至敦煌   11 西藏拉萨输公司
2 拉萨运输三队   12 公安局
3 格尔木办事   13 书店
   处招待所   14 市场
4 拉萨运输二队   15 饭馆
5 公共汽车站   16 市招待所
6 旅社   17 百货商店
7 商店   18 火车站
8 饭馆   19 查点站
9 旅社   20 至拉萨
10 拉萨运输一队

always welcome. Nearby are various hotels (Lushe); spartan affairs, cheap and close to the truck depots which are also worth a try, although their accommodation is primarily for drivers.

Shopping
If you are Lhasa bound and haven't already stocked up on food, clothing and medicines, remember, Golmud is your last chance. Try the department stores and Friendship Store across the street from the Municipal Guest House for chocolate, canned food, cigarettes (Golmud has an extraordinary range of imported foreign cigarettes, such as Dunhill, Capstan, Marlboro), medicines (there are plenty of Chinese medicines available for coughs, diarrhoea, skin complaints) and warm clothing (hats, thick overcoats, sweaters). The market has plenty of fresh fruit and vegetables.

Getting There & Away
Air Golmud is a stopover for flights on the Lhasa-Xian run. Advance booking is usually necessary and tickets are in limited supply. Tickets are available from the ticket service at the Municipal Guest House. The Lhasa-Golmud-Xian flight in theory flies in both directions on Wednesdays and Saturdays, but these flights are frequently cancelled and routed via Chengdu from Xian. The cost is Y390 Lhasa-Xian, Y230 Lhasa-Golmud, and Y190 Golmud-Xian (all fares quoted are one way).

Rail Once a military railway run by the PLA, the line from Golmud to Xining is now open to foreigners. There are two trains daily – sometimes limited to one a day by maintenance work. Local price for hard-seat on the direct train is Y15.20. The train takes a leisurely 25 hours to reach Xining via the northern shore of Kokonor (Qinghai Lake). For the train timetable see the Xining section of this chapter.

Bus Golmud-Lhasa is a 30 to 50 hour trip, and it's Russian roulette whether you get (a) the ticket, (b) the actual ride and (c) whether the bus is mechanically fit to complete the ride.

Trains arriving from Xining are met at the station by buses for Lhasa. Some of these run direct to Lhasa through the night with one driver, or two if you are fortunate. Prices vary but an average ticket price is Y59. The buses are highly unreliable. One American staggered into his room in Lhasa after a 60 hour marathon. His bus was already ailing within minutes of departure and three breakdowns later the driver and passengers spent a night in the open. Next morning a tow was organised back to Golmud where the driver promised to find another bus. A few hours later the weary passengers could only groan when they were asked to board the same vehicle which had been hastily made roadworthy again. After yet another breakdown, the wreck was revived and eventually limped into Lhasa making gross mechanical noises. Another bus, after the usual saga of breakdowns, sustained a snapped back axle.

Truck Hundreds of trucks pass through Golmud every day, bound for Lhasa, Xining, Dunhuang, Lanzhou and beyond.

For trucks to Lhasa you should try the Lhasa Transport Company; No 1, No 2, and No 3 truck depots (there are more); and any parked trucks which look ready to leave in your direction. If you are issued with an official ticket, the standard price is Y40-45 RMB. If you organise a private deal, be prepared to bargain down from much higher figures. Most trucks leave between 4 and 9 am. Drivers may offer to pick you up at your hotel, but it is safer to be where the truck is, well before the time you have arranged. The passenger checkpoint is a long walk out of town (about three km) so leave at the crack of dawn and station yourself beyond it, if you want to thumb a lift.

For trucks to Dunhuang and Liuyuan you can try No 2 and No 3 truck depots or get out on the road early. To Dunhuang the price is about Y22; to Liuyuan, about Y28. About 15 km out of Golmud there is, reportedly, a checkpoint (open 9 am to noon; 3 to 6.30 pm) which sometimes shows foreigners a sign in English, telling them they have to return to Golmud.

For trucks to Xining, Lanzhou and other destinations it is best to check number plates of parked trucks, ask around at depots or just stand on the road. Don't despair, everybody finds a ride eventually, although you may find a stranger ride than you'd imagined. An Englishwoman travelled 50 hours on the Lhasa route in the back of a truck with a friendly group of 20 Tibetans, and a large goat which kept the crowd on its toes since it could control neither the timing nor the direction of its bodily functions.

Getting Around

Within Golmud there is a desultory, unreliable bus line running from the station, past the Municipal Guest House, across to the Golmud Guest House and up to No 3 Truck Depot. There is also a Land Rover taxi which plies the same route. If these aren't available, you'll have to hitch on a walking tractor, hire a bike or just take a long walk.

Staging-point Xining

Xining (2275 metres) is the capital of Qinghai Province with a population of 570,000 and an area of 350 square km. The centre of life in Xining is the main street, running from Xining Daxia Hotel due west to the large traffic circle at Ximen (East Gate).

The square near the station is frequently used as a setting for macabre rallies where criminals are publicly sentenced before massive crowds. Heavily armed, white-gloved soldiers stand on the back of trucks holding shaven-headed criminals – some tearful, others defiant – by the scruff of their necks to face a crowd that relishes entertainment. Officials sit with microphones behind a long table on the entrance steps and deliver the sentences which are echoed back and forth across the square. The spectacle ends when the trucks roar off in a long convoy, sirens blaring, to the execution site where a shot in the back of the head finishes the day. By late afternoon posters have appeared all over town with newly printed details of the criminals, their crimes and the final flourish of a crimson tick.

Information

CITS (tel 23901 –700) is in the front building of Xining Binguan (Hotel). The office is well stocked with material on China and has a wall map of Xining. The official here speaks English but service is slow. I was advised that it would be quicker for me to buy tickets at the station. Tours are arranged to places on and around Qinghai Lake. Minibus tours (minimum eight passengers, otherwise no tour) cost between Y32 and Y78, depending on the route and number of days.

CAAC (tel 77434) is on the main street, just past Xinhua bookstore.

Bank The Bank of China is also on the main street, a short distance from the mosque. It is open from 9 am to noon and 2.30 to 6 pm, closed on Wednesday morning and all day Saturday and Sunday. Money changers also roam the streets and/or you could take a short walk down a side-street, diagonally across from the bank, and visit the cloth market.

Public Security is open from 9 am to noon and 2.30 to 6 pm. The staff speak excellent English, readily provide extensions and know the the rules of the permit game which they observe thoroughly.

Xinhua bookstore is on the main street

opposite the main department store. Maps are available here. **The Foreign Languages Bookstore** is on your left after crossing the bridge at the western end of the main street. A large selection of translated works are available here but, interestingly,the map section at the back is out of bounds to foreigners.

Things to See

Xining is without stunning sights within the city proper. Most travellers use it as a staging-point. Still, there is a charm to the frontier-post atmosphere of this city and you might be content to stroll the streets, rewarded by the occasional sight of Tibetans, Tu, Mongolians, Salar or Kazakhs.

Dongguan Mosque is on the main street. Built in the Ming Dynasty (1368-1644) in the style of a Chinese palace, this is one of

Xining Climate Chart			
Month	Average °C	Highest °C	Lowest °C
Jan	-7.7	0.9	-13.8
Feb	-4.6	3.5	-10.6
Mar	1.8	9.3	-3.6
Apr	8.3	16.3	1.8
May	12.3	19.8	6.2
Jun	15.3	22.7	9.1
Jul	17.2	24.3	11.3
Aug	16.8	23.9	11.4
Sep	12.2	18.5	7.8
Oct	6.7	13.9	1.5
Nov	-0.3	7.1	-5.8
Dec	-6.2	2.1	-12.1

the largest mosques in north-western China. On Fridays the mosque is packed with worshippers. The **Beishan Monastery** lies north of Xining on a mountain top with superb views. **Hutai** (Tiger Terrace) is in the western part of the city. Bus No 9 stops close to it. **The People's Park** has a dilapidated zoo and a boating lake. Bus No 1 stops at the entrance.

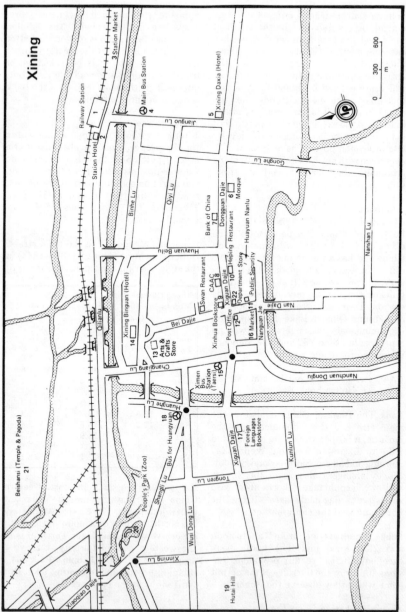

Xining

Railway Station

Station Hotel

1

2

3 Station Market

Main Bus Station

4

5 Xining Daxia (Hotel)

Jiangou Lu

Binhe Lu

Qiyi Lu

Gonghe Lu

Nanshan Lu

Bank of China

7 Dongguan Dajie

6 Mosque

Huayuan Beilu

Huayuan Nanlu

Xining Binguan (Hotel)

Swan Restaurant

CAAC

8

9 Xiguan Dajie

Heping Restaurant

10

Department Store

22

Public Security

Qilianlu

Bei Dajie

Xinhua Bookstore

Post Office

12

16 Market 11

Nan Dajie

Nanguan Jie

Changjiang Lu

13 Arts & Crafts Store

14

Ximen Bus Station (Taxis)

15

Nanchuan Donglu

Huangye Lu

18

Bus for Huangyuan

Xiguan Dajie

17

Foreign Languages Bookstore

Kunlun Lu

Tongren Lu

Wusi Dong Lu

Shengli Lu

People's Park (Zoo)

20

Xining Lu

19 Hutai Hill

Beishans (Temple & Pagoda) 21

Xiaoqiao Dajie

0   300   600
m

1	火车站	12	大什字邮局
2	车站饭店	13	省工艺美术服务部
3	火车站商场	14	西宁宾馆
4	汽车站	15	西门汽车站
5	西宁大厦	16	西大街商场
6	清真大寺	17	省外文书店
7	中国银行	18	湟源车站
8	民航售票处	19	虎台
9	新华书店	20	人民公园
10	和平餐厅	21	北禅寺
11	公安局	22	大什字百货商店

巧克力　Qiaokeli

成份: 可可豆, 可可脂, 磷脂,
奶粉, 砂糖, 和香兰素。

(義利)
北京市义利食品厂

8205

Space Invader chocolate

Places to Stay

Xining Binguan (tel 23901) is in a large, tranquil compound with a pleasant garden at the back. To get there take bus No 9 from the railway station and get off at the fifth stop. This is the largest hotel in Xining with 300 rooms and over 1000 beds. At the gate there is a taxi office. The rear building contains reception, accommodation, Chinese and western restaurants (breakfast, 7.30 to 8 am; lunch, 12 to 12.30 pm; dinner, 6.30 to 7 pm), shops, telephone service, etc. The front building houses CITS, an interpreting bureau and other offices. A bed in a three-bed room costs Y7 FEC. Ask at the desk for details of the Xining Binguan disco. To reach the city centre, walk uphill around the crescent-shaped park in front of the hotel and ride bus No 3 for one stop.

Xining Daxia (tel 77991) has 220 rooms and 560 beds. Take bus No 1 from the station and get off at the second stop. There is less comfort here but a bed in a four-bed room costs Y3. Left luggage facilities are on the ground floor. Hot showers can be elusive. *The Station Hotel* is on the right of the station square when you leave the station building.

Places to Eat

For a change from the bland fare and hushed surroundings of hotel restaurants, walk along the main street and plunge into any of the market areas. You can buy kebabs with flat bread, Muslim noodles (*lamian*), dumplings and seafood soup. A tasty, local dish is 'mutton eaten with the hands' (*Shou Zhua Yang Rou*). In the morning look for fresh yoghurt and a sweet barley dish called *tianpei* – if you happen to have measles, this is supposed to be a good cure.

The *Swan Restaurant* is 10 minutes from the Xining Binguan. Walk up Beidajie St toward the main street until you see a sign on your left pointing down a side street. The menu here, officially titled: 'Menu of China: Western Style of Swan Room', offers translated exotica. Item No 22, 'A Photograph of the Whole Family', has been reduced from Y2.80 to Y2.50, or perhaps you'd prefer 'Dregs of Pork Fat and Chinese Cabbage'.

On the north side of Ximen (East Gate) roundabout there is an excellent dumpling (*jiaozi*) restaurant. The *Heping Restaurant*, a couple of blocks east of the main department store is also worth visiting. In the early evening there is plenty of activity and a wide variety of food stalls in the station area.

Things to Buy

If you are heading for Tibet, stock up in Xining. The main department store has a great variety of goods. As is now the case in many Chinese cities, the Friendship Store is disappointing. Leather goods (shoes, boots, bags) and exotic medicines (musk, Chinese caterpillar fungus and pilose antler) are special buys. For last minute purchases, there's a large department store at the left of the station square.

Getting There & Away

Air There are regular flights from Xining to Beijing and Lanzhou. To Beijing (with stop-overs in Taiyuan and Lanzhou), departures are on Saturday and Sunday, Y222 one-way. From Xining to Lanzhou, the fare is Y24 one-way (departures; Friday, Saturday, Sunday). Other air-transport centres are at Lanzhou (Lanzhou-Xian-Guangzhou Y284, three flights weekly), and Xian which is well-connected with the rest of China (also with a charter-flight to Hong Kong on Sundays, HK$1070 one-way).

Train Trains run direct from Xining to Golmud, Baoji, Xian, Lanzhou, Zhengzhou, Qingdao, Beijing and Shanghai. There is a special ticket window for foreigners at the station.

Golmud to Xining

Train No	Dep	Arr
508 (slow)	1819	1932 (next day)
304 (direct)	1146	0900 (next day)

Xining to Golmud

Train No	Dep	Arr
507 (slow)	0740	0810 (next day)
303 (direct)	1746	1446 (next day)

From Xining

Destination	Train No	Dep
Beijing	122	1233
Lanzhou	302	0805
Qingdao	104	1824
Shanghai	178	1648
Xian	276	1412

Rail Distances from Xining

Beijing	2098 km
Chengdu	1172 km
Golmud	781 km
Guangzhou	3021 km
Lanzhou	216 km
Shanghai	2403 km
Xian	892 km
Zhengzhou	1403 km

Bus The long-distance bus station – walk straight ahead out of the station for 50 metres and it's on your left – is unwilling to sell tickets to foreigners. Those interested in hitching could take a city bus to the end of the line and start there. Buses to Huangyuan (51 km west of Xining on the Golmud road) leave at 7 am from the north side of the roundabout on Shengli Lu. Buses to Taersi leave frequently from Ximen bus station.

Getting Around

Three wheelers and taxis are available at the station. Xining Binguan has a taxi office and a special shuttle bus for the station which is probably only for group tours. Bus No 1 runs from the railway station, past Xining Daxia, all the way down the main street and then continues to the People's Park. Bus No 9 is useful since it leaves from the station and passes Xining Binguan (get off at the fifth stop).

AROUND XINING

Taersi Lamasery

Taersi, or *Kumbum* (Tibetan – one hundred thousand images) was built in 1577 and is one of the six great lamaseries of the Gelukpa (Yellow Hat) sect. Tsongkhapa, founder of the Gelukpa, was born here. The present Dalai Lama was born nearby in 1935.

In the 17th and 18th centuries Taersi was a teeming religious centre with over 3000 monks. Between 1967 and 1979 the lamasery was closed and the remaining monks were imprisoned or banished. Chueshu, a 'living Buddha' from Kumbum was sent to prison for 21 years in 1958 but has since returned. Today, the buildings are being renovated but the number of monks in residence is less than 500. Temple festivities take place on days determined by the lunar calendar in January, February, April, June and September.

Six temples are open. The main temples are: The Grand Temple; The Lesser Temple; the Great Hall of Meditation; The Flower Temple and The Nine-Chamber Temple. The eight stupas at the entrance to the monastery complex are called the *ruyi* stupas. The creation of butter sculptures with extraordinary detail is a specialty of this monastery.

Tickets must be bought at a small window beneath a large map of the monastery area opposite the eight stupas. It is possible to stay at the monastery in converted monk's quarters close to the eight stupas. Rooms at ground level tend to be damp. The friendly staff charge Y7 per bed. Giant portions of excellent food are served in the dining room.

Taersi is a 45-minute bus ride (26 km) from Xining. Buses leave from Ximen Bus Station in Xining at frequent intervals between 7 am and 6 pm. On one trip I

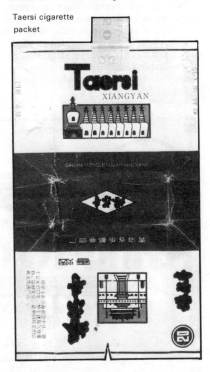

Taersi cigarette packet

watched a furious conductress jump off the bus in pursuit of a farmer attempting to slip off without paying. The irate lady threatened to beat him over the head with his pickaxe, newly acquired at the market. Perhaps it was the fear of damage to his shiny pickaxe which made the man pay on the instant. The bus drops you, not at the monastery, but in the main square of Huangzhong. This is where you catch the bus back to Xining.

To reach the monastery, walk up the hill for about one km. On the way you pass rows of stalls selling trinkets, antiques, yoghurt and assorted tourist trappings. At the eight stupas, turn right into the monastery complex. Photographers around the stupas specialise in hiring out pseudo Tibetan clothing to giggling Han Chinese for an 'ethnic' snapshot.

Pilgrims to Taersi follow a circuit clockwise around the wooded hills above the monastery buildings. You may not have the time or energy to prostrate about six km but it is a peaceful walk. At the end of the circuit, close to the eight stupas, is a large chorten with hundreds of carved prayer stones. The surrounding hills are great for hiking.

Qinghai Lake

With an area of over 4000 sq km, this is the largest saltwater body in China. Bird Island (Niaodao), at the western edge of the lake, is famed as a paradise for ornithologists. Thousands of birds, including such rare species as the black-necked stork, congregate here during late spring and early summer. To protect the birds, unescorted tours of the island are not allowed. CITS in Xining can arrange tours to the island and include other destinations if required.

If you want to visit the northern part of the lake on your own (it's not officially encouraged), try taking the Golmud train and hop off about three hours later at Ketu which is an hour's walk from the lake. If you decide to take to the road you will probably be refused a ticket on the Xining to Golmud bus. In this case, try hitching from Huangyuan to Daotanghe, then continue along the southern edge of the lake to Heimahe. From Heimahe (where

Flying to Moon toilet paper

limited accommodation is available) to the lake is only a few km. If you are continuing to Golmud, the only noteworthy stop is Chaka (just over two hours from Heimahe). About four km from Chaka is a famous salt lake (Yanhu) with open-face salt mines.

Other

Ledu (Quxiansi Monastery) Ledu is 63 km east of Xining. Buses run direct from Xining, or take a train.

Tu Autonomous County In late 1985 it was announced that two monasteries (Youning monastery and Wufeng monastery) had been renovated and opened in The Tu Autonomous County about 50 km north of Xining. The construction of Youning monastery was ordered in 1602 by the 4th Dalai Lama. One hundred lamas of the Tu nationality are now in residence (the Tu nationality has close links with the Tibetans).

Laoye Shan This is a scenic mountain area 40 km north of Xining. Buses run from Xining.

Linxia & Xiahe Linxia (Labulong Monastery) and Xiahe (Labrang Monastery): these two Tibetan monasteries, added to permit lists in 1985, are in Gansu province, but right next to the border with Qinghai. Buses run from Lanzhou. Labrang Monastery has received good reviews from the few that have been there – they describe it as highly active and vital.

QINGHAI-SICHUAN HIGHWAY

The Qinghai-Sichuan Highway runs from Xining to Chengdu. At Maniganggo the road joins the Sichuan-Tibet Highway (refer to the separate route description in the Sichuan Routes chapter).

Although places like Yushu may open soon, it is still rare for individuals to be granted permits. If you stay long in one place, 'the men in green' may want to spoil the trip. Xining and Chengdu are both open cities at each end of the highway – a point worth raising to justify your presence in these remote areas. Keep moving, arrive late, leave early, and stay low on the outskirts of small towns. Take food and warm clothing. The bus from Xining to Yushu takes two days. From Xiwu (30 km from Yushu) to Chengdu allow three days.

XINING TO MANIGANGGO

Staff at the long-distance bus station in Xining have been instructed not to sell tickets. They refer you to CITS who flip the idea away with the closed area argument. A local bus leaves from Xining for **Huangyuan** at 7 am from the north side of the roundabout on Shengli Lu. Huangyuan is a large town with shops, restaurants and a hotel on the main street. At the bottom of a short hill just before the town, the road forks right into Huangyuan and straight ahead for Daotanghe. The first 30 km of this road are under repair. Perhaps road is not the right term for this section. It is atrocious and can take over four hours. After climbing out of a river valley, the route improves and crosses the RiYue mountains at RiYue Shankou (3452 metres) about 10 km before Daotanghe.

Daotanghe is a junction for the roads to Golmud (via Heimahe on the southern edge of Qinghai Lake) and Yushu (via Madoi). There is a small shop, a restaurant, a truckers' hotel and a drowsy checkpoint here. The literal translation of Daotanghe is 'back-flowing river'. Most rivers in China flow from west to east, but this one is an exception. According to legend, when the Chinese Princess Wen Cheng was en route to Tibet to marry King Songtsen Gampo she burst into tears when she saw her homeland blocked by Riyue Shan. The God of Rain was moved to send a shower. The tears and rain combined to form a stream which followed the Princess on her journey westwards.

The road continues for an hour out of the plateau and over another pass to **Gonghe**. Gonghe is a large county capital,

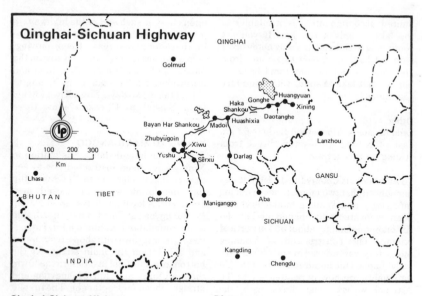

Qinghai-Sichuan Highway	Distances	
	intermediate	*cumulative*
Xining 西宁		
Huangyuan 湟源	52 km	52 km
Daotanghe 倒淌河	51 km	103 km
Gonghe 共和	42 km	147 km
Haka Shankou 河卡山南	101 km	248 km
Huashixia 花石峡	174 km	422 km
Madoi 玛多	75 km	497 km
Bayan Har Shankou 巴颜喀拉山口	121 km	618 km
Zhubyugoin 竹节寺	111 km	729 km
Xiwu* 歇武	51 km	780 km
Serxu 石渠	91 km	871 km
Maniganggo 马尼干戈	193 km	1064 km

*From Xiwu a road leaves the Qinghai-Sichuan Highway for Yushu. 玉树

now open with a permit. If you favour a low profile, don't stay at the Guest House (*Zhaodaisuo*) but try the seedier hostels opposite the bus station or get yourself dropped off at the entrance to town, just before the checkpoint (*Dianchazhan*), and try the Muslim hostel. Buses to Xining (Y4), Madoi (Y11.20) and Yushu (Y24.70) run daily. Try the trucks which stop outside the bus station or jump a

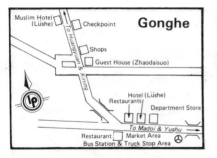

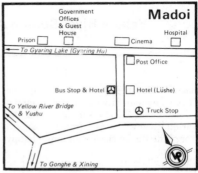

monstrous cinema which reportedly cost Y700 million to build. Armed guards patrol the roof of a prison near the government office compound. Shops here are uninteresting. The best place to stay is opposite the bus stop which also has a hostel. The truck stop is a five minute walk down the street and then left. Trucks also stop outside the bus stop. Many trucks bypass Madoi altogether, so you may be better off walking a couple of km back to

walking tractor or a horse cart out of town from where you can flag down passing traffic.

Between Huangyuan and Gonghe no sight is more wondrous to the lonesome hitcher than the huge convoys of – rub your eyes and look again – brand new Mercedes trucks (tankers and flat beds) purring past. When one of these Rolls-Royces of transport in Qinghai actually stops to give you a ride, paradise is tangible. Forgotten are the long, back-breaking night rides in the back of a Jiefang coal truck.

From Gonghe the road runs up to another plateau to **Haka** which is a shabby collection of restaurants, shops and a hostel (trucks and buses stop here). From Haka to the pass over Haka Shan (3900 metres) is a short ride. The road twists and turns over the mountains while far below yak trains follow the old road which runs straight. From the pass you descend across a plateau to **Wenquan** (Hot Springs) which has comfortable hostels (one is run by the PLA) and restaurants. The highway then crosses Anyêmaqên Shan going over a pass (5300 metres), past a large lake down to Huashixia which has a major checkpoint. From Huashixia there is a road branching off past Mt Maqên Kangri (6282 metres) to Darlag and continuing into Aba (528 km) in Sichuan province. From Aba there are buses to Chengdu.

About an hour after Huashixia you reach **Madoi**. This is a dull place at an altitude over 4000 metres dominated by a

the main road. Goloks – the nomadic, Tibetan tribesmen from this area – dressed in wild outfits ride into town to watch foreigners who are probably stranger than anything they see at the cinema.

Madoi is of special importance as a base for those interested in visiting the source area of the Yellow River. From Madoi to Gyaring on Ngoring Lake is about 44 km. Hitch a ride on a truck, arrange to hire a vehicle from government offices or take a guide and a horse. Gyaring Hu Commune has a fish factory with a dormitory, reportedly the only place to stay near Gyaring. Roads in this area are frequently washed out. If you visit during November, there is a Frozen Fish Festival when truckloads of Tibetans come here to fish for scaleless Huang. From Ngoring Lake to Gyaring Lake is another 20 km and to reach the actual source you will need to mount a virtual expedition through the

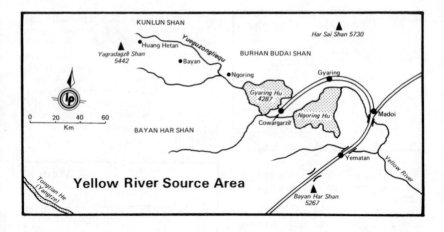

Yellow River Source Area

marshy Xingsu Lake area and up the Yueguzongliequ River. Recent research indicates that the real source may be the Kariqu River which rises from the eastern foot of the Bayan Har mountains – happy searching!

From Madoi the route continues up to the pass at Bayan Har Shankou (5082 metres), past Zhubgyü going to Xiwu. Here the road forks: east to Sêrxü, straight ahead for **Yushu**. Security is tight in Yushu, so, if Sichuan province is your goal, change transport here. Xiwu has a large, renovated monastery. From Xiwu to Sêrxü the road is currently under repair. Sêrxü is in Sichuan province. There is no bus service so try the truck depot or the truckstop/hostel (*Tiemushe Luguan*) for lifts. The highway continues through Chola Shan to **Maniganggo** where it joins the Sichuan-Tibet Highway. From here you can travel to Lhasa via Chamdo (ask at the Chamdo Transport Company truckstop) or to Chengdu via Kangding (ask at the Sichuan Transport Company truckstop).

YUSHU

This is the capital of Yushu Autonomous Prefecture and worth the 30 km detour from Xiwu. However, the 'men in green'

are super-fast at picking up non-permit-holders. First you are questioned (one official speaks English) then your passport is confiscated and a written self-criticism follows and a bus ticket is arranged for the next bus back to Xining. If you have to wait a day, you will be allowed to wander the town accompanied by a Tibetan security official. Two letters are provided when you leave: one is a pass for hostels and checkpoints, the other is for Public Security in Xining where your passport is sent by special courier. Also included in the service are free rides around town in

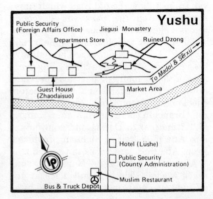

Public Security's motorcycle/sidecar combination complete with blue light.

Yushu (3700 metres), known in Tibetan as Jyekundo, lies in a picturesque river valley surrounded by high mountains. To the right of the department store there is a street leading up through the old part of town to a stream. A steep path climbs up to the ruined Dzong and Jiegusi Monastery. From here there are fine views of Yushu (note the large, prison-like structure to the north). Friendly monks will show you around the monastery which is undergoing total renovation.

The market down by the river is a good place to meet up with Tibetans keen to trade, barter or just laugh. Yushu, according to connoisseurs, is 'worm capital'. The worms are caterpillars collected during hibernation between April and July. July specimens are considered of inferior quality – the tail end. Boiled in wine, these caterpillars (Chinese: *DongchongCao*) are highly prized as a remedy for consumption and general debility. One jin (about 500 grams) equals 3000 broken specimens or 1800 whole ones (much preferred) and sells for about Y200. There is a huge annual fair at Yushu, lasting five days from 25 July. Vast crowds of nomads trek in specially for horse races, archery contests, Tibetan opera and dances.

The most comfortable place to stay is the *Guest House* (*Zhaodaisuo*), conveniently close to Public Security. There is a shabby hotel, just off the street about 500 metres before the bus station. The bus station has a good Muslim restaurant. The bus to Xining leaves from here every other day at 7 am. Buy your tickets the day before (Y28.70). One foreigner who did **obtain a permit for Yushu was a German naturalist researching asses . . .**

Xinjiang Routes

Completed by the PLA between 1956 and 1957, the Xinjiang-Tibet Highway traverses the desolate Ali (Ngari) region before crossing the Kunlun mountains to Kashgar. Now that the Qinghai-Tibet Highway has been turned into a newly asphalted speedway, there is even less traffic on this route, particularly between Shiquanhe and Lhasa. From Lhasa to Kashgar (probably the best direction to travel the highway), a direct run averages nine days.

Ali, sometimes called the roof of the roof of the world, is very sparsely populated with little more than 50,000 inhabitants in an area of 30,000 square km – so take a bulging food bag and adequate clothing for altitudes exceeding 5000 metres. One doughty American left Lhasa to hitch through this region with the largest, heaviest suitcase (full of goodies from Hong Kong) I have ever seen. But he made it and was last heard of in Ladakh. Many of the truck drivers on this route carry rifles which they use to shoot game. Yecheng and Shiquanhe are the only two towns of any stature on the entire route. Not surprisingly, the 'men in green' are quick to pick up and fine the 'paperless'.

LHAZÊ TO SHIQUANHE

For a description of the route from Lhasa to Lhazê see the Nepal Route chapter.

After Lhazê you have to cross the river by ferry to take the Xinjiang road in the direction of Coqên. The ferryman lives in the building on the other side and may help with a meal and arrange onward transportation. The road runs to Raka, then turns abruptly northwards past large glaciers to Coqên. After skirting Zhari Namco (Zhari Lake), the highway joins the main Amdo-Shiquanhe road at Dongco. Continuing through Gêrzê, the route climbs round the foot of Nganglong Kangri (6596 metres), and passes Gêgyai,

a town divided into two halves separated by about two km. The road then crosses the Sênggê Zangpo river (source of the Indus) and dips down into the Shiquanhe. This is the prefectorial capital – a bland, newly developed town with a geothermal power station. The local authorities are vigilant (various travellers have been fined for lacking permits) so the less time spent here the better.

To continue into Xinjiang, take the northern route out of Shiquanhe. However, the sights which are a real 'must' in the prefecture are reached by taking the southern road out of Shiquanhe towards Burang. The southern road passes through Gar to Namru which is the turn-off for Zanda. Allow a day to travel from Shiquanhe to Zanda which is the site of Toling monastery and a convenient base from which to visit the eerie ruins of the capital of the ancient Guge kingdom at Tsaparang.

TSAPARANG

The persecution of Buddhism by King Lang Darma during the 9th century scattered the followers of Buddhism far away from Central Tibet. The kingdom of Guge, founded in 866, became a focal point for the preservation and re-introduction of Buddhism. Yeshe Ö, a king of Guge who later abdicated to become a monk, sent the Lotsawa (translator) Rinchen Sangpo to India to study. On his return in 978, Rinchen Sangpo encouraged the revival of Buddhism and he is credited with building, amongst others, the monasteries at Tsaparang and Toling. Yeshe Ö, who had been captured and held to ransom by the king of Garlog, refused to be ransomed and instead, urged that the immense sum of gold collected for his release be used to bring the renowned Indian pandit Atisha to Tibet.

Atisha (Jowoje Palden Atisha)

After much deliberation Atisha finally arrived in Tibet in 1040 and spent two years at Toling Monastery where he created a resurgence of interest in Buddhism which eventually spread all over Tibet. Although Central Tibet became, once again, the principal focus of Buddhism in Tibet, Tsaparang and Toling retained their importance within Western Tibet as political and religious centres until the 17th century.

According to some sources, a two year siege by Kashmiris led to the fall of Tsaparang and the destruction of the Guge Kingdom. According to others, the King of Guge angered his lamas by favouring a Portuguese missionary priest, Father Andrade, who had arrived in 1624. Jealous of the favour, the lamas revolted during Father Andrade's absence and in the ensuing factional fighting, the kingdom of Guge tore itself apart. Today, more than 300 years later, all that remains is a huge complex of caves, living quarters and temples, some of it in an excellent state of preservation, the rest in ruins.

From Namru the road continues south through Moincêr to Burang. From Shiquanhe to Burang takes an average of two days with an overnight stop in Moincêr. Laga monastery lies 29 km south of Burang but the main attraction of Burang is its proximity to Mt Kailas and Lake Manasarovar – two of the most sacred sites in all Asia.

MT KAILAS & LAKE MANASAROVAR

For Hindus, Jains, Buddhists and adherents of Bon this region is the abode of the Gods and has, for thousands of years, been a goal of utmost sanctity for pilgrims.

Mt Kailas (6714 metres), known in Tibet as Tise (The Peak) of Kang Rinpoche (Jewel of Snows), is the home of the Hindu God Shiva and his consort Devi; for Tibetans, it is the home of the God Demchog and his consort Dorje Phangmo. It is here, according to legend, that Milarepa, a great Tibetan Yogi and master of Tantric Buddhism, vied with Naro-Bonchung, a grand master of Bon, to prove the superiority of Buddhism. Many contests took place, but the final one was to see who could first reach the summit of Mt Kailas at the crack of dawn. Riding his *damaru* (ritual drum) Naro-Bonchung flew towards the peak only to be overtaken at the last second by Milarepa. Naro-Bonchung was so astonished that he let go of his drum which crashed down the mountain leaving a vertical scar – a distinctive feature of the south face.

Two lakes, Manasarovar (also called Mapam Tso) and Rakastal, lie at the southern foot of Mt. Kailas. Rakastal is associated with the forces of darkness, whereas Manasarovar represents the forces of light. Also in this region are the sources of four of Asia's major rivers:

Senge-Khambab, 'river issuing from the lion's mouth' – the Indus;
Mapchu-Khambab, 'river issuing from the peacock's mouth' – the Karnali;
Tamchok-Khambab, 'river issuing from the horse's mouth – the Brahmaputra (Tsangpo);

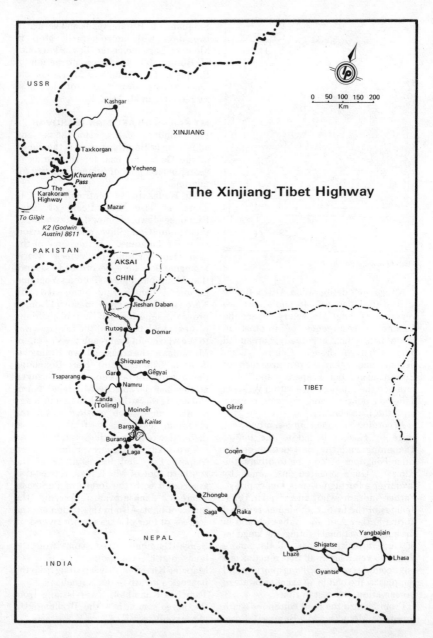

The Xinjiang-Tibet Highway

Xinjiang-Tibet Highway   Distances

	intermediate	cumulative
Lhasa 拉萨		
Shigatse 日喀则	340 km	340 km
Lhazê* 拉孜	151 km	491 km
Raka 拉嘎	241 km	732 km
Coqên 措勤	242 km	974 km
Gêrzê 改则	278 km	1252 km
Gêgyai 革吉	385 km	1637 km
Shiquanhe 狮泉河	112 km	1749 km
Rutog 日土	117 km	1866 km
Domar 多玛	149 km	2015 km
Jieshan Daban 界山大坂	136 km	2151 km
Mazar 玛扎	456 km	2607 km
Yecheng 叶城	249 km	2856 km
Kashgar 喀什	249 km	3105 km

*From Lhazê the old Lhasa-Ladakh route (usually avoided by trucks heading for Xinjiang) runs parallel with the Himalayas to Burang:

Lhazê 拉孜		
Saga 萨嘎	293 km	293 km
Zhongba 仲巴	145 km	438 km
Barga 巴嘎	387 km	825 km
Burang 普兰	104 km	929 km

Distances for towns on or connected with the Xinjiang route:

Lhasa-Kashgar**	3105 km
Lhasa-Shiquanhe**	1749 km
Shiquanhe-Burang	435 km
Shiquanhe-Kashgar	1356 km

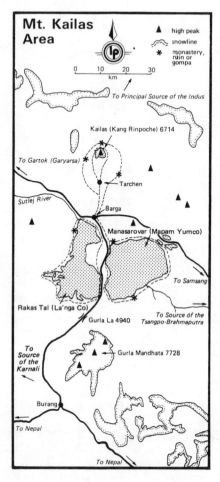

Mt. Kailas Area

▲ high peak
〰 snowline
✱ monastery, ruin or gompa

0 10 20 30
km

To Principal Source of the Indus

Kailas (Kang Rinpoche) 6714

To Gartok (Garyarsa) ✱

✱ — Tarchen

Sutlej River

Barga

✱ Manasarovar (Mapam Yumco)

To Samsang

Rakas Tal (La'nga Co)

To Source of the Tsangpo-Brahmaputra

Gurla La 4940

To Source of the Karnali

Gurla Mandhata 7728

Burang

To Nepal

To Nepal

Lanchen-Khambab, 'river issuing from the elephant's mouth' – the Sutlej.

Pilgrims perform *parikarama* (circumambulation in a clockwise direction) around Lake Manasarovar (4588 metres) and Mt Kailas. The pilgrim route from India to Mt Kailas reopened in 1981, after a closure of some 20 years. The first group of Indian pilgrims found the sacred buildings of the area somewhat damaged.

Many Indian pilgrims approach on a trek from Burang, taking about two days from Burang to Lake Manasarovar. After crossing the foot of Mt Gurla Mandhata (7720 metres) at the Gurla pass, there is a superb panoramic view of the region before a descent to the lakes. During the circuit around Lake Manasarovar (total area about 350 square km), pilgrims pick up pebbles or fill containers with the holy water. Both are prized gifts on their return. Ritual bathing in the lake is also performed to wash away sins. One circuit takes about three days (100 km).

The final and most arduous parikarama is that of Mt Kailas which takes between two and three days (55 km). It is said that those who complete this circuit 108 times are assured entry into Nirvana. Most Tibetans attempt either three or 13 circuits. At the other extreme are fanatical prostrators; it takes between 15 and 25 days to rip the clothing to shreds on a full stomach-circuit.

Although Mt Kailas intrigued turn-of-the-century travellers and geographers intent on solving its river-system riddle, and although it is arguably the most sacred mountain in Asia, to unbelievers Mt Kailas is little more than an interesting geological specimen. It consists of stratified conglomerate masses, with a distinct gully running down the south face from the summit, which cuts across a horizontal rock-band and earns Kailas the name of the 'swastika mountain'. There are four faces to the pyramidal mountain, each matching a compass point, and likened to the facets of a great jewel: the eastern face is believed to be crystal, the western ruby, the southern sapphire, and the northern gold.

SHIQUANHE TO KASHGAR
From Shiquanhe the Xinjiang-Tibet Highway runs north to Rutog, passes Bangong Lake (renowned for its Bird Island) and crosses the Kunlun mountains over Lanak pass (5406 metres). This area around Aksai Chin is specially sensitive

since it is the subject of a border dispute with India. India claims that 56,000 square km of its territory is at present under Chinese control, a large chunk of that figure being in the Aksai Chin area. This bleak and uninhabited area is so remote that the Indian government did not find out the Chinese had built a road through it until two years after the event. Mazar is close to K2 (8611 metres) – the second highest peak in the world. The trek from Mazar to the base camp (4300 metres) on the Sarpo Laggo River takes six days. The trek ascends the Sumkwat Gorge, crosses the Aghil Pass (5300 metres), drops down to the Shaksgam river and continues along it until the junction with the Sarpo Laggo river.

From Mazar the highway crosses the Chiragsaldi Pass (5400 metres) and the Akazu Pass (3550 metres) to reach Yecheng. This is a large town with vigilant authorities who have fined foreigners between Y100 and Y150 for lacking permits and then turned them back (this applies especially for those coming from Kashgar). From Yecheng it is a flat run around the Takla Makan desert to Kashgar.

Staging-point Kashgar

Kashgar, also called Kashi, was once a major halt for caravans on the Silk Road. It is now a prosperous commercial centre with a population composed of Uighur, Tajik and Kirgiz nationalities. Here it is the Han Chinese who are in the minority. As of 1984, permits for Kashgar have been easily obtainable.

Things to See
The Bazaar The bazaar area lies around the Id Kah mosque and square. Merchants and dealers beckon, haggle, swear and doze. Items for sale include carpets; pewter, brass, and copper articles; Yengisar daggers; fresh and dried fruits; local tobacco sold with papers (the local gazette torn into thin strips) to roll your own; and imported and smuggled cigarettes.

An astounding sight, not to be missed, is the Sunday animal market in a large field about half an hour's walk east of the main bazaar. Amidst clouds of dust and the thunder of hooves, a biblical-looking event takes place. Donkeys, horses, camels, Karakoram goats, fat-tailed sheep, cattle – the market has them all. Camel carts lurch off carrying door-frames and window-frames . . .

Since many of the locals make the pilgrimage to Mecca, there is a good market for money changing in the bazaar. Dress as you would for any Muslim country. Western ladies clad in shorts, T-shirts or see-through blouses have had their breasts and backsides tweaked by cheeky or irate locals.

The Id Kah Mosque The mosque, recently renovated, has a strong central Asian atmosphere. A strange assortment of beggars, pilgrims and mullahs take refuge in the shady courtyard. During the Korban festival (late August-early September) a band of musicians perches precariously on top of the portal, whilst a wild assortment of nationalities gyrate below.

The Abakh Khoja Tomb To reach this tomb takes about an hour on foot from the Kashgar Binguan. The tomb of Xiang Fei, a concubine of the Emperor Qianlong, and those of her relatives are in the mosque. The cemetery behind the mosque has some holes in the graves with the occasional bone poking through. Tickets cost Y0.50 and a drowsy guide provides a laconic tour: 'concubine mother . . . concubine father . . . concubine brother . . . other brother . . . '

Places to Stay
Kashgar Binguan provides standard accommodation in a huge compound. One massive disadvantage is its location about an hour's walk from the town centre. A bed

in a four-bed room in the block next to the entrance costs Y6. Hot showers are only available on Monday, Thursday, and Saturday from 9.30 pm to 10.30 pm. The No 1 building has more comfortable, less noisy doubles with hot water available daily. If you don't fancy walking into town, horse and donkey cart drivers will give you a gallop for between Y0.20 and Y0.50.

Other hotels with basic facilities are the *Tuen Park Hotel* and the *Renmin Hotel* – both close to the town centre.

Places to Eat

Kashgar Binguan has a restaurant serving expensive and mediocre food. The *Tuen Park Hotel* also has a restaurant. In the bazaar and on the main streets are stalls and restaurants selling kebabs with flat bread, *lamian* (noodles with meat) and *samsa* (pastry with mutton). There seems to be an obnoxious bug in Kashgar responsible for dire attacks of 'Xinjiang Belly' amongst travellers.

Getting There & Away

Air There are daily flights from Kashgar to Ürümqi (Y215).

Bus Buses run daily at 8 am from Kashgar long-distance bus station to Ürümqi via Aksu and Korla. Tickets cost Y38.90 and the trip takes 3½ days. Buses also run to Daheyon (one hour's ride from Turfan). Tickets to other destinations such as Yengisar, Yecheng and Hotan are not readily sold – there appears to be a branch of public security right at the bus station.

Trucks Trucks are also a possibility (try the truck stop just past the bus station) but the authorities are quick to pick up those without permits travelling off the Ürümqi route outside of Kashgar. Hitchers have been tailed out of Kashgar and heavy fines have been imposed on travellers picked up en route to the Pakistan border.

THE KARAKORAM HIGHWAY

Although not yet officially open for the exit/entry of foreigners, the odd tour group or individual is, in fact, beginning to trickle through the Khunjerab Pass (4800 metres) from Pakistan. The Karakoram Highway runs south to Gilgit (and con- to Rawalpindi) and north to Kashgar. It's 320 km from Gilgit via Karimabad to the Khunjerab Pass, and 955 km from Rawalpindi to the Khunjerab Pass. Although Chinese and Pakistani nationals are allowed along the route from Kashgar to Gilgit, few foreigners have got through – most are turned back due to the military sensitivity of the region (from both sides). Recently the Chinese started to upgrade the road as part of the Beijing's plans to build a modern 'Silk Road' to promote its foreign trade with Europe and West Asia. Both China and Pakistan maintain that the Karakoram Highway is strictly a trade route. Indian authorities, however, discount the trading aspects and are worried about the strategic implications, especially as China also announced plans to improve communications and transport in the regions straddling Ladakh. There are several connecting routes from China into Ladakh. In addition, missiles with a range of 1000 to 3000 km have been deployed in three places in Tibet, as well as in parts of Xinjiang Province.

In late 1985 it was announced that officials would open the Karakoram Highway to foreigners 'soon'. The glacier-flanked Khunjerab Pass has spectacular scenery, with the Pamir Mountains on one side, and the Karakoram Range on the other. It was through these mountains that Indian and Chinese merchants used to bring diamonds to Europe, and, in the other direction, the way Buddhism came to China several thousand years ago. If the Karakoram Highway does open, it would be a novel way to exit or enter China (and slip down into Tibet), and would revive the great overland route from Europe to Asia.

Glossary

Unless otherwise noted, terms are in Tibetan (rendered phonetically). Some Sanskrit terms have been emphasised because they are already well known in the west.

(T) = Tibetan
(S) = Sanskrit

Amdo – north-eastern portion of ethnic Tibet, a large chunk of which was annexed as Qinghai Province by the Chinese in 1928.

Amitabha (S) – Buddha of endless life; *Opame* (T). The Panchen Lama is believed to be a reincarnation of Amitabha.

Atisha (S) – Atisha Dipankara Srijnana, Indian Buddhist teacher who visited Tibet in 1042 and re-established Buddhism there.

Avalokitesvara (S) – the Bodhisattva of Compassion; *Chenrezig* (T).

Balpo – Nepal, also Balyul.

Bardo – the time between life and death.

Barkhor – inner pilgrim-circuit in Lhasa.

Bodhi (S) – enlightenment, from which comes the word Buddha, meaning The Enlightened One.

Bodhisattva (S) – a being who compassionately refrains from entering Nirvana in order to save others. Worshipped as a deity in Mahayana and Vajrayana Buddhism.

Bodpa – a Tibetan.

Bon – animist religion in Tibet before arrival of Buddhism.

Bultog – soda, an ingredient of butter tea.

Bumpa – ceremonial water pot.

Cha – tea.

Chagar – 'White World Region': India.

Cham – masked dance.

Champa – Buddha of the Future, or *Maitreya Buddha* (S).

Chanag – 'Black World Region': China.

Chang – Tibetan beer, brewed from barley and millet.

Chang-Tang – the northern steppes of Tibet.

Chenrezig – the patron saint of Tibet and the principal Bodhisattva of Vajrayana Buddhism; *Avalokitesvara* (S). The Dalai Lama is believed to be a reincarnation of Chenrezig.

Choga – thick coat worn by Tibetan nomads, also *chupa*.

Choi – teaching; *Dharma* (S).

Chorten – a small temple containing religious images; *Stupa* (S).

Dalai Lama – title conferred by Mongol Chieftan, Altan Khan, in 1578. In Mongolian, 'Dalai' means 'Ocean', so 'Ocean of Wisdom' is the general rendering of Dalai Lama.

Darlog – pole for prayer-flags.

Deva (S) – male god; *Lha* (T).

Devi (S) – goddess, usually consort of Shiva. In Tibet, Lhamo is the most eminent goddess, protectress of Lhasa and the Gelukpa order.

Dolma – One of the most important Vajrayana goddesses, consort of Avalokitesvara; *Tara* (S). *Dolmachangmo* (White Tara) and *Dolmakarma* (Green Tara).

Dopka – nomad, dweller of the black tent.

Dorje – thunderbolt symbol, usually made of brass, and used as a weapon against the powers of darkness.

Dri – female yak.

Drilbu – ritual bell, with half a Dorje as a handle.

Drukyul – 'Dragon Lady': Bhutan.

Dung – conch horn.

Dzong – fortress, and residence of former district governor (*Dzongpon*).

Gelukpa – the Yellow Hat Sect, founded by Tsongkhapa in the 14th century. It became Tibet's most powerful sect; also *Gelugpa*.

Geshe – a doctor of divinity.

Gompa – lamasery or monastery.

Guge – kingdom founded in western Tibet during 9th century, destroyed in 17th century.

Guru (S) – master or teacher.

Gyalpo – leader. The Dalai Lama is also known as *Gyalpo Rinpoche*, leader of the Gelukpa Sect.

Jokhang – main temple in Lhasa, also *Tsug-lag Khang*.

Kagyupa – religious order founded by Marpa, 11th century.

Kailas – holy mountain in western Tibet, also *Kang Rinpoche*.

Kalachakra (S) – a Vajrayana text and god, 'Wheel of Time'.

Kangling – human bone trumpet.

Kanjur – Tibetan 'Bible' or Canon of Buddhist Law, 108 volumes.

Karmapa – a sub-order of the Kagyupa, with abbots distinguished by their black hats.

Kashag – Council of Ministers directly responsible to the Dalai Lama.

Kham – eastern Tibet.

Khampa – inhabitant of eastern Tibet.

Khata – ceremonial white scarf, presented as a gift.

Kjangchag – prostration.

Korlam – clockwise circuit of sacred places.

Korlo – wheel, symbolises setting into motion of the teaching; *Chakra* (S), psychic centre.

Kumbum – pagoda of 100,000 images.

Lama – general term for a monk, or for a fully-ordained monk who has become a master.

Lamaism – Tibetan Buddhism.

Lapcha – pile of stones marking top of a pass, *Obo*.

Lhakhang – temple or chapel.

Lingkhor – outer pilgrim circuit in Lhasa.

Losar – New Year.

Lotsawa – translator.

Mahakala (S) – a Vajrayana god, protector of the tent; *Gonpo* (T).

Mahayana (S) – a form of Buddhism adopted in Tibet, 'The Great Path'. It aims at the liberation of all beings.

Mandala (S) – mystic circle, design or cosmogram used in meditation and initiations, and symbol of collective consciousness; *Chilkor* (T).

Mani – the mantra *Om Mani Padme Hum*, a phrase usually addressed to Buddha or to Avalokitesvara, his Tibetan incarnation. Generally translated as 'Hail to the jewel in the heart of the lotus'. Mani-stones have this mantra inscribed upon them.

Manichorkor – prayer-wheel containing mantra.

Manjusri (S) – one of the most important Buddhist deities, Bodhisattva of Wisdom; *Champai Chang* (T).

Mantra (S) – prayer formula, chant or spell.

Momo – steamed tsampa dough, usually with meat in the middle, like dumplings.

Namchuwangdan – sacred 'sign of the 10 powers' used in temples.

Nechung – name of Tibetan state oracle and monastery close to Lhasa.

Ngari – province of western Tibet.

Nirvana (S) – personal or self liberation, the state beyond sorrow.

Norbulinka – summer residence of the Dalai Lama in Lhasa.

Nyingmapa – a religious order founded around the 10th to 11th centuries by combining various older sects and traditions.

Padma (S) – lotus.

Padmasambhava (S) – great master of the Tantra, founder of the Nyingmapa order.

Panchen Lama – title of the Abbot of Tashilhunpo Monastery in Shigatse, and the most important incarnation after the Dalai Lama. Also known as the Tashi Lama.

Phurpa – magic dagger, ritual implement used in Bon exorcism.

Po – Tibet (also *Bod, Bodyul, and Khawachanjijul*– 'Land of Snow').

Rigma – female consort complementing a male deity; *Shakti* (S).

Rinpoche – blessed, or jewel.

Sakyamuni (S) – title of Guatama Buddha, 5th century BC, also sage of Sakya tribe.

Sakyapa – religious order founded 11th century, Red Hat Sect. The term Red Hat also applies to two previous orders – the Nyingmapa and Kagyupa.

Shambhala – a legendary kingdom to the north of Tibet where the Kalachakra teachings are kept.

Shiva (S) – one of the two main Hindu gods, also revered by Buddhists. The other god is Vishnu, the preserver.

Sutra (S) – a scripture or book containing doctrines.

Tantra (S) – a teaching or system of Vajrayana Buddhism.

Tantric Buddhism – see Vajrayana.

Tenjur – commentaries on the Kanjur or Canon of Buddhist Law, in 225 volumes.

Thangka – painting on cloth, often sacred.

Tsampa – roasted barley-flour, a staple food in Tibet.

Tsang – region in central Tibet. There were two sectors: the western part (called *Tsang*, with chief city Shigatse) and the eastern part (called *Ü*, capital at Lhasa) which together formed *U-Tsang*, the Lhasa Valley area.

Tsong Khapa – great reformer of Tibetan Buddhism and founder of the Gelukpa order. Lived 1357-1419.

Tsongombo – Kokonor, or Qinghai Lake.

Tulku – a living Buddha.

Vajra (S) – thunderbolt *Dorje* or diamond-like substance.

Vajrasattva (S) – name of an important Buddhist deity, 'thunderbolt-being'.

Vajrayana (S) – an esoteric form of Buddhism that employs radical steps as a shortcut to obtaining enlightenment (the Diamond Path).

Visvavajra (S) – a ritual implement known as the double-thunderbolt.

Yab-yum – a position of sexual union, signifying compassion and insight, seen in tantric deity statues and frescoes.

Yak – male Tibetan ox.

Yama – Hindu God of death; in Tibet, Lord of the Dead and King of Religion.

Yidam – in Tantric Buddhism, the individual's personal deity and protector, usually chosen for him or her by a lama.

Yoga (S) – spiritual system common to both Buddhism and Hinduism, and emphasising rigorous mental and physical discipline.

Index

N – Nepal
Q – Qinghai
S – Sichuan

T – Tibet
X – Xinjiang
Y – Yunnan

Map references are in **bold** type

Akazu Pass (X) 249
Amdo (T) 230
Anyêmaqên Shan (Q) 241
Arun River (T) 186

Baihanchang (Y) 223
Bam Tso (T) 162
Bamda (T) 217
Bangong Lake (T) 248
Baqên (T) 218
Barabise (N) 201
Batang (T) 219
Baxoi (T) 217
Bayi (T) 218
Bomi (T) 217
Burang (T) 244

Cangshan mountains (Y) 223
Chagpori (T) 133
Chamdo (T) 212-213, 215-218, **216**
Chang La (T) 180-181
Chang Tang (T) 33
Chengdu (S) 204-209, **206**
Chiragsaldi Pass (X) 249
Cho Oyu Base Camp (T) 185
Cona (T) 156
Coqên (T) 244

Dagzê (T) 150
Dali (Y) 221-223, **222**
Damxung (T) 229
Daotanghe (Q) 239
Dêgê (S) 213, 214-215
Dêngqên (T) 218
Dêqên (Y) 224
Dinggyê (T) 193
Doilungdêqên (T) 228
Doya La (T) 186
Dunhuang (Q) 232
Dzakar Chu River (T) 179

Emei Shan (S) 209
Erhai Lake (Y) 223

Everest Base Camp (N) 184-185
Everest region 175-187, **176-177**

Ganden (T) 149
Garzê (S) 214
Gejiehe (Y) 224
Gêgyai (T) 244
Golmud (Q) 230-232, **231**
Gongbo'gyamda (T) 218
Gonghe (Q) 239-241, **241**
Gyabrag Glacier (T) 185
Gyantse (T) 157-163, **157**

Haka (Q) 241
Haka Shan (Q) 241
Heimahe (Q) 238
Hengduan Shan (Y) 224
Huangzhong (Q) 238
Huashixia (Q) 241

Jarmalinka Island (T) 139
Jianchuan (Y) 220
Jinsha River (Y) 224

Kailas mountains 34
Kama Valley (T) 185
Kangding (S) 212
Kangba Plateau (T) 219
Kangmar (T) 162
Karakoram mountains 33
Kashgar (X) 249-250
Kathmandu (N) 199-201
Khamba La (T) 191
Kharta (T) 185-186
Kharta River (T) 186
Kodari (N) 198
Koko Nor (Q) 34
Kunlun mountains 33
Kunlun Shankou (Q) 230
Kunming (Y) 221
Kyichu River (T) 125
Kyichu Valley (T) 150

Lak Pa La (T) 193
Lancang River (Y) 224
Leshan (S) 209
Lhasa (T) 125-149, **128-129**
Lhasa River (T) 139
Lhünzhub (T) 156
Lijiang (Y) 224
Litang (T) 219